T0340380

Gastronomy and Local Development

Gastronomy, particularly gourmet tourism, is widely acknowledged as having a powerful impact on local development. Public policies have developed in response to research, highlighting gastronomy as key in a successful tourism economy.

However, research thus far has not fully explored the underlying mechanisms of gastronomic tourism, in particular the marketing and perception of quality, on economic development. This book considers how the quality of products, places, and experiences contributes to the desirability and competitiveness of gourmet touristic destinations. The contributors present theoretical and empirical studies to create an original conceptual framework for regional development based on the quality of products, of places, and of touristic experience. It also examines the ways in which quality is linked to identity, diversity, innovation and creativity.

With an interdisciplinary approach, this book will be of interest to researchers in tourism and hospitality, regional studies, and human geography, as well as to tourism development professionals and policymakers in the areas of rural and local development.

Nicola Bellini is Professor of Economics and Management of Tourism at La Rochelle Business School and Professor of Management at the Scuola Superiore Sant'Anna, Pisa.

Cécile Clergeau is Professor of Management, IAE, University of Nantes, and Honorary Chair of the Francophone Association of Tourism Management.

Olivier Etcheverria is Associate Professor at the UFR ESTHUA "Tourisme et Culture," University of Angers.

Routledge Advances in Regional Economics, Science and Policy

For more information about this series, please visit
www.routledge.com/series/RAIRESP

Gastronomy and Local Development

The Quality of Products, Places and Experiences

Edited by Nicola Bellini, Cécile Clergeau and Olivier Etcheverria

Routledge
Taylor & Francis Group

LONDON AND NEW YORK

First published 2019
by Routledge

2 Park Square, Milton Park, Abingdon, Oxfordshire OX14 4RN
52 Vanderbilt Avenue, New York, NY 10017

Routledge is an imprint of the Taylor & Francis Group, an informa business

First issued in paperback 2020

Copyright © 2019 selection and editorial matter, Nicola Bellini, Cécile Clergeau, and Olivier Etcheverria; individual chapters, the contributors

The right of Nicola Bellini, Cécile Clergeau, and Olivier Etcheverria to be identified as the authors of the editorial material, and of the authors for their individual chapters, has been asserted in accordance with sections 77 and 78 of the Copyright, Designs and Patents Act 1988.

All rights reserved. No part of this book may be reprinted or reproduced or utilised in any form or by any electronic, mechanical, or other means, now known or hereafter invented, including photocopying and recording, or in any information storage or retrieval system, without permission in writing from the publishers.

Notice:
Product or corporate names may be trademarks or registered trademarks, and are used only for identification and explanation without intent to infringe.

British Library Cataloguing-in-Publication Data
A catalogue record for this book is available from the British Library

Library of Congress Cataloging-in-Publication Data
Names: Bellini, Nicola, editor. | Clergeau, Cécile, editor. | Etcheverria, Olivier, editor.
Title: Gastronomy and local development : the quality of products, places and experiences / edited by Nicola Bellini, Cécile Clergeau and Olivier Etcheverria.
Description: Abingdon, Oxon ; New York, NY : Routledge, 2019. | Series: Routledge advances in regional economics, science and policy ; 28 | Includes index.
Identifiers: LCCN 2018027460| ISBN 9781138731998 (hardback) | ISBN 9781351743945 (pdf) | ISBN 9781351743938 (epub) | ISBN 9781351743921 (mobi)
Subjects: LCSH: Food tourism. | Gastronomy--Economic aspects. | Economic development.
Classification: LCC TX631 .G37 2019 | DDC 641.01/3--dc23
LC record available at https://lccn.loc.gov/2018027460

ISBN: 978-1-138-73199-8 (hbk)
ISBN: 978-0-367-66509-8 (pbk)

Typeset in Bembo
by Integra Software Services Pvt. Ltd.

Contents

Figures

Tables

Contributors

Magda Antonioli Corigliano is Professor and Director of the Master in Tourism Economics at the Bocconi University, Milan.

Nicola Bellini is Professor of Economics and Management of Tourism at La Rochelle Business School and Professor of Management at the Scuola Superiore Sant'Anna, Pisa.

Sara Bricchi teaches at the Master in Tourism Economics at the Bocconi University, Milan.

Ignazio Cabras is Professor in Entrepreneurship and Regional Economic Development at the Newcastle Business School, Northumbria University, and Research Associate at ESSCA École de Management, Angers.

Cécile Clergeau is Professor of Management, IAE, University of Nantes, and Honorary Chair of the Francophone Association of Tourism Management.

Katie Ellison is BA Candidate in Business with Economics at Newcastle Business School, Northumbria University.

Olivier Etcheverria is Associate Professor at the UFR ESTHUA "Tourisme et Culture", University of Angers.

Marie-Eve Férérol holds a PhD in geography from University Blaise Pascal - Clermont-Ferrand II.

Anne-Emmanuelle Fiamor is a Postdoctoral Researcher in socio-anthropology of food at the University of Toulouse 2 Jean Jaurès.

Robert Lanquar is a former UNWTO civil servant and presently teaches at the La Rochelle Business School. He is CEO of Cordoba Horizontes.

Isabel Lopes Cardoso is a Researcher at the Centre for Art History and Artistic Research of the University of Évora and at the Institute of Contemporary History of the Universidade Nova de Lisboa.

Cecilia Pasquinelli is a Postdoctoral Researcher in Urban Studies at the Gran Sasso Science Institute, L'Aquila.

Jérôme Piriou is Assistant Professor at the La Rochelle Business School.

Evelyne Resnick is Marketing Professor and Researcher at ISG Bordeaux - ISERAM (Institute for research in business management).

Marielle Salvador is Assistant Professor at INSEEC Business School (Lyon).

Christel Venzal is Associate Professor of Geography at the University of Pau and research fellow at the UMR PASSAGES of the CNRS.

1 Introduction

Nicola Bellini, Cécile Clergeau, and Olivier Etcheverria

Browsing through our various national dictionaries, gastronomy is defined as "the practice or art of choosing, cooking, and eating good food" (Oxford), "the art or science of good eating" (Webster's), "the set of rules and customs concerning the preparation of food; the art of cooking" (Il Devoto–Oli: our translation), and "the knowledge of everything related to cooking, the organisation of meals, the art of tasting and enjoying dishes" (Larousse: our translation). Looking back at the Greek origin of the word, gastronomy communicates the appropriateness of giving rules (nomos) to our feeding needs. Even more interestingly, the first appearance of this word in the works of authors such as Archestratus and Atheneus establishes a clear link between gastronomy and lifestyle dimensions, such as philosophy, luxury, and travel (Davidson and Jaine, 2014). Talking about gastronomy is thus not the same as talking about food or even local food as the mere (and conservative) search for some authenticity rooted in history. "Gastronomy adds a search for quality, expression of taste and pleasure in eating" (Vitaux, 2007: our translation).

> Gastronomy is neither "good" nor "haute" cuisine. It is the setting in order (nomos) of eating and drinking, thus transformed into the "art de la table". In this last expression, ambiguity is deliberately maintained between the two meanings, old or modern, of the word "art": the interests of the cook and the gourmet are united here and, if the former is promoted artist, the latter sees his function elevated to the rank of art critic.
>
> (Ory, 1993: our translation)

Gastronomy is enacted by artisans and artists, producers, chefs, and eaters whose discourses participate in the dynamics of traditions, cultures, and imaginaries. In this book, we propose our own definition of gastronomy as, "A system of discourses and imaginaries constructed upon agricultural food products and their culinary transformations, upon relations to the table, and upon the cultures of the food put into the mouth." As such, it is a powerful identity marker and definitively contributes to shaping a heritage, developing tourism (Bessières, 1998), attracting tourists with greater resources (Etcheverria, 2014a; Pérez Gálvez et al., 2017), and influencing the way tourists experience a destination (Kivela and

Crotts, 2006; Etcheverria, 2014b). And finally, it is a growing component of tourism destination attractiveness (Etcheverria, 2008, 2014c; Sormaz et al., 2016).

This book investigates the relationship between gastronomy and local development. We do not attempt to provide here a summary definition of how we perceive local development, but it is clear to us that among the many facets discussed in the literature, some are especially relevant in a discourse involving gastronomy: the issues of environmental and social sustainability; the relationship between local identities and globalisation; the role of creativity and cultural heritage; the significance of local diversities, facing regional and national centralisation, and so forth.

Nothing illustrates the geographic, sociocultural, and economic impacts of gastronomy better than the cases of those chefs who have made the deliberate and motivated choice to set up their restaurants in isolated territories that would generally be considered unsuitable for the development of an internationally renowned restaurant, and who decisively contribute to activating (or re-activating) these territories by providing an attractor to tourism and leisure mobility (Etcheverria, 2011). The relevance of this relationship has dramatically grown, mostly (although not exclusively) due to the increasing importance of gourmet tourism as a significant component of the overall growth of tourism in the contemporary economy, and as an engine of economic development at the local level. As the World Tourism Organization (UNWTO) recently stated, "Gastronomy is a distinctive and strategic element in defining the image and brand" of tourist destinations (UNWTO, 2017). In France, as well as in many other countries, political, socioeconomic, and cultural actors voiced their increased awareness of gastronomy's potential to boost new dynamics in local development. The attention to food heritage, to the territories' recipes, products and restaurants, and to gastronomic imaginary has become a common feature of more and more tourism promotion initiatives at the local level. In France, a powerful accelerator was the 2010 inscription of the "Gastronomic meal of the French" on the Representative List of the Intangible Cultural Heritage of Humanity. This decision created extraordinary momentum around gastronomy, whose role – as the French Prime Minister Edouard Philippe put it in a speech in January 2018 – is a "State business" ("*une affaire d'État*"). This prominence is also due to its privileged role in providing access to local diversities.

However, this new relevance raises a number of managerial and policy issues that academic research has started to investigate only recently. This book is part of one of the initiatives undertaken in this context: the international workshop on "Gastronomy and local development" launched in 2012 at the UFR ESTHUA Tourisme et Culture, University of Angers (Clergeau and Etcheverria, 2013a) aimed at instigating an innovative discussion on the scientific foundations of research on the functions of gastronomy with regard to development at the local scale. In the organisers' perception, fresh, groundbreaking research contributions were needed, notwithstanding the significant advances achieved in recent years (thanks to, amongst others, the studies of Hjalager and Richards (2002), and Corvo (2015)). The research agenda itself needed to be redefined or at least refocused. A second workshop was held at

La Rochelle Business School in November 2015 under the scientific direction of the editors of this book. This provided a significant opportunity to outline the present research agenda, thanks to the discussion on a wide range of case studies from several European and non-European countries. Starting from the results of the Angers workshop, which clearly indicated that quality is a key factor in determining these effects, the participants at the La Rochelle event were invited to focus their discussions on the multifaceted role and meaning of quality. Quality – as it emerged from these discussions – is a social construct that interacts and co-evolves with gastronomy as a system of discourses and imaginaries and, while taking place in systems that go far beyond the local framework, are nurtured by local communities, local customs and cultures, and local geographic characteristics.

The quality issue has been, and will always be, closely linked to gastronomy. Quality lies at the heart of the system for at least three aspects of gastronomy: its relation to health; the need for and rigour of product standards; and the relevance of the service dimension, including the staging and "servicescape" of the gastronomic experience. In fact, as management research has repeatedly pointed out, service quality is a complex and multidimensional concept (Gronroos, 1984; Zeithalml et al., 1990). From the provider's point of view, quality focuses on the "product" and refers to a range of physical and technical (and therefore codifiable and measurable) specifications of the service, and within this approach, attempting to understand and manage the tangible elements that contribute to service quality. These tangible elements can greatly differ in nature: the organoleptic features of food products or their production processes; the quality of tables and chairs, decor and dishes; other infrastructural aspects (accessibility, parking); or the waiting time in the restaurant. Such an approach also allows constructing social conventions about quality that can be certified through "quality labels" (Eymard-Duvernay, 1989). From the consumer's (and tourist's) perspective, quality takes on a more subjective character and stems from the gap between perceived benefits and expectations. Quality is recognised when expectations are met or even exceeded in the service experience, thus positively surprising the customer – the so-called "wow effect."

Models have been proposed to structurally formalise the analysis (and several exercises are available in the literature regarding the most famous, the SERVQUAL model). Yet, in the case of tourism and gastronomy, possibly more than in any other case, both perceptions and expectations are shaped by a complex web of psychological, sociological, and situational factors that define the conditions in which the service is delivered. In gastronomy, perceptions will be heavily influenced by individual factors, such as the personal disposition and level of knowledge that makes the gourmet an "educated customer." Expectations will be shaped by the same set of factors, reflecting differences among people, times, and cultures. In a gastronomic experience, however, their dynamics may also produce expectations of an implicit or fuzzy nature that are unrealistic or taken for granted (Ojasalo, 2001). In turn, these expectations may negatively influence the final quality perceptions to the extent that they conflict with the chef's own path to creativity.

Inspired by a user quality approach, and within the context of our research about gastronomy and local development, we suggest that quality depends on the combination of three dimensions: the quality of *products*, of *places*, and of *experiences*. These all contribute to the readability, attractiveness, and competitiveness of gourmet destinations. The joint qualification of product and place helps build reputation and attractiveness through the image and discourse associated with and diffused by the product, and is therefore part of the quality of the tourist experience. The debates held during the workshops about the combination of these dimensions showed that quality is a complex construct, that is gradually been shaped and questions about identity, about diversity, and about innovation and creativity.

Quality is clearly linked to *identity*, as branding strategies increasingly refer to local taste preferences as a crucial immersion vector for tourism experiences. Research is providing new insights into the way in which local products, know-how, food culture, production landscape, dynamics, and cultural heritage can contribute to the identity of restaurants. The incorporation of these elements transforms the gastronomic experience into a privileged insight for temporary residents (i.e., tourists) of the identity of the place and its permanent residents.

Quality, however, is also linked to *diversity*, as it cannot be confined within any "rusticity" stereotype. The joint quality of products and places stems not only from the originality of a certain production, but often also from the uniqueness of the underlying socioeconomic relations. Producers, suppliers, transformers, distributors, restaurateurs, chefs, and tourists forge links that, beyond economic relations, shape a staged web of images and imaginaries – i.e., a *gastronomic atmosphere* (Clergeau and Etcheverria, 2013b). Researchers are increasingly investigating the importance of this socioeconomic dimension of the local management of diversity. This is embodied particularly in proximity dynamics, knowledge and know-how assets, learning mechanisms, vocabularies, or shared representations. Sociologists suggest that different social groups may associate different symbolic meanings with local food quality. Furthermore, through food, local cultures interact with global consumption and open themselves up to the coproduction of a variety of tourist experiences.

Finally, quality is increasingly linked not just to the preservation of identities, local specificities, and preferences, but also to *innovation* and *creativity*. As discussed in the workshop, when combined with technical innovation and entrepreneurial creativity, gastronomy has the potential to be a powerful tool to revitalise agro-food economies and cityscapes. Gastronomy may be part of successful luxury and lifestyle hospitality, but it also contributes to alternative ways to experience quality – e.g., through social eating – and therefore to new business models.

The quality-focused research agenda on gastronomy is not without challenges, three of which clearly emerged from the workshop discussions. The first concerns the need to better understand how gastronomy (as distinguished from mere local food and cooking) is an increasingly "democratic" phenomenon, involving more than the traditional, passionate expert elite, and is rather a significant cultural and economic part of the travel experience across a wider range of social groups.

A second challenge derives from the geographic diffusion of gourmet tourism. These days, every country in the world counts on gastronomy to foster tourism development. There is a need to more closely investigate what drives this – i.e., the extent to which we are simply witnessing a creative imitation of the more established European models as opposed to alternative patterns, linked to the creative reinterpretation of very old culinary specialties for the global traveller.

The third and final challenge concerns the potential for collective action and the way in which public policies should be reassessed. What is to be done? Looking beyond standard practices of tourism promotion, a number of partly new issues are emerging, such as the role of selective quality labels, of education, of research, and so forth.

This book is structured around the three aforementioned questions raised by quality. In *Part I*, the link between quality and identity is first investigated by Clergeau and Etcheverria (Chapter 2), who question the possibly virtuous identity circle between a restaurant and a territory, and the way tourists can learn about the place within the dramaturgy of the gourmet experience that takes place in the restaurant. Férérol (Chapter 3) shows how gourmet tourism can be synergistic with a territorial brand strategy for a French region that is attempting to reinvigorate its own image. Venzal (Chapter 4) discusses how in another French region the quality of local products has become a vector of development through their integration in tourism destination management.

Lopes Cardoso (Chapter 5) looks at the case of Alentejo (Portugal) and shows how the region's gastronomic identity is reflected in the unique setting of Casa do Alentejo in the country's capital. Lanquar (Chapter 6) provides a critical view of the identity emerging from the gastronomic dimensions of local festivals in Spain in the era of globalisation. Finally, Salvador (Chapter 7) questions authenticity perceptions; in her view, tourists identify the characteristics of local products as quality signals and attributes, which then become the vectors of an authentic tourism experience.

Part II explores the link between quality and diversity. Etcheverria (Chapter 8) discusses the impact of a visionary entrepreneurial project (a restaurant and school-farm) in the Zhejiang Province of China, showing the relationship between enhancing local biodiversity and educating people to tasting diversity. Piriou (Chapter 9) presents the case of Cognac and its region to show the different ways territorial quality is synergistic with the success of this product and its producers. Based on a field study in southern France, Fiamor (Chapter 10) examines two types of local development induced by two different food production strategies, analysing the diversity of social meanings associated with local productions.

Part III discusses the link between quality on the one hand and innovation and creativity on the other. Cabras and Ellison (Chapter 11) explain how the revival of micro and craft breweries in Britain is providing new economic opportunities for local economies and tourism development. Bellini and Resnick (Chapter 12) show how innovation can also be detected in the experiential luxury approach in wine tourism, although with a potential weakening of the local link. Pasquinelli (Chapter 13) critically discusses an innovative way of embedding gastronomic experiences in local brandscapes through Eataly's urban poles of taste. Finally, Antonioli Corigliano and Bricchi (Chapter 14) question the impact of social eating initiatives by exploring to what extent new technologies help to experience authentic regional food and wine, and the local gastronomic culture.

Acknowledgements

The editors are grateful to all the authors who contributed to this volume. The participants of the 2015 workshop at La Rochelle, including those whose papers are not included here, provided an exceptionally stimulating opportunity for discussion and knowledge-sharing that has been decisive in shaping our work.

Special thanks are due to Groupe Sup de Co La Rochelle, which hosted the conference and supported the production of this book, and particularly to its then Director General Daniel Peyron. We would also like to thank UFR ESTHUA Tourisme et Culture at the University of Angers and its director, Professor Philippe Violier, for their support.

Finally, we are grateful to Jacqueline Fuchs for her patient and excellent editorial work.

References

Bessières J. (1998). Local development and heritage: Traditional food and cuisine as tourist attractions in rural areas. *Sociologica Ruralis*, 38(1), pp. 21–34.

Clergeau, C. and Etcheverria O. (eds). (2013a). Gastronomie et développement local. *Mondes du Tourisme*, 7, pp. 12–83.

Clergeau, C. and Etcheverria O. (2013b). La mise en tourisme et le développement local par la création d'une atmosphère gastronomique. Analyse à partir du cas de Vonnas. *Mondes du Tourisme*, 7, pp. 52–67.

Corvo, P. (2015). *Food culture, consumption and society*. Basingstoke, Hampshire: Palgrave Macmillan.

Davidson, A. and Jaine T. (2014). *The Oxford companion to food*. 3rd edition, Oxford: Oxford University Press.

Etcheverria, O. (2008). San Sebastian: Capitale gastronomique parmi les capitales gastronomiques. In Csergo J. and Lemasson J.-P. (eds), *Voyages en gastronomies. L'invention des capitales et des régions gourmands*. Paris: Autrement, pp. 171–182.

Etcheverria, O. (2011). Les tensions fondatrices du développement local autour du restaurant Bras à Laguiole: "centralité", qualité et créativité. *Norois*, 219(2), pp. 57–71.

Etcheverria, O. (2014a). Le cuisinier Olivier Roellinger, les épices et l'immatériel touristique. In Clergeau, C. and Spindler, J. (eds), *L'immatériel touristqiue*. Paris: L'Harmattan, pp. 225–246.

Etcheverria, O. (2014b). Mykonos: Lieu d'expérimentation touristique de la relation gastronomie-monde. *Via@Tourism Review*, 6.

Etcheverria, O. (2014c). Du vignoble à la destination oenotouristique. L'exemple de l'île de Santorin. *CULTUR Revista de Cultura e Turismo*, 8(3), pp. 188–210.

Eymard-Duvernay, F. (1989). Conventions de qualité et formes de coordination. *Revue Économique*, 40(2), pp. 329–360.

Gronroos, C. (1984). Strategic management and marketing in the service sector: A service quality and its marketing implication. *European Journal of Marketing*, 18(4), pp. 36–44.

Hjalager, A.M. and Richards, G. (eds). (2002). *Tourism and gastronomy*. London: Routledge.

Kivela, and J. and Crotts J. (2006). Tourism and gastronomy: Gastronomy's influence on how tourists experience a destination. *Journal of Hospitality and Tourism Research*, 30(3), pp. 354–377.

Ojasalo, J. (2001). Managing customer expectations in professional services. *Managing Service Quality*, 11(3), pp. 200–212.

Ory, P. (1993). La gastronomie. In Nora P. (ed), *Les lieux de mémoire*. Vol. III, López-Guzmán T.*Les France*, Paris: Gallimard, pp. 3743–3769.

Pérez Gálvez, and J.C., Jaramillo Granda M., and Reinoso Coronel J. (2017). Local gastronomy, culture and tourism sustainable cities: The behavior of the American tourist. *Sustainable Cities and Society*, 32, pp. 604–612.

Sormaz U., Akmese H., Gunes E. and Sercan A. (2016). Gastronomy in Tourism. *Procedia Economics and Finance*, 39, pp. 725–730.

UNWTO (2017). Second global report on gastronomy tourism. http://cf.cdn.unwto.org/sites/all/files/pdf/gastronomy_report_web.pdf

Vitaux, J. (2007). *La gastronomie*. Paris: Presses universitaires de France.

Zeithaml, V.A., Parasuraman, A. and Berry, L.L. (1990). *Delivering quality service: Balancing customer perceptions and expectations*. New York: Simon and Schuster.

Part I

The link between quality and identity

2 The identity quality of restaurants

An affordance to the tourist ecumene?
The example of the Christopher
Coutanceau restaurant in La Rochelle

Cécile Clergeau and Olivier Etcheverria

1. Introduction

The identity quality of restaurants is a perception in the minds of those who enjoy cooking, eating out, and discovering local food products. However, this notion lacks a clear definition, and analyses of the impact of identity quality on tourism development at the local level are scarce and do not go nearly enough into depth. Professionals and academics agree on the importance of the quality of agricultural food products, recipes and dishes, food and wine pairings, as well as their ability to represent a territory and translate its identity into a memorable experience for tourists. The inclusion of the French Gastronomic Meal in the UNESCO Representative List of the Intangible Cultural Heritage of Humanity on 16 November 2010 led to important research into gastronomy as a form of heritage. As Requier-Desjardins (2009: 2) affirms, heritage often leads to highlighting its link with identity and cultural diversity. At the same time, the numerous policies aimed at boosting the profile of localised agricultural food products, local recipes, and the taste preferences of indigenous inhabitants are all inspired by the same quest for identity, guided by the desire for affirmation, recognition, and differentiation as part of the heritage-conversion process. Even if many researchers and specialists seize on this question of identity linked to the heritage-conversion logic and combined with issues of local development and qualitative orientation, the concepts applied are still not well defined, and the methods used are not precise enough.

Suggesting there is a link between a restaurant and its identity at the local level supposes that we imbue the restaurant with an identity quality. To paraphrase Sgard (1999), this suggestion implies that "that restaurant" perfectly defines, compared to others, "that territory" and/or "that social group," and only that one, and that this territory and/or social group can be recognised in "that restaurant." However, the mechanisms underlying this process of reciprocal designation and recognition are currently poorly explained in literature. This is why we suggest going further, defining the identity quality (of restaurants) and analysing it as a means of allowing tourists to enter into a relationship with the tourism ecumene: as an *affordance*.

Our case study is based on the Christopher Coutanceau restaurant in La Rochelle. It proudly boasts two Michelin stars, has done so for more than thirty years, and is an institution in La Rochelle. This restaurant, which employs thirty people, was completely renovated in 2017 (with an investment of 1.2 million euro) and reaffirmed its local anchorage by using the services of artisans from the region. This example seems to us emblematic of restaurants in which a chef has made the place more than simply a flagship – it has become a true vector of a sensory connection between a territory, its producers, and tourists.

Our empirical method is part of an interpretative approach that fosters understanding in the construction of knowledge. We rely on documentary studies, participant observations, and interviews with the restaurant's two business partners, as well as tourism stakeholders in La Rochelle.

2. Identity quality as a trajection system

2.1. *About tourism ecumene*

In his introduction to the study of human environments, Berque (1987: 17) describes ecumene as "the whole and the condition of human environments ... a relationship: the ecological, technical and symbolic relationship between humanity and the terrestrial situation." His work has inspired research in tourism geography, which has since used the term *tourism ecumene* (Équipe MIT, 2005) to designate sites used for the purposes of tourism. Berque emphasises that in ecumene, things exist only in so far as human beings give them meaning through their own existence. Likewise, in tourism ecumene, things only exist because tourists give them meaning through their recreational projects and experiences. Berque then refers to the trajectivity of things, "which is not a pure phenomenology, and not even a simple projection of the human subjectivity of things; it gives them a real understanding of their physical scope" (Berque, 1987: 240). This understanding involves the inter-relations that everyone has with the elements in their environment. They are not simple objects that exist alone, irrespective of the existence of the individual, but interrelations between the individuals and their environment, such as the roughness of a rock face that is only touched by a mountaineer. Berque was inspired by Gibson's work:

> What encouraged me to look at trajection was the notion of affordance, coined by James Gibson. These are the properties that the environment offers (affords) our perception and at the same time of the capacity it possesses (affords) to influence or to interact with these properties.
>
> (Berque, 1987: 246).

Berque's work, transposed to the tourism dynamic of sites famous for their high-quality food, encouraged us to look at affordance as a vector of the interaction between tourists and the place. Our previous work on the gastronomic atmosphere in Vonnas (Clergeau and Etcheverria, 2013) allowed us to show that such an environment is an intentional construction of Chef Georges Blanc to promote the gourmet experience for tourists. In relation to this analysis, we put forward the hypothesis that this construction is organised by and around a set of relations and interrelations, connecting the local actors, the permanent inhabitants, and the temporary inhabitants (i.e., the tourists). We therefore suggest analysing the affordance as a vector of, and support for, these interrelations. In other words, we suggest considering that a material or immaterial object constitutes an affordance if it conceals potential (whether real or ideal) interrelationships that will make sense for each tourist according to their recreation project (Clergeau, 2015). We also suggest keeping the term "making sense" in all its iterations – not just its intellectual meaning, but also its emotional, psychological, and sensory meanings.

It appears then that a restaurant, which tells the local story in a sensory way, is an incubator of relationships between the place and every tourist who includes a visit in their recreational project. Research into the tourist experience suggests that a good time spent in restaurants that value local cuisine undeniably contributes to positive and unforgettable memories in tourists' minds and helps them appreciate the destination (Tsai, 2016).

We suggest here that it is not just the business, the chef, the cuisine, and the service that constitute the salience of the restaurant and make it attractive, but the identity quality of this restaurant, which represents a specific place, awakens the senses of taste and smell, and uses colours and sounds – all of which in turn represent the permanent and temporary inhabitants connected to the place. This testifies to an internal relationship with the food placed in the mouth and, more broadly, a local identity; and it requires a second look at the concept of the identity quality associated with restaurants.

2.2. The identity quality of a restaurant as a trajective affordance

Quality is defined as the ability of a product or service to satisfy customers. Such a definition requires researchers to emphasise the subjective nature of quality (Parasuraman et al., 1985; Zeithaml, 1988; Pine and Gilmore, 1998; Benavent and Evrard, 2002): Consumers evaluate the service (or product) in terms of their expectations, their experiences, their perception, and the reality. This is exactly the same with tourism and gastronomy (Clergeau et al., 2014). Quality depends on some objective characteristics of the service but also on more subjective ones: the tourists' expectations, their perceptions and experience, the atmosphere of the restaurant, its thematisation, relations with the staff in the dining room, the characteristics of the food served (Bitner, 1992; Bonnefoy-Claudet, 2006; Pageau, 2006; Heide et al., 2007; Wall and Berry, 2007; Ha and Jang, 2010; Sarra et al., 2015).

Consumer quality appraisal is a well-covered topic in literature (Boyer and Nefzi, 2009), highlighting the multiple dimensions – or attributes – of quality

(Parasuraman et al., 1985; Sirieix and Dubois, 1999). These dimensions refer to the distinctiveness consumers expect, which they identify and formalise from the characteristics of the goods or services. In relation to food, Grunert et al. (2001) suggest, for example, a typology of dimensions according to whether they are related to pleasure (hedonism), health (hygiene), practicality, or the production process (including animal welfare). The information economy (Nelson, 1970; Darby and Karni, 1973) classifies dimensions according to whether they emerge from research (quality that can be checked before consumption), from experience (quality that is proven by the consumer's experience), or from a belief (quality that cannot be formally proven but in which the consumer fully believes). In the absence of information, labels guide consumers in their choices and strengthen their belief in the quality of the service or product consumed (Larceneux, 2003). In the context of gastonomy, it depends on the expertise of the gastronomic guides who rank the restaurants and thereby influence the expectations of diners.

These different dimensions of quality have a constructed nature (Grunert et al., 2001), linking product knowledge, consumer experience, and subjective creation for individuals and their social group. They are subject to evolution: for example, the search for sustainable consumption is nowadays a key element of quality assessment not referred to in the twentieth century. Maby (2007), referring to the quality characteristics of food products, notes that they exist in many forms. Some are technical and technological and therefore measurable, while others are symbolic and immaterial, relating to imaginary concepts. He refers to "abstract forms" of quality using the example of wine. Rooted in a real territory, wine owes its measurable attributes, such as its organoleptic aspects, to the qualities of the land. In addition, wine is accompanied by an oeno-cultural discourse that idealises it and is a metaphor for the territorial effect: "The wine contributes to the construction of the global territorial representation, it gives and it receives, because this representation – enriched by all the other territorial components – helps to cement its own representations" (Maby, 2007). The author further suggests there is a specific "interactivity identity" relating to the quality of wine.

It is in this sense that we evoke the idea of identity quality for a restaurant. We consider that the quality of a food product encapsulates not only the identity of the producer, but also that of the diners who consume it as both a food and its associated taste. In an osmotic logic, the identities of producers and diners therefore enrich the qualities of the agricultural food product itself. The organoleptic characteristics of the product as such reflect the taste characteristics of the producer and the diners, as both permanent and temporary inhabitants, while also reflecting local taste preferences – the internal taste relationship of a localised social group, by which we mean its identity. In the case of a restaurant, the diners' identities combine with those of the chef who values the culinary products. As such, it is the communication and imagination of producers, chefs, and diners that enrich the quality of the agricultural food product. It is for this reason that we refer to the aesthetics of the agricultural food product. For the producer, as well as for the chef and the diner, these identities are viscerally and emotionally connected to the place, and hence strongly rooted geographically.[1]

A restaurant is a place for intersubjectivity, the meeting point for communication and imaginary, but also a place for sensory experimentation with agricultural food products, recipes, the aesthetics of dishes, as well as the environment in which the desire to eat and drink is born. The restaurant presents itself as the crucible of identity interactivity, which we call its identity quality.

3. The Christopher Coutanceau restaurant in La Rochelle

The Coutanceau restaurant boasts a score of 16.5 and three 'chef's hats' in the Gault&Millau guide:

> Aiming for a fourth hat, Christopher Coutanceau is today well placed to secure it for the region. The establishment, which was made famous by the present owner's father Richard, gets better every year thanks to the welcome provided by Nicolas Brossard, clearly identifying it as a great restaurant.[2]

From the opening paragraph, the food critics highlight Christopher Coutanceau's local roots. The restaurant represents a family, a story, and a city. With his partner Nicolas Brossard, the owner has made his local roots, as well as his links with the site and to those who promote it, a real guarantee of quality:

> The Charente Maritime region is my identity, my inspiration, and the sea is my garden. I try to explain the place using products from the sea, all those *maigre*, langoustines, scallops … straight from the ocean which stretches away from you when seated at your table.[3]

3.1. The identity quality of the Coutanceau restaurant

"My culinary identity is La Rochelle," says Christopher Coutanceau.[4] He therefore incorporates fragments of his personal identity (a system of values, aesthetic appreciation, the use of imaginary) and his La Rochelle background (he was born there) and applies these to the agricultural food products he chooses for his kitchen and his restaurant: "Everything must be local for us. Even the salt for cooking. It is sea salt straight from the Île de Ré."[5] The producers are, in fact, chosen as much for their technical skills in producing agricultural food products (the vegetables are grown to order) as for their identities, their personal qualities, and their socio-cultural qualities. "My suppliers are also my friends," Christopher Coutanceau likes to point out, and his childhood pals have now become fishermen selling their catches at the

La Rochelle auction house. "What is important for me are the human values we share," he says, insisting that, "All the details of one's character are important."

His ideas clearly highlight the importance of identity interactivity linking the agricultural food product and the actors in the food chain, the upstream producer and the downstream consumer (either a chef or a diner), including the serving staff in the dining room. This identity attribute related to the quality of agricultural food products is an added value, first for the local culture and then for the place. "My cuisine tells you about the place, it tells the local story," says Coutanceau. "My intention is for people to taste the culture, to taste the flagship products from the place." The flagship products are prepared in his unique way and reflect the identity that he projects. As such, we can clearly see that the producers, chefs, dining-room staff, and diners (both permanent and temporary inhabitants) are therefore in a common quest for identity.

This patient work with suppliers is outlined in Coutanceau's book *Carnet des saveurs en Charente-Maritime*, published in 2010, in which he introduces fourteen local producers he considers to be the most original and emblematic of local know-how. This is in fact the story of a remarkable partnership, started by Christopher's father Richard Coutanceau and directly involved in developing the restaurant's gourmet reputation. A large part of the history of La Rochelle is therefore included in the story – so much so that, in a metonymic logic, the Coutanceau restaurant is La Rochelle and La Rochelle is the Coutanceau restaurant. We can see here how a name can come to represent an entire city.

3.2. The Coutanceau restaurant's gourmet reputation

The restaurant's gourmet reputation (and that of the Coutanceau family itself) is directly related to the identity quality of the agricultural food products used in the food served. The story of the development of this gourmet reputation began in the early 1980s with Richard Coutanceau, who began making himself known and recognised (with one Michelin star in 1980) for his work at the *Hôtel de France et d'Angleterre*.

The mayor of La Rochelle, Michel Crépeau, had the idea of locating the restaurant on Concurrence Beach: "The city owned this old pergola on the beach which they wanted to renovate and bring back to life. He came to see me about it." the chef Richard Coutanceau says[6]. His cuisine was based on the appreciation of fish, shellfish, and crustaceans caught off the coast of La Rochelle. The stylistic identity is vintage in origin and, according to his son, the langoustine tartar he invented more than thirty years ago is still on the restaurant's menu today.

This is an unprecedented culinary use of langoustine, which is, first, an extremely high-quality product when alive, with both a strong iodine and sweet flavour; and, second, a remarkable spatial identifier (it comes directly from the port at La Cotinière). The product's taste qualities add to the "power of symbolic evocation, the delicacy of its sensory effects or the variety of its metaphorical representations" (Maby, 2007). Richard Coutanceau was awarded a second Michelin star in 1986.

"The restaurant's cuisine is linked to the history of the town of La Rochelle," says Christopher Coutanceau. The whole restaurant then gradually became a gourmet showcase for La Rochelle through its use of local food products, their identity qualities, and the identities of producers and fishermen, thanks to the communication and imaginary gastronomy provided by the head chef and his colleagues in the dining room. The identity qualities expressed by the serving staff and in their gastronomic imaginary are also very important.

This staging of local products is facilitated with the intrumentalisation of the wonderful view of Concurrence Beach: A large picture window turns the restaurant into a sort of shop-window on the beach, the ocean, and their riches. It is "a decor which changes several times a day," Christopher Coutanceau likes to say. The communication and the imaginary linked to Concurrence Beach and the ocean's landscape – and used by Christopher Coutanceau, Nicolas Brossard, and his serving team – is a hitherto unseen form of contextualisation within the restaurant industry.

This contextualisation is reinforced by the new decor that invites diners into an identity experience (in the strict sense as well as in the figurative sense). The restaurant's Website mentions:

> Upon arrival, there is a real sense of immersion. The totally new decor plunges us into the exciting world of the seabed of the two-star chef Christopher Coutanceau and his partner Nicolas Brossard. They envisaged, in collaboration with the ABP Architects, a setting inspired by the sea, a world that deeply fascinates them. The new decor with sand-covered walls, a ceiling inspired by the seabed, an abyss of blue carpet, over 800 suspended plant-like lamps that move as they would in the depths from white to yellow.... The tableware and cutlery also evoke aquatic elements, such as water droplet-shaped plates and fishermen's knives. Everything has been thought through down to the very last detail and is made to measure. A table art that reflects the chef's marine creations.[7]

As such, the symbols and their values and the socio-cultural imaginary of the place constitute the intangible flavour of the Coutanceau restaurant. The restaurant's anchorage in a site is metaphorised by Christopher Coutanceau in the way he matches the properties of the place ("There is a strong and unique identity of La Rochelle", he says) with the properties of the restaurant. The chef achieves this anchorage by using his former personal knowledge (he was born there) and by renewing his relations to the city, the countryside and the sea (he practices underwater fishing). And, finally, at the same time, he idealises his cultural roots. The long-term anchorage and steadfastness are important: "This restaurant has had two stars for thirty-four years. It's the oldest two-Michelin-star restaurant to have never lost one," says Christopher Coutanceau.

The restaurant has had strong media interest. It has become a recognisable landmark, positioned on a beach like a lighthouse, an identifiable site where one can find flagship products whose identity quality is valued in the cuisine. It is the food critics (in the role of transmitters) and the political actors (in the role of broadcasters) who have directly contributed to constructing the restaurant's gourmet reputation by instilling the identity message and the emblematic image.

Diners, both the permanent and temporary inhabitants, via social networks, actively participate in generating notoriety for the restaurant. In 2014, the Coutanceau restaurant was ranked fourth in the top-ten most popular gourmet restaurants in France and was given the highest score by internet users posting reviews on TripAdvisor (Traveler's Choice Award). An article in *Capital* magazine dated 7 October 2014 offered the opinion of one of the contributors: "The setting is simply extraordinary.... The layout of the tables, intelligently placed facing the ocean, gives the opportunity to admire the action of the waves during your meal."[8]

These comments and imaginaries of the restaurant are based on some idea of distinction. The restaurant is a landmark distinguishing the quality products, quality cuisine and service, and the quality town. It is an identifying, symbolic, and allegorical marker establishing the very essence of its identity quality. This has come about thanks to strong roots and geographical proximities visible in the use of local supply chains, but also thanks to organised proximities (Boschma, 2005), particularly the social and cognitive ones, explained by the development of a professional network of producers who are also "friends" and "family members."

The uniqueness of the site, represented by the restaurant, contextualises the experience and guides diners in their tasting, their sensory and aesthetic pleasure. The restaurant's reputation, patiently developed, and the fruit of this identity interaction with the site and those who value it, as well as the agricultural food products, is used as a signal to tourists. The identity quality, the real reason for its prominence – or reputation – allows tourists, in conjunction with their recreational aims, to discover, appropriate, and feel they are part of La Rochelle.

4. The identity quality of the Coutanceau restaurant as a tourist affordance

4.1. An affordance . . .

The search for an unusual experience in an unusual geographic location is explicit among tourists, a demand to which tourism destinations try to respond by promoting the qualities of the site, their identities, and local products, particularly agricultural food products. The social groups that promote them also find that tourism is a good way of renewing their local identities (Debarbieux, 2012).

The way in which tourists discover the Coutanceau restaurant, with identity as a key aspect (the recreational project is based on the discovery of something different somewhere different), allows us to recall that tourism is an activity dominated by coproduction. The production of a tourist experience (and especially a gourmet experience) is the result of a coproduction process related to the tourist's identity and linked to their relationship with otherness.

The restaurant is therefore an essential element of the tourist ecumene (Équipe MIT, 2005), understood here not only as a set of places inhabited by tourists but also, as Berque emphasises (1987: 17), a "relationship" – in this case, the relationship between tourists and tourist sites, and those who promote them. Indeed, the identity quality of the restaurant, as an affordance, allows tourists to arrive at the site through gustatory discovery and incorporation, to experience emotions, and to undergo a sensory and memorable experience. This enables the trajection whereby an object in itself becomes a tourist object, which is to say it helps accomplish a recreational tourism project. Specifically at the heart of this recreational project, the question of identity and identification is essential. In the gastronomic sector, a restaurant is really a place for gourmet experimentation through contact and relationships; conversations with the chef, serving staff, and other diners; in a specific context of hospitality; with otherness and multiculturalism exacerbated by the opportunity to do something different (the tourist activity) somewhere different (the tourist site).

Tourism actors (including chefs and restaurateurs) directly or indirectly, voluntarily or involuntarily, provide, through the restaurant, an affordance and the possibility of interrelationships that promote, through the gourmet experience, the tourist experience itself. Identifying the restaurant as an affordance is a way of facilitating access to the restaurant itself as well as to the tourist area in which it is situated.

4.2. ... as long as it is perceived as such

Studies on experiential marketing (Kotler, 1973; Holbroock and Hirschman, 1982; Lemoine, 2004; Caru and Cova, 2006) show that experiences are acquired in an atmosphere of tangible and intangible objects, affecting the senses and the emotions, but also social relationships. The restaurant as a tourist affordance is constructed through many components: sensory signals (taste primarily, then olfactory, oral, visual, tactile), architecture and decor, the associated landscape, human relationships (the welcome, service, advice and information, discussions), identities (products, the cuisine, the chef and the dining-room staff, the diners), as well as the information and imaginary provided, distributed, and asserted. That is to say, the restaurant as tourist affordance has great potential for interrelations between tourists and the tourist site, which makes "sense" in the context of the recreational tourism project.

However, this affordance must be perceived as such by tourists. As Greeno points out in relation to Gibson's thesis,

> The term *affordance* refers to whatever it is about the environment that contributes to the kind of interaction that occurs. One also needs a term that refers to whatever it is about the agent that contributes to the kind of interaction that occurs. I prefer the term *ability*.
>
> (Greeno, 1994: 338).

Berque probably would not express such reserve, considering that as the affordance is trajective, it only exists for the individual: A small indentation on a rock wall will not be a draw for the novice mountaineer. Nevertheless, Greeno's remark allows us to question the possibility that tourists perceive the restaurant as a trajective affordance.

This question concerns the tourists' acquisition of tourism skills and their progressive ability to use objects from their unfamiliar tourist environment as affordances. Studies on tourism management show that accumulated tourism experience makes tourists better able to appreciate it and be drawn to unfamiliar places and objects (Clergeau et al., 2014). Nevertheless, tourism stakeholders must endeavour to make objects appropriable for tourists. The case of the Coutanceau restaurant shows us how gastronomy actors manage to do just that.

They do so first by way of theatricalisation (Clergeau and Etcheverria, 2013). Holbrook and Hirschman (1982) show that the production of a consumer experience is akin to a dramatic art in the generic sense of the term, while Filzer (2002: 19) identifies three constants that we can interpret as actions aimed at offering affordances: the stage (the theatricalisation), the plot (the story the product narrates), and the action (the relationship between the consumer and the product). Theatricalisation includes not only the setting but also the stage: It involves the serving-staff in a controlled distribution of information and imaginary (both gastronomic and tourist-related) as well as gestures that support and stimulate them. Laurent Lesavre (2013: 27) specifies that what is interesting in the use of a theatrical technique in a company "is its living and breathing character (with an emotional charge), the fact that it creates a sense of surprise, that it concerns as much an emotion as a sense of reason and that it seems to facilitate long-term recollections."

This dramaturgy, which is precisely the catalyst behind the Coutenceau restaurant, uses a multitude of registers (cognitive, sensorial, affective, emotional) to garner the tourists' attention, to create an experience, to generate emotion, and to allow them to enter into an emotional and sensitive relationship with the territory: The picture window allows tourists to admire the immensity of the Atlantic Ocean; the langoustines relate to the port at Cotinière; the salt reminds them of the salt marshes on Île de Ré; the iodised potato references the producers from Noirmoutier as well as the unique local soil. The territory, with all its component elements (physical, historical, cultural), its myths and its messages, is on display in the narrative, in the action, in the relationships, and in the emotion. These experiences are now offered to tourists, in association with a hotel in La Rochelle, to combine a gourmet getaway with a short stay, the chef's cuisine, and a visit to the town.

The culinary and service arts in a restaurant can be seen as a dramaturgical skill, putting a local identity into narrative and emotion, and allowing them to interact with each tourist. This offers a quality and identity framework that is beneficial to the tourists and that ultimately includes them in the dramatic composition: They become stakeholders in the quality and identity of the restaurant through their gastronomic activities and then subsequently share their experiences via social networks or with their close acquaintances. They may even at times influence the recipes and ingredients used in dishes. Although this is not the case with Christopher Coutanceau, chefs sometimes have to rework typical local cuisine to suit the tastes of international tourists (Sinha et al., 2016). The narrative and its theatricalisation are reworked and adapted depending on whom they are intended for.

Theatricalisation aims to arouse curiosity and thus facilitate the affordance. Cochoy (2011) confirms that curiosity is generated, and – more – is grasped, activated, and awakened. He refers to an inquisitive differentiation:

"The propensity for people to be surprised, to be attracted by something unknown, to opt for novelty, to love surprises."

(Cochoy, 2011:56)

Hence, the (identity) quality of the serving staff in the dining room is essential:

"We know the quality of products, first one-dimensional" (good or bad, as Akerlof (1970) revealed) "and then plural" (according to Lancaster (1975)). "We should henceforth, thanks to the flow of dispositions between humans through things, rediscover the quality of people, in the original sense, which is to say people who incorporate or are attributed qualities. The qualification effort is twofold: whereas economics and sociology have exhaustively described the qualification of products and the social space involved, we need to describe the symmetrical operation for the qualification of people."

(Cochoy, 2011: 186, authors' translation).

In addition to a theatricalisation effort, chefs must develop their fame. The restaurant, like a theatre, has qualities that are exclusively revealed by the experience and the beliefs associated with this experience. So is the identity quality. It is revealed to tourists at the very moment they participate, taste, feel, and are moved by the show being performed and its staging. It is only revealed, however, if the gourmet tourists believe that what they taste – and what they experience – has an extraordinary and unique dimension they will then be able to share with their close friends and family. As with any artist, the chef-playwright operates in what can be called, borrowing the words of Saunier (2015), an "economy of fame": They live in a world of communication, and the qualities of their work are only revealed by experience and by social beliefs. Recognition, fame, and reputation are required for them to connect with and maintain the virtuous circle of identity interactions between their work and gourmet tourists.

This fame comes in different forms: commercial success, recognition by experts and tourists -on social networks, recognition in national media, and symbolic recognition with stars awarded by the Michelin Guide. As is the case in many art forms, the symbolic qualities of the work – and in particular its identity quality – are defined through the role of the artist as a person (Clerc, 2010; Saunier, 2015), by his/her career, his/her identity. Christopher Coutanceau and his partner have operated a real reputational work (Saunier, 2015) aimed at managing the reputation of the restaurant, the chef, and his cuisine, and at the same time, at guiding, maintaining, and enriching it. This is undertaken with consideration for the dual nature of reputation (Beuscart et al., 2015): the cognitive (with reference to the components of social consideration, the values and beliefs that guide it) and the metrological nature (with reference to the systems that underpin it). The Coutanceau restaurant therefore pilots a real reputational work by highlighting the chef, publishing a book, giving interviews, contributing to social media, sticking to the proven techniques that support the reputations of great chefs (food guides, the *Relais & Châteaux* network), and articulating his desire to compete for a third star.[9] This reputation is knowingly created and based around identity quality.

The chef likes to refer to his local origins: "As a citizen of La Rochelle, Christopher Coutanceau grew up facing the Atlantic Ocean."[10] He presents himself as "a cooking fisherman"[11] and reminds us that La Rochelle has influenced his identity. Presenting the new decor to the press, Nicolas Brossard and his partner explained that it aimed to provide an "immersion within this maritime world that is part of the childhood, the job, and the passion of the chef. It is his universe."[12]

5. Conclusion

With the example of the Coutanceau restaurant in La Rochelle, we have explained the definition of identity quality and have analysed it as a trajective affordance allowing gourmet tourists to interact with the town. We have clarified that this identity quality can only be applied (and therefore appreciated) if it is dramatised and supported by a real reputable technique. Our study develops the idea that the identity quality of a restaurant constitutes an affordance for the tourist ecumene. Such a property of identity quality is a challenge for restaurant owners but also, and certainly, for tourist destination managers.

In La Rochelle, Christopher Coutanceau's brother, Gregory, who shares the same passion for cooking, has himself set up several restaurants. The family is therefore variously present and active in the town. However, La Rochelle does not rely solely on the fame of its restaurants to develop its attractiveness. A brief look around the town, as well as meetings with tourism development stakeholders, revealed that the identity dynamics into which the Coutanceau restaurant fits are not conveyed by the public tourism actors, raising questions on the dynamics of local tourism development and their leverage.

Notes

1 In this sense, Jacques Maby insists that, "As such the territory seems to me to be primarily a question of spatial identity produced by society, and particularly by geographers, and based on identity indicators."
2 https://fr.gaultmillau.com/restaurant/restaurant-christopher-coutanceau?locale=fr-FR.
3 https://www.relaischateaux.com/fr/france/coutanceau-charente-maritime-la-rochelle.
4 Interview conducted in June 2015.
5 Interview conducted in June 2015.
6 Interview published in *Les Echos*, 2011.
7 Translated from the restaurant's website https://www.coutanceaularochelle.com/.
8 https://www.capital.fr/lifestyle/les-dix-restaurants-francais-preferes-des-utilisateurs-de-tripadvisor-966647.
9 "Who wouldn't want to win the World Cup?" he replied to journalists who questioned him about this possibility. From an interview with *Sud Ouest*. http://www.sudouest.fr/2017/02/16/nouveau-decor-etoil-e-cote-mer-3202071-1391.php.
10 From the restaurant's website.
11 From the restaurant's website.
12 From an interview with *Sud Ouest*. http://www.sudouest.fr/2017/02/16/nouveau-decor-etoil-e-cote-mer-3202071-1391.php.

References

Akerlof, G.A. (1970). The market for "lemons": quality uncertainty and the market mechanism. *The Quarterly Journal of Economics*, 84(3), pp. 488–500.

Benavent, C. and Evrard, Y. (2002). Extension du domaine de l'expérience. *Décisions Marketing*, 28, pp. 7–11.

Berque A. (1987). *Ecoumène, Introduction à l'étude des milieu humains*. Paris, Belin.

Beuscart, J., Chauvin, P., Jourdain, A. and Naulin, S. (2015). La réputation et ses dispositifs: Introduction. *Terrains & Travaux*, 26(1), pp. 5–22.

Bitner, M.J. (1992). Servicescapes: The impact of physical surroundings on customers and employees. *Journal of Marketing*, 56, pp. 57–71.

Bonnefoy-Claudet, L. (2006). *Les effets de la thématisation du lieu sur l'expérience vécue par le consommateur: Une double approche cognitive et expérientielle*. Thèse pour le doctorat en sciences de gestion, Grenoble: Université de Grenoble.

Boschma, R.A. (2005). Proximity and innovation: A critical assessment. *Regional Studies*, 39(1), pp. 61–74.

Boyer, A. and Nefzi, A. (2009). La perception de la qualité dans le domaine des services: Vers une clarification des concepts. *La Revue des Sciences de Gestion*, 237–238(3), pp. 43–54. doi:10.3917/rsg.237.0043.

Caru, A. and Cova B. (2006). Expériences de consommation et marketing expérientiel. *Revue Française de Gestion*, 2003/3(162), pp. 99–113.

Clerc, A. (2010). Entre artiste idéalisé et personne incarnée: Les figures de l'écrivain nées des rencontres avec les lecteurs. *Terrains & Travaux*, 17(1), pp. 5–21.

Clergeau, C. (2015). Atmosphère des destinations touristiques, propositions pour une analyse stratégique. *4ème colloque sino-européen du tourisme.* ESTHUA Tourisme et Culture, Université d'Angers, July 2015.

Clergeau, C. and Etcheverria, O. (2013). La mise en tourisme et le développement local par la création d'une atmosphère gastronomique. Analyse à partir du cas de Vonnas. *Mondes du Tourisme*, 7, pp. 52–67.

Clergeau, C., Glasberg, O. and Violier, P. (2014). *Management des entreprises du tourisme, stratégie et organisation*. Paris, Dunod.

Cochoy F. (2011). *De la curiosité. L'art de la séduction marchande*. Paris: Armand Colin.

Darby, M.R. and Karni, E. (1973). Free competition and the optimal amount of fraud. *Journal of Law and Economics*, 16, pp. 67–88.

Debarbieux, B. (2012). Tourism, Imaginaries and Identities: reversing the point of view. *Via. Tourism Review*, (1). http://journals.openedition.org/viatourism/1191.

Équipe MIT. (2005). *Tourismes 2. Moments de lieux*. Paris, Belin.

Filzer, M. (2002). Le marketing de la production d'expérience: Statut théorique et implication managériales. *Décisions Marketing*, 28, pp. 13–22.

Greeno, J. (1994). Gibson's affordances. *Psychological Review*, 101(2), pp. 3336–3343.

Grunert, K.G., Juhl, H.J. and Poulsen C.S. (2001). Perception de la qualité en alimentaire et rôle des labels. *Revue Française du Marketing*, 183/184, pp. 181–196.

Ha, J. and Jang S. (2010). Effects of service quality and food quality: The moderating role of atmospherics in an ethnic restaurant segment. *International Journal of Hospitality Management*, 29, pp. 520–529.

Heide M., Laerdal K. and Gronhaug K. (2007). The design and management of ambience: Implications for hotel architecture and service. *Tourism Management*, 28, pp. 1315–1325.

Holbrook, M.B. and Hirschman, E.C. (1982). The experiential aspects of consumption: Consumer fantasies, feelings, and fun. *Journal of Consumer Research*, 9(2), pp. 132–140.

Kotler, P. (1973). Atmospherics as a marketing tool. *Journal of Retailing*, 49(4), pp. 48–64.

Lancaster, K. (1975). Socially optimal product differentiation. *American Economic Review*, 65(4), pp. 567–585.

Larceneux, F. (2003). Segmentation des signes de qualité: Labels expérientiels et labels techniques. *Décisions Marketing*, 29, pp. 35–46.

Lemoine, J.F. (2004). Magasins d'atmosphère: Quelles évolutions et quelles perspectives d'avenir? *Revue Française du Marketing*, 198(3/5), pp. 107–116.

Lesavre, L. (2013). *Scènes de management. Le théâtre au service de l'entreprise*. Grenoble: PUG – Collection: Management et Innovation.

Maby, J. (2007). Le vin, argument identitaire du territoire. Conférence pour la société géographique italienne. https://jacquesmaby.wordpress.com/2007/01/13/le-vin-argument-identitaire-du-territoire/.

Nelson, P. (1970). Information and consumer behavior. *Journal of Political Economy*, 78, pp. 311–329.

Pageau, F. (2006). Ambiance des restaurants et expériences touristiques. *Téoros*, 25(1), pp. 43–49.

Parasuraman, A., Berry Leonard, L. and Zeithaml V.A. (1985). A conceptual model of service quality and its implications for future research. *Journal of Marketing*, 149, pp. 41–50.

Pine, II B.J. and Gilmore, J.H. (1998). Welcome to the experience economy. *Harvard Business Review*, 76(4), pp. 97–105.

Requier-Desjardins, D. (2009). Territoires – Identités – Patrimoine: Une approche économique? *Développement Durable et Territoires*, Dossier 12, http://developpement durable.revues.org/7852.

Sarra, A., Di Zio, S. and Cappucci, M. (2015). A quantitative valuation of tourist experience in Lisbon. *Annals of Tourism Research*, 53, pp. 1–16.

Saunier, E. (2015). Produire la valeur artistique dans une économie de la notoriété. Le cas d'Amélie Nothomb. *Terrains & Travaux*, 26(1), pp. 41–61.

Sgard, A. (1999). Qu'est-ce qu'un paysage identitaire? In *Paysages et identités régionales. De pays rhônalpin en paysages*. Textes réunis par C. Burgard et F. Chesnet (eds). La passe du vent, Valence, France.

Sinha, N., Chaudhury, H.R. and Mazumdar S. (2016). Understanding gastronomic taste of cosmopolitan consumers: Study on Bengali themed restaurants in Kolkata. *XIMB Journal of Management*, 13(1), pp. 1–20.

Sirieix, L. and Dubois, P-L. (1999). Vers un modèle qualité-satisfaction intégrant la confiance? *Recherche et Applications en Marketing*, 14(3), pp. 1–22.

Tsai, C.T. (2016). Memorable tourist experiences and place attachment when consuming local food. *International Journal of Tourism Research*, 18(6), pp. 536–548.

Wall, E.A. and Berry, L.L. (2007). The combined effects of the physical environment and employee behavior on customer perception of restaurant service quality. *Cornell Hotel and Restaurant Administration Quarterly*, 48(1), pp. 59–69.

Zeithaml, V.A. (1988). Consumer perceptions of price, quality and value: A means-end model and synthesis of evidence. *Journal of Marketing*, 52(3), pp. 2–22.

3 Gourmet tourism as part of a territorial branding strategy

The example of Auvergne

Marie-Eve Férérol

1. Introduction

Supermarkets have used branding strategies for decades, and over the last fifteen years or so, regional authorities have followed suit. Now part of a globalised economy and dominated by market laws, regions have no other choice but to endeavour to stand out in an effort to attract new residents and potential investors. To achieve this, local stakeholders adopt marketing policies largely based on regional resources that come in many forms: material or immaterial, innate or constructed (e.g., Pecqueur and Gumuchian, 2007; François, 2008; Fabry, 2009).

Cultural resources (Ritchie and Zins, 1978; Landel and Sénil, 2009; Meyronin and Berneman, 2010), and gastronomy in particular (Csergo and Lemasson, 2008), are among the resources to exploit to increase regional attractiveness and develop tourism. Food products, recipes, and cookery expertise form "a whole that constitutes a strong and distinctive element and can lead to positive differentiation associated with image, quality and reputation" (Fabry and Zeghni, 2014). As Clergeau and Etcheverria illustrated at the conference dedicated to gastronomy and local development in 2012, gastronomy generates numerous effects, both tangible and intangible, at the regional level. For example, it can heighten the permanent or temporary attraction of people or businesses and lead to a new relationship between urban and rural areas, the redevelopment of landscapes, the construction of regional symbols, or the redefinition of the local image through everything that is tasted or touched.

In light of this, the current chapter aims to explore the contribution of gastronomy, and more generally gourmet tourism, in the context of territorial branding. Like Lemasson (2006) and Etcheverria (2014), we refer to "*tourisme gourmand*" or gourmet tourism,[1] since this covers a wide range of approaches, from culinary tourism with its focus on authenticity and nutrition, to gastronomic tourism, which is more rooted in the quality of produce and the search for pleasure (Jacobs and Smits, 2007; Racine, 2012; Barrère, 2013). The term "gourmet tourism" also allows us to address issues such as the level of service offered in Michelin-starred restaurants and farm-taverns (part of agritourism[2]), and ways of staging regional produce, such as organising events.

This study focuses on the Auvergne region in central France, which alongside other regional authorities has opted for territorial branding.[3] The *Auvergne Nouveau Monde* brand, first conceived and operationalised at the end of 2011, places strong emphasis on the quality of products, places, and experiences for new arrivals and tourists to enjoy. As such, this strategy perfectly suits the context of our research. At the outset, this brand was intended to primarily boost tourism, but local stakeholders quickly expanded the initiative to include all economic sectors.

The chapter is structured as follows: Our literature review first lays out the specific conceptual framework adopted. We then present the region under study and its territorial branding approach. The subsequent sections present our findings from the semistructured interviews with relevant stakeholders and the analysis of documents (websites, internal documents, brochures, etc.) from various sources (regional authorities, development agencies, Regional Tourism Development Committee, etc.) to answer our research questions: What products and recipes can Auvergne emphasise? What makes these markers of identity? Is there a form of gourmet tourism specific to Auvergne? And if so, how can the territorial brand benefit from it? Finally, we discuss some potential contributions that gourmet tourism can offer.

2. Conceptual framework

We begin by developing our case study but first offer a succinct account of the primary concepts referred to in this chapter. The relevance of this conceptual framework has been highlighted by some authors, such as Brisson (2012: 34):

> The relevance of the destination branding theoretical framework is seen in the numerous connections that can be drawn between the concepts of destination branding and gastronomic tourism. In fact, a number of studies have established a connection between these two concepts, meaning that destination branding theory has already been used to explore and explain various gastronomic tourism phenomena.... Moreover, many scholars have stressed the importance of ensuring that the food and drinks of a particular place are utilized to brand it with a distinct gastronomic identity that will ultimately contribute to its competitiveness as a destination.
> (Fox, 2007; Stewart et al., 2008; Henderson, 2009; Lin et al., 2011)

2.1. Regional and tourist appeal

Globalisation has led to competition and competitiveness on all levels (municipalities, regions, etc.) and across all domains (industry, tourism, etc.). Public authorities now compete to find the most ingenious ways to boost the appeal of their regions (e.g., Hatem, 2004; Fabry, 2009; Poirot, 2010). As Fabry (2009: 57) states,

The attractiveness of a region is based on three pillars – its productive fabric, its residential fabric and its tourism – which are promoted with unequal efforts: tourism is often overlooked, which is not true of the economy or productivity. A region is said to be attractive if it is capable of drawing in businesses and capital for productive purposes and people for residential purposes. Tourist appeal is more complex as it requires both mobile segments of the population and tourist-related businesses for most of its services. However, the attractiveness of a particular destination must not be disassociated from the general challenge of boosting regional appeal.

Like any economic activity, tourism contributes to a region's general development: first, because it generates economic opportunities through job creation and the consumption of goods and services; second, because it forms part of the residential economy through temporary or permanent installations. According to Duhamel (2013: 50), "tourism is an activity that generates populations." In the same vein, by promoting events and material and immaterial heritage, tourism helps improve the region's image by showcasing its best qualities, fundamental in a context of regional competitiveness and competition.

2.2. Territorial appeal and branding

The objective of regional development is to promote and/or create distinctive resources, skills, and amenities that enable a region to stand out from its competitors and gain a competitive advantage (Veltz, 2004; Pecqueur and Gumuchian, 2007; Fabry, 2009; Gómez et al., 2015). Numerous researchers, particularly Pecqueur and Gumuchian (2007), have recently highlighted the existence of two types of regional resources: generic resources, which can be easily reproduced elsewhere, and specific/innate resources, which have a direct link with the region. The former are indicative of the stakeholders' capacity to create infrastructures and organise themselves (e.g., as a cluster), while the latter represent the region's DNA, its geographic and social characteristics, and its identity.

This implies that the creation of a territorial brand is a means of boosting development, providing visibility to the region's resources and initiatives (Aaker, 1996; Sexto et al., 2001; Gollain, 2011; Meyronin, 2015). According to Lorenzini et al. (2010: 541),

> Many studies have indicated the brand as a competitive factor for destinations. Territorial brands are a particular type of brand that have been addressed also in the literature on place branding and on sustainable development focusing on ecotourism and on the use of local products for tourism development. As Neto (2007) states, the building of territorial brands is a way of promoting the territory as a tourist destination, but also, and mainly, to attract investments and populations, to promote the

companies located in it as well as their products and to increase the portfolio of established companies.

A territorial brand performs several functions:

It serves at once a defensive function to differentiate a product from competitor products, and a symbolic function as a marker of identity that embodies a promise. It creates financial value and in that respect is an important resource (products "Made in France" for example) but it is also a process that involves mobilising everyone in support of a shared project that is expressed through values.

(Rochette, 2012: 7)

Ultimately, territorial brands themselves become an intangible resource generating non-financial and then financial value. In particular, for regions with strong tourism, branding has several benefits. As Brisson (2012: 34) states,

Branding can assist a place in becoming associated with a unique identity as well as help it deliver memorable experiences to travellers, thus allowing it to better compete with other destinations. Branding can also build awareness for a destination, reduce consumer anxiety and risk about undertaking travel, and encourage repeat visits by building loyalty (Kolb, 2006). Other advantages of destination branding for places could include more effective tourism promotion, a larger profile in the media, and the development of an atmosphere where innovation and investment is prized.

(Anholt, 2007)

Landel and Sénil (2009) argue that for a territorial brand to act as a driver of attractiveness, two factors are essential: "In a context of widespread competition between regions, quality and innovation are essential drivers of competitiveness." This quality requirement is also emphasised by other authors (Lorenzini et al., 2010; Lin et al., 2011; Gheorghe et al., 2014).

Territorial brands can be considered as emotional and iconic brands, since they convey a content of authenticity, quality and typicality.... Since territorial brands aim to promote an image of quality and sustainability of the territory they refer to, they can be considered as a tool of place branding. As Kavaratzis and Ashworth (2005: 511) state, "part of place branding is about using the qualities of local products to ascribe meanings and associations to the place."

(Lorenzini et al., 2010: 542)

Another relevant factor is the explicit link between the brand and the region's identity, which distinguishes the region from its competitors (Lin et al., 2011; San Eugenio, 2013). Furthermore,

A consumer who perceives the identity of a brand to be attractive is more likely to identify with the brand and incorporate that identity. In the consumption of a product or service that is highly visible, brand attractiveness is expected to play a significant role in CBI (customer brand identification) given the hedonic qualities associated with the enhancement of one's self.

(So et al., 2017: 642)

2.3. Gastronomy as a driver of territorial/destination branding[4]

Across the world, even in countries little known for their gastronomy (such as Sweden; Bonow and Rytkönen, 2012), gastronomic or culinary resources (regardless of which term is used) are becoming tools for local development and "strong territorial markers" (Leroux, 2016). "A food identity can be used to market and brand a region as a culinary tourism destination and give a taste of a locality" (Bonow and Rytkönen, 2012: 3). The World Tourism Organization (UNWTO) survey commissioned in 2012 revealed that for more than 88% of its members, gastronomy is a strategic element in defining the brand and image of a destination. Several studies have also highlighted the importance of gastronomy discourses in generating regional appeal (Hillel et al., 2013).

2.3.1. A return to terroir produce: a response to globalisation and poor diet

Linked to increasing mobility and globalisation, we are currently beholding the relative internationalisation of food products, resulting in the homogenisation of tastes. "In today's globalizing world, many have spoken out to express fears of cultural homogenization and a loss of diversity" (Blakey, 2012: 51). Some authors go even further: "Globalisation poses a threat to local gastronomic identity and image" (Mak et al., 2012: 3). However, paradoxically, we are seeing a return to terroir[5] produce, symbolic of the quest for identity in modern society (Blakey, 2012; Williams et al., 2014).

> Globalisation acts in a contradictory way here: on the one hand, it does favour the development of internationally standardised dishes (pizza, hamburgers, nuggets, sushi, tabbouleh) but on the other hand, in recent moves to differentiate territories, it also encourages the development or the renaissance of once-forgotten regional cooking.
>
> (Knafou and Anton Clave, 2012)

Often required to move several times within their lifetime and swept up in the whirlwind of globalisation, people look to food for a sense of rootedness. As many of today's urban dwellers once lived in the countryside, we are witnessing a return to nature, a "myth where the desire for nature and the past is seen as a counter tendency to globalisation, and associated urbanisation; it is an escape from technology-based society and a reconnection with one's 'roots'" (Steinmetz, 2010: 21).

Disappointed by industrial products (Salvador-Pérignon, 2012; Gheorghe et al., 2014; Williams et al., 2014) and in response to health scandals, consumers also increasingly opt for wholesome cultivation methods, integrated farming, and, if possible, local produce. "Getting 'back to nature' is also a reflection of an increased distrust of modern agricultural production methods and processed foods with the use of chemicals and food additives" (Steinmetz, 2010: 21).

2.3.2. Gastronomy: a strong identity marker with value added

Gastronomy in its broadest sense falls under the category of cultural resources, whether material or immaterial. "Gastronomy may help to reveal structuring elements of a country and of a culture" (Knafou and Anton Clave, 2012). Varying from one region to another, gastronomy underpins comparative advantage and thereby constitutes a driver of attractiveness. "Local and regional food could give added value to the destination and contribute in this way to the competitiveness of the geographic area" (Jiménez-Beltrán et al., 2016: 1). Such interregional diversity can first be explained by the different terroirs that give food products their distinct taste and appearance (Flores, 2007). Recipes, often handed down from one generation to the next, are a testament to a certain know-how (or "craft"), to our ancestors' capacity to sublimate products that in some cases appeared to have no great intrinsic value (Bessière, 1998). Cultural legacy, collective memory – our food heritage is a formidable vector of identity, uniting people from a given territory through the products they eat and the way they eat them.

Gourmet tourism is a way of showcasing a region's cultural resources to the greatest number of people. "The food is part of the social and cultural heritage of peoples, and that it reflects a certain style of living in different geographical areas and that gastronomy is something rooted in their own culture and tradition (Mitchell and Hall, 2006)" (López-Guzmán et al., 2014: 95). Boiţă (2014: 398) argues, "Gastronomic tourism is a part of cultural tourism, both through her traditional and culinary values, including at the same time tourism in urban areas and rural ones with its various specific activities." Gourmet tourism gives tourists the opportunity to savour new dishes (in restaurants or farm-taverns), discover new produce at events with a focus on the local terroir, or take an interest in manufacturing methods while visiting agro-food production plants.

2.3.3. Gourmet tourism: a new kind of tourism

In recent decades, tourist practices have shifted towards the experiential. Tourists no longer simply want to see things being done (for example, watching craft workers in the medinas in north Africa), they want to play an active role. The precepts of tourism in the twenty-first century are seeing, doing, and learning in a context of collaborative production and encounters.

If in the past mass tourism was the main way of its manifestation today tourism is practiced in small groups who look to live new experiences but keep in mind the environment. ... Nowadays, tourists are more experienced, have sufficient funds allocated to travel, have more free time. Through tourism they can escape the daily routine of their lives and they sink into a whole new world full of freedom and new things. More and more tourists in the world are seeking to learn new experiences. Gastronomy is such an experience.

(Gheorghe et al., 2014: 12)

The tourist experience now aims to awaken all the senses, and the key advantage of gastronomy for holiday destinations is that it stimulates our sense of smell, taste, touch, and sight (e.g., Beaudet, 2006; Steinmetz, 2010).

Food involves all the senses of taste, smell, touch and sight and this helps to provide for, and fulfil, visitors' need for new sensations. Greater symbolic significance is also often attached to the occasion. As Long (2004: 22) explains, food "engages one's physical being, not simply as an observer, but as a participant as well." Thus, it is the hedonic and aesthetic nature of food in tourism, for the sake of experiencing it in itself, that satisfies sensibilities, rather than what the food represents in satisfying hunger.

(Steinmetz, 2010: 34)

It is therefore unsurprising that gastronomy has become a key consideration when choosing holiday destinations.

Several researchers (e.g., CIET-UNSAM, 2008; Steinmetz, 2010; Gheorghe et al., 2014; Williams et al., 2014) point to the particular profile of gourmet tourists who are educated and have a relatively high income. They are more open to visiting new places, better informed, and less reluctant to experiment with unknown customs. This segment of the population holds the key to deciphering other cultures and drawing comparisons. "Culinary tourism is an authentic experience of a sophisticated lifestyle in a pleasant environment, associated with the good life and the economic wellbeing of consuming exclusive, high-quality locally grown products" (UNWTO, 2012: 7).

Although brief, this literature review reveals that gastronomy can boost a destination's appeal, serving as a strong identity marker. We use the territorial brand *Auvergne Nouveau Monde* as a concrete illustration of our research and to reveal a virtuous circle: quality – identity – territory. Food or culinary products can guarantee a certain level of quality, which in turn has a positive impact on the origin of such products. The reverse can also be true. Before we continue, we now briefly present the region under study.

3. Auvergne: a region intent on boosting its appeal

Auvergne is a mid-altitude mountainous region that is sparsely populated, and its rural areas are home to more than a third of its population and jobs. It is part of the "Diagonale du Vide" (diagonal of emptiness) that stretches from Extremadura to the Belgian Ardennes region. Its characteristics are not conducive to a high level of attractiveness and make it a territory that is often mocked or derided by certain Parisian journalists.

3.1. A region with little general appeal…

Over the last few decades, Auvergne has been described in various ways depending on the prevailing views of what is politically correct. "Underprivileged" in the 1970s, it became "fragile" in the 1980s and is now considered "sensitive" (Chignier-Riboulon, 2007). Referring to its handicaps within an open economy in which competition is the norm, these semantic shifts always come back to one central point: Auvergne's marginality, whether in demographic or economic terms.

With an average of fifty-two inhabitants per square kilometre, the Auvergne demographics are morose. However, after many years of decline, the region saw the population increase by 26,423 between 2006 and 2015 to a total 1,362,367. This increase, although lower than the national average, is due to migratory surplus. Auvergne is a region in which natural population growth is weak if not stagnant: The birth rate is low (9.9% in 2013) and the population is ageing (+60-year-olds represented 29.7% in 2015).

In economic terms, Auvergne is well down the ranks. With a GDP of €34 billion in 2012, it ranked nineteenth among all French regions, just ahead of Franche-Comté, Limousin, and Corsica. Its job structure reflects the region's traditional economy, with 5.2% of jobs in the agricultural sector in 2015 (twice the national average). Although the tertiary sector is the most significant, representing 72.1%, the range of services is incomplete, with a very large public sphere but inadequate services for business. However, the region boasts a strong productive sector (22.7%, compared to an average 19% in metropolitan France), driven by companies with an international presence (Michelin, Limagrain). Unfortunately, the region fails to sufficiently capitalise on this strength, leading Chignier-Riboulon to comment that for politicians in Auvergne, "the cows are more iconic than our high-tech companies!" (2002: 14).

Thankfully, this rather gloomy outlook is tempered by one of the great strengths of Auvergne: the tourism sector.

3.2. …despite strong tourist appeal

Partly due to its thermal history, Auvergne has long welcomed tourists. Despite the social tourism image that for a long time clung to this region, in recent years Auvergne has managed to become an appealing destination with a wide range of tourist practices linked to its natural, cultural, and historic heritage: skiing, thermalism and/or cures, hiking and swimming in rural areas, gastronomic experiences, visits to museums and castles, and participation in nationally and even internationally renowned festivals (such as the short film festival), not to mention the Pal wildlife reserve and the scientific theme park Vulcania. Such a rich choice of activities explains the relative balance in visitor numbers throughout the year: 22% of revenue generated in winter, 22% in spring, 36% in summer, and 20% in autumn.

As its isolation has been attenuated (even if the situation remains critical in terms of the railway network), the region is now easily accessible by road. This explains why the most faithful clientele is from Rhône-Alpes (16%) and two historic sources of visitors: Ile de France (19%) and greater western France (17%, including the Centre, Pays de Loire, and Poitou-Charentes regions). Overall, the vast majority of visitors are French (86%), and one of the challenges facing the tourism sector in Auvergne is attracting a greater number of foreigners. Another challenge is to broaden the spectrum of tourists: Currently the two traditional groups are families and pensioners.

Although in the 2000s tourist revenue in Auvergne was relatively strong, professionals from the sector and elected representatives remained wary and shared certain concerns driven by the economic crisis brewing (and continuing to brew) in France. Furthermore, as Botti (2011: 86) pointed out, "the extent of tourism in a region depends first and foremost on its tourist appeal." The Regional Council therefore decided to conceive a territorial brand – *Auvergne Nouveau Monde* (ANM) – with the objective of promoting the region's strengths. At the outset this brand was intended to benefit the tourism sector, so the Regional Tourism Development Committee (CRDT, 2013)[6] was initially responsible for it.

3.3. Boosting appeal with a territorial brand

Similar to other regional authorities,[7] Auvergne chose marketing tools and practices to boost its appeal, opting for a territorial brand. The first stage (not described in detail here) involved establishing an identity profile that would reveal the personality of the region and its inhabitants, with the objective of standing out from other regions. The second stage entailed a SWOT-type analysis. In addition, consultancy firms were brought in to determine the region's image both within and outside its "borders." Ultimately, the positioning Auvergne chose was an alternative development approach that represented a departure from the focus on intensive productivity. The current trend favouring soft power and soft attitudes (e.g., slow food movement[8]) is evident in the comments made by those behind the brand.

3.3.1. "A new tourism model"

The tourism sector has a privileged position in the brand's orientation, given that tourism often plays a showcasing role. If tourists can be attracted, then so can companies, which can also contribute to the residential economy through secondary homes or establishing a permanent presence. Those behind ANM, including CRDT (Regional Tourism Development Committee), see tourism in Auvergne as

> a natural, high-quality tourism that rejects excessive visitor numbers and imbalances both in time and space. Tourism built on sharing and exchanges, one that is authentic and personalised in respect of regional identities and which favours fulfilment, whether that of local inhabitants or visitors. ... Away from mass tourism, Auvergne must offer the public a new world in which visits provide a twofold benefit, that of affordable and active holidays for families first of all, but also that of a region that is refreshing, lifts the spirits and invigorates all those who come for a weekend or extended summer holidays.
>
> (CRDT-REGION AUVERGNE, 2011: 58 and 89)

The tourism that ANM promotes perhaps corresponds to what some researchers call "alternative tourism". According to Steinmetz (2010: 25),

> Alternative development models of tourism based on local sustainability have emerged in the wake of the negative outcomes associated with the globalisation of the industry. Such "alternative" models represent an attempt to maximise equitable economic benefits of tourism for local people and reduce the sociocultural and environmental impacts of traditional tourism models. Holden (2006: 127) has identified the following characteristics of alternative tourism models: (1) The pace of development is directed and controlled by local people rather than external influence, and development is small scale with high rates of local ownership. (2) Environmental conservation is important with the minimisation of negative social and cultural impacts. (3) Linkages to other sectors of the local economy such as agriculture are maximised, thus reducing the reliance on imports. (4) There is emphasis on attracting a market segment that is interested in education in the local culture and environment, and willing to accept local standards of accommodation and food.

The tourism ambitions underlying ANM cover environmental protection and quality of life: favouring open-mindedness, replenishment, and invigoration, being able to enjoy open and accessible wildlife, good value for money, unusual experiences, leaving the well-trodden path, etc. Although this brand positioning – perhaps overly focused on ecotourism and the emphatic expressions associated with the brand – may leave some feeling a little perplexed (Férérol, 2017), the emphasis on authenticity, well-being, calm, and unpolluted spaces is likely to be positively perceived by certain segments of the population. Those being targeted by CRDT and ANM are of course the region's traditional visitors (families and pensioners), but above all young urban dwellers from higher socioprofessional categories who have begun to appear in the region over the last five years or so.

3.3.2. The values promoted by the Auvergne brand

According to CRDT, and the ANM association[9] that took over the initiative when the Regional Council decided to expand the brand to cover all economic sectors, a new society – "a new world" – is currently emerging in response to the perverse effects of globalisation and rampant urbanisation. The economic and financial crisis and the explosion of new technologies have modified people's expectations and practices.

> With globalisation, the economic and financial crisis, and the expansion of the Internet and social networks, the world is changing... A new world is now emerging: a world that is more balanced, more human, one that no longer wants to create material wealth without protecting the environment or without contributing to human fulfilment. It is another model of development that is driving a new life and work philosophy, a model for a more balanced society that puts humans back at the centre of its projects, creating harmony between society, culture, work, tradition and innovation... Auvergne wants to embody this ideal world. It can achieve this thanks to the values which are deeply embedded in its identity and which it has successfully preserved.[10]

Ultimately, Auvergne wants to embody an "ideal world" based on five values: idealism (defend and express another world vision through actions), naturality (maintaining close links with nature), sharing (generating links, favouring exchanges and solidarity), demanding standards (perpetuating a sense of rigour and an emphasis on quality) and creativity (encouraging the artistic and creative movement).

In a publication edited by Clergeau and Spindler (2014), Sotiriadis ponders why holiday destinations do not capitalise on aspects of culinary tourism in their branding by using it as a cultural symbol and a formative element of their image. We complement this discussion by exploring whether Auvergne's gastronomy can represent the five values underpinning the *Auvergne Nouveau Monde* territorial brand. To do so, we first consider whether the region's culinary and gastronomic resources have sufficient potential and whether gourmet tourism truly exists here:

> Not all destinations seem capable of providing authentic gastronomic experiences. Hjalager and Corigliano (2000), who offer a comparative model for evaluating a destination's potential to become gastronomically attractive, consider existence of cuisine (a product of historical processes and on-destination natural and cultural resources) to be a prerequisite for success. In practice, this is not always the case.
>
> (Hillel et al., 2013: 200)

4. What products and recipes can Auvergne promote?

The cuisine in Auvergne, listed in a 2011 food and culinary heritage inventory[11] as having ninety-two terroir products and forty-seven traditional recipes,[12] can be traced back to traditional rural cooking, the food of the poor. Paradoxically, this proves an attractive characteristic:

> Food seen as rustic and natural is enjoying new popularity. A single dish, simple and abundant in quantity, was once characteristic of poverty as it was a response to the challenge of meeting daily needs, but is now seen as typifying robust and reassuring rustic nourishment.

> (Bessière, 2006: 17–18)

4.1. Dishes and recipes for the poor...

Auvergne is a largely mountainous region with harsh winters that make cultivation and the movement of people difficult. Its geographic and economic conditions have meant it has never enjoyed opulent farming. As a result, people had to "make do" with what they had and settled for products such as potatoes, legumes, cabbage, pork products, and cheese. Using these unrefined ingredients, recipes were developed that have since become iconic in the region (Figure 3.1): stuffed

Figure 3.1 Auvergne's four most iconic dishes

cabbage, *potée*,[13] *truffade*,[14] *pounti*,[15] amongst others. Traditional desserts include apple *pompe* and *milliard*, which at the beginning of the twentieth century was deemed "inedible for tourists.[16]" Luxurious confectionery (candied fruit and fruit jellies from the Limagne orchards, which in their heyday were intended for clients of the region's thermal spas in the nineteenth and twentieth centuries) are also a regional tradition.

As the Clermont geographer Mazataud (1997: 94) so accurately put it, Auvergne's cuisine was

> food for physical labourers who had to display great strength during the hay harvest. Today's nutritionists would have 100 reasons not to recommend such a diet, but they bite their tongues for they are aware of the value of this food that links us to the rustic ancestry that is dormant within us.

Moreover, most of the products used in the region's traditional recipes are of high quality, and many have been awarded certified status.

4.2. ...but made with products now recognised for their quality

As part of a territorial approach centred on know-how and geographic origin, food production under official quality labels has risen sharply since 2000 (the most spectacular increase being that of protected designation of origin [PDO] labels: +114%), now representing 23% of all production in Auvergne. This makes it the third-ranked region in France behind Franche-Comté and Limousin. A total 14% of production enjoys controlled designation of origin (CDO) status (e.g., St-Pourcain wines, green lentils from Le Puy), and 1% has protected geographical indication (PGI) status (e.g., Charolais du Bourbonnais, Velay poultry, etc.). This qualitative approach has made it possible to secure *Label Rouge* certification for several products, including cured ham, blonde lentils, beef from the Salers breed of cattle, as well as *Conformité Produit* (product compliance) certification for products such as *tripoux* and mountain pork.

In addition to certification, products are also promoted by other means. One example is the "*Sites Remarquables du Goût*" ranking. In 1995, four ministries (culture, tourism, environment, and agriculture) compiled a list of around one hundred production sites throughout France that met four criteria: a high-quality iconic regional product with a strong reputation and history; the presence of exceptional heritage in architectural terms and/or linked to the product; facilities in place to inform members of the public about the links between the product, local cultural heritage, landscape, and people; and organised stakeholders with an impact on each of the four relevant dimensions (agriculture, tourism, culture, environment). Auvergne is home to five "*sites remarquables du goût*"[17]: Billom for its pink garlic, Ambert for its *fourme* (cheese), St. Nectaire and Salers for their eponymous cheeses, and Le Puy for its green lentils.

Those who initiated the *Auvergne Nouveau Monde* brand have refused to allow it to become a tool for certification,[18] and hence it is not used to attribute labels –e.g., *"Produit en Auvergne"* – as other regions have done (*"Produit en Bretagne"* or *"Savourez l'Alsace – produit du terroir"*) to promote their agricultural produce. However, the region does benefit from the presence of a certain number of food products recognised for their quality through various appellations or certifications. As Hillel et al. (2013: 201) comment, "the French AOC system is the quintessential example of materialization of cultural identity."

Getting others to enjoy a type of cuisine means locals must enjoy it first. The people of Auvergne are proud of their cuisine and refer to it when explaining their attachment to the region. Is this identity rooted in gastronomy a way of standing out in an era of globalisation? This is a question worth asking given the recurrent use of identity in the Regional Council and CRDT discourses: The term *"identitaire"* appears nineteen times in the regional plan for tourism development, six of which are part of references to gourmet tourism.

5. Is there gourmet tourism in Auvergne?

In 2007, Auvergne was ranked fifth among the regions in France most associated with gastronomy (Lévy, 2014). Seven years later, 41% of respondents in France described it as the perfect region to discover farm produce and terroir products (Novamétrie, 2014 for the CRDT). In both cases, the region owes its results to the multiple facets of its gourmet tourism (Férérol, 2014). To appropriately identify these, we adopted the methods of Jacobs and Smits (2007: 2), who recommend taking into account four elements: infrastructure (restaurants, farm-taverns, farms, etc.), activities (tastings, guided tours, etc.), events (festivals, fairs, etc.), and structures (private or public, formal or informal) to promote and develop this type of tourism. In some respects, this method reflects the four major perspectives of gourmet tourism of Mak et al. (2012: 5),

> The growing body of literature of food consumption in tourism can be distinguished into four broad perspectives: food as a tourist product/ attraction, tourists' food consumption behaviour/pattern, tourists' dining experiences, and tourists' special interests in various food and beverages and related events/activities in destinations (e.g., food tourism, wine tourism, food events).

5.1. Stakeholders behind the tasting of Auvergne products

5.1.1 Rise in the number of Michelin-starred restaurants

In 1990, the Michelin Guide did not include a single two-starred or three-starred restaurant in the region (Bailly and Hussy, 1991). Twenty-five years later, Auvergne is proud of the fifteen Michelin-starred chefs operating here, making it the thirteenth region in France. However, in terms of ratios, whether number of inhabitants or number of tourists, Auvergne makes it into the top ten.

The presence of these chefs is important as they play a key role in building the region's image by placing regional cuisine centre stage and gaining media publicity for their work and the products they use. "Any tourist region that uses tourism as a key part of its local development strategy should take into account the promotional effect of these stars in French gastronomy" (Callot, 2002: 53).

5.1.2. *"Les Toques d'Auvergne" and "Tables Régionales d'Auvergne"*

The Association des Toques d'Auvergne currently represents around forty chefs, some award-winning and others who run simple bistros. The association was founded some thirty years ago in Clermont-Ferrand and, at the time of writing, was chaired by the Cantal-based Michelin-starred chef L.B. Puech.[19] It operates with two watchwords: openness and solidarity. Despite their differences, all the chefs are intent on promoting Auvergne's gastronomy.

> To promote the gastronomy of Auvergne, there has to be a certain proximity between restaurant owners. The Association des Toques d'Auvergne is an umbrella group for restaurants across the entire region and is committed to producing high-quality food made using the finest regional products. Each stakeholder has a role to play at their own level to celebrate the culinary virtues of Auvergne. Indeed, our restaurants resemble our landscapes: the materials, wood, volcanic stone ... all form part of this.[20]

The *Tables Régionales d'Auvergne* is a Regional Chamber of Agriculture initiative operating on the same basis as *Les Toques*. The thirty or so restaurant owners who make up this network are committed to putting Auvergne's gastronomy centre stage. Their menus include specialities based on traditional local recipes using regional produce, examples include salmon roulade with *fourme, lapereau* with Charroux mustard, and snail *cassolette* with Côtes d'Auvergne wine and gentian.

5.1.3. *Farm-taverns: ideal locations to discover Auvergne's terroir produce*

The regional products celebrated in traditional restaurants, whether high-end or not, are also served in farm-taverns, the "ideal setting to appreciate them" according to Mazataud (1997: 94). "For tourists, these are places for discovery and initiation into terroir produce" (Callot, 2002: 55). Around fifteen of these farm-taverns belong to a national association known as *Bienvenue à la Ferme* with 282 farmers and 317 growers from Auvergne (respectively 4.4% and 3.5% of nationwide subscribers). The aim of this association is to introduce people to France's terroir produce, whether on trips to farms or local markets. To guarantee the high quality of products promoted, the farmers and growers are committed to fully respecting sustainable development.

In Auvergne, just 2% of farms have diversified their activities to include accommodation and catering (DRAAF, 2013[21]). As in other regions (for example, 4% in Aquitaine and 2.9% in Midi-Pyrénées), the proportion dedicated to agritourism is therefore very low. Mindful of this situation, the Regional Council wanted to support this sector for several reasons:

> Agritourism is an activity that can favour agricultural diversification in a certain number of geographic sectors. . ... The world of farming is in a state of crisis, resulting in falling revenue for farmers. The solutions proposed by the Regional Council include strengthening the link between the farming and tourism sectors. However, there is inadequate knowledge of agritourism services and insufficient publicity around life on the farm, even though it is something that is in sync with contemporary consumer trends and the focus on natural aspects, organic produce, regeneration and short stays. As a result, farm visits now represent an offer in their own right, reflecting the identity of our region and corresponding to new consumer trends, thereby responding to an economic need.
>
> (CRDT, 2011: 7 and 93)

5.2. Promoting terroir produce through tourism

In terms of initiatives promoting terroir produce, Auvergne is no exception.[22] This is true particularly during the summer season, when it hosts a large number of events (e.g., Saint-Cochon in Besse, Fête des pancettes in Gerzat) as well as local markets. There is nothing exceptional about these events, but they contribute to tourism and the destination's appeal by providing entertainment that combines gastronomy with a warm atmosphere. However, the economic benefits they generate are very difficult to assess. The only reliable indicator is visitor numbers. For example, more than 10,000 people attended the *Fête des cornets* (biscuits filled with Chantilly cream) in Murat or the *Fête du bleu* ("bleu" cheese) in Riom ès Montagne.

Tourist routes are also a good way to promote local heritage, whether culinary or not (Beaudet, 2003). Like most tourist routes in France, since 1997, the objective of the cheese route in Auvergne (one of the most iconic symbols of the region for the French and Europeans alike – Novamétrie, 2014) is to promote regional specialities – in this case, the region's PDO cheeses: *Cantal, St-Nectaire, Fourme, Salers* and *Bleu d'Auvergne*. This route, which crisscrosses two of the region's departments[23] (Puy de Dôme and Cantal), is dotted with forty stop-off points that include farms, cheese shops, and cooperatives.

Such diverse facilities give tourists the chance to learn more about the lives of the farmers and their traditional know-how, as well as how the cheeses are made. Furthermore, at each destination, a small commercial space is available to purchase high-quality cheeses that must meet strict specifications to benefit from PDO status. Bessière (2006: 20) states that underpinning these purchases is the desire to support short distribution chains: "Through the act of purchasing products at farmers' markets or on the roadside, or tasting them on site, consumers feel as though they are escaping the laws of the market, short-circuiting the commercial distribution chain." Finally, to note is that visitor numbers along this route are satisfactory: 70,000 visitors have stopped off at one or more of these destinations. This is unsurprising, since "gastronomic routes are very popular tourism products" (Gheorghe et al., 2014: 14).

Visiting a tourist area is often linked with purchasing a souvenir as a way to remember an enjoyable experience or offer gifts to friends, ranging from postcards to iconic ornaments to regional produce. In economic terms, the purchase of food souvenirs can be significant.[24] In Auvergne, tourists have a strong appetite for terroir produce. According to a survey conducted by a local newspaper, cheeses, candied fruit, wines, and cured meats are among the top ten souvenirs that tourists purchased (*La Montagne*, 01/09/2014).[25]

5.3. Auxiliary tourism: industrial agro-food tourism

Industrial agro-food tourism is auxiliary to gourmet tourism. "The production and processing of certain food products can generate tourism either in the form of museums or organised visits to workshops or factories, described by some as industrial tourism or economic discovery" (Bessière et al., 2013: 76). Industrial tourism, which has enjoyed a boom in recent years in France (eight million tourists), attracts families as well as pensioners and students keen to discover the secrets behind the manufacture of the products they consume.

In Auvergne, a few companies have climbed on board by opening their doors to members of the public. The most high-profile example is without doubt Volvic, part of the Danone group. The third best-selling mineral water producer in France recorded visitor numbers of 83,000 in 2013. Other examples include the Pastillerie de Vichy,[26] the Bourdon sugar plant (the oldest active sugar plant in metropolitan France), and the Pagès distillery, which since 1859 has made its famous verbena liqueur.

It is clear that Auvergne enjoys gourmet tourism, yet this is hardly mentioned by those behind the ANM brand. The only sentence in a tourist brochure that refers to it states,

> Here, vines abound on river banks and hillsides, medicinal plants are transformed into exquisite liqueurs, cheeses are the stars of our high plateaux, meats and lentils enjoy PDO status, and we avidly consume the beneficial waters filtered by our volcanoes. Savour the expressive flavours of our local produce with short distribution circuits. Discover the renewal

of talents and cuisine that is at once rooted and open to the world. Now that's the art of living!

Furthermore, while "heritage and the art of living" is one of the six priority areas[27] in the region's approach to tourism, corresponding to the expectations of more elderly tourists and foreign visitors (German, Belgian, and British) (CRDT-REGION AUVERGNE, 2011: 94), a notable lack of visibility of Auvergne's gastronomy is evident in the way the *Auvergne Nouveau Monde* brand is advertised. In the next section, we will endeavour to show how those behind the brand could better exploit gourmet tourism and make it an identity marker for the region.

6. Discussion: what contribution can gourmet tourism make to Auvergne to boost its appeal?

6.1. Idealism: making human concerns a priority

The new life philosophy Auvergne promotes is evident in the documents used to publicise the brand:

> The Auvergne model, away from unbridled consumption, has resisted fads and all forms of bling – initially worshipped but quickly scorned. ... Here in Auvergne, we have not forgotten that an environment of the highest standards makes fertile ground for humans to flourish and that human fulfilment is central to the development of an economy and tourism of excellence. Here in Auvergne, we have chosen to generate growth with wisdom and simplicity in a way that respects nature and humans; the fundamentals – friendship, family, vitality, shared moments of happiness and non-commercial values – flourish here.[28]

These principles relate to the fundamentals of sustainable development, the possibility of promoting local economic development, and the benefits of short distribution chains with an emphasis on quality and proximity. The gourmet tourism, by some of its aspects, could legitimise this lifestyle. Our position is based on the work of Gheorge et al. (2014):

> Recently, the cuisine has become an indispensable element in knowing the culture and lifestyle of a territory. Cuisine embodies all the traditional values associated with the new trends in tourism: respect for culture and tradition, a healthy lifestyle, authenticity, sustainability and feelings associated with it.
>
> (Gheorghe et al., 2014: 14)

In Auvergne, there is one very well-known case of local economic development revolving around the presence of a major Michelin-starred chef. In a relatively remote area, at the border between the Haute-Loire and Ardèche departments, Régis Marcon (awarded three Michelin stars) managed to bring his childhood village, with a population of just 250, back to life. His decision to set up a restaurant here was in fact an ideological move. He had a strong attachment to his homeland and was intent on returning there and regenerating it. Alongside his two brothers – one of whom is the mayor (and president of CCI France) and one of whom is an MP – his aim was to initiate a local development project through gourmet tourism. In the village of St-Bonnet-le-Froid, Marcon manages several facilities: three high-end hotels, two restaurants, a pastry and tea salon, a bakery, and a holiday centre. These have all generated jobs for dozens of people, including fifty at the Michelin-starred restaurant. His success has already led to the creation or preservation of other food-related businesses (e.g., butcher and cheese shop), with more on the way.

As well as maintaining the commercial fabric and services sector in the area, Marcon's activities promote "local food resources through the use of ingredients produced locally or regionally" (Marcilhac, 2011: 50) and offer de facto support to the farmers and other stakeholders from the agro-food sector, both locally and regionally, through the purchases generated: goat's cheese from Dunières, snails from Grazac, Bourbonnais chickens, *fourme* cheese produced on a farm near Ambert, and so forth. While Marcon is a strong advocate of culinary localism, this development is also a reflection of the evolving practices of major chefs in line with the new expectations of their clientele.

> With the rise in fears surrounding food, new demands are being expressed, including and perhaps above all by high-end clients: nowadays there can no longer be any doubt about the quality and traceability of products. This is where the local producer comes in, providing proof of the freshness and source of the products used.
>
> (Brochot, 2008: 99)

The ideal the brand supports is that the farmers in Auvergne can continue to live here. "Culinary tourism has positive economic impacts, especially for rural areas. Promoting food tourism in rural areas helps local farmers, producers and small business owners and helps these rural economies to diversify" (Blakey, 2012: 51). "Local artisan production can contribute to secure local employment and keep rural communities alive. It offers opportunities for development even to poor and depressed regions through a new agricultural model" (Bonow and Rytkönen, 2012: 3). Thus far, the figures point to a certain level of crisis in Auvergne: year-on-year decline in agricultural operations of 2.1% since 2000 and the disappearance of 67% of farms between 1970 and 2010 (DRAAF, 2013). The developers of the ANM brand are banking on the new behaviour of consumers who are aware that local purchases form part of economic development. They therefore hope that agritourism through visits to farms and farm-taverns can help diversify farming revenue and thereby provide a breath of fresh air to farmers in Auvergne. Unfortunately, according to the director of the CRDT, the region's policy to support agritourism has so far had little success, with just ten applications filed each year. Moreover, as one of our interviewees pointed out, this path is attracting mainly well-off farmers who are already in a position to invest, rather than those with modest incomes.

6.2. Naturality: a return to rural routes and the preservation of nature

The second value the brand promotes is naturality. Local stakeholders emphasise the Auvergne landscape dominated by blue (lakes and thermal springs) and green (volcanoes, forests, and pastures). They argue that this omnipresent nature provides opportunities to regenerate mind and body. How can this perspective be linked to the facets of gourmet tourism?

Due to the continued importance of farming, this region has many well-maintained spaces. Maintaining the landscape is vital, with both consumers and tourists who often draw a link between the quality of destinations and the quality of products.

> The development of agritourism, rustic dining options and itineraries with themes that focus on terroir products have in recent years helped establish close links between the landscape and epicurean pleasures. It is as though the quality and renown of a product or meal were revealed through the quality of the landscape.
>
> (Beaudet, 2006: 13)

UNWTO (2012: 11) even states, "The destination is the backbone of the gastronomic offer. Tourism product contains environmental values, landscape, culture, traditions, local cuisine. Identification of the culinary landscape with tourist destination represents one of the challenges of creating tourism products."

Shocked by multiple food scandals and reflecting the rise in environmental concerns, consumers/tourists look for products that respect the environment and have a local origin. This is just as true in France as it is in the rest of the world (Dumas et al., 2006; Gheorghe et al., 2014; Velissariou and Mpara, 2014).

> The last decade marked a turning point characterized by the consumer trends in an increasingly higher manner towards the ecological and traditional products. . . . In Europe the traditional products have a very good image, a fact that led to increasingly higher demand for these products. Higher demand is also explained by the fact that the products are containing fewer additives and not containing genetically modified ingredients.
>
> (Gheorghe et al., 2014: 18)

PDO cheeses perfectly reflect the current climate, with an emphasis on sustainable production methods (short distribution chains, reduced use of fertilisers, etc.). According to Route des Fromages d'Auvergne,

> PDO implies a close link with the terroir. To strengthen this link, the specifications for PDO-certified Cantal and St.-Nectaire cheeses, for example, require the cows used for the cheese to be born and bred in the area covered by the appellation. Similarly, the feed given to the animals must be produced within the same area. The proportion of concentrates given to cows is controlled and limited. These criteria, by limiting the input entering the PDO zone and by guaranteeing ranching methods, ensure the zone is protected from any artificialisation. Not to mention the fact that by restricting the milking, manufacturing and breeding zone etc., carbon emissions, in particular due to transport, are significantly reduced. Furthermore, the importance of grass in these specifications has a direct impact on the landscape. The presence of herds within the framework of such practices helps maintain open spaces which are characteristic of Auvergne's mountain landscape.[29]

The tourists' appetite for products that respect the environment encourages farmers to use more wholesome production methods. Organic farming is beginning to take hold in Auvergne. Although the share of the sector is slightly below the national average (4%), there are now twice as many organic farms as there were in 2000, with 3.4% of the region's farms producing in accordance with the specifications of organic farming, ranking Auvergne eleventh among French regions. This percentage is clearly set to rise as 745 farms are considering converting over the next five years, a significant trend that corresponds to customer needs. "The purifying and therapeutic images associated with the countryside can now be found in the consumption and search for 'wholesome,' 'natural' products" (Bessière, 2013: 79). This observation is perfectly in line with the regeneration dimension of the Auvergne brand.

6.3. Sharing: closer social bonds

As mentioned in Section 2, the brand is intended to improve the image of Auvergne and its inhabitants. In opinion surveys, the typical Auvergne resident is seen as rustic and inward looking. Yet, the region has often been a place of refuge and its inhabitants have shown their generosity, as attested by Georges Brassens's well-known song, *Toi l'Auvergnat*: "*Elle est à toi cette chanson, Toi l'Auvergnat qui sans façon, M'as donné quatre bouts de pain, Quand dans la vie il faisait faim*".[30]

There are many different ways of sharing: at celebrations, at meetings between tourists and residents at their place of work, or in business dealings between the various professional stakeholders of gourmet tourism. Such encounters correspond to the brand's emphasis on sharing as a way of promoting the human dimension, exchanges, and solidarity. As the previous section mentions, Auvergne is home to many events in celebration of its terroir produce.

Beyond the mere act of consuming, the tourist experience is also expressed through discovering the people who inhabit a region.

> A journey of experiences is on a close connection with a lifestyle that includes experimenting, learning from different cultures, accumulation of knowledge and lessons learned, by eating, about the qualities or attributes related to culinary tourism, and culinary specialties produced in the region visited.
>
> (Gheorghe et al., 2014: 13)

Getting to know a tourist destination's cuisine is a way for visitors to learn more about others, understand some of their characteristics, and attain a sense of the "spirit of the place."

> Consuming the food of other people and borrowing from their culinary practices may provide a sense of the place visited and be seen as a symbolic consumption of a region or a place, facets of its climate, history, customs and scenery.
>
> (Bonow and Rytkönen, 2012: 4)

Indeed, as Bessière (2006: 21) states, "The success of meals shared in farm-taverns or in guesthouses appears to be an expression of a desire to communicate through the context of food, reflecting a kind of nostalgia for shared meals." It is on such occasions that tourists enjoy true experiences, and it is more about exchange than consumption. Such "intimate" tourism is the very foundation of slow travel, which respects two principles: taking time and immersing oneself in the place. Michelin-starred chefs also play on the importance of closer bonds, as evident in some of Marcon's cookery school courses, which transform into voyages to discover the local territory through mushroom-picking excursions.[31]

Finally, the owners of farm-taverns can also act as prescribers for local producers, just as restaurants do. "It is often in non-Michelin-starred restaurants that tourists get information about local produce. Without the barrier of renowned status, chatting with staff or the owner is a good way to get tips about where to buy products" (Salvador-Pérignon, 2013: 29). Gourmet tourism thereby favours closer links between restaurant owners and suppliers. This proximity is clear in Marcon's comments:

> Here we get to meet the producer, we can chat with him. That has a big influence on us, we work differently. We encourage people to produce. We have a team of support staff and we want to ensure they make a living.
>
> (Marcon, quoted by Callot, 2002: 53)

Getting to know producers and how they produce ultimately facilitates contact between restaurant owners and their customers, to whom they have a story to tell (the history of the area, the history of the people who live there, and the personal history of the producer).

6.4. Demanding standards: when work is synonymous with quality

Auvergne pioneered sustainable development. Due to a certain level of poverty, the people here were forced to save money and adopt rigorous manufacturing standards so the objects would last. Promoting this durable quality is therefore central to the aims of the brand's developers. This rigour in know-how is also reflected in the local food heritage.

The dishes presented in Section 4 may be simple, but they are made using quality produce. This is an important asset for Auvergne, as for any tourist destination. "Local cuisine is an important factor in terms of holiday quality" (Gheorghe et al., 2014: 13). "The products become unique and acquire identity. The consumer refuses to substitute these products with others which are similar" (Velissariou and Mpara, 2014: 255). Certification not only facilitates the sale of the products concerned, and at an above-average price (once production constraints have been taken into account), but also ensures traceability, "natural" and characteristic flavours for consumers. This is very important against the backdrop of food crises – "Consumers are interested to know the origin of products and the method of production, because in this way ensure their health and safety and the safety of their children" (Velissariou and Mpara, 2014: 255) – and regional competitiveness. "Appellations are undeniably a factor in international competition, a way of recognising and promoting the economy of terroirs, while at the same time helping the regions concerned to acquire tools of competitiveness linked to quality" (Dumas et al., 2006). Furthermore, the quality of the terroir produce helps restaurant owners improve customer satisfaction levels, just as the quality of their dishes reflects the quality of the products used to make them.

6.5. Creativity: inventive chefs portray a dynamic region

Lastly, to modernise the region's image, local public stakeholders have insisted on the value of creativity. Restaurant owners and chefs in the region make an important contribution: With intense competition, integrating creativity into their work has become essential to promoting their gastronomic heritage. They transform simple products into refined dishes by combining them with other flavours. In the words of Régis Marcon, "using local produce, chefs must prove they are creative and have imagination to promote this gastronomic heritage" M[32] The following dishes proposed by the award-winning chef are examples of this: lobster cassoulet with green lentils from Le Puy-en-Velay, quinoa cake with mushrooms, verbena jelly with green lentils, or skewered bananas with morel caramel. Through their actions, restaurant owners, whether Michelin-starred or not,[33] are thus in harmony with the creativity promoted by the brand's developers. To generate publicity for the region's culinary arts, *Les Toques d'Auvergne* often organises public events. Once every year, in unique locations (summit of Puy de Dôme in 2013, national centre for stage costumes in Moulins in 2014), the association organises a "toque-chaud" (word play: "warm chef's hat/talk show") with a gala dinner or a more affordable "picnic" for €25 (in 2013: salmon sushi with green lentils from Le Puy, boletus tart, and verbena, chocolate and pear dessert).

Nevertheless, creativity does not end with the innovative dishes or actions of Michelin-starred chefs. CRDT also encourages farmers who cater for tourists to offer innovative and ecoresponsible accommodation that celebrates naturality without sacrificing modern comforts (spa, Wi-Fi): treehouses, isolated former cheese-making huts on the volcanic plateaux (Figure 3.2), etc. In time, these will form part of the Nattitude network that the region has developed as a way of generating visibility for accommodation options that promote the brand's values: exceptional locations (charismatic villages, natural parks, etc.), architectural and decorative qualities (charm, comfort, originality), an environmentally friendly approach (choice of building materials, consistent waste management, etc.), wellness activities (spa, yoga classes, sophrology), close links with the region (short distribution chains, organic produce), a warm welcome, and knowledge of the region. CRDT and ANM target young urban dwellers from the higher socioprofessional categories by mixing the trendy with the rustic: "So long riads, fincas and palazzis, this summer treat yourself to the cabin lifestyle! Refuges are the new thing, with the rich and famous getting back to basics. Primitive is the new chic!"[34] The Nattitude programme is about creating an atmosphere that is a source of plenitude and can stimulate all the senses. This evokes the notion of "theatricisation" that Etcheverria (2014, 2015) emphasised – "Turning a place into a tourist destination requires the ability of hotel and restaurant owners as well as tourist promoters to offer temporary inhabitants a true experience (Pine and Gilmore, 1998)" (Etcheverria, 2015: 237).

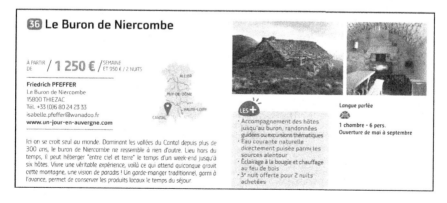

Figure 3.2 Example of a Nattitude accommodation option

Our analysis points to the fact that gourmet tourism is in sync with the values of the ANM territorial brand. It lends Auvergne an image of quality and conviviality, proving the role it plays in tourism marketing in support of regional development. In this context, each stakeholder benefits: Producers are delighted to see their expertise achieve recognition, tourists find the experiences and authenticity they seek, local inhabitants can be proud that outsiders are taking an interest in them, and all local stakeholders can benefit from the publicity for the quality of life that the region boasts, thus attracting new investors and customers.

7. Conclusion

Auvergne is a rural territory *par excellence* and belongs to the group of regions that feel excluded from globalisation and the positive dynamics it generated. But this is a region that also refuses to be beaten, developing a territorial brand to boost its attractiveness and demonstrate that development outside of metropolitan areas with high levels of circulation is possible. The second challenge facing this brand is combatting the clichés from which the region suffers and restoring the balance between perceptions and reality. This explains the name chosen for the brand: *Auvergne Nouveau Monde*.[35] Use of the adjective *nouveau* (new) is an indicator that the region has initiated a shift and plays on the element of surprise:

> This semantic choice is not neutral, for language constructs territories. By adopting the word "new" and associating it with Auvergne, we are steering the actions of all stakeholders. At first glance, these two terms may appear to be antonymous, given that the image of Auvergne has not previously embodied modernity.
>
> (Rochette, 2012: 15)

Meyronin (2015) stated that of more than 5,600 territorial brands, 86% fail within a year of their launch. *Auvergne Nouveau Monde*, which has existed for six years now, has therefore enjoyed a good start. Furthermore, according to Nicolas Bordas (vice-president of TBWA Europe), this is the only other brand outside of Brittany that benefits from positive perceptions (*La Montagne*, 21/01/2017).[36] ANM espouses a new life philosophy and, according to those who developed it, also reflects Auvergne's qualities. The links between territorial brands and gourmet tourism are part of a virtuous circle. But which of the two has the stronger impact on the other? On the one hand, "gastronomy can be promoted with a view to boosting attractiveness" (Lévy, 2014: 78), and when it is of high quality, can legitimise a territorial brand. On the other hand, "territorial brands are seen as a framework of trust, guaranteeing quality" (Marcotte et al., 2011: 210), which can have an impact on the products of that territory. In any case, the concomitance of high-quality products, locations, and experiences generates value based on territorial quality, which Mollard et al. (2001) define as the combination of the intrinsic quality of a product and its rootedness in a specific place with its own history and know-how.

Ultimately the brand's developers would do well to follow the advice of Nicolas Bordas, who recommends a communications approach focused on the notion of "recharging one's batteries in Auvergne" and "an expression that would capitalise on the idea that Auvergne is beneficial for both mind and body. Mens sana in corpore sano. Let us not forget after all that Blaise Pascal was born in Auvergne!"[37]).

Notes

1 "Culinary, cuisine, or gourmet tourism are all expressions fundamentally employed in a synonymous manner to gastronomic tourism in the literature" (Brisson, 2012: 17).
2 Agritourism covers all tourist activities (accommodation, restaurants, and the sale of products or services, such as leisure, sports, and cultural activities) available at active farms (as defined by the Comité Régional de Développement Touristique d'Auvergne, 2011).
3 In this research, we refer to territorial/place branding, an approach that entails associating a brand name with a specific region (e.g., OnlyLyon, L'Originale Franche-Comté, L'Ain mon luxe au naturel).
4 As Brisson notes in her thesis, "The term destination branding is sometimes referred to synonymously, or with slight variations, as place branding, place marketing or destination marketing" (2012: 29).
5 "While there is no literal translation into English, the French use the term terroir to describe the combination of place and food characteristics. Long (2004, p. 25) defines the concept of terroir as an integral part of 'region' – that is, a French term used to describe 'the combination of soil, climate and culture that gives wine and food products defining characteristics of place'" (Steinmetz, 2010: 31).
6 J.-F. Jobert, director, interviewed on 19/03/2014.
7 Brittany was the first French region to develop a territorial brand.
8 "The inception in 1989 of the 'Slow Food Movement' in Paris represents a celebration of the 'local' and the efforts of individual communities to protect traditional food heritage against the fast-food trend. The 'Slow Food Movement' is an international body set up in the defence of biodiversity, promoting local food worldwide in an effort to preserve not only traditional methods of food production and preparation but also to conserve cultural identities" (Steinmetz, 2010: 21).
9 Jean Pinard, interviewed on 06/05/2014.
10 http://www.auvergne-nouveau-monde.fr/qui-sommes-nous
11 "All of the material and immaterial facets that constitute food cultures and are defined by the group as a shared heritage" (Bessière, 2013: 38).
12 Hyman, M. (2011). Auvergne: *Produits du terroir et recettes traditionnelles* (L'inventaire du patrimoine culinaire de la France). Paris: Albin Michel.
13 A mixture of meat, potatoes, and vegetables boiled in stock.
14 Fresh Cantal *tomme* (cheese) combined with diced potatoes, not to be confused with *aligot*, a dish that is found more in the Aveyron department and southern Cantal and is made with mashed potatoes.
15 Prunes and pork or veal served with green chard leaves and various herbs.

16 Comments made by a Touring Club correspondent at the beginning of the twentieth century, as she explained that tourists were turned off by the unpitted cherries in this *clafoutis* from the Auvergne and Limousin regions (Csergo, 2006: 9).

17 Remarkable taste site.

18 L. Wauquiez, president of the new Auvergne-Rhône Alpes region (result of a merger between the two former entities in 2016), is nonetheless considering launching a brand that would promote local (and perhaps organic) products (*Le Progrès*, 08/10/2016).

19 Telephone interview, 04/03/2014.

20 Marcon (2017). http://www.auvergne-tourisme.info/articles/rencontre-avec-regis-marcon-635-1.html.

21 Regional department for food, agriculture, and forestry.

22 In a survey conducted by Gheorghe et al. (2014: 18), 79% of respondents attributed importance to gastronomic events, 62% to gastronomic routes, and 59% to fairs with local products.

23 France is divided into regions, which are then divided into departments (*departements*).

24 According to Eurostat, an estimated one-third of tourist expenditure is on food products (Knafou and Anton, 2012; Gheorghe et al., 2014; Velissariou, 2014).

25 https://www.lamontagne.fr/clermont-ferrand/loisirs/2014/09/01/fromages-vins-ou-couteaux-chaque-ete-les-touristes-ramenent-des-souvenirs-de-leur-sejour_11125971.html.

26 Each year, this lozenge plant hosts between 7,000 and 8,000 visitors who come to learn how the famous sweets are made.

27 The five others are: outdoor activities, well-being and regeneration, agritourism, motorcycles, and *nattitude* accommodation.

28 www.auvergne-tourisme.info/articles/manifeste-pour-un-modele-auvergnat-4-1.html

29 www.fromages-aop-auvergne.com/-Route-des-Fromages-.

30 "This song is for you, Auvergnat, who didn't think twice about giving me four bits of bread, when times were hard".

31 However, these courses are not easily affordable: €410 for a two-day course ("Cooking mushrooms, from picking to plate").

32 http://www.auvergne-tourisme.info/articles/rencontre-avec-regis-marcon-635-1.html.

33 Eleven stars awarded in Auvergne in 2017, including one three-star (Marcon) and two two-star restaurants (Beaudiment and Vieira).

34 http://madame.lefigaro.fr/evasion/refuge-cabane-primitif-vacances-chic-280515-96652.

35 Since writing this chapter, some changes have taken place. In the summer of 2017, it was decided that the *Auvergne Nouveau Monde* brand would become simply the **Auvergne brand** and that the logo would change to reflect the graphic charter and colours of the new expanded Auvergne Rhône Alpes region. The region's president, L. Wauquiez, asked F.X. Montil (who holds a position in the Cantal Departmental Council and originally worked as an agro-food engineer and a territorial marketing specialist) to join the *Auvergne Nouveau Monde* association and generate new momentum to "proudly display the colours and values of Auvergne. ... Auvergne is an opportunity for Rhône-Alpes and its voice must not be swallowed up by the larger region. On the contrary, the flag of Auvergne must fly high and the people of Auvergne must be proud of their powerful lands" (La Montagne, 21/04/2017 and 10/07/2017). Apart from these changes, the brand's values have remained the same, as has the association's president, former industrialist, P. Laurent, and the financing, the main source of

which is the Regional Council (budget of around €500,000, including €475,000 in subsidies).

36 https://www.lamontagne.fr/clermont-ferrand/politique/2017/01/23/changer-cler mont-ferrand-en-clermont-auvergne-oui-dit-nicolas-bordas_12252792.html.
37 Ibid.

References

Aaker, D.A. (1996). *Building strong brands*. New York: Free Press.
Anholt, S. (2007). *Competitive identity: The new brand management for nations, cities and regions*. Basingstoke, UK: Palgrave Macmillan.
Bailly, A. and Hussy, C. (1991). La diagonale gourmande. *Mappemonde*, 2(91), pp. 48–49.
Barrère, C. (2013). Patrimoines gastronomiques et développement local. *Mondes du Tourisme*, 7, pp. 15–36.
Beaudet, G. (2003). Les routes touristiques: Entre marketing territorial et valorisation identitaire. *Teoros*, [online] 22(2). https://teoros.revues.org/1747.
Beaudet, G. (2006). La géographie du tourisme gourmand. *Teoros*, 25(1), pp. 10–14. http://teoros.revues.org/1298?file=1.
Bessière, J. (1998). Local development and heritage: Traditional food and cuisine as tourist attractions in rural areas. *Sociologia Ruralis*, 38(1), pp. 21–34.
Bessière, J. (2006). Manger ailleurs, manger local. *Espaces*, 242, pp. 16–21.
Bessière, J. (2013). Quand le patrimoine alimentaire innove. *Mondes du Tourisme*, 7, June, pp. 37–51.
Bessière, J., Poulain, J.P., and Tibère, L. (2013). L'alimentation au cœur du voyage. *Mondes du Tourisme*, March, pp. 71–82.
Blakey, C. (2012). Consuming place: Tourism's gastronomy connection. *HOHONU*, 10, pp. 51–53.
Boiţă, M. (2014). Gastronomic tourism management revitalizer factor of the tourism offer. *Academica Brâncuşi Publisher – Economy Series, Special Issue Information Society and Sustainable Development*, pp. 398–401.
Bonow, M. and Rytkönen, P. (2012). Gastronomy and tourism as a regional development tools: The case of JÄMTLAND. *Advances in Food, Hospitality and Tourism*, 2(1), pp. 2–10.
Botti, L. (2011). *Pour une gestion de la touristicité des territoires*. Baïxas: Balzac Edition.
Brisson, G. (2012). *Branding Prince Edward County as a gastronomic niche tourism destination: A case study*. Thesis, Ottawa: University of Ottawa.
Brochot, A. (2008). Haut lieu touristique, haute gastronomie, haute clientèle: Le tiercé gagnant de la côte d'Azur? In Csergo, J. and Lemasson, J.-P. (ed), *Voyage en gastronomie*. Paris: Autrement, pp. 90–101.
Callot, P. (2002). Tourisme et gastronomie: Le fabuleux destin d'un mariage réussi. *Cahier Espaces*, 76, pp. 52–58.
Chignier-Riboulon, F. (2002). L'image de la ville auvergnate. In Edouard, J.-C. (ed), *L'Auvergne urbaine*. Clermont-Ferrand: Presses Universitaires Blaise Pascal, pp. 11–27.
Chignier-Riboulon, F. (2007). La nouvelle attractivité des territoires: Entre refus du fatalisme et mouvement protéiforme. In Chignier-Riboulon, F. and Semmoud, N. (ed), *Nouvelle attractivité des territoires et engagement des acteurs*. Clermont-Ferrand: Presses Universitaires Blaise Pascal, pp. 9–20.

CIET-UNSAM. (2008). *La gastronomía como atractivo turística y factor de desarrollo.* http:// www.unsam.edu.ar/escuelas/economia/CIDeTur/boletines/Estudio%20Tom%C3% A1s%20Joff%C3%A9%20-Parte%201.pdf.

CRDT. (2013). *L'économie du tourisme en Auvergne.* Clermont-Fd: CRDT.

CRDT-REGION AUVERGNE. (2011). *Schéma régional de développement du tourisme et des loisirs 2011–2015.* Chamalières: Région Auvergne.

Csergo, J. (2006). Quelques jalons pour une histoire du tourisme et de la gastronomie en France. *Teoros,* 25(1), pp. 5–9. http://teoros.revues.org/1297?file=1.

Csergo, J. and Lemasson, J.-P. (2008). *Voyages en gastronomie: L'invention des capitales et des régions gourmandes.* Paris: Autrement.

DRAAF. (2013). Memento de la statistique agricole: Auvergne. *Agreste,* 125, pp. 33.

Duhamel, P.H. (2013). *Le tourisme: Lectures géographiques.* Paris: La Documentation Française.

Dumas, L., Menvielle, W., Perreault, J.D. and Pettigrew, D. (2006). Terroirs, agrotourisme et marketing. *Teoros,* 25(1), pp. 34–49. http://teoros.revues.org/1317?file=1.

Etcheverria, O. (2014). Le tourisme gourmand: Un tourisme qui associe cuisine, vin et gastronomie. *Revue Espaces,* 320, pp. 60–68.

Etcheverria, O. (2015). Le cuisinier O. Roellinger et l'immatériel touristique. In C. Clergeau and J. Spindler (eds), *L'immatériel touristique.* Paris: L'Harmattan, pp. 225–246.

Fabry, N. (2009). Clusters de tourisme, compétitivité des acteurs et attractivité des territoires. *Revue Internationale d'Intelligence Economique,* 1, pp. 55–66.

Fabry, N. and Zeghni, S. (2014). *La gastronomie: Atout de développement économique et touristique durable? 5èmes journées du tourisme durable dans le cadre du 3ème colloque international de l'UNESCO.* Université de Barcelone, 16–19 juin 2014 (texte aimablement fourni par les auteurs).

Férérol, M.E. (2014). *L'Auvergne gourmande: Une réalité touristique? 5èmes journées du tourisme durable dans le cadre du 3ème congrès de l'UNESCO.* Université de Barcelone, 16–19 juin 2014.

Férérol, M.E. (2017). Auvergne Nouveau Monde: Le pari gonflé d'une région en quête d'attractivité. In N. Bernard, P. Duhamel and C. Blondy (eds), *Tourisme et périphéries. La centralité des lieux en question.* Rennes: Presses Universitaires de Rennes, pp. 61–76.

Flores, M. (2007). La identidad cultural del territorio como base de una estrategia de desarrollo sostenible. *Revista Opera,* 7, pp. 35–54. http://www.redalyc.org/pdf/675/ 67500703.pdf.

Fox, R. (2007). Reinventing the gastronomic identity of Croatian tourist destinations. *International Journal of Hospitality Management,* 26(3), pp. 546–559.

François, H. (2008). Durabilité des ressources territoriales et tourisme durable: Vers quelle convergence? *Géographie, Économie, Société,* 10 (1), pp. 133–152.

Gheorghe, G., Tudorache, P. and Nistoreanu, P. (2014). Gastronomic tourism: A new trend for contemporary tourism? *Cactus Tourism Journal,* 9(1), pp. 12–21.

Gollain, V. (2011). *Guide du marketing territorial.* Supplément de *la Gazette des Communes,* n° 2091.

Gómez, M., Lopez, C. and Molina, A. (2015). A model of tourism destination brand equity: The case of wine tourism destinations in Spain. *Tourism Management,* 51, pp. 210–222.

Hatem, F. (2004). Attractivité: De quoi parlons-nous? *Pouvoirs Locaux,* 61, pp. 34–43.

Henderson, J.C. (2009). Food tourism reviewed. *British Food Journal*, 111(4), pp. 317–326.

Hillel, D., Belhassen, Y. and Shani, A. (2013). What makes a gastronomic destination attractive? Evidence from the Israeli Neguev. *Tourism Management*, 36, pp. 200–209.

Hjalager, A.-M. and Corigliano, A. (2000). Food for tourists – Determinants of an image. *International Journal of Tourism Research*, 2(4), pp. 281–293.

Hyman, M. (2011). Auvergne: *Produits du terroir et recettes traditionnelles* (L'inventaire du patrimoine culinaire de la France). Paris: Albin Michel.

Holden, A. (2006). *Tourism studies and the social sciences*. Oxon: Routledge.

Jacobs, H. and Smits, F. (2007). Le tourisme culinaire: Un fort marqueur territorial. 6èmes Rencontres de Mâcon Tourismes et Territoires, pp. 6. http://www.recherche-macon nais.org/tl_files/irvsm/pdf/Colloques/6eRencontresMacon/Jacobs.pdf.

Jiménez-Beltrán, F.J., López-Guzmán, T. and Cruz, F.G.S. (2016). Analysis of the relationship between tourism and food culture. *Sustainability*, 8(418), p. 11. http://www.mdpi.com/2071-1050/8/5/418.

Kavaratzis, M. and Ashworth, J. (2005). City branding: An effective assertion of identity or a transitory marketing trick? *Tijdschrift voor Economische en Sociale Geografie*, 96(5), pp. 506–514.

Knafou, R. and Anton Clave, S. (2012). Gastronomy, tourism and globalisation. *Via (3) International Interdisciplinary Review of Tourism*. http://viatourismreview.com/wp-con tent/uploads/2015/06/Tourisme_gastronomie_mondialisation_EN.pdf.

Kolb, B.M. (2006). *Tourism marketing for cities and towns*. Burlington, MA: Elsevier Butterworth-Heinemann.

Landel, P.-A. and Sénil, N. (2009). Patrimoine et territoire, les nouvelles ressources du développement. *Développement durable et territoires*, 12. https://journals.openedition. org/developpementdurable/7563.

Lemasson, J.-P. (2006). Penser le tourisme gourmand. *Teoros*, 25(1), pp. 3–4. http://teoros.revues.org/1288?file=1.

Leroux, E. (2016). Management du tourisme durable: Attractivité du territoire, patri-moine et gastronomie. *Management & Avenir*, 3(85), pp. 109–112.

Lévy, M. (2014). La gastronomie locale: Un atout touristique à ne pas négliger. *Espaces*, 320, pp. 76–80.

Lin, Y.C., Pearson, T.E. and Cai, L.A. (2011). Food as a form of destination identity: A tourism destination brand perspective. *Tourism and Hospitality Research*, 11(1), pp. 30–48.

Long, L. (2004). A folkloristic perspective on eating and otherness. In L.M. Long (ed), *Culinary tourism*. Kentucky: The University Press of Kentucky, pp. 3–25.

López-Guzmán, T., Hernández-Mogollón, J.M. and Di Clemente, E. (2014). Gastro-nomic tourism as an engine for local and regional development. *Regional and Sectoral Economic Studies*, 14(1), pp. 95–102.

Lorenzini, E., Calzati, V. and Giudici, P. (2010). Territorial brands for tourism develop-ment. *Annals of Tourism Research*, 38(2), pp. 540–560.

Mak, A.H., Lumbers, M. and Eves, A. (2012). Globalisation and food consumption in tourism. *Annals of Tourism Research*, 39(1), pp. 171–196.

Marcilhac, V. (2011). Revitalisation d'une économie locale et stratégie familiale: Le cas Marcon à St Bonnet le Froid. *Norois*, 2(219), pp. 41–56.

Marcotte, P., Bourdeau, L. and Leroux, E. (2011). Branding et labels en tourisme: Réticences et défis. *Mangement & Avenir*, 7(47), pp. 205–222.

Mazataud, P. (1997). L'Auvergne gourmande. In *Guide Bleu Auvergne*. Paris: Hachette, pp. 40–47.

Meyronin, B. (2015). *Marketing territorial: Enjeux et pratiques*. 3rd ed. Paris: Vuibert.

Meyronin, B. and Berneman, C. (2010). *Culture et attractivité des territoires*. Paris: L'Harmattan.

Mitchell, R. and Hall, C. (2006). Wine tourism research: The state of play. *Tourism Review International*, 9(4), pp. 307–332.

Mollard, A., Pecqueur, B. and Lacroix, A.J. (2001). A meeting between quality and territorialism: The rent theory reviewed in the context of territorial development. *International Journal of Sustainable Development*, 4(4), pp. 368–391.

Neto, P. (2007). Strategic planning of territorial image and attractivity. In A. Matias, P. Nijkamp and P. Neto (eds), *Advances in modern tourism research*. New York – Heidelberg: Physica Verlag, pp. 233–256.

Novamétrie. (2014). *Image et notoriété de la destination Auvergne Enquête pour le CRDT*. Paris: Novamétrie

Pecqueur, B. and Gumuchian, H. (2007). *La ressource territoriale*. Paris: Économica.

Pine, B.-J. and Gilmore, J-H. (1998). Welcome to the experience economy. *Harvard Business Review*, 76 (4), pp. 97–105.

Poirot, J. (2010). L'attractivité des territoires: Un concept multidimensionnel. *Mondes et Développement*, 1(149), pp. 27–41.

Racine, A. (2012). Le tourisme durable par la voie culinaire. http://veilletourisme.ca/2012/12/12/le-tourisme-durable-par-la-voie-culinaire/.

Ritchie, J.-R. and Zins, M. (1978). Culture as determinant of the attractiveness of a tourism region. *Annals of Tourism Research*, 5 (2), June, pp. 252–267.

Rochette, C. (2012). L'approche ressources et compétences comme clé de lecture du processus d'élaboration d'une ressource originale: La marque territoriale. *Gestion et Management public*, 1, pp. 4–20.

Salvador-Pérignon, M. (2012). Tourisme culinaire et valorisation des produits artisanaux: Vers un tourisme durable. *Mangement & Avenir*, 6(56), pp. 114–133.

Salvador-Pérignon, M. (2013). Expérience vécue chez un chef étoilé et achat de produits locaux par les clients. *Mondes du Tourisme*, 8, pp. 19–32.

San Eugenio, J. (2013). Fundamentos conceptuales y teóricos para marcas de territorio. *Boletín de la Asociación de Geógraficos Españoles*, 62, pp. 189–211.

Sexto, C.F., Arce, C.M., Vazquez, Y.G. and Vázquez, P.G. (2001). El territorio como mercancía. fundamentos teóricos y metodológicos del marketing territorial. *Revista de Desenvolvimento Economico*, 5, pp. 68–79. http://www.revistas.unifacs.br/index.php/rde/article/view/618/498.

So, K.K.F., King, C., Hudson, S. and Meng, F. (2017) The missing link in building customer brand identification: The role of brand attractiveness. *Tourism Management*, 59, pp. 640–651.

Sotiriadis, M. and Van Zyl, C. (2014). Évènements culinaire et éléments immatériels. In C. Clergeau and J. Spindler (eds), *L'immatériel touristique*. Paris: L'Harmattan, pp. 271–296.

Steinmetz, R. (2010). *Food, tourism, destination differentiation: The case of Rotorua (New-Zealand)*. Thesis, University of Auckland.

Stewart, J.W., Bramble, L. and Ziraldo, D. (2008). Key challenges in wine and culinary tourism with practical recommendations. *International Journal of Contemporary Hospitality Management*, 20(3), pp. 302–312.

Velissariou, E. and Mpara, E. (2014). Local products and tourism gastronomy in rural areas. 9th MIBES International Conference, 1 June 2014, pp. 253–265. http://mibes. teilar.gr/proceedings/2014/Velissariou-Mpara.pdf.

Veltz, P. (2004). *Des lieux et des liens*. La Tour d'Aigues: L'aube poche essai.

Williams, H.A., Williams, R.L., Jr. and Omar, M. (2014). Gastro-tourism as destination branding in emerging markets. *International Journal Leisure and Tourism Marketing*, 4(1), pp. 1–18.

World Tourism Organization. (2012). *Global report on food tourism*. Madrid: UNWTO.

4 Analysing the links between identity and quality as vectors of local economic development in rural mountain areas

Christel Venzal

1. Introduction

As researchers, we have been involved in various projects that establish partnerships between different actors and public or private organisations. These active research experiences have enabled us to investigate local development strategies, mainly in rural medium-altitude mountain areas. In these projects, aimed at local economic development, we have observed that identity and quality are issues that regularly emerge in the discourses, discussions, and meetings, but are never clearly defined by those actors we meet or interview. Therefore, rather than specifically describing each of the areas studied, our aim here is to investigate, experimentally and for the research purposes, the methods and organisational approaches of the various local actors. The common starting point for all these projects is a "shared" view of local development. According to Pecqueur (1994: 92, author's translation), "Local economic development (LED) refers to any process for mobilising actors that results in the development of strategies to adapt to external constraints, based on collective identification with a culture and a local territory." We therefore studied the organisational forms and approaches that different local actors aim for to achieve local development through partnerships and network-building. Our research method is based on territorial analysis principles. We first applied a so-called "sensitive" approach to the area studied through field observations, landscape interpretation, photographic reporting, and mapping projections. The next phase involved documentary research to select the variables to investigate. The survey phase followed with a series of interviews and meetings or discussion workshops that validated – or rejected – our initial assumptions. For each of the projects, we held a workshop to review the results with the various actors to help them define coherent strategic guidelines. Based on case studies that reflect this approach, this chapter presents an experimental selection of three local areas (Alpes-de-Haute-Provence, the Vercors Massif, and the Upper Ossau Valley in the western Pyrenees, see Figure 4.1) and four types of organisation with different competences and means of action (Geopark, private company, the Regional Nature Park, and a municipality). For each case study, we set out the previously stated and transverse aims regarding identity, local product quality, and tourism, with the latter a long-standing objective as a driver of local development. As Jean-Robert Pitte (1993, author's translation) wrote:

> The future, initially with a French flavour, probably lies more in the idea of quality, understood not in terms of luxury products but rather as products that are "authentic original, and reflect the environment and the people who brought them into being.

Resulting in

> Landscape quality, in other words, landscapes that vary with each physical and human setting and are well maintained both in valleys and hilly or even steeply sloping areas. These landscapes are an outstanding asset for tourism based on discoveries and encounters, and the only ones in France where future development still beckons, all our other mountain and coastal areas now being so heavily built-up.

This aspiration is reflected in the demand for quality in local products, landscapes, and therefore tourist offerings, and an approach we set out to investigate experimentally in our rural medium-altitude study areas.

In an article published in 2004, Guy Di Méo and colleagues discuss the symbolic relationship between landscape and identity: "Like heritage and economic values, landscapes, as mediators of the relationship between people and their groups and the local areas to which they belong and in which they live, are highly effective symbols of identity" (author's translation). Some of the actors we interviewed during the study referred to "a kind of mountain world of our imagination." In our study of the Upper Ossau Valley, we also noted this representation of mountain-dwellers and the idea that tourists mainly came to the area due to its specific landscapes. To be recalled is that mountain tourism is in fact a fairly recent phenomenon based on the concept of developing mountain-related practices. Tourism in mountain areas was initially based on developing ski resorts. Over fifty years, some 320 ski resorts were built by public authorities.[1] The Alps are the most highly developed tourist region with a wide range of amenities. Tourism in mountain areas is therefore highly competitive, and the everlasting questions for tourist professionals are the same everywhere: How do we attract tourists to our destination, and how do we keep them there? France is still the world's leading ski destination, but it has now been shown that many people visiting skiing areas do not actually ski. Tourist offices and other actors consequently offer different activities in these areas, some of which are based on the attractiveness of local produce. These actors are beginning to realise that developing ski resorts is not necessarily the most suitable policy for the future and are thus looking to tourist strategies with an emphasis on summer activities, such as hiking, discovering mountain landscapes, and trying out local produce. In fact, all

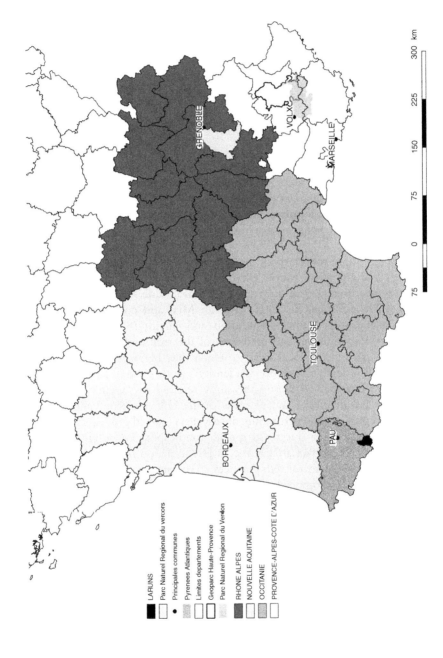

Figure 4.1 Three types of areas studied

these areas offer more or less the same things for tourists: wonderful landscapes, local produce (cheese, wine, pâtés, sausages, etc.), the architecture of mountain villages, local heritage, hiking trails, and so on. This type of project demands an adjustment in the mentality of the host communities, as shown by the approach that Anne Leroy developed on boosting the dynamics of the countryside through tourism. She notes that, "Rural tourism relies on people's desire to find out about different ways of life, and different local areas especially, which implies that projects that do not involve local populations have no place in this type of tourism" (Leroy, 2001: 91, author's translation). The organisations (businesses, local government agencies, and natural area managers) described in this chapter all tend towards the same strategic goal of high-quality tourism that strives to involve local communities and their competences in a tourism policy based on (re)discovering local products and local areas to support local development.

We therefore compared the projects that the Vercors Regional Nature Park launched in cooperation with tourism professionals around the "Inspiration Vercors" trademark with the strategic aspiration towards "a new way of positioning tourism" that the stakeholders in Upper Ossau Valley expressed. Discussions with actors in the Vercors helped us to understand the importance of their networking efforts to support the goal of local development. As Pecqueur (1994: 107, author's translation) notes, "A network is the flow of exchanges, material or otherwise and monetary or not, that links partners together." Clearly, development cannot happen without active cooperation, without a common goal, and especially without the desire to join forces through a network. The approach that Olivier & Co (a food company specialized in olive oil and its by-products) adopted and the development of the Haute-Provence Geopark support this view of working towards local development through networks and partnerships. After a diagnosis of tourism in the Upper Ossau Valley, and as a continuation of the study, we proposed preparing a tourism strategy geared to the idea of developing networks and partnerships between actors and cross-cutting projects (tourism clusters, cultural and gastronomic events, digital curation of local features, and an interpretation centre on the heritage of the Ossau region). The research we conducted in the mountains areas of Haute-Provence and Vercors proved invaluable in formulating the strategic challenges in support of the proposals we made to the Ossau decision-makers. These decision-makers find themselves addressing similar problems (young people moving out of the area, climate change, competition between local areas, etc.) and their tourism strategies are underpinned by the same identity symbols: local landscapes and local products. These policies all seek to adapt tourism offerings to external constraints (political, economic, real estate, climate change, etc.). This chapter presents the results of these analyses of local areas by cross-referencing them successively with quality- and identity-related topics. The first part focuses particularly on our study of the tourism experiences involving the identification of local products. In the second part, the analysis leads to the question of landscape quality. Finally, in the third part, we put forward the idea of local trademarks to guarantee the quality of all tourism amenities in these areas.

2. Local products and the tourist experience

Tourism is not only a matter of statistics; it has become a global phenomenon. Every country, city, town, or village wants to develop tourism and become *the* place to visit. Tourism is a source of income and also stands for peace and quality of life. "Tourism is no longer just the expression of leisure choices for an affluent minority but a core element in modern society, increasingly recognised as a primary economic driver in all countries" (Middleton et al., 2009: 14–15). Tourism is no longer a matter for the public authorities alone, as local communities themselves are increasingly involved. However, this does not mean that local authorities working with tourist operators can turn any outstanding or unique area into a tourist destination.

> A tourist destination is generally defined as any territory that has an organisation or structure (accommodation, transport, tourist services, etc.), to receive tourists who come to spend at least one night. A tourist destination therefore differs in essence from a place of transit or a place visited. Nevertheless, even once the aim of receiving tourists has been established, tourist destinations come in highly varied forms.
>
> (Lesne and Zins, 2009: 82, author's translation)

To this definition we add the observation of Etcheverria (2016: 9, author's translation) with reference to the MIT research[2]: A tourist destination is a place transformed over time by temporary mobility and spatially by the tourist amenities introduced. What makes a true tourist destination is the ability of local actors to transform an ordinary, everyday place into something special. This implies a long period of study, negotiation, organisation, partnership-building, infrastructure development, and so forth. Developing a tourist project needs time: time for analysis, to reach agreement on policies, to develop professional services and appropriate products, and set up specialised companies.

According to Condevaux et al. (2016), this development requires all actors to commit to working together in the interests of the local area. Tourism is a recent phenomenon in which many mistakes have been made. Tourism generates pollution, damage to the natural environment, short-term profits and exponential benefits, but it is also synonymous with freedom, well-being, and social encounters, thanks to the contributions of the host communities. This point is now essential in all tourist strategies. In research on tourism and sustainable development, the question of hospitality and identity has become fundamental. Tourism is based on human relationships: It can be expressed, on the one hand, in terms of a community that agrees to meet and welcome visitors; and on the other hand, visitors who want to discover an area and meet the local community, try out its way of life, its local products, etc. Our study builds on the quality of local products as an essential component of sustainable development and attractiveness to tourists, together with the quality of landscapes and the close involvement of the local communities themselves. Nevertheless, "A region and its food or wine production may not in themselves be sufficiently appealing or attractive to warrant visitor interest" (Croce and Perri, 2010: 60). The local community may appreciate a local product that visitors do not, due to different sensitivities arising from their identity, their nationality, their education, their culture, their history, their heritage, and so forth.

In terms of surface area, 80% of France is classified as rural. In these areas, local politicians and actors aspire to tourism as a strong driver of development. This idea has been reinforced in the last twenty years by the aims of EU programmes. In her analysis of local tourist development, Gerbaux underlines the essential role attributed to the subsidies granted to rural areas for tourist development. The support provided under EU programmes such as LEADER is intended "to develop high-quality tourism that promotes the local culture and heritage; to enhance the value of local dynamics and local products and to support small and medium enterprises" (Gerbaux, 2001: 77, author's translation). Local areas are encouraged to identify their heritage, especially by enhancing the value of typical products that are part of local culture – products that had often been forgotten or transformed into industrially processed goods to cater for postwar consumer demand. The idea is to revive products based on regional or local know-how to support local development, through tourism if possible. As Christian Barrère (2013: 32, author's translation) notes in an exhaustive review of gastronomic heritage, "Promoting the value of natural products, emphasising the link between products or recipes and local areas and the idea that they are part of the national, regional or local heritage are all responses to consumer demand for identity." Consumers want food products that are "authentic and natural." They want to know and understand where the products they buy come from. A product, therefore, tells them about its producer, how it was made, and about local know-how. Product traceability is discussed, and reference is increasingly made to the image of the production area as a guarantee of product quality, represented in advertising material of rural landscapes described as "authentic." Most French regions therefore offer the same tourist attractions, organised around nature, landscapes, and visits to farms and wineries.[3] At the same time, some regions have realised that local products are important resources that can distinguish their own rural areas from others. Tourist strategies for these territories are being improved by an emphasis on the charm of their landscapes together with the quality of their local products. Nevertheless, this strategy cannot hope to attract tourists successfully unless the local products are well prepared and produced. Even if local operators want to market a destination through promoting local products, this will not make tourists automatically choose the area (see Croce and Perri, 2010). This type of strategy can only succeed if all the actors involved work towards the same end. Quality thus becomes the common "corporate" goal to achieve for local produce as well as for sports activities, heritage, and other local attractions. To complete this analysis, we quote the research of Batat and Frochot (2014: 4–10, author's translation):

> A successful experience involves the consumer, engages the five senses, has a meaning for the individual and produces memories. And it is not only evaluated by the clients' level of satisfaction but more and more through the intensity of the memory and the pleasure that it will permeate.

To further elaborate on the idea of tourist experiences supported by well-identified local products, we cite the example of *Olive Ecomuseum in Volx* (Alpes de Haute-Provence, southeast France). As explained on its website, the idea behind the *Première Pression Provence* (PPP) concept is to encourage French people to experience and buy French olive oils. Olivier Baussan,[4] who created the concept, reminds us that olive oil comes primarily from Italy and Spain (both substantial olive producers), while France produces only a small propor-tion of the world's olive oils. Only 3% of olive oil consumed in France is made in Provence; overall, only 5% comes from France. Large manufacturers there-fore buy olive oil from Spain, where it is produced on a large scale. The aim of the PPP concept is to develop fair trade in Provence. Fair trade does not exist only in developing countries, such as South America or Africa. For Olivier Baussan, fair trade can "start right at home in other words, in France and specifically Provence, Fair trade is the way PPP helps olive oil producers sell their precious product by reducing the number of intermediaries." The idea behind PPP is quite simple: "PPP is the only intermediary between the producer and the consumer, and reducing the number of intermediaries allows a reduction in price." PPP olive oil prices are the same as farm prices. This point is very important for the trademark. The marketing strategy is also quite simple: classifying the products by specific origin rather than by flavour.

All the olive oils sold in the PPP shop are from Provence. The system is based on three taste categories: *fruité vert, fruité mûr,* and *fruité noir.* The exhibitions at the Olive Ecomuseum in an old lime kiln showcase the concept. The exhibition is based on "the living culture of a tree: the olive." Associated with the shop and the ecomuseum is a restaurant in which tourists can enjoy meals prepared with olive products. This is an instructive example of exploring a marketing and commercial approach to organise a value chain for a local product.

Before Olivier Baussan and his PPP concept, olive oil producers in Prov-ence sold their produce directly to consumers from their farms, sometimes online but mainly to cooperatives. They sell olive oil produced in a specific area, such as *le Moulin de l'Olivette* in Manosque in the Alpes de Haute-Provence (southeast France),[5] an olive oil mill founded in 1928. They produce olive oil using a traditional process, and their website explains that they sell their oil directly from producer to consumer. The olive oils are all selected from orchards belonging to producers in the terroirs of Haute-Provence and safeguarded by a protected designation of origin (PDO). PPP's marketing does not mention the PDO, instead placing emphasis on the producers and direct sales. The website shows pictures of all their producers presented as partners in a team working to offer a wonderful olive oil experience. Due to their rare and unique flavours, the olive oils are presented like famous wines. Olivier Baussan's initial concept was based on well-known images of Provence, such as lavender. He again chose a newly fashionable product, olive oil, which had experienced economic difficulties fifteen years ago, to increase the attractiveness of both Provence and his own company. The concept is simple but very effective, and this example can be compared with the way regional cuisine is evolving. According to Christian Barrère (2013: 29, author's translation), "It seeks to exemplify a return to rural roots and to promote direct producer-to-consumer circuits, using location and culinary specialisation to surf the wave of the new trend for worshipping nature and respecting the environment." The aim in these examples is not to promote a small local area or a typical village, but to sell an entire experience in a destination marketed through its symbols (lavender, olives, etc.) and the quality of its local products. Quality and partnerships are essential in these marketing strategies.

3. Local produce and landscape quality

In our study on the development of the geotourism concept in the Natural Geological Reserve of Haute-Provence (NGRHP), we identified the link between landscape symbols and local products. In our research, we linked the idea of geotourism with Tilden's (1957) concept of "heritage interpretation." Geotourism is promoted in areas of geological interest with well-defined boundaries and a large enough surface area to serve local sustainable development. These areas, called "geoparks," include a number of geological heritage sites or "geosites." Through a systemic and spatial analysis of the foundations of the geosites located in NGRHP, we found they encompass different features associated with their geological, historical, and economic interests, as identified by specialists in sites of this type. We devised a model for a geosites indicator that takes geological history, events, and processes into account, as well archaeological, environmental, historical and cultural values. We found that signposts, information panels, etc., constituted the first interface in an interpretation system between a geosite and a tourist. We compared this first approach with the definitions of geosites used in Quebec and the "geotop" concept promoted in Switzerland. We then identified the central role of the NGRHP area, now labelled the "Haute-Provence Geopark," thanks to its inclusion in the UNESCO Geoparks Network. An analysis of the functions of this geopark, defined as part of local sustainable tourism development, was essential to identify the interests of the local actors involved in the geotourism strategy. We considered that geotourism complements cultural tourism through its scientific contributions. The second interface mediating between a geosite and a tourist are the local actors involved. One of the reasons for developing geotourism is to encourage sustainable tourism. Since 2001, the European Geoparks Network has worked with UNESCO to develop a Global Geoparks Network. In 2017, UNESCO's website explained that

> a UNESCO Global Geopark uses its geological heritage, in connection with all other aspects of the area's natural and cultural heritage, to enhance awareness and understanding of key issues facing society in the context of the dynamic planet we all live on, mitigating the effects of climate change and reducing the impact of natural disasters. By raising awareness of the importance of the area's geological heritage in history and society today, UNESCO Global Geoparks give local people a sense of pride in their region and strengthen their identification with the area. The creation of innovative local enterprises, new jobs and high quality training courses is stimulated as new sources of revenue are generated through sustainable geotourism, while the geological resources of the area are protected.[6]

The UNESCO network includes some 118 geoparks in 33 countries. The aim of the network is to boost local economies through local sustainable development.

> The UNESCO World Heritage and Sustainable Tourism Programme is a new approach based on dialogue and stakeholder cooperation where planning for tourism and heritage management is integrated at a destination level, the natural and cultural assets are valued and protected, and appropriate tourism developed.[7]

When the geotourism idea was launched in the 2000s, the founders of Europe's geoparks based their tourism strategy on people's appreciation of quality local produce, such as olive oil. They raised awareness of the olive oil producers' difficulties among European and national authorities to obtain subsidies and develop partnerships with local producers. Images of geological landscapes (volcanoes, mountains, fossils) were used to develop a local trademark. This fair-trade story (like the PPP concept) in the 2000s was the beginning of a global network recognised by UNESCO. It was also the start of our work on associating quality local products with landscapes in mountain areas. "Tourists are consumers of landscapes, but they are also consumers of local products, as long as local actors know how to establish the link between local produce and their landscapes" (Derioz, 2004: 160, author's translation).

To analyse another possible connection between landscapes and local products in mountain areas (outside the Geoparks Network), we conducted a study on the Upper Ossau Valley, near the Spanish border in the western Pyrenees, in the district of Laruns (Figure 4.2). Laruns itself is a small town of 1,326 inhabitants, but the Laruns district is extensive, with a surface area of 250 km². The local economy is mostly based on hydroelectric production,

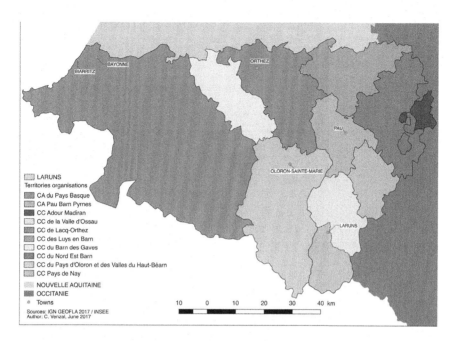

Figure 4.2 The Pyrénées Atlantiques and the district of Laruns

agriculture, and tourism. The district runs a tourist train, called the *Petit train d'Artouste*, along a route near the Spanish border. This historic tourist railway was actually built in 1920 to transport workers and equipment for the eight-year project to build the Artouste dam. In 1932, the local authorities decided to open the railway to the public. Since then, tourists have been able to visit the mountain area in the heart of the Pyrenees National Park at an altitude of 1240m to 2000m without any real physical effort. In summer, they can view the dam and admire Lake Artouste. In all seasons, tourists (and skiers in winter) can observe the 2884m Pic du Midi d'Ossau from the Artouste cable-car station, which is the starting point of the railway journey in summer. Laruns thus offers two tourist attractions throughout the year: the Artouste railway in summer and the Artouste ski resort in winter.

The Ossau range has manifest attractions as a geological site: the Pic du Midi d'Ossau can be described as a geosite that also attracts people because of its specific geological and historical features. The peak is a very significant local symbol: It is known to locals as "Jean-Pierre," which refers to the myth of Jean and Pierre, twin brothers who were shepherds in the Ossau range and responsible for preventing attacks by barbarians. The Pic du Midi d'Ossau can be seen from a considerable distance – for example, from the Boulevard des Pyrenees in Pau (Figure 4.3). For host communities, the peak has become a

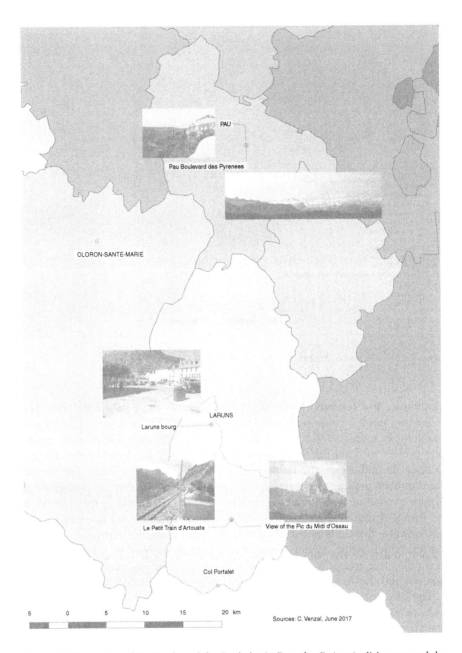

PAU

Pau Boulevard des Pyrenees

OLORON-SANTE-MARIE

LARUNS

Laruns bourg

Le Petit Train d'Artouste

View of the Pic du Midi d'Ossau

Col Portalet

5   0   5   10   15   20 km

Sources: C. Venzal, June 2017

Figure 4.3 Illustration of the Boulevard des Pyrénées in Pau, the *Petit train d'Artouste*, and the Pic du Midi d'Ossau

symbol of *their* Pyrenees, their identity, and their way of life, and it has been adopted by economic and political actors in their communication strategies. This geosite has become part of the tourism economy. Images of the peak are used in most tourist brochures on the Bearn region (the tourist offices in Pau or Oloron-Sainte-Marie, for example). At the start of our investigations, the Pic du Midi d'Ossau was not recognised by local actors (intermunicipal bodies, Laruns municipal authority) as contributing to the area's attractiveness to tourists. To quote Gravari-Barbas and Graburn (2012, author's translation), "While their definitions refer primarily to the way they imagine the places where tourist activities take place, it would be a mistake to ignore the way they imagine local practices or actors involved in tourism." Identifying tourist representations of Ossau was therefore the first step in our explorations in relation to the economic estimation of tourism in the Laruns area.

Tourism in the Ossau area is concentrated in the summer (80%) and mainly revolves around nature and sports, which are very dependent on the weather. Among the tourists we surveyed, 38%[8] had come to the Laruns area for just one day, 17% had come for a week, around 9% for three days, and 8% for two days. The most usual form of holiday accommodation was in furnished apartments (60% outside the Laruns or Ossau areas), 28% rented an apartment in Laruns, and 4% in the villages of Eaux-Chaudes, Fabrèges, and Gabas. Around 57% of visitors to Laruns had come by coach. If we add this figure to the number of campsites, about 60% of visitors to Laruns we interviewed were campers. Among all visitors, 80% indicated nature as their main motivation, 25% mentioned the *Petit train d'Artouste*, and 16% mentioned the border with Spain (we asked them to choose two answers). In this initial survey, none of the visitors mentioned the local gastronomy or even local produce, such as cheese, as a motivation for their trip, even though some local shepherds have the Ossau Iraty PDO label (Maizi and Amilien, 2007). Tourists' activities focused on hiking (60%), photography (40%), nature sports (55%), mountain-biking (12%), and discovering the local heritage (30%). Some 60% of visitors interviewed had already visited the area. The first aspect they mentioned was the Ossau landscapes, which for most represented a change in their everyday scenery. They described their sense of engagement with these landscapes that changed the focus of their daily lives and the enjoyment of being in a protected natural environment.

To conclude this first survey, we would say that tourism in the Ossau area and Laruns can be described as contemplative. At the time, our study did not make any links between tourism and local activities or local farm produce. We therefore decided to investigate the local tourist economy in the following summer. In 2012, seventy-seven retailers were registered in the Laruns area. We selected and contacted fifty-six retailers as relevant to our investigation and received forty-six responses. Of this sample, 58%[9] were family businesses; 12.5% spoke only French and not even a few words of Spanish; 75% were open all year round, but 30% closed their shops in the autumn or Easter holidays; 86% believed they were dependent on tourism; 28% admitted they had no interest in a tourist strategy; and 20% had no relationship with the Laruns tourist office. These responses and observations showed very wide differences in the quality of commercial offerings in this sector of the Pyrenees. Most restaurants in Laruns did not even offer their customers a chance to try the local sheep cheeses. To quote the article of Kadri et al. (2011:13) published in the *Encyclopaedia of Tourism* (Jafari, 2000: 144–145):

> A destination, as distinct from an origin or a market, refers to a place where tourists intend to spend time away from home. The geographical unit visited by tourists as a destination may be a self-contained centre, a village or a town or a city, a region or an island or a country. A destination may also be a single location, a set of multi-destinations as part of a tour, and it may even be mobile, as in the case of a cruise.

With reference to this definition, our surveys show why Laruns can be classified as a tourist destination: Tourists pass through, buy some bread or ordinary local products, enquire about tourist information on hiking and the *Petit train d'Artouste*. Yet there are tourists who return, sometimes year after year. Returning tourists mentioned the quality of the Ossau landscapes, which they rediscover anew on each visit. However, at this time, it was evident that tourists did not associate quality and protected landscapes with local products. The question of quality has become essential to raising awareness of operational tourist strategies that help promote local development in Laruns. Our research approach to local development refers to Vachon and Coallier (1993: 92, author's translation), who emphasise the human element in development strategies:

> Local development is a dynamic process driven by attitudes and behaviours centred on action, rather than by a series of predetermined procedures organised into a closed system. Local development is a strategy in which the actors involved are the beneficiaries. It is implemented in different areas where human and physical resources are very diverse and where aspirations and priorities as regards development create specific problems. These strategies are evolutionary processes that need to be continually assessed and adjusted.

After this new step in our investigations, we proposed a turning point to the Laruns municipality and devised their tourist strategy around the Ossau geo-spot as a symbol of the local heritage, quality, hospitality, and local produce. The idea is quite simple: Tourists are attached to this region because of its well-preserved natural environment, its wonderful scenery, and its sports activities, while the host community is attached to "our Ossau" (as they called the peak in our interviews), to their land, their landscapes, their traditions, and their local products. The arguments are based on quality tourist products developed in association with the host community.

If life is good for the host community in a tourist destination, it will automatically be more attractive in the eyes of potential tourists. They too will want to live there, even if only temporarily, and experience the host community's culture at first hand. Visitor satisfaction with their experience will create a sense of attachment and an emotional bond with their holiday destination.

(Croce and Perri, 2010: 62)

The making of a true tourist destination is impossible without the increasingly essential support of local actors and host communities. As Clergeau and Etcheverria (2013: 53, author's translation) explain,

The making of a tourist destination is at least partly based on the capacity of local actors to share their knowledge, standards and values with temporary residents, and to make their culture and their identity an essential part of the tourism project.

As shepherds contribute significantly to the area's identity, we decided to investigate their perceptions of tourists and tourist development on their land and their farms.[10] Shepherds look after their flocks all year round and have to milk their ewes twice a day. Some shepherds in the Ossau area take their flocks up to the mountain pastures from May to September and make summer cheese there. Régis Carrère told us that he stopped making cheese in June to protect his ewes and their lambs. He had decided to take over his parents' farm a few years previously but did not want to carry on working with a large number of sheep and cattle, preferring to manage a small flock of one hundred sheep on his own. He milks his sheep each day by hand. He works on the principle of making quality cheese but without seeking to obtain the Ossau Iraty PDO label. Carrère sells 60% of his cheeses directly to consumers from his farm, at the roadside, or his mountain hut in the summer, and also to restaurants in Pau (the main town in the western Pyrenees), Pessac (near Bordeaux), and small supermarkets in Pontacq (western Pyrenees). The other 40% of his cheeses are sold indirectly through dairy refiners in Toulouse and Tournefeuille (Haute-Garonne *département*) and Luz (Hautes-Pyrénées). Thus, Carrère does not sell his cheeses in any of the shops in Laruns even though his farm is in this district. During our investigations, we noted that restaurants or food retailers in Laruns mentioned local cheese but not "Laruns" cheese on their menus or in shops. Carrère is not the only Laruns shepherd who does not sell his produce in his own village. Why? For Carrère, the reason is simply the low quality of the products sold by local retailers, and his opinion is the same for those sold under the Ossau Iraty PDO label. Some shepherds produce pure ewe's cheese without any certification and some choose to adopt the PDO concept. As in the case of the PPP project, the shepherds we interviewed wanted to produce quality products from their region but without having to comply with top-down directives in which they do not recognise their own production methods; however, they admit that communication under the Ossau Iraty label is effective for both cheese and tourism.

Carrère and other local shepherds we interviewed make cheese according to traditional methods without having to comply with external directives. Because these cheeses all have their own character, the system works, provided the shepherds do not seek to increase their production and therefore the scale of their operation. Most shepherds in this district like to receive people on their farms or at their mountain huts during the summer, but they insist that this is because they like meeting people, and not to promote the image of the traditional shepherd with his beret and his woollen vest – even though most of them, including Carrère, do wear a beret every day. This is a very significant point, indicating that communication on tourism should not be about turning traditions into conventional images to sell a destination. Tourism should be thought of as encounters between real people that can challenge tourists' representations, and not in terms of hackneyed images like beret-wearing shepherds. Carrère explained that the aim of the Laruns cheese fair in October is to present and sell only quality cheese from the Ossau region.

The Laruns cheese fair was first mentioned in 1843 and takes place each year on the first weekend of October. Since 1950, the village has held traditional events in the covered market, including cattle markets and parades with performing bears or costumed characters. Cheeses are exhibited on Sundays and judged by panels of experts for a national competition. Since 1990, local retailers have introduced entertainments based on pastoral life as well as local gastronomic specialities, such as the traditional *poule au pot*, a local dish of boiled fowl attributed to Henri IV. For the last twelve years, local shepherds have managed this fair focused on the central subject: Ossau cheese. Only selected quality cheese can be sold at the fair. In addition, the organisers invite different partners each year from other pastoral regions or countries. All restaurants offer local dishes on their menus, such as ham, cheese, or stewed fowl. According to the local authorities, some 15,000 visitors are expected each year. During our investigations on the 2015 fair, we counted about 8,000 visitors. The weather was quite bad and it was difficult to obtain a reliable count without automatic counters on the roads or at the entrances to the village. Only pedestrians are allowed into the centre of the village. The fair is very regional: 51% of visitors interviewed during our survey (out of 182 people)[11] were from the Pyrénées Atlantiques department and about 90% from the Nouvelle-Aquitaine region, 69% of those interviewed had come with a group of family or friends, 38% stayed for the weekend, 35% for only a day, and 13% slept at their friends' or family's homes. About 10% had come by coach: Some 120 coaches were parked around the centre of Laruns. Of the visitors we interviewed, 84% had come to buy cheese, 41% had come for the first time, and 34% came each year. In the answers, and especially the comments we collected, the Laruns cheese fair was associated with local produce. People's motivations for coming to Laruns and to the fair were to buy or taste the local produce and watch the entertainments that were well identified as revolving around pastoral life. They thought that their purchases directly helped shepherds and those living in the Ossau Valley. They also wanted to show support for traditional as opposed to industrial products: 90% knew that the cheeses sold at this fair were produced in the Ossau Valley, which to them is proof of quality.

In conclusion of this survey, the Laruns cheese fair is a local agricultural and traditional event but cannot be considered an established tourist attraction. In the last few years, the Laruns tourist office has organised cheese and wine tastings as a way of strengthening the fair's attraction. To do so, the tourist office persuaded Laruns shepherds and wineries within the Jurançon geographic designation (near Pau) to provide their products for a combined tasting event. Each Saturday morning, a group of twenty tourists can try out Ossau cheeses together with the sweet white Jurançon wines. This tasting is a real tourist experience, where the shepherds and winegrowers explain their products and how to enjoy them in combination. These producers all rally around the same quality requirement. Visitors to the Laruns fair can be described as food-lovers because they enjoy eating and drinking, but not necessarily as "gourmets" or those who not only enjoy good food, but are also very knowledgeable about fine cuisine and fine wines.[12]

This survey also shows that the Laruns fair is a local attraction, but that the entertainments offered do not make the area an outstanding tourist destination. The local people who get involved in tourism do so because tourists visit their localities, but they do not really have a coherent plan to organise their area for tourism to support local development. To do so, a destination needs to manage and organise the involvement of all those concerned. As Croce and Perri (2010: 63) explain, each separate component of a destination "is clearly identified, and organised and managed by public and private operators working in synergy. It is not a closed system providing a fixed model." Hence, even though all the people we met during these investigations seem to be certain of the quality they offer, it cannot be said that Laruns is an outstanding or even a quality-level tourist destination. Among the tourist offerings in Laruns, the only example that aims for quality in tourism is the recently opened Hotel du Pourtalet.[13] This hotel offers a complete experience: fully renovated premises, tastefully redecorated rooms, a panoramic restaurant, a spa, friendly staff, and a location in an outstanding protected natural landscape near the Spanish border. In 2016, the young hotel manager recruited a new chef (Thibaut Repéto) and obtained the *"maître restaurateur"* label. They also run a small shop for local products including cheeses, *charcuterie* from Lahouratate, a well-known butcher, and products from the Eaux-Chaudes soap factory. These items are all labelled as products from the Ossau area, so it is clear that the district and its people are capable of putting together tourist products of excellent quality. But what they need is some new inspiration and to learn how to work together. The "tourism cluster" concept could be a trigger to achieve this. As Fabry and Zeghni (2012: 99) describe,

A tourism cluster corresponds to a space for coordination and institutional arrangements which in return make the destination visible (to tourists) and readable (to stakeholders). The aim is to develop a coherent source of support for the actors involved and to facilitate the emergence of a common system of priority values. … A tourism cluster, when considered from the point of view of the local area as a whole, becomes a place in which local actors become the stakeholders by creating and managing their resources themselves.

The concept of a tourism cluster gives new meaning to a local area by transforming it from a mere geographic or administrative district into an attractive tourist destination. This renewed perception essentially relies on local area management in the spirit of a corporate development plan. All actors, and not only those involved in tourism, have a direct interest in the development of their area via different projects that usually involve a local trademark as a sign of quality.

4. Trademarks to market a local area and its specialities

As mentioned above, a local area cannot become a tourist destination without the involvement of all those directly and indirectly involved. The cluster concept can help them be considered as members of a larger network. A cluster represents all the relationships between host communities and tourists that quality tourist experiences demand. A cluster is a guarantee of shared values:

The fact that these businesses are all members of the same network means that there is an explicit agreement to share the same values, objectives and standards, to adhere to the same rules and to adopt the same criteria towards business practices.

(Croce and Perri, 2010: 68)

Defining these shared values requires a jointly agreed diagnosis of a shared area. A local area analysis, such as that presented in Figure 4.4, will include all the traditional factors, such as spatial patterns, organisation, population surveys, types of operators, and environmental analyses. To produce a shared diagnosis, all the connections between all these components have to be considered, and the local way of life and local identity have to be understood as essential factors of a tourist product. It is assumed that a host community chooses to live and work in a mountain area because of the quality of life. In the cases studied, this way of life is linked to local products, culture, traditions, heritage, and "eco-gastronomy," a concept defined as an alternative to consumerism based on interactions between humans and food and the effects these interactions produce. The aim is to obtain healthier and more sustainable food and, at the same time, reduce the environmental impacts of both production and

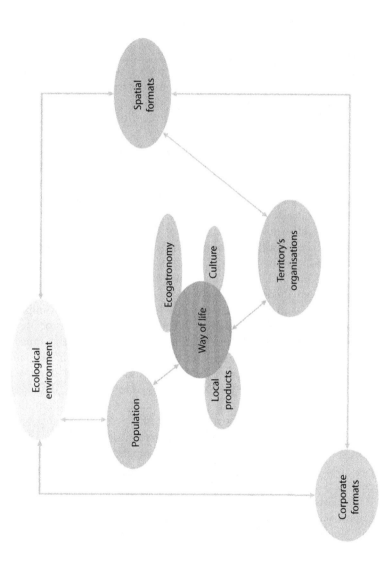

Figure 4.4 Local area analysis, a fundamental phase in the organisation of tourism clusters (inspired by the tourism system of Dewailly and Flament, 2000)

consumption (Harvey et al., 2004). Ecogastronomy can connect the actors involved and the host community to their ecological environment through local products and recognition of the local culture. In this approach, protected landscapes are part of the development of the ecotourism experience. Marketing will combine protected landscapes and local products to symbolise quality. A well-preserved landscape then becomes a guarantee of quality.

> Gastronomic tourism must therefore take on the symbolic load of its "terroir" just as other tourism sectors reflect symbolic images of their destinations; but in the case of gastronomic tourism, the region's natural and socio-economic characteristics must also be protected.
>
> (Croce and Perri, 2010: 75)

The sustainable tourism projects run by the Vercors Regional Nature Park (PNR) illustrate this concept. The Vercors PNR was created in October 1970 and covers 205,806 hectares, including 17,000 hectares classified as a nature reserve. The altitude of the park ranges from 180m to 2453m at the summit of the Rocher Rond peak. The Vercors PNR covers eighty-five municipalities, including forty-eight in the Isère department and thirty-seven in Drôme. The gateways to the PNR are Grenoble, Crest, Roman, Saint Marcellin, and Vinay. The region is divided into eight natural areas and four mountain ranges: Trièves, Vercors Drômois, Royans Isère, Royans, Drôme, Gervanne, Diois, and Northern Piedmont. The Vercors' PNR web page[14] explains that the park encourages and supports companies and economic actors implementing sustainable development principles. Protected landscapes associated with environmental and architectural integration are part of the quality image that PNR seeks to promote. According to Perrin-Malterre (2015: 96, author's translation), "Vercors is in a phase of stagnation and concerned about seeing a decline in tourist numbers. The park's priority is to revitalise the destination by making it more sustainable." The park's web pages also mention that this sustainable positioning demands a redefinition of the values the area wishes to promote, but also greater consistency and better coordination between partners. "On a more positive note, regional competition and the synergy of complementary products help to raise the overall quality of the visitor's experience and the products on offer in all destinations" (Kivela and Crotts, 2006: 375). This point relates to the principles of tourism clusters entailing a quality approach. The focus of the Vercors PNR tourist project is on its trademark slogan, *"Inspiration Vercors."* This trademark identifies a network of tourism actors supported by the Pamplemousse consultancy (based in Annecy) and by the head of the park's tourism department, Mathieu Rocheblave, who is adept at getting tourism operators (tourist offices and district tourism committees) around the table with operators in the tourist sector. During our interviews, he said that they are increasingly recognised as stakeholders by the PNR team. This aspiration of the PNR towards sustainable tourism is evidence of a movement in search of a new impetus in an area that has become a victim of its own success (working people from Grenoble move into the PNR area every year). The resulting urban sprawl has had an impact on tourist practices, with more and more people visiting just for a day rather than a week as they used to. The discussions around the Inspiration Vercors trademark led to more upstream work on links between local authorities and a longer-term view of sustainable tourist development. According to the managers and elected representatives of the Vercors PNR, the trademark has had a federating effect and allows shared public and private governance. To manage the trademark, the stakeholders share common values. Rocheblave underlines that in addition to learning new skills, the various actors put in a great deal of effort to reach this point. The main goal is achieving a common position that will preserve the specific features of each tourist area. The park acts as coordinator, even project incubator, by mobilizing all the stakeholders to turn Vercors into a true tourist destination. Inspiration Vercors aims above all to federate as many tourism actors as possible who identify with sustainable development values. Vercors Tourisme is the organisation responsible for nationally promoting PNR's values under the Inspiration Vercors banner. Inspiration Vercors is an initiative that aims to be more collaborative and participatory than the application of the principles of the national PNR brand.

It was pointed out to us, however, that all products with the Inspiration Vercors label adhere to the principles of the national PNR brand. Inspiration Vercors strongly underlines the image of the Vercors range. Like the Pic du Midi d'Ossau, the Vercors geosite is a presence in the mind of each inhabitant promoting the PNR values. The Vercors range is inhabited by rural and "neo-rural" populations with a common duty to preserve its heritage and natural landscapes for future generations. The members of the Inspiration Vercors network act as ambassadors for the area. They exemplify the spirit of friendliness that the park wanted us to experience during our investigations and meetings. The park's sustainable tourism project is organising around the Inspiration Vercors trademark and its operational axis of tourist promotion and communication between the park, with its elected representatives, and its economic partners. All the actors, partners, and stakeholders we met told us that the most important point was the standard of quality of tourist offerings and local products. For example, about fifty members of Inspiration Vercors participate each year in the Paris agricultural show to present local products along with the local tourist offerings. This event has become essential to the life of the network and to demonstrate the connection of each member to the sustainable tourism development project.

These examples bring the spirit of UNESCO's Geopark Network to mind, which is also associated with the idea of quality tourism experiences. The UNESCO label is a mark of guaranteed quality across the world. The rules of the UNESCO label are based on the identity of candidates. If a geological area wants to be part of this world network, it must have outstanding features. Candidacy is only possible after lengthy consideration of the local identity, protected landscapes, and the natural and human heritage. In the UNESCO

Geopark Network, the question of identity in connection with local development is essential for all candidate areas. As Chamard (2014: 145, author's
translation) notes:

> The identity of an area is its DNA, a set of signs, of cultural features, of
> 'codes' that give a group a sense of being part of the same team, define its
> personality and its character and make it unique in the eyes of both
> inhabitants and visitors.

All the geosites in this network are classified as world heritage sites and most
are unique and extraordinary. The network promotes the involvement and
excellence of host communities as a means of achieving sustainable local
development. The Geopark managers anticipated the emergence of globally
competitive tourism: Rather than promoting countries, they involve geological
areas in local sustainable development through geotourism – a concept that
promises unique experiences in sites of outstanding geological and historical
interest managed by local actors working closely with host communities. These
areas seek to become tourist destinations identified by the UNESCO label, an
aspiration that relates to the approach of Bédard (2011, author's translation):

> In a context of increasingly competitive tourism worldwide, local or
> regional destinations now play a key role. Rather than a country, visitors
> choose an attraction, a resort, a city, or a region. They recognise destina-
> tions by their brand or image. The various actors involved within a
> destination are increasingly aware of the importance of seeking excellence
> to improve their competitive position.

The geopark label is also a tool to promote development and cohesion
around a shared project, to optimise the link between knowledge and
enhanced value.[15] To join the network and propose a true tourist product
based on quality and experience, geoparks have to identify not only the
"specific character" of their geosites as areas of outstanding geological interest,
but also their local history, communities, inhabitants, traditions, and heritage.
This type of label involving different actors in a local development approach
based on local products, landscapes, heritage, and host communities helps to
clarify the local tourist offerings. To quote Real and Garcia (2014: 77):

> Some rural areas are launching a new generation of labels to simplify the
> message and streamline top-heavy systems. These labels are intended to
> preserve both the identity and the cultural, social and environmental
> resources of these local areas with a view to their development. . . .
> Thanks to their contribution to local rural development, the most impor-
> tant labels are those that aim for quality in all aspects of their locality. The
> idea is to make their strategy visible through a label that can guarantee
> (within and outside the area) the tangible and intangible quality of the

goods, services, natural and cultural heritage, and institutional elements that a rural area offers to consumers.

The UNESCO Geopark Network helps tourists identify destinations by making connections between the quality of the geosites and the local products, tourist activities, heritage interpretation, and so forth. These sites are of interest not for their geology alone, but also because they offer real discovery through interpretations of the geology, which provide them with cues to anticipate the earth's future.

In the case of the Ossau Valley and Laruns, the local authorities and tourist office have limited scope to adjust the problematically low standard of their tourist offerings. However, during our investigations, we identified a common culture that converges towards tourism. To improve their tourist products, we advised local actors to base their output on images of Ossau and to change the scale of their tourist promotion and communication. In 2015, we put forward the idea of a local trademark, *"Ossau Pyrénées Tourisme,"* to the Laruns local authorities and other actors involved to help them envisage tourist development on a broader scale. The idea of developing tourism on the larger scale of the Pyrenean range, for example, is quite modest, but the trademark would show that all those involved share the same aspiration to quality products. This trademark could trigger ideas for developing a true tourist destination for food-lovers (gourmand destination), organised around quality local products and outstanding landscapes. The idea was met with enthusiasm in Laruns, but the trademark had not been released at the time of writing. The actors concerned in Laruns and Ossau are in conflict over their tourist development strategies, and the lack of local dialogue is crippling the development of a unique local tourist experience. These actors were unable to agree on joining a local network (such as a cluster or any other form of involvement) focusing on sustainable develop-ment. They want their village to be identified as a tourist destination but are focused on their own particular approaches to traditions, language, and heritage. These are real difficulties that are slowing down local development.

5. Conclusion

The analysis in this chapter highlights a number of strategic lessons on harnessing identity and quality to support local economic development. We noted that local development cannot manifest without creating networks amongst the actors concerned. However, such partnerships cannot simply be decreed by the relevant institutions; they must be based on local consensus. The actors must analyse their local area to define a common identity and cross-cutting aims. Furthermore, several studies have established that quality is now an essential component in such projects, encouraging more discerning expectations among actors as to the local products and type of tourism to be promoted in their areas. Consumers demand greater transparency in agricultural products; they appreci-ate local products, marketing systems that connect them more directly to producers and actors actively involved in quality. Responding to demand, especially in tourism, requires the use of local area analysis techniques and strategic concepts suited to each component of the area in question, and not relying on ready-made models. For any local development project, especially for rural mountain areas, it has become fundamentally important to link the quality of local products, landscapes, and the tourist experience. Since tourism products in rural mountain areas are very similar, it has become essential to develop a certain level of quality to attract visitors to particular areas. In other words, the "human factor" is more and more indispensable. The beauty of a landscape alone will not sell its cheeses, spring water, or any other local product; recognition of the local area and its people acting in accordance with common identity values are just as important. Local people may be satisfied with their products, landscapes, and the place where they live, but these alone are not enough to make tourists decide to stay for a few days or even stop for lunch. A local area and those who live there are understood through values, quality, and their identity. Most of those talking about identity associate it with the idea of quality but find it more difficult to identify the essential relationship between this and effective and sustainable local economic development.

Finally, trademarks and labels have developed considerably across France, more or less successfully, and with greater or lesser popularity among actors and consumers. To improve their performance, these regional or local trademarks require a shared diagnosis and strategic guidelines to emphasise the ideas of identity and quality to support the actors concerned who need to work together to agree on a shared diagnosis of their identity, heritage, and way of life. If local actors do not know who they are, where they come from, and why they live in these regions, tourists will not choose to stay there either. However, for most local and regional trademarks, these phases can be lengthy, resulting in neglected or superimposed labels that are more confusing than helpful to tourists and consumers. In these local areas experiencing development difficulties, designing a label that will guarantee a certain standard of quality demands local involvement based on a well-recognised identity. In our investigations, we identified projects that aim for local sustainable development based on a strategy. These projects are built on specific and outstanding mountain landscapes and rural areas. Local public and private actors play a crucial role in producing tourism of this type. In all the projects we studied, high-quality local products are increasingly the key to a complete tourist experience. The introduction of trademarks encourages local actors and host communities to join forces towards a common end, which is essential for their approach to be sustainable.

Notes

1   Source: http://www.domaines-skiables.fr/.
2   Équipe MIT (2002), Tourismes 1. *Lieux communs*, Paris, Belin; Équipe MIT (2005), Tourismes 2. *Moments de lieux*, Paris, Belin; Équipe MIT (2011), Tourismes 3. *La révolution durable*, Paris, Belin.
3   Italy is the world's leading wine producer and France is still in second place. http://www.lemonde.fr/economie/article/2016/10/20/vin-malgre-une-produc

tion-en-baisse-de-12-la-france-reste-numero-deux-mondial_5017289_3234.
html.

4 https://www.ecomusee-olivier.com/notre-histoire. Olivier Baussan is the creator of *L'OCCITANE* and *OLIVIERS & CO.*

5 http://www.moulinolivette.fr/.

6 http://www.globalgeopark.org/aboutGGN/6398.htm.

7 http://whc.unesco.org/en/tourism/.

8 Source: Gallioz S. (2011). Design: G.S. The sample for this survey comprised 400 individuals. To carry out the study, Sylvain Gallioz stayed in around four different hiking sites each Tuesday and Friday during 8 weeks in summer season.

9 Source: Charlotte Genet (2012).

10 In 2015, a study was conducted with shepherds in the Laruns area to assess their views on tourism. In October 2015, a group of seven students working on heritage promotion undertook a study of the Laruns cheese fair where they interviewed 182 visitors (optimum sample: 323 responses). A heritage interpretation plan was explored in 2016, resulting at the end of 2017 in a project proposal for a complete interpretation exhibition in the old train station in Laruns. This research project employed five trainees and three staff on fixed-term contracts (six months each) to investigate the Laruns area and was a unique opportunity to explore all the aspects of the local area with all the necessary support, time, and resources.

11 Source: Students taking the Master *Valorisation des Patrimoines, étudiants option Mise en tourisme* and *C. Venzal, 2015–2016.*

12 Cf. definition in the *Larousse Cobuild English Learner's Dictionary.*

13 http://www.hotel-pourtalet.com/.

14 http://parc-du-vercors.fr/fr_FR/les-actions-1109/le-parc-au-salon-de-l-agriculture-2682.html.

15 http://www.geopark-monts-ardeche.fr/decouvrir-le-geopark/presentation-du-geopark-geopark/un-geopark-qu-est-ce-que-c-est-geopark.html.

References

Barrère, C. (2013). Patrimoines gastronomiques et développement local: Les limites du modèle français de gastronomie élitiste. *Mondes du Tourisme*, 7, pp. 15–36, http://tourisme.revues.org/178.

Batat, W. and Frochot, I. (2014). *Marketing expérientiel. Comment concevoir et stimuler l'expérience client.* Paris: Dunod.

Bédard, F. (2011). L'excellence des destinations. *Téoros*, 30(1), pp. 9–11.

Chamard, C. (2014). *Le Marketing Territorial.* Louvain-La-Neuve: De Boek Supérieur.

Clergeau, C. and Etcheverria, O. (2013). La mise en tourisme et le développement local par la création d'une atmosphère gastronomique. Analyse à partir du cas de Vonnas. *Mondes du Tourisme*, 7, pp. 52–67.

Condevaux, A., Djament-Tran, G., and Gravari-Barbas, M. (2016). Before and after tourism(s). The trajectories of tourist destinations and the role of actors involved in "off-the-beaten-track" tourism: A literature review. *Via@Turism Review*, 1(9). http://viatourismreview.com/2016/10/avantetaprestourisme-analysebiblio/.

Croce, E. and Perri, G. (2010). *Food and wine tourism.* Wallingford, Oxgfordshire: CABI.

Derioz, P. (2004). Le paysage, une ressource territoriale emblématique mais ambiguë. *Conférence proceedings: La notion de ressource territoriale*, Domaine Olivier de Serres, Le Pradel, 14–15(20), pp. 155–163.

Di Méo, G., Sauvaitre, C., and Soufflet, F. (2004). Les paysages de l'identité (le cas du Piémont béarnais, à l'est de Pau). *Géocarrefour*, 79(2), pp. 131–141.

Équipe MIT (2002). *TOURISME 1 Lieux communs.* Paris: Belin.

Équipe MIT (2008). *TOURISME 2 Moments de lieux.* Paris: Belin.

Équipe MIT (2011). *TOURISME 3 La Révolution Durable.* Paris: Belin.

Etcheverria, O. (2016). Le tourisme "gourmand" existe-t-il? *Téoros*, 35(2), http://teoros. revues.org/2968.

Fabry, N. and Zeghni, S. (2012). *Tourisme, territoires et développement.* Bruxelles: De Boeck.

Gerbaux, F. (2001). Le développement touristique local entre régulations sectorielles et gestion territorial. In Bensahel, L. and Donsimoni, M. (eds) *Le tourisme, facteur de développement local.* Grenoble: Presses Universitaires de Grenoble, pp. 70–87.

Gravari-Barbas, M. and Graburn, N. (2012). Imaginaires touristiques. *Via@Turism Review*, 1, http://www.viatourismreview.net/Editorial1.php.

Harvey, M., McMeekin, A., and Warde, A. (2004). *Qualities of food.* Manchester University Press, Manchester, pp. 176–191. https://en.wikipedia.org/wiki/Eco-gastronomy#cite_note-3.

Jafari, J. (2000). *Encyclopaedia of tourism.* London: Routledge.

Kadri, B., Khomsi, M., and Bondarenko, M. (2011). Le concept de destination. *Téoros, Revue de Recherche en Tourisme*, 30(1), pp. 12–24.

Kivela, J. and Crotts, J.C. (2006). Tourism and gastronomy: Gastronomy's influence on how tourists experience a destination. *Journal of Hospitality & Tourism Research*, 30(3), pp. 354–377.

Leroy, A. (2001). Tourisme et économie rurale: Le tourisme rural peut-il (re)dynamiser nos campagnes? In Bensahel, L. and Donsimoni, M. (eds) *Le tourisme, facteur de développement local.* Grenoble : Presses Universitaires de Grenoble, pp. 89–106.

Lesne A. and Zins, M. (2009). Evaluer les destinations touristiques dans un contexte de multiplication des expériences offertes aux touristes internationaux. In Lemasson, J.-P. and Violier, P. (eds) *Les Rendez-Vous de Champlain, Destinations et Territoires, Coprésence à l'œuvre.* Vol. 1, pp. 81–91. Montreal: Presses de l'Université du Quebec

Maizi, P. and Amilien, V. (2007). Les tribulations d'un bien commun. *L'AOC Ossau Iraty*, symposium on *Les terroirs: Caractérisation, développement territorial et gouvernance*, Aix-en-Provence.

Middleton, V.C.T., Fyall, A., Morgan, M., and Ranchhod, A. (2009). *Marketing in travel and tourism.* Elsevier Buttenworth-Heinemann, Oxford, UK.

Pecqueur, B. (1994). Le système local des acteurs: Émergence du développement économique local, in Marc-Urbain Proulx, *Développement économique. Clé de l'autonomie locale.* Les Editions Transcontinental inc. et Fondation de l'Entrepreneurship, Québec.

Perrin-Malterre, C. (2015). Comparer l'organisation d'un sport de nature dans deux espaces protégés. *Sciences Sociales et Sport*, 1(8), pp. 79–101. doi: 10.3917/rsss.008.0079.

Pitte, J.-R. (1993). Des productions de qualité dans un paysage de qualité: Un défi pour le monde rural français. *L'aménagement Foncier Agricole et Rural*, 79, pp. 19–22.

Real, E.R. and Garcia, D.G. (2014). Towards a 2nd generation of quality labels: A proposal for the evaluation of territorial quality marks. *Labellisation et mise en marque des territoires*, Presses Universitaires Blaise Pascal, CERAMAC 34, pp. 71–88.

Tilden, F. (1957). *Interpreting our heritage.* Chapel Hill: The University of North Carolina Press.

Vachon, B. and Coallier, F. (1993). *Le Développement Local. Théorie et pratique. Réintroduire l'humain dans la logique de développement.* Gaëtan Morin, Itée, Québec.

Venzal, C. (2013). *Diagnostic touristique de la Haute-Vallée de l'Ossau : le territoire de Laruns.* Convention de recherche Mairie de Laruns/Société Altiservice/UPPA-SET.

5 The real and imaginary Alentejo

Overlapping perspectives on the various strategies for agricultural and tourism development in this Portuguese region[1]

Isabel Lopes Cardoso

1. Introduction

The name Alentejo comes from *Tejo*, the Portuguese word for the River Tagus that marks the region's northern border, preceded by the adverb *além*, meaning "beyond." Thus, Alentejo literally means "Beyond the Tagus" and evokes an external, detached vision of a region located off the beaten track. The origin of the name dates back to the founding of Portugal (in the twelfth century) when the territorial conquest progressed southwards from the north. Since that time, both the central political powers and the capital city of Lisbon, which was built on the north side of the River Tagus, have almost always considered Alentejo as an outlying region. In the nineteenth century, during the 1820 Liberal Revolution, and with the later advent of emerging nationalism in Europe, Portugal sought to ensure its economic independence. The state therefore designated Alentejo as an agricultural region dominated by the monoculture production of wheat. This decision was made without taking into account the complex reality of the biophysical capacity of the local environment or the social organisation that had developed there in close symbiosis with nature. Later, during the Estado Novo period from 1933–1974, the notion of Alentejo as the "breadbasket" of Portugal was used as a propaganda tool to underpin the dictatorship's policy. The third historic period that sealed the transformation of the Alentejan countryside into an intensive farming area began when Portugal joined the European Economic Community (EEC) in 1986 and the Common Agricultural Policy (CAP) came into force. A hundred years of this monoculture-focused production policy therefore almost eradicated *montado*, a sustainable agro–silvo–pastoral ecosystem that for centuries played a crucial role in mitigating the desertification process (Wilson, 2009)[2]. Indeed, this thousand-year-old, man-made regional ecosystem now struggles to maintain its resilience and is much debilitated, currently awaiting inscription on the UNESCO World Heritage List. Moreover, whereas the *montado* ecosystem had both enabled the settlement of people and helped to develop a unique, almost thousand-year-old regional culture characterised particularly by its cuisine, the intensive farming of the region caused local populations to abandon Alentejo and led to the area's rapid desertion.

Since the beginning of the twenty-first century and the creation of Alqueva, Europe's largest artificial lake, the outstanding beauty of the monoculture landscapes and the region's status as one of the "least populated places in Western Europe" have been promoted to tourists who are touted the scenario of a land where "time has stood still," which is "authentic," "intact," and the perfect place to "be happy." With its living space emptied of permanent inhabitants, the region's brand image as now conveyed by the media and tourism sector (unlike that of the "breadbasket") reflects an unrealistic authenticity and sense of tradition that ignore the thousand-year-old ties forged between people and this poorly productive biophysical environment.

In terms of local development, an exploratory study of the terrain conducted in central Alentejo in 2014 in association with landscape architect Carapinha revealed the limits of this marketing operation: In fact, a number of the rural tourism units visited belonged to absentee property owners (mostly from Lisbon). They had made the property their second home but used rural tourism as a front to benefit from the subsidies available for building renovations. Instead of contributing to a better quality of life for Alentejan inhabitants and to the region's local development more generally, the breadbasket image and the concept of rural tourism making good use of monoculture landscapes have in reality intensified the desertification of the region (22.8 inhabitants/ km^2 in 2016).

Based on historiographic, iconographic, and literary sources, the first part of this chapter offers a historical view of how a landscape and its representations can be orchestrated as instruments of power and an external vision that determine the economic and social future of a region, even to this day. We will then focus on a precise geographic location, the Herdade do Freixo do Meio farm in Montemor-o-Novo. This is a local agricultural development project based on a qualitative, environmentally friendly approach to the land via the reintroduction of the *montado* ecosystem. Going against popular opinion and the standard practices prevailing in the region, Alfredo Sendim rehabilitated the *montado* ecosystem at Herdade do Freixo do Meio, returning it to the memory of an identity predating the fictional breadbasket, emphasising the ties between respect for nature, quality of place, product quality, quality of life, and local development. In opposition to the deadly, closed-off landscapes created by intensive monoculture on poor-quality soils, Herdade do Freixo do Meio proposes the living, resilient, and multifunctional landscapes that are the result of *montado*. The data supporting Sendim's experience were collected during an exploratory study conducted with Carapinha and in discussions with Sendim after his presentation at the study day held at the Calouste Gulbenkian Foundation in Paris (10 December 2014) on the topic, "Heritage, Landscape, and Food Tourism" (*Patrimoine, Paysage et Tourisme Gourmand*). Additional data were obtained via informal interviews conducted at his shop in Lisbon, the analysis of press and blog articles, and consultation of the Herdade do Freixo do Meio and the Montemor-o-Novo municipality websites. The final part deals with Casa do Alentejo in Lisbon and its role as a showcase for the external identity of the region. Located in the historic centre of the capital city, Casa do Alentejo is dedicated to the preservation of Alentejo and promotes its culture to a wide audience, particularly via gastronomy with its restaurant, tavern, and shop. While fully acknowledging that it seeks to benefit from the tourism trade, Casa do Alentejo is critical of the tourist boom's predatory effect on the historic centre of Lisbon. It attempts to differentiate itself from this by providing quality products and services. The data presented here were collected during informal individual interviews conducted since 2014 with the management and employees of Casa do Alentejo and during *in situ* observation sessions. This information was supplemented and cross-referenced with my own personal experiences as a patron of the venue for thirty years, the analysis of press and blog articles, and consultation of studies on Casa do Alentejo and its website.

2. Landscapes of power, local development, and why one man's happiness is not another man's gain

Today, Alentejo is appreciated for its aesthetic qualities as a tourist destination. Over several years, the British daily newspaper, *The Guardian*, devoted long articles in its "Travel" section to the region, and these are regularly republished in the Portuguese press. In a column published in *Público* in 2012, the historian Paulo Varela Gomes (2014) noted, however, that the increasing infatuation with Alentejo, particularly amongst Portuguese city-dwelling tourists, was acting as a direct counterpoint to the "transgenification" occurring in the northern country areas of Portugal as described by the geographer Domingues (2013). In preference to the now fully urbanised but formerly bucolic regions lying to the north west of the Tagus, today's tourists opt for the "magical landscapes" of an imaginary Alentejo "where time has stood still," and evoking historical heritage, cultural, environmental, and recreational values. Tranquillity ("unspoilt") nature, tradition, and authenticity are the much sought-after attributes of this new "lost paradise" (Van der Ploeg, 1997), but in reality the region is characterised by its "intermediary landscapes" (Tuan, 1974; Silva, 2007), which are neither wild nor urban – and are in fact a combination of agricultural zones, forested areas, reservoir basins, and houses (with swimming pools).

This idyllic and idealised image, so aesthetically pleasing from the outside, glosses over the reality of the rural world in general, and Alentejo in particular: poverty, lack of employment and services, school closures, agricultural bankruptcy, the abandonment of farms, and depopulation. As Alentejan landscape architect Carapinha (2014) notes, the publicity campaign slogan describing Alentejo as a place "to be happy"[3] does not necessarily mean that the region is a place where one actually *is* happy. Her remarks about the region's landscapes and its various representations corroborate the analysis of the anthropologist Cauvin-Verner (2006) that tourism objects reflect the tensions produced by intersecting contradictory strategies and desires. Thus, the tourist who seeks and sees authenticity and tradition in a so-called unchanged Alentejan land-scape (because it has not been urbanised) is, in truth, enthralled by a relatively recent landscape, developed at the end of the nineteenth century and whose layout has greatly contributed towards the region's desertification and the emigration of its inhabitants. The ecological and social memory of the multi-functional, lively and dynamic pre-nineteenth-century Alentejan countryside, where different social classes developed a *modus vivendi* thanks particularly to "the full range of wasteland resources ... capable of sustaining a human group" (Silbert, 1966: 471), was abandoned in favour of the still-dominant production method – that of a closed, intensive, and massively subsidised[4] monoculture that almost exclusively benefits large-scale private entrepreneurs. Ironically, it is these uniform, smoothed-out, sluggish landscapes with their 193.1% aging rate that delight the current temporary inhabitants: tourists in search of authenticity and tradition as a means of escaping – just for a while – from the pressures of the fast-paced and erratic city life.

Today's Alentejan monoculture landscapes were developed from scratch barely a hundred years ago and are reminiscent of what Mitchell (2002) describes as a landscape of power. Their aesthetic beauty makes tourists oblivious to the complex thousand-year-old ancestral culture (i.e., considered by Alentejans to be authentic and traditional), which is based on close ties between communities and their natural environment. This symbiotic relationship gave rise to *montado*, which influenced the unique culinary culture that was a genuine mark of identity for the region. Today, *montado* is in an ailing condition and awaits its inscription on the UNESCO World Heritage List, while the region's cuisine has been made the subject of the Alentejo Gastronomy Charter published in 2011. This collection of more than 1,000 recipes has drawn attention to the fact that Alentejan gastronomy and the quality of its products are closely linked to, and even depend on, the resilient *montado* system. In other words, the unique character of Alentejan cuisine could disappear if the region's tourism marketers continue to use images and practices that associate monoculture landscapes with traditional Alentejan know-how and way of life. In fact, such traditions are rooted in an entirely different – multifunctional – relationship with the land. Thus, if that which marketers seek to promote is to be saved (particularly sustainable development[5]), a certain number of historical truths must first be reintroduced in the region's narrative.

2.1. Local agricultural development and the "breadbasket" concept as a tool for the orchestration of power relations

It was always a particular feature of Alentejo that a large proportion of the land was owned by a small number of people. The geoclimatic characteristics (gentle slopes, poorly productive soils and subsoils, water scarcity) and historic factors relating to property laws (a concentration of large areas of land held by a handful of owners) explain the low population levels in a territory that covers around 33% of the country's entire surface area. These conditions also determined the humanisation of the countryside pastures based on the Mediterranean triad of wheat, olive oil, and wine dating back to the *urbis, ager, saltus, sylva,* and *latifundiae* of the Latin landscape (Carapinha, 2014). From this symbiosis of ecological factors came a landscape that was diversified not only in its morphology but also in its productivity. The historian Mattoso and his colleagues (2010) reiterated that the Alentejo described in pre-nineteenth-century documents was very different to the image that has been developed and propagated since, with its emphasis on the breadbasket notion (and other monocultures) as a solution for this southern, underdeveloped region. Indeed, the archives teach us that between the High Middle Ages and the modern era, Alentejo[6] was an economically dynamic entity. Along with farming the land's raw materials, and in close collaboration with the land, residents raised animals and invested in processing facilities (wool, olives, milk, and cork), and there was a thriving commercial trade. At that time, the Alentejan countryside and economy were multifunctional and multiproductive structures in which the fallow lands played an important role because they facilitated the gathering of all sorts of food supplements that are still the hallmarks of the regional cuisine.

Recent history has forgotten the link between the local communities and this poor, fragile biophysical environment that operates according to its own rules. Cereal crops have always played an important role in the Alentejan economy, but they were sown on appropriate soils[7] and combined with other crops. From the nineteenth century onwards, this dynamic link was supplanted, as successive governments propagated the idea of Alentejo as the nation's breadbasket. Silbert (1966) lists the limits and failures of the policy's various experiments. In his chapter focusing on the wheat trade, the historian emphasises, for example, that at the start of the nineteenth century, the protectionist measures undertaken by the Liberals to make the country economically independent[8] came up against the reality of Spanish cereal imports authorised by the terms of the 1757 free trade agreement. He also points out the region's geoclimatic constraints. According to him, the cereal trade was occasionally clandestine and created traffic flows which varied in both size and direction depending on the harvest, or in other words, the weather. Silbert argues that referring to Alentejo as the "bread basket of Lisbon" is far too simplistic. Not only because the capital received most of its wheat supplies from elsewhere, but also because wheat from Lisbon was occasionally sent to supply Alentejo when the harvest was bad. De Oliveira Marques (1971) also suggests that with regard to the provision of food to the nearby capital of Lisbon, "the high price of transport added such a cost to Alentejan wheat that it ceased to be competitive in comparison with imported wheat."

Towards the end of the century, the 1899 law on cereals established protective measures for nationally grown wheat, but the results were disappointing despite the use of fertilisers and an increase in the size of the area cultivated (Pais et al., 1976). The poor soils quickly became depleted, and self-sufficiency was never achieved. The same thing happened with the wheat campaigns promoted and subsidised by the Estado Novo,[9] which began at the end of the 1920s and shaped the regime's agricultural policy until the 1960s (Freire, 2008). The "absentee" owners of the large-scale estates (*latifundio*) who lived in the capital city and constituted an unfailing source of support for the dictatorship, made their living principally from trade, real estate, and banking. As their land-based properties were mostly used for leisure purposes, they were not directly interested in the government's agricultural policy. Nevertheless, it was certainly in their interest to make a number of ostensible concessions to the breadbasket project and to contribute to its use as a political instrument aimed at absorbing the large throngs of migrants arriving from other regions in the country – a phenomenon that was a stain on the dictatorship's image as protector of the nation. Thus, the large-scale landowners agreed to rent out their less fertile and fallow lands to the peasant farmers. The research conducted by the anthropologist Cutileiro (1971) and the novels of Fonseca (1943)[10] and Nobel laureate in Literature Saramago (1980) provide insight into the permanently conflictual social climate that reigned amongst the rich landowners, the sharecroppers (*seareiros*),[11] the poor temporary Alentejan agricultural workers, the migrant agricultural workers, and the gypsies.

These conflicts were regularly hushed up by the regime's censorship system to promote the mythical image of the breadbasket that was widely adopted and disseminated by travel literature and advertising in accordance with the principles imposed by the Estado Novo propaganda (Rosas, 2001; Rodrigues, 2014). The writing and pictures in Portuguese travel guides (Proença, 1927), as well as those published in France (Papy and Gadala, 1935; Chantal and Santos, 1950), Germany (Glassner, 1942; Seligo, 1959), England (Chantal and Santos, 1953; Fodor's Modern Guides, 1967), and Switzerland (Job, 1956), all contributed to the smoothing effect and development of the external view of the Alentejan countryside that is still held by Portuguese and foreign tourists today.[12] The guidebooks refer to the "physiognomic simplicity" of the plains and their "truly outstanding capacity for wheat growing" and also draw parallels with the concept of fertility and the biblical symbolism of bread. The harvesters became the emblematic figures of the vast, "fiery and fertile" Alentejo described in the travel guides. From the end of the nineteenth century and throughout the twentieth century, Portuguese painters[13] and writers[14] from different schools (naturalist, realist, and neo-realist), with differing ideological viewpoints ranging from glorification to denunciation, all produced the same image of these heroes labouring beneath a "searing," "enamel blue sky" with its "ferociously dazzling light" as they carried out their "work of the damned" amidst "the resounding silence of the plains baked by the 50° heat." At this particular point in the Alentejan symbolism and narrative, the region's positive image as the breadbasket and its negative counter-image of poverty and underdevelopment become entwined. For, although these "damned beings" carried out the noble task of harvesting at the height of the heat, they belonged to the most impoverished lower social classes. They were associated with extreme poverty, within a structural framework in which the division of land and socioeconomic organisation were profoundly inequitable, where agricultural workers with precarious temporary employment status were legion, and where their main preoccupation was the struggle for survival (Baptista, 1994). In 1970, these people still accounted for 82% of the Alentejan agricultural population, which also included 2% of overseers and 16% of small independent farmers (Guichard, 1990).

2.2. From the breadbasket to local tourism development, or the persistent fiction of the landscapes of power

The Carnation Revolution brought the Estado Novo to an end in 1974. The large-scale landowners were expropriated and Alentejo underwent the Agrarian Reform.[15] However, Europe remained watchful, and Portugal gradually edged its way towards membership of the Common Market (EEC) in 1986. Years of contradictory policies from the Common Agricultural Policy (CAP) then ensued, and these contributed greatly towards the desertification of the region (Wilson, 2009). Many farms disappeared and the trend continued towards a concentration of activity in large farms (which became agricultural companies). Since then, and with the creation of Europe's largest artificial lake (Alqueva), a new myth has emerged: that of tourism, the twenty-first-century panacea that is supposed to make up for the decline in agricultural business. It is noteworthy that the Estado Novo's use of the breadbasket concept, and the dual image of the very catholic[16] dyad of blessing/domination that was so beneficial to the business of the absentee landlords and the government, never fostered the development of tourism. The country's elite kept tourism for other areas of the country, particularly the Algarve, to maintain Alentejo as their own exclusive preserve.

At the beginning of 2014, the Portuguese National Institute of Statistics estimated that 2014 would be the region's best year for tourism – an estimate that would subsequently be confirmed. In 2016, hoteliers recorded 1,165,758 guests (21,252,625 for the whole of Portugal), i.e., twice the number as in 2009.[17] Alentejo is in vogue, especially with the Portuguese who make up the largest percentage (two-thirds) of tourists in the region.[18] As the nation's former Arcadia (the North) gradually becomes more urbanised, so Alentejo emerges as the final outpost of authenticity (with its idealised rural associations), where one can enjoy the tranquillity of nature with the family or as a couple (lovers or seniors). Here, one can enjoy contemplation of the "dark sky,"[19] indulge in the local cuisine, participate in wine-tasting sessions and bread-making workshops (a concept that combines Alentejo's breadbasket image as "the land of bread" with the globalised, city-dwellers' fashion for making one's own bread), and visit architectural heritage sites and theme parks. As far as foreign tourists are concerned, the "authentic" Alentejo is often synonymous with a journey back in time, luxury hotels, wine, and the charm of a poor, scarcely populated region (Choat, 2014[20]).

The National Strategic Plan for Tourism (PENT 2006–2015) identified gastronomy and wine as strategic products for the development of tourism in Portugal. Along with Douro, Alentejo is the second largest wine-producing region in the country[21] and is also the region with the largest number of wine tourism establishments. On 8 September 2014, in a post for *In Vino Viajas*, a Brazilian blog about "wine culture and quality tourism," which has followers in 105 countries and claims to be the tenth-most-consulted website on wine in Brazil, self-styled "journalist and wine connoisseur" Ruschel wrote: "The Alentejo region in Portugal has been voted the world's best wine growing destination by the readers of America's biggest newspaper, USA Today."[22] To explain the reasons leading to this choice, the author reiterates the arguments cited by the *USA Today* journalists and lists the reasons that enchanted their readers: the region's beauty, the wide range of wine-cellar showrooms (seventy wineries across the region in 2014), fully serviced hotels, excellent restaurants (sometimes offering a selection of fifty wines from eight subregions,[23] accompanied by local cheeses from Serpa, Évora, and – as in the case of Enoteca de Redondo – Nisa), fantastic wines, and well-tended vineyards, all set against a backdrop of "vast, undulating plains, peppered with cork oaks and olive trees and whitewashed villages." The imagery conveyed by readers reprises the stereotypes established by the regional tourism directorate's various campaign messages. They see "a region where time has stood still." "In summer, the swaths of golden wheat blanket its southern reaches and flecks of wild flowers provide a tapestry of colour and fragrance," and the hills are "sprinkled with medieval hamlets and the shells of once mighty castles built to protect the frontier." Their conclusion is that "despite its tantalizing allure, this is still one of the least visited areas of Portugal."

According to Raposo (2016), the son of Alentejans who migrated to the industrial belt to the south of Lisbon in the 1960s, it was only in the twenty-first century, with the construction of the Alqueva dam, that Alentejo finally gained recognition. Alqueva constitutes the latest major transformation of the region. Raposo sees this as a future opportunity for ordinary Alentejans and considers it a means of escaping from a two-century-old history of oppression and economic, social, political, and moral violence. But in 2010, the seminal study of Serdoura et al. (2010), which examined the main strategic axes of the urban and architectonic sustainability of the Alqueva Plan and its exploitation for tourism purposes, revealed the absence of any overall strategic vision for the region – an affirmation subsequently corroborated by the former regional director of culture (Carapinha, 2014). Environmental conservationists considered the felling of one million trees in 2001 prior to the construction work to be the greatest ecological crime ever perpetrated in Portugal (Serdoura et al., 2010). The conservationists advocated a progressive, staggered operation that would enable both the protection and regeneration of the often unique flora and fauna. It is clear that the large companies (the current main landowners) prevailed, and that for them a change in the Alentejo region's natural environment constitutes a *sine qua non* condition and a guarantee of productivity within the global consumption market.

The extreme drought experienced throughout the entire country in 2017, and the prediction of long periods of successive years of drought in the future, divides expert opinion with regard to Alqueva. For some, Alqueva saves a large part of the Alentejo region by guaranteeing – finally – that it has access to a regular water supply; but for others, Alqueva has come too late because the region was already too far along the process of desertification, to the extent that even the *montado* ecosystem could not survive.[24] As always, whenever concerning Alentejo, two conflicting views emerge: the first seeks to use Alqueva to develop short/medium-term tourism projects of more or less colossal proportions[25] and will continue intensive farming; the second points to the historical geoclimatic reality and advocates a return to a multifunctional approach. This would be based on an overall sustainable plan for Alentejo, within which Alqueva would be considered as just one of many factors and not as the central feature of the short-term vision. The fact remains that the work that Pinto Correia (2007) conducted over the last few years demonstrates the residents' preference for the multifunctional use of the countryside and the territory, a reduction in the size of farms,[26] and the diversification of crop cultivation (Surová et al., 2016).

3. Towards a redefinition of Alentejan identity based on multifunctionality

3.1. The Herdade do Freixo do Meio development project: a reaffirmation of agriculture's role as a source of food, and the association of quality of life with ecofriendly products

With its twenty-eight-year history, the Herdade do Freixo do Meio project (1990–2018)[27] led by Sendim is not only a wonderful story, but also a living laboratory and testament to the successful reconstruction/preservation of the thousand-year-old *montado*[28] ecosystem for the benefit of the local community. This experience reconnects with the region's ancestral history and demonstrates that this ecosystem is perfectly adapted to the Alentejan climate and soil conditions. Its story is a reaffirmation of "Mother Earth" agricultural practices in combination with what might be described as the gourmet delight of organic produce. Product quality and quality of life by respecting nature are the principles guiding Sendim's activity.

Alfredo Sendim is the grandson, on his mother's side, of an Alentejan large-scale landowner. In an interview for the newspaper *Público*[29] he explained how his family was exiled to Spain during the Carnation Revolution (1974). He was just eight years old. On his return from exile, Sendim studied animal husbandry at the University of Évora (1984–1989). He enjoyed student life and the local society in the city, both of which were undergoing great change. "My friends were in favour of cooperatives"; they opposed the return of property to the absentee large-scale landlords and "private property." Nevertheless, in 1990, just shortly after his graduation, he found himself in conflict with his friends' logic and took over the family farm. Sendim says that the existing cooperative, dating back to the days of the Agrarian Reform, "func-tioned very well," but it required "the cooperation" of the family. During an interview held in preparation for the *Landscape, Heritage and Food Tourism Conference*,[30] Sendim said that several former cooperative workers still work at Herdade do Freixo do Meio and that he is proud to demonstrate that private property can be good for the community. He believes in collective responsi-bility, but based on individual responsibility. He prefers the slogan, "the land for those who respect her" to the Agrarian Reform slogan of "the land for those who work on her."

> Private property is meaningful only if the wealth it creates benefits the common good. In Portugal, more than 30% of the agricultural land lies abandoned and that is unacceptable in a country which imports more than 30% of the food products it consumes.[31]

Today, Herdade do Freixo do Meio is a label for organic production (100% since 2001) and a model in the agro-ecology domain. The farm is also a reference of the intangible cultural heritage of the Mediterranean diet that has been inscribed on UNESCO's Representative List since 2011.[32] This is because the farm not only produces all the foodstuffs it uses (except for fish) but also because it implements "a set of skills, knowledge, rituals, symbols and traditions concerning crops, harvesting,... animal husbandry, conservation, processing, cooking, and particularly the sharing and consumption of food".[33] By rehabilitating the *montado* ecosystem at Herdade do Freixo do Meio (and while awaiting its inscription on the World Heritage List[34]), Sendim (2015) contributes to the continued presence of the Mediterranean diet on the Intangible Heritage List because he shares the values recognised by UNESCO:

> The Mediterranean diet emphasizes values of hospitality, neighbourliness, intercultural dialogue and creativity, and a way of life guided by respect for diversity. It plays a vital role in cultural spaces, festivals and celebra-tions, bringing together people of all ages, conditions and social classes.[35]

It was a very long journey before Sendim managed to breathe new life into 500 hectares of *montado*, which he cultivates in all its complexity, just as they did 150 years ago before the idea of turning Alentejo into the nation's breadbasket ever emerged. To revive this thousand-year-old man-made eco-system (proof that humans do indeed "know better than Nature"), Sendim first had to acknowledge that his "technical-mechanical-chemical" university training would not suffice to enable him to single-handedly create jobs and develop his farm. Portugal had joined the EEC in 1986 and had therefore signed up to the Common Agricultural Policy (CAP). In this context, and following the logic of increasing numbers or the size of a productive area to be profitable, Sendim began by increasing his initial flock of 1,000 sheep to 5,000.

But he then had to buy tonnes of foodstuffs to feed these animals. It was then that an old man made this remark to him: "A hundred years ago, when this property provided food for 200 people, only two things were ever brought in here: salt to preserve the food, and iron." Everything else was produced and transformed on-site. Seeing that he was incapable of making his business profitable, Sendim decided to effect a strategic reversal and reintroduced the *montado* agro-ecosystem. This was a deliberate, well-thought-out act that drew upon his experience of the land,[36] his training in the management and sales of agricultural products acquired in Greece and in Spain, and his master's degree in agrarian economics from the University of Évora.

In contrast to the simplification of processes inherited from the industrial revolution and its corollaries (the intensification of production and profitability), Sendim uses complex crop cultivation and activities in association with the idea of living well off one's own produce. Herdade do Freixo do Meio functions "like a savannah." Trees, bushes, and pastures make up a complex mosaic of crops, large numbers of animals, fruits, wines, almonds, and different horticultural species.

> Here we have an agro-forestry structure where the dominant factor is the Mediterranean diet: olive oil, cereals, and pâtés. Our strength comes from this complexity. In this way, the montado system is sustainable. It existed well before [the current fashion for] organic agriculture. We have chosen to stop destroying the countryside which we love and have designed a model which also creates jobs.[37]

The exploratory survey we conducted (Cardoso Lopes, 2014)[38] showed twenty-one people from the region working at the farm, including a German geographer. Today, there are more than thirty workers.[39] These jobs are in different sectors of the farm's agro-system: production, transformation, and distribution. Sendim deals with the marketing communication himself. A man of conviction, with a convincing manner, he gives talks free of charge whenever asked to do so. He has also given classes in the management and sale of agricultural products at the university. With almost thirty years' experience, he has gained the sense of perspective required to confirm the success of what has become his life's work, but which he sees as a social project based on the principles of mutual support, symbiosis, and "competitive cooperation, just as can be found in nature." He recently installed 340 solar panels, and these are expected to contribute to making Herdade do Freixo do Meio energy self-sufficient. The investment will be recovered within three years, and the energy bill has already decreased by two-thirds.

The Herdade do Freixo do Meio label includes three hundred food product references available for sale on-site at the farm, as well as in the farm shop located in a section of the covered market hall of Lisbon's former wholesale market[40]– a currently fashionable place for food tourism in the Portuguese capital. As a man of his time, Sendim has also developed online sales of his products and set up several order delivery points in Montemor-o-Novo, Évora, Lisbon, and its region. The CSA (community supported agriculture) programme established between Herdade do Freixo do Meio and the CCIAM research centre at the Faculty of Science in Lisbon is a benefit and risk-sharing programme related to production at Herdade do Freixo do Meio. It is now in its sixth year. Each cycle lasts six months (spring/summer), during which shares in production match the producer's participation (i.e., the products that are effectively provided) and the commitment of the subscribing coproducer (the products that are actually bought/consumed). Subscribing to shares implies ownership of a fraction of the farm's food production. Any citizen may participate. Established on this basis, the network now includes more than a hundred subscribers. "This is an alternative to the market, with food being understood as a common good."[41] Sendim's entrepreneurial innovation serves to secure the future of his social economy business model but is also a structurally inherent element of agroecology and its development model. "The ecosystem needs Man," and Sendim has therefore created a micro-enterprise project. Eight such projects are currently in operation at Herdade do Freixo do Meio. The families live on the farm and are involved in various types of production (bakery, cooking, preparation/processing vegetables, poultry slaughter, and cured pork meats). Product distribution is managed by the shop in Lisbon, the various sales points, and the direct distribution process via the CSA programme, which Sendim hopes to develop further as part of the transition towards a cooperative for sustainable production and consumption.

As a man with strong beliefs grounded in scientific and historic facts, Sendim has spent over ten years testing ways of transforming acorns (which can be eaten like chestnuts) into all sorts of food products: flour (made with raw or roasted acorns), bread, toast, biscuits, cakes, dried acorns, frozen raw shelled acorns, frozen raw unshelled acorns, coffee made from acorns, hamburgers, meatballs, and pâtés.[42] There are more than ten varieties available at the farm. Sendim is not the only person to restore this fruit that was once a widespread source of food before the potato came to Europe in the sixteenth century. The No Ponto website (http://noponto.pt), which provides information about a research project on Portuguese cakes, sweets, and desserts, reports on a baker in Alandroal, a small Alentejan village close to the Spanish border, who has been using acorn flour[43] for several years to make the famous *pastel de nata* (custard tarts). For his part, Sendim has not opened an organic restaurant at Herdade do Freixo do Meio, but he does serve a national stew dish known as *cozido à portuguesa*, which showcases the farm's organic meat, pulses, cereals, and horticultural products. Provided on an all-you-can-eat basis to groups of more than ten people, the stew is served with bread, olives, and "strong" wine from the farm.

The latest corporate objective[44] at Herdade do Freixo do Meio relates to tourism with an educational purpose. In the 2014 exploratory study mentioned earlier, Sendim defined the concept of "tourism in rural areas" as "a short-term experience of the past and present within the context of the rural reality," and he links this closely to the notions of "history, montado, diet, traditions and challenges." With this new direction in his activity, Sendim seeks to provide solutions for "all those who show an interest in the development of sustainable human communities." At the time of the study, he provided a house capable of accommodating up to four people. The house was rented out as a single unit, and individual rooms could not be booked. Today, faced with increasing demand, he now receives up to fourteen people in Casa da Malta and in the ecohostel, and up to one hundred people in the ecocamping area, thus providing sleeping accommodation for "people wishing to experience adventure tourism, to try out this kind of agriculture, help out with the work in the fields and understand the montado concept."[45]

Herdade do Freixo do Meio now draws about 20,000 people a year to the parish of Vale de Figueira. A large proportion of these visitors come to attend two annual events that are both free of charge: the Spring Meeting (held since 2005) and the Autumn Meeting (since 2011). The former is held on or around the symbolic date of 25 April, which commemorates the 1974 Carnation Revolution and marks the end of the almost fifty-year-long winter of dictatorship under António Oliveira Salazar. In this way, Sendim inscribes the memory of his own family's expropriation in collective history and relives it in a positive manner: "In the end it turned out to be a good thing, it obliged my brothers and I to study so that we could find work and take responsibility for ourselves."

> We are part of a cosmic project on this planet, a very clear strategy which is the system of life. We have the capacity to understand nature and, just as the soil created very complex ecosystems, we too can create even more complex ecosystems and we can make a true paradise here, a true Eden. Our function is to understand and enhance nature. To have this awareness gives me huge satisfaction and peace. We humans are the new soil and we can make a difference on this planet for the better, and build.[46]

At this stage of reflection, associations can be made between Sendim's project and the concepts of the *Planetary Garden* and the citizen-gardener figure evoked by the French landscape architect Clément (1999),[47] as well as the Global Landscape concept proposed by the Portuguese landscape architect Telles (2011).[48] Sendim implements three central aspects from the visions of Clément and Telles (Batista and Matos, 2013) within his project: recovering the memory of a place and its contribution to the consolidation of cultural identity; acceptance of the "Garden-Planet" as a dynamic ecosystem in ever-constant transformation, comprising both different timescales (chronological, biological, and recreational) and spaces (pastoral, wild, and domesticated); and humans as actors with special responsibility for managing their relationship with nature, and also as planetary gardeners who are obliged to act at the local level but do so in the name and in full awareness of the entire planet and its global landscapes. The close articulation between the region of Montemor-o-Novo and the concepts of identity and quality of life that underpin Sendim's project constitute a paradigm that therefore extends beyond local boundaries and is propelled into the global sphere. Casa do Alentejo, the only regional cultural centre still remaining in Lisbon, also seeks, in its own way, to achieve this same purpose.

4. *Casa do Alentejo* in Lisbon: a showcase for Alentejan identity and an external actor for local development?

Casa do Alentejo (House of Alentejo) in Lisbon will soon celebrate its one-hundredth anniversary. Founded under the name of Grémio Alentejano in 1923 during the First Republic (1910–1926) by the Alentejan elite based in the capital – many of whom were landowners who would later support the Salazar regime – the centre's declared objective was to promote the region's culture. However, this official objective concealed a complex reality that reflected the stratification of Alentejan society, with each social layer having different political visions and ambitions for Casa do Alentejo. Verdugo, vice-president of Casa do Alentejo in 2013, tells the Portuguese News Agency Lusa[49] that elite members had access to a barber "providing manicure and shoeshine services" as well as dances and games of chance (which were clandestine at the time). For the poor Alentejan migrants in the capital, a medical centre and a primary school were established. In honour of its charitable work, in 1939 during the Estado Novo, Casa do Alentejo received the award of Officer of the Order of Charity. Moreover, it was the de facto host for cultural activities, including the first (in 1943) of a series of subversive antidictatorship talks held at the home of the neo-realist writer Dionísio (1916–1993)[50] by the intellectual opponents of Salazar's dictatorship. After 25 April 1974 and the Carnation Revolution, Casa do Alentejo became "an associative space … with its doors wide open to the world" and the "charity of the old regime" was finished. Today, you can go in wearing a tie or not, and you can have lunch or dinner, attend the Sunday dance, listen to Alentejan music[51] or choral groups, visit and take photos, enjoy a glass of wine with bread and olives, have a coffee or a beer, or read a newspaper in the library.[52]

As a multipurpose cultural centre, Casa do Alentejo organises, promotes, and hosts book presentations, poetry readings, temporary exhibitions, themed conferences, gastronomy weeks, art/literature/photography competitions, artisanal craft exhibitions, and special weeks devoted to different Alentejan municipalities.[53] In 2013 the centre had about 2,250 members.[54]

In 1981, when the palace building (which, in the meantime, had been listed as a "building of public interest") was acquired from the descendants of the noble family that had built it in the seventeenth century, Casa do Alentejo started to develop its restaurant service with the aim of acquiring a source of income in addition to its membership fees. "Without this commercial component, we would never have been able to keep the House open," Verdugo emphasised. At first, the restaurant was only frequented by the Alentejan community and national tourists, particularly from the north of the country. For them, stopping in Lisbon and trying a different kind of food in an exceptional setting and at a price that was affordable for the average salary[55] had a preholiday feel about it and came to represent a compulsory stopover or ritual. The same was true for the inhabitants of Lisbon, while for Alentejans, it was their home away from home. But the restaurant was given new commercial impetus when funding had to be found to renovate the roof of the building.[56] Since then, prices have aligned with international tourism standards,[57] and this has led to creating a tavern that opens on to a small interior patio and offers affordable prices to members and young people. The blogosphere reveals the dissatisfaction of former Portuguese customers, particularly Alentejans, who no longer relate to the new pricing policy in the restaurant (whose activity is outsourced) and who criticise not only the quality of the service (deemed unwelcoming and "in a hurry to get rid of the customer") but also the quality of the food (considered unexceptional and not specifically Alentejan). "This is not Alentejo." Hence, it is within the more discreet confines of the tavern that the members of Casa do Alentejo, and all those who know and love the sociability of Alentejan gastronomy, prefer to gather. And it is here that they come to enjoy a regional-style meal, chat together, relive their memories, and have a drink. Of the people who frequent this place, 80% are regular patrons, comprising members and young people who mostly consume *petiscos*, or Alentejan tapas. The geographer Ribeiro pointed out that for the average Alentejan, eating signified, above all else, filling one's stomach to stave off the feeling of hunger. "And, as we all know, hunger sharpens ingenuity" (Carvalho, 2013). Since antiquity, the Alentejan peasant farmer has embellished his meagre soup by garnishing it with all kinds of locally grown herbs and grasses: purslane, chard, broadleaf dock, thistles, asparagus, pennyroyal, water mint, etc. Strabo, the Greek geographer, referred to the region as a "paradise for herbal grasses" (Carvalho, 2013). These plants enhance every meal, especially the bread-based dishes (such as the *migas* salad or *açordas* broth) that the patrons of the tavern at Casa do Alentejo enjoy eating.

From their perspective, foreign tourists particularly appreciate the building's antiquated interior (the Arabic patio, the Louis XVI-style Room of Mirrors, the neo-Renaissance style salon, the seventeenth-century panels of blue and white azulejo tiles, and the library). The building and its 120-seat restaurant are famous and featured in guidebooks and online forums. A Canadian blogger living in Berlin gives her impressions:

> I'll be completely honest. I have not eaten a meal at Restaurant Casa do Alentejo in Lisbon. Just let me tell you just why I want to eat here someday. Situated in a former 17th century Moorish palace, Restaurant Casa do Alentejo is popular simply because of the atmosphere and surroundings. I was lucky enough to be able to do a quick inspection of

the restaurant while on a walking tour with Urban Adventures. I didn't want to leave. I wanted to stay for the afternoon, sip some *vino verde* and learn more about the history of the place. Once a palace, it's since been used as a school, casino and now a restaurant. Locals come to relax here, play cards and read a newspaper. Cultural events are also held on premises from time-to-time. When you arrive, you feel as if you've entered paradise. A sanctuary in the busy city of hot and sexy Lisbon.[58]

In winter (November – February), 50% of the clientele at Casa do Alentejo are Portuguese and 50% are foreigners. However, the latter account for 80% of those frequenting the centre in summer (May – September).[59] In 2014, the management recorded an average of 16,000 visitors per month, half of whom had eaten a meal on-site (85% at the restaurant and 15% in the tavern).[60]

"The average price of a three course meal is about 20 euros. They serve traditional Portuguese food with a focus on the Alentejo region. The online reviews seem to be mixed – check out their rating on Trip Advisor."[61] Among the five most popular main dishes eaten in the restaurant, three are not specifically Alentejan (oven-baked cod fillet, grilled fillet of salmon, and veal steak).[62] The other two dishes (*carne de porco à alentejana*, or Alentejan pork, and grilled lamb cutlets) honour two livestock animals that belong to the *montado* countryside. With regard to the former, when the Romans occupied the Iberian Peninsula, they were surprised by the taste of the local pork, which was fed on acorns. The recipe for *carne de porco à alentejana* celebrates this exceptional meat, and its pairing with clams reminds us that Alentejo was once a land in which cultures intersected and products circulated between the interior lands and the Atlantic sea coast, particularly via the Guadiana River route. But it is in their choice of desserts that visitors show the greatest curiosity for the region's gastronomy. *Sericaia* (also known as *Sericá* or *Cericá*) is a typically Alentejan recipe made from flour, eggs, sugar, and a large amount of cinnamon and is often accompanied by candied prunes. Of mysterious origin (India or Brazil), this moist cake with a cracked surface was first made by two convents in two different cities (Vila Viçosa and Elvas – they both dispute who invented the original recipe). The same goes for the almond cake *Toucinho do Céu* (literally, "Bacon from Heaven"), which became known nationally but may well have originated in Alentejo. Made in all the convents, it is one of the most highly reputed traditional desserts in Portugal. The recipe for this creamy flan is based on eggs and sugar and originally included a dash of pork fat, which has now been replaced by butter. The third cake that makes up the assortment of Alentejan desserts tourists frequently choose is a tart made from curd cheese (*tarte de requeijão*). These convent recipes are a throwback to a time before 1834, the year when the religious orders were expelled from Portugal, as well as a reminder of the region's elite to which the clergy belonged. In 2017 Casa do Alentejo opened a shop selling local products. This is outside the main building, and its esplanade opens directly onto one of the most highly frequented pedestrian streets in the historic centre of Lisbon. The manager, a young Alentejan, has performed an ethnographic analysis that shows that "different realities intersect" at the sales point and *in situ* eatery. Wine is the most popular product. On-site, it is mostly consumed by "mature-aged couples" looking for a quiet place in the midst of the countless restaurants hailing customers. They willingly allow themselves to be guided by the owner's advice. In his opinion, the German and English tourists "are easier to convince than those from France." The French need to taste more wines before making their final choice. Often enamoured with Douro wines, which are not available in the shop, French tourists end up having a beer instead. On the other hand, Brazilian tourists are savvy consumers who are knowledgeable about wine and the region. In general, when they go to the shop, they do so knowingly and often after having taken a trip to Alentejo. They may spend up to 200 euros at a single time. In addition, foreign tourists account for 80% of customers buying olive oil from the shop. For their part, Portuguese customers come specifically to buy bread and Serpa cheese. They account for 20% of the clientele and are regulars, as in the case of the older woman who travels across Lisbon every week to buy her bread or the elderly gentleman who comes to buy cheese to give as a gift each time he has to consult his doctor. The Portuguese find the other products expensive, but they are prepared to pay a little more for one of them – namely, Delta coffee, which costs 90 cents (instead of 70). The shop sells up to 250 coffees a day, particularly on days when shows are held in the two nearby performance halls (Coliseu and Politeama).

Keen to improve the service and to increase sales of regional products, the manager of the shop explains that the employees are currently being trained to improve their technique in slicing ham (another Alentejan speciality) to reduce waste. Tastings and sales of specifically Alentejan products are offered on the pavement outside and at the entrance to the shop. These activities are currently being expanded. Sold only by small local producers (using organic farming methods or not), products such as arbutus berries and liqueur are difficult to find. The periodic tasting campaigns advertised by Casa do Alentejo's shop are organised on a profit-sharing basis. They also serve as a showcase for producers and incorporate Casa do Alentejo's goal as an external promoter of Alentejan culture and actor for local development. However, this remains a long-term project because, as the managers of Casa do Alentejo remarked, a network of regular regional suppliers who can guarantee supplying Casa do Alentejo with quality local products needs to be developed.

5. Some concluding but entirely provisional remarks

In October 2017, the daily newspaper *Diário de Notícias* devoted a series of articles to the "Iberian Peninsula economy" in which it predicted that after the olive tree and the vine, the new fashion would be for dried fruits – with almonds (which have become the second biggest permanent Alentejan crop) at the top of the list. Large agricultural companies are investing in the expansion of almond trees "because we must develop economies of scale." Their intensive monocultures dominate, thanks to subsidies and their more-or-less colossal tourism projects. On the other hand, small- and medium-sized entrepreneurs find it difficult to make their mark due to the lack of a general policy plan for the region – a situation already criticised by Serdoura (2010) – and as a result, they either migrate or emigrate. Within this context, Sendim and his farm, Herdade do Freixo do Meio, represent both the history and the future of the region. By reviving the memory of the multifunctional *montado* ecosystem of the past, and by putting this system into practice for nearly thirty years, Sendim indicates a way that could be a political project for the region and that could stabilise the population. For its part, Casa do Alentejo is the showcase for the complex reality of Alentejo today. The region struggles to define an overall, long-term economic policy that could coordinate the various initiatives and enable the region to make the most of its resources. The interviews conducted with various personnel at Casa do Alentejo (the management, qualified employees in the restaurant and shop) reveal their considerable lucidity with regard to the work left to be done before Casa do Alentejo can be transformed into an embassy for the region and its local development. To fully achieve this aim, and to reduce dependence on the passing tourist trade, Casa do Alentejo must be able to draw upon an overall strategy and a network of local producers that have yet to be established.

Notes

1 This chapter is an essay that I started in 2014 as part of a post-doctoral project on Landscape and Heritage financed by FCT, Lisbon, Portugal (SFRH/BPD/65877/2009). I would like to thank Olivier Etcheverria for his proofreading of the text and for his unfailing support and encouragement, despite the change in my professional circumstances. My thanks also go to: Nicola Bellini, Cécile Clergeau, La Rochelle Tourism Management Institute (France), Philippe Violier, Benjamin Taunay, University of Angers (France), Shen Shiwei, Ningbo University (China), CHAIA University of Évora (Portugal), and the Calouste Gulbenkian Foundation/Délégation en France (Paris) for their financial and logistical support that enabled me to participate in the various conferences held in the three countries referred to in the text.

2 "The Portuguese montado is an agrosilvopastoral system quite similar to the dehesa in Spain, and covering in Portugal most of the Southern region of the country, Alentejo. The trees in the montado are cork or holm oak, and the system is mostly acknowledged due to the cork production, but also due to its singular savanna-like land cover pattern, its multiple and complementary productions, the support of a diversity of ecosystems services and its biodiversity". https://www.researchgate.net/publication/225125237_Introducing_the_montado_the_cork_and_holm_oak_agroforestry_system_of_Southern_Portugal.

3 The short promotional film, "*Alentejo, tempo para ser feliz*" (Alentejo, time to be happy), won the bronze medal at the Tourfilm-Riga 2014 tourism film festival, in the "Ecotourism" category. Started in 2007, this festival annually honours the best tourism advertising films for products, cities, countries, and regions.

4 Since Portugal joined the EEC in 1986, there have been successive and intensive cultivation of sunflowers, olive trees, vineyards, and more recently, almond trees.

5 The National Strategic Plan for Tourism (PENT) 2006–2015 decreed that the development of sustainable tourism was a major challenge for Portugal.

6 Particularly the northeastern section and centre of the region (Portalegre-Évora).

7 The clay soils in Beja and the Campo Maior are the best.

8 The desire to protect national cereal crops was one of the principles of the Liberal Revolution of 24 August 1820, which brought absolute monarchy to an end.

9 Regarded by some as a dictatorship, or as regime with a "taste for totalitarianism" by others, the Estado Novo was led by António Oliveira Salazar. In 1928, Salazar was appointed Minister of Finance for the military dictatorship that preceded the Estado Novo regime. Having been appointed head of the government in 1932, Salazar established the Estado Novo in 1933.

10 A reference to the author's first novel. Subject to censorship, Fonseca was obliged to change the novel's ending.

11 A *seareiro*, or sharecropper in English, is a farmer who rents out land and has a right to a portion of the crop. Cf. Vale de Almeida,1996, p. 28.

12 The authors of the German and English guidebooks (Glassner and Fodor respectively) both thank the Secretariat of National Propaganda (known as the "SPN" and later as "SNICPT") for its "inestimable contributions and suggestions," thereby testifying to the (preventive and retroactive) control and censorship exercised by the Estado Novo in tourism, the press, advertising, performing arts, literature, exhibitions, and radio. Suzanne Chantal, a French journalist and novelist was married to the Portuguese journalist José Augusto (dos Santos), who was the correspondent for several Portuguese daily newspapers and radio stations, as well as the Portuguese tourism representative in Paris during the Estado Novo period.

13 Silva Porto (1850–1893), José Malhoa (1855–1933), Alberto de Souza (1880–1961), Dordio Gomes (1890–1976), Bernardo Marques (1898–1962), Cândido Teles (1921–1999), Júlio Pomar (1926–2018).

14 Fialho de Almeida (1857–1911), Alves Redol (1911–1969), Manuel da Fonseca (1911–1993), Etelvina Lopes de Almeida (1916–2004), Mário Ventura (1936–2006), José Saramago (1922–2010), amongst others.

15 The Agrarian Reform began at the end of 1974, with the first instances of land occupation. The process expanded and continued until 1976. In total, 1.1 million hectares of land were occupied, expropriated, and nationalised in the regions of Alentejo and Ribatejo. The Barreto Law brought these occupations to an end in 1977. From 1980 to 1990, the former owners regained most of their lands. The Agrarian Reform process had a long-lasting impact on the Alentejan psyche and has left enduring scars. Today, there is still one place near Beja where the Agrarian Reform continues to exist. On lands formerly belonging to the Herdade Machado farm, forty-five farmers cultivate 1,700 hectares of land rented from the State after their nationalisation. The farmers' contracts, which were signed in the 1980s, are due to end in 2018. See http://www.agroinfo.pt/ainda-se-mantem-viva-a-reforma-agraria-de-sa-carneiro/ and https://www.dn.pt/lusa/interior/reforma-agraria-ainda-dura-numa-herdade-do-alentejo-40-anos-apos-lei-barreto-8650612.html.

16 The Catholic Church was one of the pillars of the Estado Novo.

17 https://www.pordata.pt/Municipios/H%c3%b3spedes+nos+estabelecimentos+hoteleiros+total+e+por+tipo+de+estabelecimento-750-4982.

18 https://www.pordata.pt/Municipios/Dormidas+nos+estabelecimentos+hoteleiros+total++residentes+em+Portugal+e+residentes+no+estrangeiro-751.

19 Regularly cited as one of the rural tourism activities to be enjoyed in the region, the Alentejan "dark sky" has even been granted European certification: www.darkskyalqueva.com, http://www.turismodeportugal.pt/Portugu%C3%AAs/AreasAtividade/desenvolvimentoeinovacao1/Pages/ReservaDarkSkyAlqueva.aspx; https://www.visitportugal.com/fr/node/73796.

20 https://www.theguardian.com/travel/2014/jul/12/-sp-portugal-alentejo-region-europe-finest-beaches.

21 http://www.winesofportugal.com/br/press-room/statistics/other/.

22 http://invinoviajas.blogspot.it/2014/09/alentejo-portugal-e-eleito-o-melhor.html.
23 *Portalegre, Borba, Redondo, Reguengos, Vidigueira, Évora, Granja-Amareleja* and *Moura*, according to the government website http://www.ivv.gov.pt/np4/56/
24 ENEG 2017 (The National Meeting of Water and Sanitation Organisations) was held in Évora, from 21 to 24 November. Filipe Duarte Santos, professor at the University of Lisbon, Faculty of Sciences, and president of the National Council for the Environment, recommended that the *montado* ecosystem should be moved to the centre of the country and that it should also be implemented in the regions that had suffered fires that year (2017).
25 Such as that of José Roquette and his group SAIP, which was never built due to the lack of bank funding (940 million euros over twenty years, for seven hotels, four golf courses, tourist villages, two marinas, one horse-riding centre, one holiday camp, with the expected creation of 2130 direct jobs and 3,000 indirect jobs).
26 Concerning the size of farms and the possession of land that characterise the Alentejan landscapes, the geographer Orlando Ribeiro (1911–1997) notes in his work of reference on *Portugal, the Mediterranean and the Atlantic* (1963, p. 168) that concerning Alentejo "nobody wanted to know how useful it would be to try experiments with land parcelling; this is why there is a predominance of large agrarian units, distant hills and scarce villages where the people are based, in the middle of the large-scale farms."
27 https://www.herdadedofreixodomeio.pt/
28 https://www.researchgate.net/publication/225125237_Introducing_the_monta do_the_cork_and_holm_oak_agroforestry_system_of_Southern_Portugal
29 https://www.publico.pt/2015/12/06/sociedade/noticia/o-que a-natureza-ensi nou-a-um-rapaz-de-lisboa-1716449.
30 The Landscape, Heritage and Food Tourism Conference (*Colloque Paysage, Patri-moine et Tourisme Gourmand*), Paris, Centre Culturel Portugais, Fondation Calouste Gulbenkian, 10 December 2014.
31 https://www.cmjornal.pt/mais-cm/domingo/detalhe/a-terra-a-quem-a-trabalha
32 Portugal was included in 2013.
33 https://ich.unesco.org/en/RL/mediterranean-diet-00884.
34 Portugal's request was submitted on 31 July 2017; http://whc.unesco.org/en/tentativelists/6210/.
35 Source: https://ich.unesco.org/en/Rl/mediterranean-diet-00884.
36 Besides Herdade do Freixo do Meio, Sendim manages several other properties/family businesses that have been recuperated over time: https://www.ipbeja.pt/eventos/sem_cnt/Paginas/oradores.aspx; http://ad16619a.hosting.net.vodafone.pt/menu1_1. html. See also the chart of the properties belonging to the Sousa Cunhal group in 2007: http://www.triplov.com/estela_guedes/2007/Freixo-do-Meio/index.html.
37 http://upmagazine-tap.com/pt_artigos/montemor-o-novo-vamos-visitar-um-amigo/.
38 By Aurora Carapinha and Isabel Lopes Cardoso on the realities of rural tourism in Alentejo.
39 https://www.agroportal.pt/politica-alimentar-comum/.
40 https://www.zomato.com/pt/grande-lisboa/herdade-do-freixo-do-meio cais-do-sodr%C3%A9-lisboa.
41 Presentation by Alfredo Sendim at the Landscape, Heritage and Food Tourism Conference (*Paysage, Patrimoine et Tourisme Gourmand*), Paris, Centre Culturel Portugais, Fondation Calouste Gulbenkian, 10 December 2014.
42 https://www.herdadedofreixodomeio.pt/produtos/categoria/26/bolota-e-produ tos-de-bolota;https://www.herdadedofreixodomeio.pt/produtos/categoria/5/con servas-vegetais.
43 http://noponto.pt/pastel-nata-bolota/.
44 Various types of production in agriculture, forestry, wine-growing, hunting animal husbandry; provision of agricultural services, the transformation and sale of meat,

horticultural, agricultural, forestry, and wine products, bread-making, and tourism and educational services.

45 http://visao.sapo.pt/actualidade/sociedade/2017-08-05-Uma-viagem-ao-Alentejo-onde-tudo-mexe-e-vibra.

46 https://eco123.info/en/portugal-en/interviews-en/interview-with-alfredo-cunhal-sendim/.

47 http://www.gillesclement.com/cat-jardinplanetaire-tit-Le-Jardin-Planetaire.

48 https://www.portaldojardim.com/pdj/2007/05/15/a-recriacao-da-natureza-entre vista-com-ribeiro-telles/.

49 http://www.esquerda.net/artigo/casa-do-alentejo-casa-que-revolu%C3%A7%C3% A3o-de-abril-devolveu-%C3%A0s-pessoas-assinala-90-anos/28188.

50 Only the first talk took place, led by the mathematician Bento Jesus Caraça (1901–1948). He was a university professor, an antifascist resistance fighter, and activist in the Portuguese Communist Party (PCP). The second, led by Fernando Lopes Graça (1906–1994), who was considered the greatest twentieth-century Portuguese composer and was also an antifascist resistance fighter and PCP activist, was interrupted by the police. http://www.centromariodionisio.org/biografia_mariodionisio.php.

51 The *cante alentejano* (Alentejan polyphonic singing) was listed as a UNESCO Intangible Cultural Heritage of Humanity in 2014.

52 https://www.esquerda.net/artigo/casa-do-alentejo-casa-que-revolu%C3%A7% C3%A3o-de-abril-devolveu-%C3%A0s-pessoas-assinala-90-anos/28188

53 http://www.casadoalentejo.com.pt/historia/.

54 http://www.esquerda.net/artigo/casa-do-alentejo-casa-que-revolu%C3%A7%C3% A3o-de-abril-devolveu-%C3%A0s-pessoas-assinala-90-anos/28188. To be a member, proof of a parental, professional or other connection with Alentejo must be provided. The average age of members is currently between 50–60.

55 The minimum wage is currently 557 euros (over fourteen months) and the average salary is 924 euros (over fourteen months).

56 Repair costs amounted to 300,000 euros (information provided by the management of Casa do Alentejo).

57 For a full meal (i.e., one which the Portuguese are used to eating at midday), with starter, main course, and dessert, the *à la carte* menu price is about 25 euros/person, not including drinks. The price of the set menu (cover charge, soup, main course) is 15 euros. http://www.casadoalentejo.com.pt/menu-restaurante/.

58 http://cherylhoward.com/2013/08/16/restaurant-casa-do-alentejo-in-lisbon-por tugal/.

59 At the end of 2014, the distribution of nationalities was as follows: France 17%; Spain 15%; Germany 14%; Brazil 13%; United Kingdom 11%; other nationalities 31% (statistics provided by the management of Casa do Alentejo in 2014).

60 Information received from the management of Casa do Alentejo in 2014.

61 http://cherylhoward.com/2013/08/16/restaurant-casa-do-alentejo-in-lisbon-portu gal/.

62 Information provided by the management of Casa do Alentejo in 2014.

References

Baptista, F.O. (1994). A agricultura e a questão da terra – Do Estado Novo à Comunidade Europeia. *Análise Social*, 29(128), pp. 907–921.

Batista, D. and Matos, R.S. (2013). O jardim planetário: Uma utopia para o século XX? In *Arte e Utopia*. Lisboa: IHA/EAC, Universidade Nova de Lisboa. http://hdl.handle. net/10174/10075.

Carapinha, A. (2014). Le paysage de l'Alentejo – Authenticité ou construction? *Patrimoine, Paysage, Tourisme Gourmand: Entre théorie et pratique. Regards critiques à partir d'un cas d'étude, l'Alentejo.* Paris: Fondation Calouste Gulbenkian (Délégation en France) (conference paper).

Cardoso Lopes, I. (2014). Déguster un repas à la Casa do Alentejo à Lisbonne ou observer le "dark sky" à Alqueva: la quête de l'authenticité à l'épreuve du reel. *Patrimoine, Paysage, Tourisme Gourmand: Entre théorie et pratique. Regards critiques à partir d'un cas d'étude, l'Alentejo.* Paris: Fondation Calouste Gulbenkian (Délégation en France) (conference paper).

Carvalho, G. (2013). Aromas e sabores do Alentejo. *De Rerum Natura.* http://dererum mundi.blogspot.it/2013/02/aromas-e-sabores-do-alentejo.html.

Cauvin-Verner, C. (2006). Les objets du tourisme, entre tradition et folklore. *Journal des Africanistes,* 76(1), pp. 187–201.

Chantal, S. and Santos, J. (1950). *Le Portugal.* Paris: Editions Odé.

Chantal, S. and Santos, J. (1953). *Portugal and Spain.* London: McGraw-Hill Publishing Company Ltd.

Choat, I. (2014),A guide to Portugal's Alentejo region, home of Europe's finest beaches, *The Guardian,* 12 July (on-line edition).

Clément, G. (1999). *Le Jardin Planétaire. Catalogue de l'Exposition Parc de la Villette, Paris 1999–2000.* Paris: Albin Michel.

Cutileiro, J. (1971). *A Portuguese rural society.* London: Oxford University Press.

De Oliveira Marques, A.H. (1971). Trigo. In Serrão, J. (ed), *Dicionário de História de Portugal.* Vol. 6, Lisboa: Iniciativas Editoriais, pp. 209–213.

Domingues, Á. (2013). Paisagens Transgénicas. In Cardoso Lopes, I. (ed), *Paisagem e Património. Aproximações Pluridisciplinares.* Oporto: Dafne Editora, pp. 223–244.

Fodor's Modern Guides. (1967). *Portugal.* New York: David McKay Company, Inc.

Fonseca, M. (1943). *Cerromaior.* Lisboa: Editorial Inquérito.

Freire, D. (2008). A Campanha do Trigo. In Paço, António Simões (ed), *Os Anos de Salazar.* Lisboa: Planeta DeAgostini, pp. 31–39.

Glassner, H. (1942). *Portugal.* Berlin-Zurich: Atlantis-Verlag.

Gomes, P.V. (2014). *Ouro e Cinza.* Lisboa: Tinta-da-China.

Guichard, F. (1990). *Géographie du Portugal.* Paris: Masson.

Job, J. (1956). *Portugal. Land der Christusritter.* Erlenbach-Zurich and Stuttgart: Eugen Rentsch Verlag.

Mattoso, J., Daveau, S. and Belo, D. (2010). *Portugal – O Sabor da Terra.* Lisbonne: Temas e Debates - Círculo de Leitores.

Mitchell, W.J.T. (2002). *Landscape and power. Space, place and landscape.* Chicago: University of Chicago Press.

Pais, J.M., de Lima, A.M.V., Baptista, J.F., de Jesus, M.F.M. and Gameiro, M M, (1976). Elementos para a história do fascismo nos campos: A "Campanha do Trigo": 1928–38 (I). *Análise Social,* Vol 12, No 46, pp. 400–474.

Papy, L. and Gadala, M.-Th. (1935). Le Portugal. *Bulletin Hispanique,* 38(1), pp. 113–114.

Pinto-Correia, T. (2007). Multifuncionalidade da paisagem rural: Novos desafios à sua análise. *Inforgeo,* 20/21, pp. 67–71.

Proença, R. (1927). *Guia de Portugal. Estremadura, Alentejo e Algarve.* Vol. 2, Lisboa: Fundação Calouste Gulbenkian.

Raposo, H. (2016). *Alentejo prometido.* Lisboa: Fundação Francisco Manuel dos Santos.

Ribeiro, O. (1963). *Portugal, o Mediterrâneo e o Atlântico*. Second Edition. Lisboa: Livraria Sá da Costa Editora.

Rodrigues, P. (2014). Tourisme, image et identité nationale au Portugal du 20ème siècle. *Patrimoine, Paysage, Tourisme Gourmand: Entre théorie et pratique. Regards critiques à partir d'un cas d'étude, l'Alentejo*. Paris. Fondation Calouste Gulbenkian (Délégation en France) (conference paper).

Rosas, F. (2001). O salazarismo e o homem novo: Ensaio sobre o Estado Novo e a questão do totalitarismo. *Análise Social*, 35(157), pp. 1031–1054.

Saramago, J. (1980). *Levantado do Chão*. Lisboa: Porto Editora.

Seligo, H. (1959). *Portugal*. München: Wilhelm Andermann.

Sendim, A.C. (2015). *Público*. https://www.publico.pt/2015/12/06/sociedade/noticia/o-que-a-natureza-ensinou-a-um-rapaz-de-lisboa-1716449.

Serdoura, F., Moreira, G. and Almeida, H. (2010). Sustainable tourism development around Alqueva Lake, in Portugal. Proceedings of the Conference on "Sustainable Architecture and Urban Development", Amman, 12–14 July, vol. II, pp. 413–428.

Silbert, A. (1966). *Le Portugal Méditerranéen à la fin de l'Ancien Régime. 18e – Début du 19e siècle. Contribution à l'histoire agraire comparée*. Paris: S.E.V.P.E.N./Ecole Pratique des Hautes Etudes.

Silva, L. (2007). À procura do turismo em espaço rural. *Etnográfica*, 11(1). http://etnografica.revues.org/1896.

Surová, D., Guiomar, N. and Pinto-Correia, T. (2016). Distinct landscape – Distinct well-being? How residents evaluate landscape, environmental and agricultural traits in two contrasting landscapes of Southern Portugal (Southern Europe). In *Landscape Values. Place and Praxis*. Galway, Centre for Landscape Studies, 29 June – 2 July 2016 (conference paper).

Telles, G.R. (2011). Paisagem global - Um conceito para o futuro. In Veríssimo Serrão A., (ed), *Filosofia da Paisagem. Uma antologia*, Lisboa: Centro de Filosofia da Universidade de Lisboa, pp. 475–485.

Tuan, Y.-F. (1974). *Topophilia: A study of environmental perception, attitudes, and values*. New York: Columbia University Press.

Vale de Almeida, M. (1996). *The Hegemonic Male, Masculinity in a Portuguese Town*, New York: Berghahn Books, pp. 28.

Van der Ploeg, J.D. (1997). On rurality, rural development and rural sociology. In H. De Haan and N. Long (eds.), *Images and realities of rural life: Wageningen perspectives on rural transformations*. Assen: Royal van Gorcum, pp. 39–77.

Wilson, G.A. (2009). *European policy and desertification: Evidence from the local scale*. Booklet Series: A, Nr. 6. Plymouth: School of Geography, University of Plymouth.

6 Gastronomy and identity in tourism development

The role of festivals in the Province of Cordoba

Robert Lanquar

1. Introduction

Jean Duvignaud (1973, 1991) describes festivals as a time that is free of the conventions and requirements of production and work. Could it be that tourism – which involves the departure of holidaymakers from their homes and the reception of national or foreign visitors – represents such a time and is it a factor for "happiness"? Even if this were the case, the tourism in question must be responsible, sustainable, inclusive, and, in today's world, connected ("smart tourism"). It must also not have any negative impact on the traditions and values of the host country (Lanquar, 2012). Such moments of happiness are experienced during visits, in the wonder evoked by a landscape or monument, through participation in an event or cultural and entertaining activity, and very often by gathering around a table to savour the cuisine and gastronomy specific to a festival or event, made with ingredients produced by the local terroir.

The purpose of festivals and local pilgrimages (*romerías* in Spanish) is to promote the feeling of belonging to a community and developing a sense of cohesion and homogeneity within a territory. In rural areas, festivals and fairs are often merged with funfairs. Some festival events also include trade fairs for local terroir specialities, gastronomic food markets, and flea markets (*mercadillos*). By incorporating all viable options, such festivals provide opportunities for a vast array of creativity and innovation and set aside humdrum reality – at least symbolically. They may also facilitate the reconstruction of a collective culture that, as in the case of Andalusia, was shattered by National Catholicism following the 1936 Civil War.

In Spain, a festival is a "fiesta" that brings people together in *tertulias* (social gatherings of family or friends and discussion groups), brotherhoods, and *romerías* organised by religious fraternities and sisterhoods. This is intended to be a time of "light and happiness" (*luz y alegría*). Today, these fiestas must incorporate aspects of globalisation and new experiences and symbols, many of which have more to do with the promotion of products and local characteristics to boost tourism and exports than representing the lives of saints, the Virgin Mary, or the Passion. Moreover, since the end of the 1970s, the democratic process has increased the secularisation of festivals in Spain. Gastronomy plays a role in this process, too, not only for its attractiveness to tourists but also due to the current interest in discovering new recipes that are locally anchored, yet open to global influences.

Many civil festivals, which formerly reflected local particularities and the main crafts and trades in the villages, towns, and cities of a given territory, were taken over by the local clergy, adapted to patron saints, and set on dates that often no longer corresponded to the realities of rural life and labour in the fields. Even local cuisine was controlled with a principle of what one could and could not eat. Yet, a festival both has and is a date; as Durkheim's disciple, Czarnowski (Paris, 1914 – New York, 1975), indicated, "It [a festival] has its heroes, saints, spirits, etc." Tourism first began to perturb such traditions from the 1970s onwards. It caused local authorities to secularise festivals, concentrate their scheduling during the tourist season, and link them to the development of artisanal and food products.

Ultimately, one may also question, as Andreas Bimmer (1993) underlined, what influence the so-called "regional identity" has on celebrations and festivals and what the role of "regionality" could be, i.e., belonging to a determined geographic territory (in our case, the Province of Cordoba). Bimmer raised the question of whether "traditional" or "modern" festivals can in fact contribute to the construction of a regional identity. We add to this by considering and evaluating the role of gastronomy and tourism in this quest for identity. Bimmer (1993) deems, as other German authors who studied, for example, the Bavarian Oktoberfest, that tourism has been a decisive factor since the end of the World War II, and this is also the case in Andalusia and the Province of Cordoba.

How can festivals contribute to the development of tourism and the food production industry? How can they contribute to sustainable rural development, especially in little-known regions in Europe (and in most advanced countries) that are being gradually divested of their populations? Festivals have mostly been studied by sociologists (Czarnowski, 1975); only recently have geographers (Di Méo, 2001) considered the role of festivals in structuring territories. It would now seem time for economists to examine the potential role of festivals in local economic development. Management and entrepreneurial development specialists should also be involved so that festivals can provide a guiding theme around which new activities can be created in the tourism, artisanal, and/or agricultural/food production sectors. How can meaningful strategies be developed to raise awareness amongst local populations so that entrepreneurs and associative groups initiate and enact such processes?

Festivals contribute to the construction of territories and consolidate their cultural and hence culinary identity (Di Méo, 2001). Festivals and local fairs are the focus of political and media attention, which also contribute to territorial cohesion. Since antiquity, festivals, fairs, and local markets have served as meeting places for eating and drinking, where people have also met to do business and trade, establish matrimonial alliances, and exchange information. This networking process is magnified today by information and communication technologies and social media.

A wide range of literature exists on this subject. Felsenstein and Fleisher (2003), based on cases in Israel, show that local festivals are more and more frequently used to promote territorial tourism, and that public authorities can use these to provide visitors with better information and assistance. Stankova and Vassanka (2015) refer to examples in Bulgaria to demonstrate that festivals increase opportunities for local production and services, which can then play a role in the sustainable economic, social, and cultural development of territories. In the case of Cordoba, while Jiménez Beltrán et al. (2016) emphasise the importance of local gastronomy in attracting international tourists to the city, and despite a wide range of literature on this subject, no mention is made in local gastronomy promotion campaigns of the role of festivals held across the Province of Cordoba (including in the capital city). This is because very little research has been conducted on the topic of festivals and gastronomy, and this is not only the case in Cordoba.

Should we therefore not reconsider more sociological concepts such as the "potlatch"? Originally a cultural form of behaviour based on giving and exchanging gifts, particularly during community meals and feasts (Deleuze, 1993; Girard, 2001), these events have been transformed by tourism. This example leads us to the main issue under analysis in this chapter.

2. The research context

Andalusia is experiencing the depopulation of its countryside areas, which is a widespread problem in southern Europe. Rural communities do not aspire to development solely for the sake of economic growth; they seek to improve their future in societal, environmental, and cultural ways. The ability of local populations to take responsibility for themselves, or to have a sense of self-progress, ensures their sustainability, i.e., the pursuit of a development process for as long as required to obtain long-term results, without deteriorating territories and their natural and cultural resources. This type of sustainable rural development, with its values rooted in traditions and ancient customs, supposes that territorial partners will abide by sufficiently long-term agreements on the aims and means available. From the culinary and gastronomic perspective, this means that the actors involved give priority to the use of locally produced specialities, locally based production and supply chains, waste reduction, energy- and resource-saving initiatives, transparency in supply chains, and so forth.

The development of Cordoba, the provincial capital, will depend on the renewal of its traditional model (Morales and Lanquar, 2014). The *Fiesta de los Patios*, or Patio Festival, has been on UNESCO's Representative List of the Intangible Cultural Heritage of Humanity since December 2012 in accordance with the 2003 Convention for Safeguarding Intangible Heritage that came into force in April 2006. The Mezquita of Cordoba had already been inscribed on the list in 1984, and this was extended to include the city's entire historic centre in 1994.[1] The city is considered a "mature destination,"[2] a term used in Spain in the 1980s to refer to coastal mass tourist destinations that had reached visitor capacity saturation and no longer offered any new attractions. This led to an unsustainable process that had very negative economic, social, and environmental impacts. Since 2010, this term can also be applied to inland destinations, such as Toledo, Salamanca, Saragossa, Seville, and Cordoba.

How can festivals in the rural regions of Cordoba be better managed so that a robust form of gastronomic tourism can be developed here? Just as in the rest of Spain and in Europe, the provincial authorities, in close collaboration with the Andalusian Junta, the Autonomous Community of Andalusia, are constrained to invest in financing celebrations, festivals, and cultural events to reinforce the identity-defining characteristics of the province's various counties or districts known in Spanish as *comarcas*. Such investment will also be required for any tourism services and products that inevitably lie off the beaten track and yet are directly connected to local festivities and celebrations. It will become a logical part of considerations for developing tourist attractiveness and competitive differentiation when seeking to attract value-adding customers from households, associations, or companies.

Tourism takes the sacred aura out of festivals, integrating them into leisure activities, shows, and tourist trails and circuits. It globalises festivals by opening them up to outsider participants. More and more of these tourists may view themselves as cosmopolitan citizens of the world, possessing multiple identities, particularly in Andalusia with its combination of Judeo-Christian and Muslim cultural heritage. Except that, from the fifteenth century onwards, most of the Judeo-Muslim aspects of local festivals have lost their meaning, and their mythology has been rewritten based either on purely Christian concepts or on more ancient tales predating the arrival of the Visigoths, such as the myth of Hercules. Even the food has changed – the Catholic Church required converted Jews and Muslims to eat pork and to follow the same culinary traditions as Christians during holy festivals.

2.1. The lack of statistics on tourist demand for festivals, romerías, and other local events

Together with food production, tourism has become the most important economic sector in Cordoba and its province. According to INE (2017), Cordoba and its province received a record 1,178,203 national and international visitors in 2016, a 3.78% increase over 2015. This represented 1,924,994 overnight stays, with the highest demand focused on the capital city of Cordoba. The villages and towns of the province only accommodated 10% of this total, i.e., 200,000 overnight stays. Currently, festivals, *romerías,* and other local events only attract local people or inhabitants of Cordoba, particularly at weekends and on national holidays. Few international visitors attend, except on special occasions such as Holy Week or in August. Now, there are no precise figures on foreign tourist attendance rates, although the National Institute of Statistics (INE) studies conducted in 2014 show that the average length of a stay in the provincial towns and *comarcas* is slightly longer than a typical stay in the capital Cordoba: 1.57 overnight stays in Cordoba compared to 1.61 stays in the rest of the province in 2013 (Source: EOH – INE).

The concentration of tourists in the city of Cordoba is very high for a province that had 792,182 inhabitants in 2013 compared to 805,757 in 2011. Cordoba city lost 5,000 inhabitants with its population declining from 328,704 in 2011 to 323,600 in 2013. There were 472,249 inhabitants in 2013 in the Province's six *comarcas* (Guadalquivir, East Campiña, South Campiña Cordobesa, Subbetica, Pedroches, and Guadiato) that include seventy-six municipalities and more than two hundred settlements, hamlets, and localities. The following towns have populations of over 20,000 inhabitants: Lucena (40,746), Puente Genil (29,093), Montilla (23,840), Priego de Córdoba (22,999), Baena (21,138), Cabra (21, 087) and Palma del Rio (20,855). Outside these main towns, the seventy-five registered municipalities range from 421 (Valsequillo) to 13, 653 inhabitants (Aguilar de la Frontera). Cordoba is one of the worst provinces in Spain for unemployment, with 20% of the active population out of work. According to INE surveys conducted in 2014, the combined total of unemployed and retirees almost equalled the working population. The Guadiato Valley recorded the highest rate of unemployment with 24.6% in 2013. The other *comarcas* have an unemployment rate of 15% – 16%.

The *comarcas* essentially pursue agricultural activities based on wine, olives, oranges and citrus fruit, and sheep and pig farming. Exceptions to this are the Guadiato Valley, which has a mining industry dating back 2,500 years, and Subbetica, whose main town Lucena, the former Pearl of Sepharad, is the powerhouse of the province's economic activity with a diversified range of industries in furniture, refrigeration, and services.

This research focuses on the issue of sustainable territorial development. To avoid the depopulation of its province, the city of Cordoba must increase its links with its surrounding *comarcas* via tourism and gastronomy. By taking advantage of the province's festivals, it should be possible to accelerate the development of culinary tourism – including tourist circuits, excursions, unique and unusual visits, and other entertaining activities based on atypical traditional games, etc. – based on local agricultural products. Such initiatives could consolidate Cordoba's image in international markets, which is precisely what the Salmorejo Brotherhood has successfully done.

The province's tourism structure was described in the Tourist Board's 2013 Development, Promotion and Communication Plan (Turismo de Cordoba, 2014) and then in the 2014 Strategic Tourism Plan for Cordoba 2015 – 2019. The structure hinges on the concept of locally produced products. These are intended to be clearly differentiated and exclusive; they must use the tourist brands and cultural, natural, or social resources connected with the destination, drawing on the different services and complementary activities available within that destination.

The other aim of these two plans is to ensure the complementarity of tourism products in the provincial capital and the various *comarcas*. The plan emphasises the need to launch products related to "festivals and popular events" in conjunction with the various local and regional institutions. This involves making an inventory and publishing a catalogue of all the information required to participate in festivals, including a precise schedule and description of the nature of each event: religious, culinary, folkloric, or other particularity. Festivals are expected to liaise with both the province's main tourist routes (religious and civil sites, wineries, etc.), and its *romería* pilgrimage destinations. *Romerías*, pilgrimages, and country festivals are indeed wonderful tourist attractions. The original meaning of the word *romería* derives from the pilgrimage of "romero" – the pilgrim who returns from Rome. The growing number of brotherhoods that organise and promote these events have recreated what Isambert (1982) described as a "structuring imaginary," a largely indeterminate set of sociohistoric and psychic figures and symbols that originally reinforced Spanish National Catholicism but are rapidly changing with the democratisation process.

3. Methodology

The analysis of local festivals in the rural areas of Cordoba is based on a questionnaire sent out to 30 tourism directors in the *comarcas* and to 150 local entrepreneurs listed by the provincial Tourist Board for promotional and communication purposes – a total of 180 questionnaires. The questionnaire focused on the awareness of the new opportunities for tourism development in the province, particularly concerning festivals and gastronomy. Its purpose was to identify which products and services, amongst others, could be used to create locally made products. Above all, the aim was to address the research problem of sustainable territorial development to avoid the depopulation of the province. In addition to ordinary questions about tourism in the province, the questionnaire included six points concerning the festivals held in each *comarca*:

- The nature of the festival's interest for tourism, whether this be popular religious traditions, popular sociocultural and civil traditions, or a combination of sociocultural, religious, and civil aspects (in a preconsolidated scheduled activity or event).
- The impact on tourism: supply and demand.
- What could be done to increase this impact?
- Which actors (folk groups, brotherhoods, or associations) promote festivals locally?
- Which events, new activities, and innovative services could be created within the respondent's *comarca* related to these festivals?
- Which products and services could be developed within the *comarca* related to these festivals, particularly regarding cuisine and gastronomy?

In addition, after analysing locally available documentation, an inventory was made of all the festivals and celebrations held in the Province of Cordoba, together with their associated local products. This enabled identifying the most significant dishes and recipes prepared for each festival.

4. Results

Thirty-five of the questionnaires collected were suitable for analysing the awareness of local authorities and tourism professionals regarding recurrent local festivals and events and their impact on the creation of products and services in outlying rural areas. This response rate of less than 20% is not statistically significant, even less so because the most complete and detailed answers came from travel agents and professional event organisers. The majority of these expressed their grievances or requests for the improvement or creation of products and services. Political leaders and those responsible for tourism in the municipalities and *comarcas* either did not want to, or did not know how to demonstrate their interest in local festivals.

Is this lack of interest due to the fact that tourism technicians do not usually organise festivals? We also attempted to talk to religious authorities and to those responsible for culture – but without any significant success. Our first observation is that there is little coordination at the municipality or *comarca* level between those involved in the organisation of festivals. Occasionally, when there are coalition governments, the responsibilities for tourism, culture, festivals, and relations with civil and religious society are given to politicians from different parties. Consequently, a complete statistical analysis of the results is not possible, and we can only highlight specific qualitative aspects.

Based on the results obtained from political leaders, tourism technicians, and professionals, the least-promoted festivals are religious ones related to local patron saints (15%). Basically, these events are of little tourism or gastronomic interest, whereas festivals of a purely local sociocultural and civil nature have more impact (30%). Religious events, such as Holy Week, the *romerías*, or well-scheduled consolidated activities have the greatest impact (55%). Some such events, which have made applications to the Andalusian Autonomous Government or Spanish State for this purpose, have been officially designated as "of tourism interest." Table 6.1 shows the festival inventory constructed by the author in association with the technicians of the Provincial Tourism Office.[3]

Most respondents primarily emphasised the need for infrastructure and equipment to facilitate tourism development in their *comarcas*, even outside of festival periods. They also indicated the lack of good signposting for towns, villages, and their attractions; more car parks are needed for private cars and tourist buses at the entrances to villages and towns. Above all, in the *comarcas* with woodlands and natural parks, respondents asked for more hiking, horse riding, cycling, and mountain biking paths.

Table 6.1 Festivals in the Province of Cordoba

COMARCA	Total number of festivals	Religious	Non-religious	Festivals of tourism interest [1]
High Guadalquivir	54	39	15	
Campiña Baena	15	11	4	1
Campina Sur	25	14	11	3
Cordoba city	8	4	4	1
Pedroches	54	40	14	5
Subbética	37	25	12	6
Guadiato Valley	21	16	5	
Middle Guadalquivir	13	7	6	
TOTAL	227	156	71	16*
		69%	31%	

1 Important to note is that by 2013, 125 Declarations of Tourism Interest had been accepted by the Autonomous Government of Andalusia, including thirty-one in the Province of Seville, one in Cadiz Province, eighteen in Malaga Province, fourteen in the Province of Cordoba, thirteen in Huelva Province, ten in Granada Province, nine in the Province of Jaen, and eight in Almeria. Furthermore, under the terms of a Joint Declaration (for Baena and Cabra in the Province of Cordoba), Holy Week has been recognized everywhere as a festival of regional interest. Declarations of Tourism Interest aim to highlight Andalusian and Spanish intangible patrimonial heritage by attracting visitors' attention to their major tourism resources.
* Including four national festivals (three religious) in Cordoba (The Patios), Lucena (The Aracelinitanes), Baena, and Cabra (Holy Week).
Source: Turismo de Córdoba – Diputación de Córdoba, 2013 in association with the author

For travel agents and event organisers, there are not enough country-inn-style hotels of either a comfortable or luxury standard, and there is a lack of rural accommodation in the *comarcas* that are far away from Cordoba city. Paradoxically, hoteliers and restaurateurs pointed out that, except in the case of a few hostelries outside Cordoba city, there is not enough customer demand in the low season. However, none of these accommodation providers make any real attempt to develop quality gastronomic offerings in the low season. Only a small number of respondents thought that local festivals and their associated gastronomy could be an additional factor to attract corporate meetings, incentive trips, or small conferences to rural areas.

Finally, we have the Guadalquivir River, which is no longer navigable beyond Seville. The irrigation systems that have made Andalusia a garden and orchard paradise in the Arab imagination are referred to in this context.

As for marketing tools, many respondents are convinced that promotional videos on CDs and USB drives are the best option. Some are just beginning to realise that mobile e-tourism is on the increase with the use of tablets and smartphones. Nevertheless, the distribution of these technologies is advancing rapidly, and by 2017 – 2018, the situation could be very different with interest for smart tourism. The Declaration of Añora of 19 October 2017 on Smart Rural Land[4] is indicative of these rapid changes.

4.1. Brotherhoods and fraternities

In the eyes of the tourism professionals, the most noteworthy festivals, and therefore the most highly attended, are of a religious nature – first, those during Holy Week, and then the local *romerías* held in hermitages: Araceli in Lucena, The Virgin of la Sierra in Cabra, Saint Isidor Labrador in Montalban or in Cañete (Campiña Sur). Lucena (Subbética) and Puente Genil (Campiña Sur) have sought to extend Holy Week by working together to create Children's Holy Week, and other communities, such as Bujalance, have followed suit.

However, some resistance was noted towards the creation of products related to religious tourism that might foster intercultural interactions. The first example is the Mezquita, Cathedral-Mosque in Cordoba, but also the Jewish heritage in Lucena (formerly known as the Pearl of Sepharad; for more than a century between the first and second millennia, this town was administered by a Jewish community) and Saint John of Avila, who was born into a converted Jewish family and pronounced doctor of law by the Vatican in November 2013. Also noteworthy is that some respondents suggested referring to Andalusian Muslim patrimonial heritage and including it in certain events and festivals outside of Cordoba, such as Medina Al-Zahra (five km from the centre of Cordoba, to be included in 2018 in the UNESCO World Heritage List), so that the whole province could commemorate its past and make use of it to promote Cordoba as a bridge between West and East.

Due to their success in the city of Cordoba, the Cross Festivals (Cruz de Mayo), held in May, have spread across the province to Añora, Bujalance, Espejo, Fernán-Nuñez, Montalban, Montilla, La Rambla, Gualdalcázar, etc. Paradoxically, many civil public holidays have been established around the patron saint of a town or village. For example, the festival of Saint Mark the Evangelist, which is held during the last week of April after Holy Week, has been successfully developed in several *comarcas* in the neighbouring Province of Jaen (shows involving bulls). Such events could contribute to a better seasonal adjustment of tourism in early spring, and associations could be made with these adjustments.

The brotherhoods and fraternities often have culinary traditions described in a recipe book produced by the Cordoba Hoteliers' Association (HOSTE-COR) for the provincial Gastronomy Days. However, Gastronomy Days devoted to garlic, game meat, beer, Iberian pork products from the Pedroches Valley, pies, stews, mushrooms, and Montilla-Moriles wines are rarely linked to local festivals.

What has been most noticeable over the last few decades is that with the strong growth in rural tourism, festivals have been created based on the host municipality's main economic activity. La Rambla is a small town of artisan pottery-makers that had more than 110 factories in 2010 – some have since closed. Having been able to create a suitable venue during the traditional Saint Isidor Labrador Festival (from 8 – 15 August), the municipality launched a

Tapas Festival in May each year to celebrate the local *morillas* speciality made with artichokes and chorizo. However, the tapas concept is widespread and of little significance in Spain, where nearly all bars and restaurants offer these with a glass of wine or beer.

The organisation of festivals depends essentially on the brotherhoods and fraternities. Several hundreds of these exist in the Province of Cordoba. These types of associations date back to the thirteenth century and were regulated by the Franco regime to perpetuate National Catholic traditions. The main confederation of these associations in Cordoba is the Association of Holy Week Sisterhoods and Brotherhoods (*Agrupacion de Hermandades y Cofradias de Semana Santa*).

Since the return to democracy, there has been an increase in the development of civil fraternities, including those for gastronomy and food tasting, such as the Salmorejo, or more bacchanalian groups in Montilla and Moriles (the Cofradia de la Viña y del Vino de Montilla and the Vid de Moriles). The Brotherhood of the Friends of the Olive Tree in Baena, which holds a special Flowering Festival celebration, is an example of this phenomenon. It was created at the start of the twenty-first century, and its president has competed for the right to create other brotherhoods, such as the Salmorejo. These gastronomic or bacchanalian brotherhoods promote Cordovan food products directly to national and international markets. They appoint ambassadors who live outside of the Province of Cordoba, inside and outside of Spain; they invite journalists and bloggers and honour well-known personalities from the worlds of politics, art, and literature.

4.2. Festivals, cultural habit, and the importance of gastronomy

As Table 6.2 shows, the locally produced specialities used during these events are quite varied.

Let us analyse the case of the Sierras Subbéticas, a nature reserve in the centre of Andalusia. It owes its glorious cultural past to its strategic position and frontier post mentality forged amidst the Christian lordships and Muslim-ruled Taïfa kingdoms – hence the long-term coexistence of different peoples and cultures within this territory.

From the Iberians and the Romans, whose archaeological remains can be found in Cabra and Almedinilla; to the Jews, Christians, and Muslims, who each left their mark here; together with the civil, military, and religious influences found in the local architecture, culture, folklore, and artisan craftsmanship – all have transformed the identity of this region and are at the base of its idiosyncrasy. In addition to a gastronomy at times based on Sephardic and/or Muslim recipes, the activities related to olive oil, wines, liqueurs, aniseed-flavoured spirits, and a wide variety of sweet pastries have become the pillars of a cultural melting pot – an open, cross-cultural zone that has preserved its ancestral legacy as a foundation on which to construct its present and prepare its future. In Almedinilla, about ten km from Priego, attempts have been made to revive this ancient legacy with an event that has been held every August for

Table 6.2 Festivals, dishes, and traditional beverages in the Province of Cordoba

Municipality	Population 2014	Festival name	Time of year	Dish/traditional drink	Local products used
Adamuz	4,398	La Botijuela	February	Miller's breakfast	D.O. Montoro–Adamuz olive oil
Aguilar de la Frontera	13,631	Popular festival	July	Tastings of wine and Matanza pork products	Wines from the Montilla–Moriles Regulatory Board
Almedinilla	2,468	Roman dinners	All year	The recipes of Marcus Gianus Apicus (first century)	Rosé wine, hydromel (mead)
Almodóvar del Río	7,977	Zoco de la Encanta	March/April	Suckling pig	Piglets
Benamejí	5,123	Our Lady of Candelaria and Saint Blas	February	Sesame seed bagel	Durum wheat flour
Bujalance	7,744	The Joyo Festival	April	Miller's breakfast	Olive oil, young beans, and dried cod
Cabra	21,001	New Harvest Olive Oil Festival	December	"Hoyo" (a ball-shaped bread loaf hollowed out and filled with vegetables and meat)	Flour, olive oil
Cardeña	1,606	Suckling Pig Festival	October	Cochifrito	Iberian suckling pig, olive oil
Castro del Río[1]	8,052	Holy Week Gourmet Cod Festival	April	Cod with garden vegetables	Dried cod, fresh beans, chorizo

Córdoba	328,041	Spring Festival / May Carnations	March–early June	Salmorejo	Tomatoes, bread, salt, garlic, olive oil
Doña Mencía	4,935	Holy Week	March/April	Rossoli	Coffee, flower liqueurs (jasmine)
Espejo	3,474	Pig slaughtering	October/November	Cooked pork meats	Pigs
Fernán-Núñez	9,801	Food fair	October	Chickpea stew	Locally grown dried vegetables
Fuente Obejuna	4,961	The Los Panchez Festival of Artisanal Crafts	October	Bakery products / Game meat products	Locally produced durum wheat, game
Fuente Tojar	800 approx.	The Caper Festival	November	…	…
Hinojosa del Duque	7,126	The Tapas Route	November		
Hornachuelos	4,660	The Tapas Route	October	Stews	Game and products from hunting
Iznájar	4,637	Holy Week	March or April	Relleno	Local ham, eggs, breadcrumbs
Lucena	42,748	Gastrofestival FOOD & JAZZ	April/May	Oxtail mille-feuille	
Luque	3,178	The Olive Tree Festival	November	Tasting of various olive oils and dishes made with these oils	Denomination of Origin local oils
Montalbán	4,472	Garlic Festival	July	Pork meats and Candle ends	
Montemayor	4,001	Livestock Festival	January		Chorizo, boudin sausage, pork meats
Montilla et Moriles	23,622 et 3,872	Grape Harvest Festival	September	Tasting of D.O wines	D.O. Montilla-Moriles wines

(Continued)

Table 6.2 (Cont.)

Municipality	Population 2014	Festival name	Time of year	Dish/traditional drink	Local products used
Montoro	9,744	Olive Tree festival	May	Tasting sessions of Hoyo with olives	Durum wheat, olive oil, olives
Nueva Carteya	5,540	Olive Oil Day	November	D.O. oil tasting sessions	
Obejo	2,012	Saint Antony Festival	January	Crustless bread with chorizo	Farmhouse bread with local pork meats
Palma del Río	21,582	The Oranges Festival	April	Cod with orange	Oranges, garlic
Posadas	7,512	The Posadas Gastronomy Days	November	El Rin Ran (Salmorejo soup)	Tomatoes, local ingredients
Pozoblanco	17,491	Our Lady of La Luna Romería	8 December for the Immaculate Conception	Hornazo (pie)	Eggs, pork fat
Priego de Córdoba	23,112	Food fair	September	D.O. oils tasting sessions	
Puente Genil	30,186	The Quince Festival	October	Cheese and quince jelly	
La Rambla	7,547	Tapas Festival	May	Morrillas	Artichokes, chorizo
Rute	10,387	Christmas in Rute	November December until January 6th (Epiphany Day)	Turron Aniseed	Almonds

Santaella	6,097	St James Festival	July	Chickpea soup and Salmorejo	White chickpeas, tomatoes
Villafranca de Córdoba	4,893	La Gran Huevada and Saint Isidore	May	Egg-based dishes and omelettes	Eggs
Villanueva de Córdoba	9,226	The Festival of Iberian acorn-fed ham from the Pedroches Valley	October	Ham-based dishes	Iberian acorn ham
Zuheros	696	Cheese Festival	September	Cheese tastings	Local and national Spanish cheeses

Source: The Author
1 This little town is home of the biggest codfish salting and drying company in Europe.

the last few years: the FESTUM Ibero-Roman festivities, where mead and rosé wines are proposed.

The success of festivals is often directly linked to funfair events held in the main towns of each *comarca*. These are accompanied by a surge of cultural practices, including songs, dance, music, and drama, as well as gastronomy and homemade-style cuisine (*casera*). Via the La Botijuela festival, which takes place mid-March and aims to promote the town's olive industry, the Adamuz municipality organises traditional song and dance performances as a way of upholding its ancestral folklore. Short (free) mule rides are also offered – mule rearing was a local specialisation that was lost due to the mechanisation of agriculture and is now being revived thanks to tourism. In association with small local salting firms, the Castro del Rio municipality (in the Guadajoz Campiña-East district) uses the artisanal Ars Olea festival to showcase its cuisine based not only on olive oil but also on dried salted cod, which, before the advent of refrigeration, was the only fish widely available to all. Ars Olea also provides a means of developing industries related to olive tree cultivation: olive wood furniture, olive oil based cosmetics, and so forth.

This takes us from cultural practices (traditions and folklore) to cultural consumption (tourism and gastronomy). Local officials do not make this one of their main objectives, except when they set up temporary workshops to encourage the creation of training courses in agricultural methods and traditional craftsmanship. Every year, at the start of April, Bujalance organises the Joyo Festival[5] – when, according to the municipality's advertising poster, attendees can enjoy tastings of bread with olive oil, cod, and beans. On this occasion, local groups sing the *pajarona*, which is similar to flamenco music but with Castilian rather than purely Andalusian tones. In fact, the Andalusian Flamenco Route begins in Bujalance with these *abandolaos*-style songs.

Thus, gastronomy is the most rapidly expanding economic activity in the Province of Cordoba. Almost all the respondents emphasised the development and promotion of gastronomy and local cuisine. First and foremost, they cited Salmorejo, which has become a symbol of Cordoba and is based on locally produced ingredients: olive oil, garlic, salt from the inland salt marshes, and breadcrumbs from wheat grown in the province. On 15 October 2008, a brotherhood – the Cofradía del Salmorejo[6] – was founded, with the support of the Friends of Baena Olive Oil Brotherhood on which it was modelled. Led by tourism professionals, this group has around a thousand members and ambassadors across the world, is a member of the Andalusian Federation of Gastronomy Brotherhoods (FECOAN), the Spanish Federation of Oeno-gastronomic Brotherhoods (FECOES), and the European Oeno-gastronomic Brotherhoods Council (CEUCO). Since 2012, it has played an essential role in running nonreligious festivals in the province. Ham, oil, wines (including Montilla-Moriles wines), aniseed, and oranges are the leading lights in these new festivals, but mushrooms (mycology), cork-based handicrafts, basketry, pottery, and glassmaking are also involved.

According to most respondents, culinary experiences should be developed via a form of exploratory tourism, including visits to wine and aniseed liqueur cellars, oil mills (*almazaras*), artisanal potters, and glassmakers. This would involve the creation of gastronomy-themed routes with workshops and mini-information centres. Some suggested that in the autumn, after All Saints Day, the provincial authorities should increase the promotion and development of the traditional Iberian pig-slaughtering period (*matanza del cerdo*), particularly in the Pedroches and Guadiato Valley counties. Some professionals have already spotted this opportunity and offer packages enabling connoisseurs of pork-cured products to choose and buy an Iberian acorn-fed pig and have it made into sausages, chorizo, and ham.

Other examples are more unusual. Moriles is a large municipality in South Campiña about sixty km from Cordoba city. The information the province provides on the festivities focuses on two events: the patronal festival, celebrated on 7 October, and the Vigil of the Feast of Our Lady of Mount Carmel in July. However, since 1997, on the initiative of the Association of the Young Friends of Moriles Wine, the festival including the Las Vinalias trade fair has been organised just after the grape harvest. This involves tasting sessions of local wines in all the wine cellars across the town and makes for a lively event with wine cellar visits, including flamenco demonstrations and tastings of typical dishes and tapas.

Fourteen km from Moriles lies Montilla, the main town in the Campiña Sur county. This town has two unmissable cultural attractions: the sixteenth-century manor house belonging to Inca Garcilaso de la Vega, an advocate of the fusing of cultures and interculturality, and the Priory of Saint John of Avila, where the saint lived until his death in 1569. Montilla is above all the capital of the denomination of origin of Montilla-Moriles wines. These wines are classified as *fino, amontillado, oloroso,* or *Pedro Jiménez* (also called *PX)*; the latter is considered the most famous and delicious of dessert wines, while the others are comparable to diverse types of sherry. Although there is a Wine Harvest Festival – (at the end of September) and the Oenology Day (in November), two events are internationally recognised: the Wine and Tapas Fair, and the Andalusian Wine-Making Industry and Gastro-Oenological Tourism Fair. These are veritable bacchanalian celebrations with a series of attractions and events. The wine-growing municipalities have also encouraged the creation of a wine route that travels across the province's southern and eastern *comarcas,* between Aguilar de la Frontera, Montilla, Moriles, Doña Mencía, Montalbán de Córdoba, Monturque, Nueva Carteya, Puente Genil, Baena, Cabra, Castro del Río, Espejo, Fernán-Núñez, La Rambla, Lucena, Montemayor, and Santaella.

Rute is an example of a municipality where the festivals are developed largely around the production of flavoured alcoholic beverages (orange, aniseed, etc.) and distilled spirits made with aniseed. Rute is located ninety-four km south of the city of Cordoba at the edge of the Malaga Province. Its main traditional festivals are those of Saint Mark; the Fair of Our Lady of la Cabeza (created in 1986), held in May; the Royal Fair; and the Festival of Our Lady of Carmel. Civil groups are involved via brotherhoods such as Our Lady of Carmel and Our Lady of La Cabeza, but more particularly via the Association of the Rute Aniseed Spirits and Liqueur Producers. The carnival is very popular in this *comarca* due to its murgas, which combine music, drama, and dance. These are performed by local groups in accordance with a mixture of Latin American customs and African slave heritage that the Spanish émigrés acquired when they fraternised, as was tolerated and permitted during the Carnival. During all these celebrations, aniseed-flavoured beverages, liqueurs, and artisanal brandies are used to make cakes, biscuits, milk jam, and diverse types of pastries, such as *piononos,* whose origin dates to the end of the Reconquista, perhaps during the Granada siege in 1490 – 1491. Certainty, these festivals struggle to survive, but due to the influx of tourists from spring to autumn, some of their production processes have been industrialised, and local professionals insist on improving their quality to ensure the continuity of their distribution in Spain and for exportation, without necessarily creating new products or events around them.

This is not the case in Palma del Rio (Middle Guadalquivir), where orange production is the dominant industry. Although the town, developed in the sixteenth century by converted Jews fleeing persecution, is the birthplace of famous matadors such as El Cordobès (Manuel Benitez) and fashion designers such as Victorio & Lucchino, the decline in attendance of bullfights has caused local authorities to create new types of festivals and events. Thus, the Month of the Orange and The Orange Day were created and are held from the end of March onwards (after the citrus harvest). Another initiative was the Orange Jam festival, a hip hop music festival attracting international artists. Unfortunately this did not last long – certainly for economic reasons but particularly due to both a lack of institutional support (the municipality was unable to manage the safety and social aspects of the festival) and rejection by local companies that viewed the event more as a source of difficulties than profit (it was a rave-style event). The new Orange Day provides a host of microevents, including dance, drama, and, above all, gastronomy using orange-based jams, confits, and tapas. This is also why the Multi-Sector Fair and the Tapas Fair, promoted internationally in Germany and in Northern European countries, now start just a few days afterwards. To note is that with the aid of the European Commission via its Rural Development Groups, the local authorities have been able to use these festivals to develop their exports of oranges and derived products.

Palma held a Flamenco Cultural week, a scenic arts market unique in Andalusia, and another fair/funfair event in August – all essentially oriented towards tourism. Furthermore, local entrepreneurs have created some very innovative initiatives: Orange3 now sells the world's best oranges over the internet and counts a Coca-Cola executive in Atlanta as one of its customers. These fruits come from the ancient gardens of Palma de Rio and are watered by irrigation wheels built by the Arabs and maintained by converted Jews. Some orange trees are more than two hundred years old and ten metres high.

Benameji is a totally separate example. On the banks of the River Genil, main tributary of the Guadalquivir and taking its source in the Sierra Nevada above Granada, this village borders the Province of Malaga. Since the Muslim period, it has always been renowned for its melons. Up to now, this reputation has not been exploited as part of the local gastronomy. The town's festival and fair are held in August and September. The local event most supported by the town's inhabitants, but hardly attended by tourists, is the Saint Mark spring festival, during which simple durum wheat bagels are made. The local authorities would like to create activities based around a museum dedicated to the Duchess of Benameji, whose extraordinarily beautiful mummified body was discovered in a local convent. This could provide the focus of a show run by local volunteers, which would also include the turbulent history of the Reconquest and that of the outlawed bandeleros, such as Jose Maria El Tempranillo, whose steps can be retraced on a route bearing his name. The idea is to develop hiking tourism packages including boxed lunches featuring the foodstuffs eaten by the outlaws: omelettes, cured pork, bread, and dried fruits.

4.3. Integrating organic and ecological trends into festival gastronomy

No respondent mentioned the terms "ecological" or "organic" in relation to festival gastronomy. However, as awareness grows amongst elected officials and tourism technicians due to pressure from civil society, farmers, and artisans who work in the organic sector, examples of "eco" or "organic" gastronomy are becoming more widespread across the Province of Cordoba.

The 31,568-hectare Sierras Subbeticas Natural Park covers eight communes of the *comarca*, including Priego and Zuheros. The latter is famous for its cave of bats, where wall paintings and engravings testify to the former presence of a large Neolithic colony. A procession to the Virgin was first recognised here in 1569. For tourism purposes, a brotherhood was re-established a few decades ago to relaunch three festivals: la Candelaria (Purification), the Annunciation and Assumption of Our Lady, and the local fair that takes place around 15 August. No emphasis has been placed on organic agriculture and ecological resources, even when a spring Cheese Festival was launched. More than 15,000 people participate in this festival, and about 8,000 kg of cheese are consumed during the three-day trade fair organised with the support of the Zuheros town hall and the Andalusian Regional Government. The fair has more than thirty producers of various types of goat's cheese, as well as traditional pressed cheeses with different processing times and herb flavours. Without any real support from the trade fair organisers or the Andalusian government, some of these artisans have proposed organic or "ecological" cheese, bread, cakes, and culinary preparations since 2010. Some of these are CAAE certified – the European certification specialised in ecological production processes designed by the Spanish organisation ENAC for the UNE-EN-ISO/IEC 17,065: 2012 standard.

Priego de Cordoba is known as the "water city" due to its many springs and fountains. It is the jewel of Andalusian baroque heritage, with its churches and monuments financed by the émigrés who returned from the Americas in the eighteenth century. The Royal Fair is held at the start of September and is devoted to food production and agricultural machinery. In addition to the religious celebrations, the most original festivities are the Fraternity of the Companions of Aurora,[7] a tradition dating back more than four centuries. It takes place at midnight on certain Saturday nights and consists of people walking the streets of Priego as they sing traditional songs dedicated to the Virgin Mary. Springs and fountains are forgotten as part of these traditions, as are the mountains, even though the two highest peaks in Cordoba Province are located here: La Tiñosa (1570 m) and El Bermejo (1470 m).[8] Priego is most strongly characterised by its olive oils. At international agricultural fairs, its extra-virgin olive oil (AOVE) is frequently honoured with prizes and awards for the world's best olive oil. Restaurateurs vaunt the use of Priego oil in their cuisine, and the Royal Fair uses it during events to which finalists of the Spanish Master Chef programme are invited.

In the north of the Province of Cordoba, at the heart of the Sierra Morena in the *comarcas* of the Pedroches Valley, Cardeña seeks to play a role both in the Cordovan cuisine that uses game meat as a key ingredient and in the discovery of its natural environment (first the Cardeña-Montoro Natural Park and then the municipality close to the Sierra de Andujar Natural Park in the Province of Jaen). The evergreen oak forests and olive groves here make it possible to rear Iberian pigs on acorns. According to the Regulatory Council of the Pedroches Valley PDO (protected designation of origin), the legs and shoulders of ham must come from Iberian breed pigs with a pedigree of a minimum 75% of the Iberian breed and a maximum 25% of the Duroc or Duroc Jersey strain. The ageing period is twelve months for shoulders and eighteen months for legs of ham. Depending on the food fed to the animals, hams are classified as *bellota, recebo,* or *cebo.* In this part of the Province, tourism products have been developed around the pig-slaughter period (*matanza del cerdo*) with its associated gastronomic specialities. Nevertheless, there is not yet a suckling pig festival, as some have suggested. In fact, according to the respondents, there has not been any real social pressure to develop this type of tourism, since such activities would disturb production. Little has been done to encourage nature-based tourism or ecotourism with rural cottage accommodation or camping and caravan sites, and even less to develop nature-focused events or festivals.

4.4. Training

Most respondents believe that guides, shopkeepers, accommodation providers, and tourism authorities are not trained to deal with visitors during festivals and fairs. In general, apart from in Cordoba, the province's capital, few speak foreign languages. However, this is changing with the younger generations, who are better prepared for international contexts. Several guides to restaurants in the Province of Cordoba in different languages have been published on the Internet.[9] Some contain a series of typical recipes, sometimes with details of their nutritional value, but no direct link to local festivals.

The University of Cordoba now offers a series of training programmes related to the development of food production and is therefore beginning to create the link between such development and gastronomy, particularly via its Chair in Food Science and Food Technology and at ETSIAM (the School of Agricultural and Forestry Engineering), which awards an engineering degree in food production in rural environments. Its aim is to foster an entrepreneurial mindset among its future engineers and thereby lead to the creation of companies whose activities could be based on festivals, fairs, and local gastronomic products and sectors.

4.5. SWOT analysis

All this information made it possible to identify the strengths, weaknesses, opportunities, and threats (SWOT) that impact rural tourism within the Province of Cordoba and hence provide ideas and projects so that local festivals can act as stimuli for gastronomic tourism.

The SWOT analysis (Table 6.3) shows that an improvement in the efficiency of the system of tourism governance is required, particularly the coordination processes between *comarcas* (counties – districts) and municipalities. This view of sustainable rural development, and from 2017 smart rural land development (with the Añora Declaration),[10] is based on the creation of synergies designed to increase the level of local self-esteem and improve the perception of quality of a given destination. It facilitates the application of a recognition and differentiation system for destinations depending on their environmental sustainability and social responsibility. This kind of gastronomic rural tourism could also become one of the key factors of developing sustainable, connected, and inclusive tourism, i.e., smart tourism.

5. Conclusions

In rural contexts, festivals represent a break with the daily routine of labouring in the fields and doing agricultural artisanal work. These breaks take several forms: they constitute a breach of conventional norms; a breach of time by allowing the past to be brought back into the present; a breach of the spatial norms that usually demarcate a community's internal and external zones; and finally, a breach of the divide between the human and the divine world. For all these reasons, tourism is a powerful factor for the development of festivals, celebrations, ceremonies, and pilgrimages. Such festivities are a sort of laboratory for future perspectives and also have an integrative and civic impact on the rural world. They must be included in a smart tourism strategy as

Table 6.3 SWOT: Rural tourism and festivals in the Province of Cordoba

Strengths

- Festivals, a strong point for tourism development
- Opportunity for creativity and innovation
- The festival or fiesta connects people with their *tertulia* groups
- Festivals contribute to the construction of territories and the consolidation of their identity
- Sustainable rural development, not just clichés
- Innovative and structuring processes initiated by local authorities and rural development groups.
- Agricultural activity based on wine, olive trees, oranges and citrus fruits, sheep and pig farming.
- *Romerías*, pilgrimages and country festivals
- Holy Week: consolidated and well-scheduled activities have the greatest impact.

Opportunities

- To avoid rural depopulation, Cordoba city must reinforce links with its surrounding *comarcas* and neighbouring provinces.
- Smart tourism – i.e., sustainable, connected, and inclusive between the capital and its territories
- A bigger role for women and young people
- Awareness of new opportunities for tourism development
- Public-private partnerships
- Baroque festivals and carnivals
- Festivals and the water culture: Guadalquivir: a centre for nautical activities and river beaches, Arab baths (*hammams*), water wheel (*noria*) route
- Mobile e-tourism and social media networks
- Muslim and Jewish patrimonial heritage
- The Three Cultures Grand Art Fair
- Grand shows involving public participation
- Development of secular and civil fraternities dealing with export products (e.g., oil, oranges, Iberian ham)
- Local cultural practices, e.g., song, dance, music, and drama, as well as gastronomy
- Increase in microevents

Weaknesses

- Lack of economic analysis of regular festivals and events
- Depopulation of the countryside
- Festivals of a religious nature are less well promoted

Threats

- Attitude of certain social groups and resistance towards the creation of more open forms of religious tourism, i.e., more ecumenical and intercultural

- Need for infrastructure and equipment
- Lack of adequate signposting
- Lack of information on tourism products and services in the province
- Marketing methods used are too traditional
- Lack of training for guides in rural areas
- The role of women and young people
- Safety and control taken over by certain social groups and local authorities
- A general lack of governance in this field

- Lack of transparency and information regarding certain festivals
- Financial and fiscal checks
- Lack of creativity for nature-oriented festivals and events
- Lack of creativity regarding products and services to be offered in the future
- Lack of knowledge about markets and the new characteristics of international demand
- Lack of understanding cosmopolitanism in the face of globalisation
- Little emphasis on cultural practices, excessive focus on cultural consumption

advocated in the Añora Declaration on Smart Rural Land of 19 October 2017. Cuisine and gastronomy play a leading role. Nevertheless, when looking carefully at recipes for festive meals, certain trends observed over the last few decades are clearly emphasised by the people interviewed for this survey:

- More and more products and ingredients from outside a given territory are being used and added to locally grown products. Although this was not highlighted by respondents, an increase in dishes with additions particularly from North Africa (couscous) and Latin America, but also from North American fast food, has been observed during these festivals. Globalisation is passing through here, too.
- Channels are now being developed for the sale of derived preserved and conserved products and for the online sale of locally produced specialities that customers have consumed *in situ*. A few pioneering experiments have been set up for extra-virgin olive oil, aperitif wines, and oranges.

Still, for the moment, in the Province of Cordoba, there is no sign of any great innovations based on organic farming or of the use of meat substitutes (for vegans or vegetarians), all of which could be showcased during festivals.

How to ensure the development of authentic tourism in the Province of Cordoba? Is there a direct, clear, and factual link to the traditional identity of the Province of Cordoba and its interculturalism as recalled by Inca Garcilaso de la Vega of the city of Montilla and based in its Jewish, Christian, and Moslem roots? As the Quebec Tourism Intelligence Network points out, "The search for authenticity is a predominant trend driving tourism because travellers are looking for unique experiences that are part of our vibrant and varied world."[11] There is no other solution than to focus on a form of rural tourism based on gastronomy, agricultural and food production resources, and culinary traditions via local festivals. Tourists currently place more and more emphasis on convivial, well-balanced encounters – i.e., harmonious and sustainable – and they want to share their gastronomic experiences through Facebook, Twitter, or Instagram.

What role should public institutions and tourism authorities have in the pursuit of a more participatory means of intervention through accompanying developments without managing them directly? This requires training local agents and professionals in the public and private sectors, who will have to learn how to generate initiatives and encourage and train potential or emerging entrepreneurs without restricting their creativity. Many have asked to overcome political discontinuities, pointing to the common good that festival development represents.

There remains the question of safety at festivals. This was not raised once by any of the respondents, tourism professionals, or local officials. As seen in the city of Cordoba, a festival can become too large and placed under financial and fiscal control under the pretext of safety, for example, to avoid the excesses that occur with the *botellon* rave parties where alcohol predominates. Today, there is also the additional risk of terrorism in the Province of Andalusia, regarded as legendary by jihadists. Furthermore, resident populations may reject tourism due to noise and other types of abuses. Everyone agrees that, for all events, a public-private partnership is needed to establish security norms and budgetary limits, thereby preventing certain festivals from generating deficits that could have repercussions on local public finances.

Finally, what can be done to avoid accentuating the gap in the next few years between "commercial fairs," where the accent is placed on the promotion and sale of locally produced specialities, and "convivial" festivals of a religious or civil nature? The secularisation of festivals is not yet complete in Spain, particularly in Andalusia, but it is happening, sometimes because a prominent role is given to the commercial sector. Most respondents requested a consistent, long-term festival events schedule and established standards to avoid any excesses. Secularisation could create better coordination between festivals and de-seasonalise these by spreading them out beyond the harvest and major religious festivals (Christmas, New Year's Day, Epiphany, and Holy Week). Such coordination would require negotiations between fraternities and brotherhoods, particularly the religious ones, for the good of everyone.

Festivals could be considered as short-, medium-, and long-term opportunities to extend a stay, especially if better coordinated. This coordination should not be restricted to collaborations between the municipalities of each *comarca*, but should be implemented between associations of municipalities. They could then work together, for example, along the River Guadalquivir between the High Guadalquivir and the lowland of the Guadalquivir (Middle Guadalquivir), as well as with the adjacent provinces of Seville, Jaen, and Malaga. In all cases, this must result in local, provincial, and Andalucía community tourism policies leveraging gastronomy and the agricultural and food production industries. They would have a positive impact on employment and investments and would create clusters capable of accelerating alliances between local economic and social activities (tourism, trade, handmade goods, food production, and technological advances). They would also enable many civilians to participate, particularly young people and women who are only just starting to play a role in the fraternities and brotherhoods. The social, political, economic, and religious powers will need to reach a consensus on the need for sustainable, connected, and inclusive development as a means of preventing the slow, yet all too real, rural depopulation of the Province of Cordoba.

Notes

1 http://whc.unesco.org/fr/list/313.
2 http://geographyfieldwork.com/TourismMatureDestinations.htm.
3 Cf. http://www.turismodecordoba.org/empresas/0106/4627/0085/patronato-provincial-de-turismo-de-cordoba.
4 https://www.smartruralland.com/. Añora is a small city in the Pedroches Valley and seventy-nine km north of Cordoba.
5 Joyo is bread dipped in oil extracted from the first pressing of the olives.
6 http://www.salmorejocordobes.com and https://cordobapedia.wikanda.es/wiki/Cofrad%C3%ADa_Gastron%C3%B3mica_del_Salmorejo_Cordob%C3%A9s.

7 The same festival can be found not far away from here in the municipalities of Cabra Monturque (but here the festival is only half a century old). In Castro del Rio, the brotherhood is called the Brothers of la Bella Aurora.

8 Priego is also the birthplace of the first president of the third Spanish Republic (1931 – 1939) and certain pro-Republican associations have attempted to develop commemorative events there.

9 https://gastronomiacordoba.com/guia-los-restaurantes-la-provincia/.

10 https://www.smartruralland.com/.

11 http://tourismintelligence.ca/2005/10/20/authenticity-what-do-they-really-want/. According to the Quebec survey, authenticity is a concept that surrounds customs and tradition. It involves making one's differences known and offering a window on one's culture, heritage, history, and any other aspect that shapes the identity of a destination.

References

Bimmer, A.C. (1993). Identité régionale et fêtes contemporaines. *Civilisations*, 42–2, pp. 243–247.

Czarnowski, S. (1975). *Le culte des héros et ses conditions sociales: Saint Patrick, héros national de l'Irlande.* New York, Arno Press. (première édition, Paris, 1914).

Deleuze, G.(1993). *Critique et Clinique.* Paris, Editions de Minuit.

Di Méo, G. (2001). Le sens géographique des fêtes. *Annales de Géographie*, 622, pp. 624–646.

Duvignaud, J. (1973). *Fêtes et civilisations.* Paris, Weber.

Duvignaud, J. (1991). 1st publication 1977 *Le don du rien.* Arles, Actes Sud.

Felsenstein, D. and Fleisher A. (2003). Local festivals and tourism promotion: The role of public assistance and visitor expenditure. *Journal of Travel Research*, 41(4), pp. 385–392. https://doi.org/10.1177/0047287503041004007.

Girard, R. (2001). *Des choses cachées depuis la fondation du monde.* Paris, Grasset.

INE. (2017). Instituto Nacional de Estadística, Hostelería y Turismo http://www.ine.es/dyngs/INEbase/es/categoria.htm?c=Estadistica_P&cid=1254735576863.

Isambert, F.-A. (1982). *Le sens du sacré – Fête et religion populaire.* Paris, Editions de Minuit.

Jiménez Beltrán, J., López-Guzmán, T. and González Santa Cruz, F. (2016). Gastronomy and tourism: Profile and motivation of international tourism in the city of Córdoba, Spain. *Journal of Culinary Science & Technology*, 14(4), pp. 347–362. https://doi.org/10.1080/15428052.2016.1160017.

Lanquar, R. (2012). Le tourisme fait-il le bonheur des nations? *Espaces, Tourisme & Loisirs*, 307, pp. 31–35.

Morales, E. and Lanquar, R. (2014). El futuro turístico de una ciudad patrimonio de la humanidad: Córdoba 2031. Revista Encontros Cientifico. *Tourism and Management Studies*, 10(2), pp. 1–15.

Stankova, M. and Vassanka, I. (2015). Raising cultural awareness of local traditions through festival tourism. *Tourism & Management Studies*, 11(1), pp. 120–127.

Turismo de Córdoba. (2014). Plan Estratégico de Turismo de Córdoba 2015–2019, una publicación con la colaboración del EIO, del Ayuntamiento de Córdoba, del FEDER. http://www.turismodecordoba.org/84/gdocumental/l15_a42_c7/plan_estrategico_turismo_cordoba2015_2019.pdf.

Turismo de Córdoba Diputación de Córdoba (2013). Plan de desarrollo, promoción y comunicación de Córdoba.

7 Local food products as vectors of authentic tourism experiences

Marielle Salvador

1. Introduction

Tourists pursue activities that allow them to immerse themselves in the lives of the local people of a city or region to live authentic experiences. Local food products are an important part of this. As Arseneault and Bellerose (2016) state, "the more an experience allows [one] to be immersed in the local culture …, the more it is considered like an authentic experience … and this immersion includes the food: we want to eat local food." In management science, Cova and Cova (2002) and Camus (2003) emphasise this dominant aspect of imaginary authenticity as a means of rediscovering the roots that modern societies have put at risk. Local products are important for any region, and according to the World Tourism Organization (2012), local gastronomy accounts for one-third of expenditure during a tourist stay. Unlike localised products that may be labelled, local products including food make no explicit mention of their geographic origin (Merle and Piotrowski, 2012) and are distinguished by the proximity between their place of production and their place of consumption (Amilien, 2005), generally between eighty and one hundred km (Merle and Piotrowski, 2012). Local products including fresh produce, such as fruit, vegetables, and meats, or processed products, such as cheese and wine, are what consumers today look for. The 2014 IPSOS study found that for 51% of French respondents, local products are better-quality products. Consumers deem geographic proximity, the origin of the ingredients, and local production in the region as a reassurance in a context of suspicion towards the agro-food industry (Fischler, 1990; Poulain, 2001).

This chapter attempts to shed light on the links between tourism experience authenticity and local products through their quality characteristics. In our view, tourists identify these local products as genuine and help make their tourist experience feel authentic. If, as Camus (2014) states, the fundamental variable of tourism authenticity is the experience, the objective characteristics would seem less able to explain such authenticity than the experience itself. However, any tourism experience is above all an experience with places, objects, and people. Thus, we posit that certain objective characteristics of products are indicators of their authenticity and, as authentic objects, participate in rendering the tourism experience authentic.

This chapter is structured in three parts. The first part highlights the characteristics of local products through the notions of quality and typicity, emphasizing the importance of anchoring the local product in the place as a factor of identity. The second part, based on the results obtained from an exploratory study, presents the signals and attributes of quality most likely to be considered as indicators of authenticity for tourists. Finally, the third part considers local products as vectors of the authenticity of the tourism experience and suggests reconsidering certain positions related to authenticity in tourism, a subject under debate for several decades.

2. Identity and authenticity of the local product through quality and typicity characteristics

The local origin of a product is expressed through temporisation (history), spatialisation (territory), socialisation (local tribes and mediators), and naturalisation (materials and human gestures) (Cova and Cova, 2002). Local products hence have their own identity, and local origin helps make them singular and typical. Wine tasting uses the term "typicity," which refers to the complex notion of terroir, to indicate a wine that is typical of its geographic provenance and grape variety. Hence, typicity is the characteristic or distinctive nature of what is typical, of what constitutes originality. Indeed, Passebois-Ducros et al. (2012), citing the study of Symoneaux et al. (2010), reveal that for nonexpert consumers, the notion of typicity refers to the place of production only, whereas the more expert they become, the more the definition includes the sensory properties of the product. Nevertheless, this anchoring in a terroir provides the product with an identity, unlike those deriving from the agrofood industry that Fischler (1990) refers to as OCNI – a French acronym for unidentified edible objects. In a context of consumer-eater suspicion, local products strengthened by this identity recreate the link between the consumer and the producer but, above all, between the consumer and the product itself. Thus, the territorial origin of a product, which reassures consumers, is often indicated on the label with an *appellation d'origine controlee* (AOC) or an indication of source. These verify the local origin of the product and sometimes proof of its quality. However, AOC and the protected designation of origin (PDO) only identify the production in a given territory but are not a guarantee of quality. Although AOC was originally a guarantee of tradition and know-how, intensive production and the use of pesticides in many AOC vineyards are contrary to this representation (Garcia, 2015). Despite the changing legislative specifications, numerous winegrowers have abandoned this label to produce natural wines. Nevertheless, origin remains a sales argument and a means of differentiating in a highly competitive sector. For consumers, local anchoring of production represents small-scale agriculture associated with the guarantee of more flavourful products (Merle and

Piotrowski, 2012) and reassures on their freshness (Gallen, 2005), which are signals and attributes of quality.

In general, consumers formulate expectations and beliefs about the performance of a product that constitute the expected quality. According to Oude Ophuis and Van Trijp (1995), each product thus has quality cues that generate beliefs and quality attributes, which are the benefits perceived in its consumption. Perceived quality is an individual's judgment of the excellence of a product (Zeithaml, 1988) and is therefore subjective and has an evaluative and relative dimension (Oude Ophuis and Van Trijp, 1995). The individual infers the quality of the product from its intrinsic and extrinsic characteristics (Sirieix and Dubois, 1999). The product is considered as the sum of a set of attributes that satisfy consumer expectations. Behaviour in relation to a product is the result of a confrontation between the consumer's perception of the product (individual-object dimension) and expectations related to a purchasing context (personal dimension). Steenkamp (1989) developed a model that distinguishes quality cues from quality attributes (Ophuis Oude and Van Trijp, 1995). Quality cues are concrete characteristics of the product (intrinsic, such as the likely taste of a fruit deduced from its colour, or extrinsic, such as price) the senses identify before consumption. Quality attributes are the abstract benefits of the product that can only be experienced by the individual.

With regard to classification, D'Hauteville (2003) suggests that visual, tactile, or olfactory signals produce evocations belonging to the register of cognitive representations rather than taste judgments, and these signals are quality cues. Indeed, in a purchasing situation, since sensory information is rarely available, the individual makes a choice based on nonsensory information, such as a brand, price, packaging, or storytelling about the product. Similarly, the local characteristic of a product may be communicated to the consumer before consumption through storytelling, packaging, or by the place or conditions of purchase. In this context, if previously informed, the consumer will discover the local side. This characteristic falls within the category of quality cues as well as quality attributes. Although the local characteristic of the product is an attribute in the sense of Ophuis Oude and Van Trijp (1995), communication around and by the local product is also a signal of quality. Local products, with some attributes and quality signals referring to anchoring in the place, are therefore likely to evoke authenticity in individuals (Figure 7.1).

Local products with some attributes and quality signals that refer to anchoring in the place can evoke authenticity in individuals. Indeed, according to Beverland (2005), both origin and typicity create the authenticity of the product. Its local origin, which is a dimension of authenticity, constitutes the identity of the product but also participates in constructing the individual's identity according to the symbolic principle of incorporation, since "we are what we eat." As with other goods, food enables the individual to connect with their social roots while serving as sociocultural benchmarks (Belk, 1990).

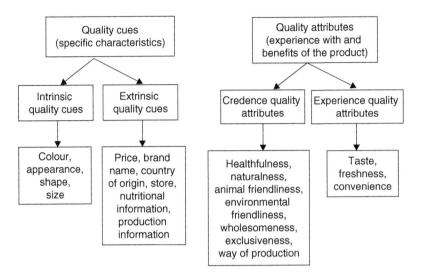

Figure 7.1 Quality cues and quality attributes

3. The local product with quality characteristics that indicate its authenticity

Camus (2003) defines authenticity as a product characteristic that connects it to an origin, that fills a gap or a dissatisfaction, and that is reinforced when the product represents a part of the consumer's identity. The author developed a scale to measure the perceived authenticity of products according to three dimensions: the origin of the product, its singularity, and the projection of the individual's values. Local products cover these three dimensions: produced in a distinct terroir, drawing its own originality, and in which individuals can project the values that are important to them (respect for seasonality, search for taste, support producers, regional identity, etc.). However, when local products lack any specific label, how does the individual tourist identify the authentic local product from amongst others? We suggest that the signals and attributes of quality of a product may constitute the signals and attributes of the authenticity of these products.

To verify this hypothesis, we carried out a qualitative exploratory study with fourteen individuals with semi-structured interviews at their place of work or at home following several experiences of buying and tasting local products during their holiday. The resondents varied in terms of age and sex. We established a guide around issues related to their search for and purchase of local products during their holiday, focusing on the signals and attributes of the quality of the local products best able to facilitate their choice. For the analysis of the collected data, we aggregated lexical units into themes and subthemes for each interview. We established a coding grid to synthesise the themes concerning the signals and attributes of the quality of local products and to ensure semantic saturation after the thirteenth interview. The first results of this study highlight that local products, through some of their signals and attributes of quality, are considered as products illustrating authenticity. However, whereas individuals' familiarity with local products in their region makes their search and purchasing relatively easy, other identification processes take place when they are on vacation.

3.1. The choice of a local product according to quality signals

In their quest for authentic local products, some interviewees referred to the creation of benchmarks via intrinsic signals of quality. According to one interviewee:

> Now, we know the difference between Espelette pepper of lesser quality that is going to be chopped, which will have this orange side that one can often see. While the one we found is small pieces of pepper with a much darker red colour, the colour that the pepper has when it dries.
>
> (Philippe)

For him, and after some experiences with the product, authentic Espelette pepper is now recognizable by its colour. Rarity, attributed to the quality of the product, is also discreetly evoked. Others, on the contrary, seem to prefer extrinsic quality cues, such as the place of sale of local products:

> When I am on vacation in Brittany I go to get the fish directly from the port, it is cooler.
>
> (Isabelle)

They seek a quality product and the distribution site is representative of this quality or the production origin. The local market is the place to find local products but also the place where the local culture can be discovered through meeting people and tastings:

> When we are on vacation, we like to go to local markets to find local products, the atmosphere, tasting, talking with people.
>
> (Geraldine)

While the place of purchase remains essential, the proximity of the product to its place of production is a guarantee of quality but also authenticity:

> Well the products from Toulouse I buy from among sellers who I know. The Tarbais beans I also buy in Toulouse, but on the other hand, Lyonnais products I will necessarily buy them in Lyon. I buy in the city where the product is located. It's part of the product's authenticity.
>
> (Arnaud)

Thus, while we can find a Beaufort cheese in Marseille today without the product's typicity being questioned, for some individuals the product would lose its property as a vector of authenticity if purchased outside its place of origin.

3.2. The choice of a local product according to quality attributes

Others create signals via intangible quality attributes, such as how the product is made:

> We went to a restaurant in Gers indicated by friends. The sommelier said to us, "If you like Armagnac, go to a place where the producer is the last one that makes everything using wood fire".
>
> (Benedicte)

There is no need for a label for a product manufactured according to the rules of the art, following ancestral know-how that a limited number of people still practice. Nevertheless, most respondents spoke of the tasting moments (tangible attribute) to obtain an idea of the quality of the product:

> We taste the product and we buy, and that is all in the spontaneity of the moment. For example, we had to go to Uzès and ended up in a market with wine producers and we could taste. It was not planned, but it was the moment.
>
> (Fabienne)

There were some attributes of quality that our respondents did not mention at all, including convenience or the environment. Similarly, the nutritional information and brand were never mentioned for local products purchased in the place of vacation. Unlike the place of purchase, country of origin or production information constituted important signals for our interviewees, such as the attributes of taste, freshness, or rarity. These quality cues and attributes therefore participate in the local product authentication process.

4. Local products, vectors of authenticity of the tourism experience

The previous section focused on the links between local products and their authenticity characteristics. Nevertheless, these products, as objects, represent a part of the tourism experience in the same way as the places visited. Indeed, experience is constituted as much by the appropriation of the place as the appropriation of the object (Roederer, 2012). Such appropriation is fundamental to making the experience memorable (Pine and Gilmore, 1999), and local products are directly involved in this appropriation. Thus, the tourist will appreciate "discovering and exploring the culture and history of a place through its food and related activities through the creation of memorable experiences" (Long, 1998). The tourist, whom Long (1998) describes as a culinary tourist, wants to have authentic experiences enabling them to capture "the spirit of the place" (Jacobs and Smits, 2007) through multiple activities, such as visits to local markets. Buying oil from a farm, visiting the factory where Armagnac is distilled in a wood-fired still, or buying the country's specialty are some examples illustrating how local products contribute to the authenticity of the tourism experience. Product search, discovery, tasting, and buying can all be authentic tourism experiences in the sense of consumer experience theory, including the setting, the intrigue around a product, and an action between the individual and the product (Filser, 2002) through purchasing or tasting.

> Like a guy at the market who will tell you the history of his production, his wine, his sausages, and you feel that it is something that is anchored in the local history.
>
> (Romain)

MacCannell (1973) introduced the concept of authenticity in the sociology of tourism in 1973. Since then, many scholars have studied tourists' quest for authenticity (Wang, 1999). However, the term remains ambiguous both for sociologists and tourism anthropologists (Cravatte, 2009). Some authors (Mac-Cannell, 1976; Harkin, 1995) emphasise the authenticity of feelings tourists experience and the authenticity they attribute to the countries and places visited (Hamon, 2005). The individual searches for "references to an imaginary situated in ancient times or in the exotic" (Warnier, 1994), whether through leisure activities or through the consumption of products. In this sense, the interest in local food in recent years is a perfect illustration. Wang (1999), citing Berger (1973), explains the concept of existential authenticity to describe this search for an ideal or a "special state of Being in which one is true to oneself, and acts as a counterdose to the loss of 'true self'". Rosselin (1994) identifies authenticity as a process of rupture. These quests for naturalness, terroir, and tradition would seem to underpin the desire to break with a daily life that no longer satisfies individuals cut off from their roots. This other exists in the individual or collective imaginary past of individuals. For Cova and Cova (2002), "the quest for post-modern authenticity is seen as a rediscovery of the local and the imagination it carries." The tourist seeks the authentic self (Brown, 1999), a "good time" to satisfy their hedonistic inclinations. Yet, this "good time" can be inauthentic, and authenticity can be staged to satisfy this need for hedonism. MacCannell (1973) explains that tourists, due to their lack of knowledge of the host country, cannot realise these stagings and therefore cannot distinguish the authentic from the inauthentic. Our study moderates these remarks in the field of food products. Indeed, individuals seem quite capable of identifying authentic local products based on the quality attributes and signals. Authenticity is the result of individual and social constructions, depending on the spatial context

(Wang, 1999; Camus, 2014), and is therefore constructive authenticity. According to Gilmore and Pine (2007), the authenticity of an offer depends on how people perceive the world. Thus, even if the object is only imaginary or a reconstruction, it can be perceived as authentic because it preserves a social, cultural, or natural heritage (Camus, 2014), which suggests that such an object possesses characteristics.

Thus, if the authenticity of an experience is relative and contextually determined (Salamone, 1997), and the definition of an authentic object may differ and depends on the age and gender of individuals, then the references are not always the same (Goulding, 2000). The tourism experience depends on the place, but also on the objects that have the objective characteristics of authenticity. Thus, while for Camus (2014), "authenticity seems less to be explained by objective characteristics than by experience produced and lived," we nuance this point of view, considering that the tourism experience integrates objects and food products. Indeed, according to Heinich (1999), "Authenticity is not authentic without an authentication procedure." Warnier (1994) specifies that these procedures are broadly understood, since they can cover labels that "certify that the product is of undoubted origin, is not an imitation and is authoritative because of the legal forms of which it is invested" (Camus, 2007). Other procedures that can signal authenticity include expert opinions, packaging, or distinctive product storytelling.

We have shown that local products, even in the absence of official certification but intrinsically anchored in a place, can be authenticated by individuals via some quality signals and attributes. Thus, the tourist experience – consisting of a setting, an intrigue, and an action – may contain objective elements of authenticity, such as local products. Indeed, individual variables, such as the level of involvement or level of expertise with respect to food products, may introduce a level of variance into our analysis, but objective characteristics exist in the authenticity of the tourist experience. Thus, if the authenticity of the experience as a function of the consumed object is authentic, then the tourism experience will also be authentic.

However, individuals are suspicious of "copies":

> In Perpignan, there are many people who sell fruits and vegetables along the road, and I prefer asking someone at a café because sometimes we have doubts, I'm not sure it always comes from local production, if people tell me they know someone and they say OK you can go, otherwise I prefer not to buy.
>
> (Yann)

Here, the signals and attributes of product quality are not enough. The authentication process according to Yann depends on a person living in the place. The relationship with local people is a means of overcoming the mistrust inherent in the commercial dimension of the authentic tourism experience. Indeed, literature shows that the difficulty of reconciling the gap between authenticity and the commercial dimension (Camus, 2003) can be reduced by the experience lived with the product through the scenery, the intrigue, and the relationship between the individual and the product (Filser, 2002). Insofar as the quest for postmodern authenticity in the sense of Cova and Cova (2002) entails rediscovering the local, it is clear that local food products play a major role. This is a question of "living the product" – not only eating it but impregnating itself through its terroir, its history; symbolically, to eat the place and live an authentic tourism experience. It is the symbolism of food, as Gallen (2005) emphasises, whereby the individual does not buy a food product to feed themselves but rather for what it represents. The local product represents the proximity with the place that one seeks to discover, to know better. Tasting a local product is to "taste the place," a way to imbibe it. For our interviewees, it represents the authenticity that they aspire to on their holiday. By appropriating the local product manufactured nearby, they take possession of the place symbolically and simultaneously transform the tourism experience into an authentic and memorable one.

5. Conclusion

Finally, if authenticity is not a stable characteristic, it is nevertheless a current demand among tourists, perceived through their social activities and interactions as well as through objects. In this context, the local product is a vector of the authenticity of the tourism experience. In the absence of official product certification, individuals create their own authentication procedures. Local products, because they are anchored in a territory, carry signals and attributes of quality, some of which are elements of authentication for tourists. Thus, the quest for authenticity of the tourism experience passes through the local products, and these play an active role as elements of such authenticity. Local products carefully selected from amongst others will then be perceived as the "true," the most authentic, local product. Hence, tasting activities, but above all, search, discovery, and purchasing, help individuals take ownership of not only the product but also the place, helping to make the experience memorable. It is therefore ultimately both the presumed authenticity of the object and the experience lived that make the tourism experience authentic.

This exploratory study should be continued to clarify these initial conclusions. Nevertheless, we can suggest some managerial guidelines for local producers and tourism operators to enhance the authenticity of their territory through local products. First, this study confirms the importance of gastronomy in tourism activities through meeting with producers – for example, visiting manufacturing sites and participating in workshops. However, while some local and regional tourism operators have created some gourmet roads, they suffer from, amongst other things, lack of communication. Second, these initial results highlight that it is less a question of official labels or other mentions than letting the consumer create their own idea. The signal sent by the place of sale is the first that must be retained. On the other hand, information on manufacturing is important, as is direct contact with an expert (real or perceived). With increasing demand for these products insofar as individuals seek to satisfy their quest for authenticity, communication must be a priority. Smaller producers are generally considered as producers of authentic products, products that will sometimes be taken back home, constituting memories that will extend the experience lived.

References

Amilien, V. (2005). A propos de produits locaux. Préface. *Anthropology of Food*, 4 May. https://journals.openedition.org/aof/306.

Arseneault, P. and Bellerose, P. (2016). *Dix tendances touristiques à l'aube de 2020*. Chaire de tourisme Transat ESG Université du Québec UQAM. https://chairedetourisme. uqam.ca/upload/files/10_tendances_tourisme_horizon_2020.pdf.

Belk, R.W. (1990). The role of possessions in constructing and maintaining a sense of past. *Advances in Consumer Research*, 17, pp. 669–676.

Berger, P. (1973). "Sincerity" and "authenticity" in modern society. *Public Interest*, 31, pp. 469–485.

Beverland, M.B. (2005). Crafting brand authenticity: The case of luxury wine. *Journal of Management Studies*, 42(5), pp. 1003–1029.

Brown, D. (1999). Des faux authentiques, tourisme versus pèlerinage. *Revue Terrains*, 33, Sept, pp. 41–56.

Camus, S. (2003). *L'authenticité marchande perçue et la persuasion de la communication par l'authentification: Une application au domaine alimentaire*. Thèse de doctorat, Dijon: Université de Bourgogne, http://www.theses.fr/2003DIJOE006.

Camus, S. (2007), La marque authentique et l'expérience de consommation, *Actes des Journées de recherche en marketing de Bourgogne*, pp. 29–44

Camus, S. (2014). L'authenticité et l'expérience dans le champ du patrimoine immatériel touristique. In Vlergeau, C. and Spindler, J. (ed) *L'immatériel touristique*. Paris: L'Harmattan, pp. 93–120

Cova, B. and Cova, V. (2002). Les particules expérientielles de la quête d'authenticité du consommateur. *Décisions Marketing*, 28, pp. 33–42.

Cravatte, C. (2009). L'anthropologie du tourisme et l'authenticité, Catégorie analytique ou catégorie indigène? *Cahier d'Etudes Africaines*, vol.193-194, n° 1/2, pp. 1–2, 193–194, 603–620.

D'Hauteville, F. (2003). Processus sensoriels et préférence gustative: Apports de la recherche expérimentale au marketing agroalimentaire. *Revue Française du Marketing*, 194(4/5), pp. 13–27.

Filser, M. (2002). Le marketing de la production d'expérience: Statut théorique et implications managériales. *Décisions Marketing*, 28, pp. 13–22.

Fischler, C. (1990). *L'homnivore*. Paris: Odile Jacob.

Gallen, C. (2005). Le rôle des représentations mentales dans le processus de choix, une approche pluridisciplinaire appliquée au cas des produits alimentaires. *Recherche et Applications en Marketing*, 20(3), pp. 59–76.

Garcia, M.F. (2015), Vin: l'AOC un peu bouchonnée, http://www.liberation.fr/soci ete/2015/04/16/vin-l-aoc-un-peu-bouchonnee_1243274.

Gilmore, J.H. and Pine, J. (2007). *Authenticity. What consumers really want*. Boston: HSB Press.

Goulding, C. (2000). The commodification of the past, postmodern pastiche, and the search for authentic experiences at contemporary heritage attractions. *European Journal of Marketing*, 34(7), pp. 835–853.

Hamon, V. (2005). Authenticité, tourisme durable et marketing. *Revue Espaces*, 228, pp. 42–56.

Harkin, M. (1995). Modernist anthropology and tourism of the authentic. *Annals of Tourism Research*, 22, pp. 650–670.

Heinich, N. (1999). Art contemporain et fabrication de l'inauthentique. *Terrain*, 33, pp. 5–18.

Jacobs, H. and Smits, F. (2007). Le tourisme culinaire: Un fort marqueur territorial. L'exemple du Canada. *Actes des 6èmes Rencontres de Mâcon "Tourismes et territoires"*, 13-15 Sept.

Long, L. (1998). Culinary tourism, eating and otherness. *Southern Folklore*, 55(3), pp. 181–204.

MacCannell, D. (1973). Staged authenticity: Arrangements of social space in tourist settings. *American Journal of Sociology*, 79(3), pp. 589–603.

MacCannell, D. (1976). *The tourist. A new theory of the leisure class*. New York, Schocken.

Merle, A. and Piotrowski, M. (2012). Consommer des produits alimentaires locaux: Comment et pourquoi? *Décisions Marketing*, 67, pp. 37–48.

Ophuis Oude, P. and Van Trijp, H.C.M. (1995). Perceived quality: A market driven and consumer oriented approach. *Food Quality and Preference*, 6(3), pp. 177–183.

Passebois-Ducros. J., Trinquecoste, J.F. and Viot, C. (2012). De l'influence du jugement de typicalité des étiquettes sur le jugement de typicité d'un vin: Une application aux vins de Bordeaux. *11th International Marketing Trends Conference*, Venise, 19–21 janvier.

Pine, B.J., II and Gilmore, J.H. (1999). *The experience economy*. Boston, Harvard Business School Press.

Poulain, J.P. (2001). *Manger aujourd'hui. Attitudes, normes et pratiques*. Toulouse, Editions Privat.

Roederer, C. (2012). *Marketing et consommation expérientiels*. Editions EMS Management & Société, Paris.

Rosselin, C. (1994). La Matérialité de l'Objet et l'Approche Dynamique-Instrumentale, dans J.P. Warnier (1994). *Le Paradoxe de la Marchandise Authentique. Imaginaire et Consommation de Masse*. Paris, l'Harmattan, pp. 145–170.

Salamone, F.A. (1997). Authenticity in tourism: The San Angels Inns. *Annals of Tourism Research*, 24, pp. 305–321.

Sirieix, L. and Dubois, P.L. (1999). Vers un modèle qualité-satisfaction intégrant la confiance? *Recherche et Applications en Marketing*, 14(3), pp. 1–22.

Steenkamp, J.B.E.M. (1989). *Product quality*. Herndon, (VA), Books International.

Symoneaux R., Perrin, L., Wilson, D., Maitre, I. and Jourjon, F. (2010). La typicité sensorielle des vins d'appellation: Comment la mesurer avec les professionnels, comment l'aborder avec les consommateurs? *Qualité et Environnement*, 142, pp. 94–101.

Wang, N. (1999). Rethinking authenticity in tourism experience. *Annals of Tourism Research*, 26(2), pp. 349–370.

Warnier, J.P. (1994). *Le paradoxe de la marchandise authentique. Imaginaire et consommation de masse*. Paris, l'Harmattan, pp. 145–170.

World Tourism Organization (2012), Second Global Report on Gastronomy Tourism, http://cf.cdn.unwto.org/sites/all/files/pdf/gastronomy_report_web.pdf.

Zeithaml, V.A. (1988). Consumer perceptions of price, quality and value: A means-end model and synthesis of evidence. *Journal of Marketing*, 52(3), pp. 2–22.

Part II

The link between quality and diversity

8 From entrepreneurship to local development by a central actor or the dynamics of the links between quality and diversity

The example of the Longjing Caotang restaurant in Zhejiang Province, China

Olivier Etcheverria

1. Introduction

In *The New Yorker* of 24 November 2008, the journalist Fuchsia Dunlop described her discovery of the Longjing Caotang restaurant in Hangzhou, China, as follows:

> One day in September, I joined the Chinese restaurateur Dai Jianjun for a foraging expedition on a remote mountainside in Zhejiang Province.... In an age of industrialization, dire pollution, and frequent food scares, the Dragon Well Manor is committed to offering its guests a kind of prelapsarian Chinese cuisine. Dai assures them that everything he serves will be made from natural ingredients, untainted by pesticides or melamine, and with no added MSG. Each morning, his buyers drive out into the countryside to collect the best of the season's produce.... He had read the work of Yuan Mei, China's Brillat-Savarin, an eighteenth-century scholar-gentleman who abandoned his career as an imperial bureaucrat to retire to Nanjing, where he designed his own garden and wrote a seminal cookbook, "Food Lists of the Garden of Contentment."... Dai decided that his restaurant would have the kind of Hangzhou dishes that Yuan Mei would have enjoyed, prepared with local ingredients according to the theories of Chinese medicine and the solar terms of the old agricultural calendar.

These extracts indicate that the Longjing Caotang restaurant can be seen as a local agricultural and rural development tool at different scalar levels in Zhejiang Province. Indeed, with this visionary entrepreneurial project and the unique philosophy of life and solidarism of its owner Dai Jianjun, this commercial establishment has become one of the sources of socioeconomic vitality in the Longjing Tea Garden area and particularly in the Waijilongshan rural district, where the restaurant is located. However, the effects of the

Longjing Caotang restaurant on local agricultural and rural development are not only visible in the area surrounding the restaurant. Indeed, they have spread 270 km southwest to the village of Suichang, where in 2009, Dai Jianjun created the Gonggeng Shuyuan school-farm that has revitalised one of the most devastated and impoverished areas in Zhejiang Province. As such, this geographically isolated hamlet, Huangniling, which is only accessible by boat, is characterised today by its resistance to the rural exodus, the original social use of its territory, and its recent modernisation.

This chapter analyses the role that Dai Jianjun has played and the importance of his Longjing Caotang restaurant in the dynamics of local agricultural and rural development in Zhejiang Province in China. Dai Jianjun's visionary entrepreneurial strategy, philosophy of life, and solidarism are reflected in the geographic spread of activities, skills, discourses, and imaginaries, with a qualitative aim based on managing the local diversity. The underlying hypothesis is that Dai Jianjun is a central actor capable of encouraging the conditions required to drive local agricultural and rural development. According to Brunet et al. (1992: 95) in "Les Mots de la géographie. Dictionnaire critique," centrality is defined as the "ownership of what is in the centre, or what is a centre" – the centre being a "point around which phenomena are distributed in space" or a "place of decision-making and power." The authors go on to explain that, "This meaning nevertheless has a spatial dimension in geography: we therefore designate the space where people and activities related to domination are most concentrated (places of real power, company head offices, activities with high added-value)." The centre is considered as a point crossed by centripetal and centrifugal forces. The theory of "central places," developed by the geographer Walter Christaller (1932) as applied to Bavaria and by the economist August Lösch (1940: 300), "exploits an implication of the law of gravitation: the condensation of centres in their levels and the regularity of their theoretical spacing." Dai Jianjun can be seen as a key personality because he has qualities, roles, and "central" values. In his Longjing Caotang restaurant, he has developed and geographically spread the "central" functions of command, coordination, and control over the rural areas near the restaurant and up to 270 km away. He directs, structures, and prioritises activities, knowledge and ideas, and the skills of several thousand small farmers. This original, specific, and specialised concentration of skills, knowledge, ideas, powers, discourses, and imaginaries explain his visionary and strongly anchored management ability to boost and value producers with a quality focus based on managing local diversity. Thus, his scope of influence has multiple effects in terms of agricultural and rural development visible at different scalar levels and spreading out from his restaurant.

For our analysis, we used a participative methodology, meeting Dai Jianjun and Zhu Yinfeng, head of the Gonggeng Shuyuan school-farm, in June 2016. Our meetings were also an opportunity to discover the typical dishes and recipes of the Zhejiang cuisine both at the Longjing Caotang restaurant over a banquet with Dai Jianjun and at a dinner prepared and shared with Zhu

Yinfeng during our stay at the Gonggeng Shuyuan school-farm. Also in June 2016, we conducted interviews with producers and tourism, hotel, and restaurant stakeholders to identify their real and ideal relationships with Dai Jianjun, the restaurant, the school-farm, and their local connections. These field interviews were aimed at providing an understanding of the spatial, socioeconomic, and cultural benefits the Longjing Caotang restaurant has had on local development in rural areas, *in situ*, and 270 km southwest.

2. At the scale level of the Longjing Caotang restaurant: qualitatively develop and orient the mainly local jobs and promote high-level training in local catering

2.1. A restaurant as a showcase for the local area

The Longjing Caotang restaurant, which Dai Jianjun built in 2004, is to the north of West Lake, around ten km from the city of Hangzhou in China's Zhejiang Province. Hangzhou, the former capital of the Song dynasty, has been recognised for centuries as a sophisticated city that has attracted poets and painters. Set in this area of urban influence, the restaurant is in a polarised rural sector. More specifically, the restaurant is situated in the Longjing ("Dragon Well") Green Tea Garden, which is today the most famous of its type in China. It was built on the site of a disused and mortgaged small-plant nursery by the Hangzhou Municipality in the Waijilongshan rural district. Surrounded by hills planted with tea trees, the Longjing Caotang restaurant includes a set of dining rooms spread around the Yuanlin garden, which means a garden set out in the style of the Song dynasty.

The word-for-word translation of Longjing Caotang is the "Longjing Rice Straw House." The second meaning of Caotang is "an educated person's hidden house." The layout of the garden ensures the aesthetic visual link between the restaurant and the surrounding landscape of tea plants.

Eight dining rooms decorated in the Song architectural style are spread around the 1.2-hectare park full of rock gardens, artificial islands, and shrub- and tree-planted borders. The restaurant consists of four individually themed rooms: Qin (a musical instrument), Qi (a game of chess), Shu (calligraphy), and Hua (painting); these four arts are skills supposedly developed by educated, distinguished, and refined individuals. There are three major reception rooms named after prominent officials: Zhuxi (Mao Zedong, head of state), Enlai (Zhou Enlai, prime minister), and Zhu De (chief of staff in the People's Army of China, 1949–1976). Finally, there is the Kurong pavilion ("rise and fall/ honour and shame"). The layout of the buildings adheres to the principles of yin-yang theory.

A quality approach characterizes the interior decoration of the dining rooms. The restaurant's reception is furnished in the Hui style, one of the best-known building techniques in southeast China. Calligraphy and paintings are widely used. These are the mediums for philosophical discussions and imaginary related to Confucianism, Taoism, and Buddhism. However, the pavilions have doors leading outside, thus visually ensuring they maintain a relationship and sense of harmony between the inside and outside. The floor in the dining rooms is made of green bricks. The tables and chairs are made of wood in the Ming style. The crockery and chopsticks were especially made to order from the kilns in Jingdezhen, the well-known porcelain-producing city and former home of the imperial porcelain administration.

The decoration of the plaster takes its inspiration from Shanshui paintings, landscapes accompanied by calligraphic inscriptions on rocks, trees, or any other geographic element. Finally, the toothpick boxes invite customers to learn about the solar food period corresponding to the day of the meal with the Jieqi system, consisting of twenty-four periods of fifteen days (Table 8.1). The total seating capacity is thirty to forty. The fixed menu is printed in the shape of a fan, and the wine list is modelled on a book from the Qin dynasty (bamboo tablets tied together with cotton thread).

A former civil servant with the Hangzhou Municipality, Dai Jianjun grew up locally. He relied on his local social network to help set up the restaurant. From the outset, Dai Jianjun has offered a range of carefully selected, high-quality catering services based on the promotion and culinary use of local, fresh, and farm-sourced agricultural products. The menu combines a rediscovery of ancient recipes and a revitalisation of Zhejiang cuisine, which is one of eight main Chinese cooking styles. (These are subdivided into four other branches – Hangzhou, Ningbo, Shaoxing, and Wenzhou – and include more than 240 dishes.)

Searching for local products and iconic recipes from Zhejiang Province, long regarded as *the* "rice and fish region," Dai Jianjun rediscovered a cookery book called "Various delights from the Sui Villa," written by Yuan Mei in 1792 (during the Qing dynasty), in which the culinary know-how, recipes, and methods for choosing and cooking Zhejiang's agricultural food products are recorded.

The shede dish (Figure 8.1), which means "abundant" in Chinese, is made only from the central part of a stalk-growing vegetable. Making a dish for four people requires around fifteen kilograms of whole plants. These tender and tasty stalks are cooked in chicken broth. Dai Jianjun also encourages his chefs to develop their creativity by reinventing iconic dishes such as dongpo pork, in which the meat is replaced by an almost forgotten local variety of squash, in this case the waxy squash. As such, for the su ("vegetal" in Chinese) dongpo (Figure 8.2), the waxy squash is cooked very slowly in a soy sauce. According to Dai Jianjun, his chefs are more skilled in discovering menu ideas than creating them.

One of the characteristic dishes served in the second half of June (at the summer solstice) is the salty and bitter duck soup: Jinchan yinling (Figure 8.3). This soup is prepared using old farmyard ducks from the Shaoxing region in Zhejiang province. The birds are salted and rubbed with ginger, then placed in a porcelain pot along with Jinchan cicadas (Figure 8.3), usually used in

Table 8.1 The Jieqi system

Period	Date	Name
1	04/02	The start of spring
2	19/02	Rain water
3	05/03	Animals waking from hibernation
4	21/03	Spring equinox
5	05/04	Clear and shiny
6	20/04	Rain for producing cereals
7	06/05	The start of summer
8	21/05	A little fattening
9	06/06	Grain beard (protecting the wheat kernel)
10	21/06	Summer solstice
11	07/07	A slight warmth
12	23/07	A hot period
13	07/08	The start of autumn
14	23/08	In heat
15	08/09	White dew
16	23/09	Autumn equinox
17	08/10	Cold dew
18	23/10	Frost falling
19	07/11	The start of winter
20	22/11	Light snow
21	07/12	Heavy snow
22	22/12	Winter solstice
23	06/01	A slight cold
24	20/01	A big freeze

medicine. The cooking process is achieved by slow steaming the mixture; it takes four to five hours. The resulting broth develops a strong, bitter taste and is deemed energizing.

The menus vary daily, depending on available ingredients, and scrupulously follow the twenty-four solar periods set out in the Jieqi system. The dishes come from the Zhejiang cuisine characterised by the extraordinary diversity of its agricultural food products.

2.2. A restaurant that boosts the local sphere of work, employment, and income

The restaurant provides benefits that translate into work, employment, and primary or secondary income. The existence and running of the restaurant effectively imply both theoretical and real needs in terms of workforce – it technically needs the local population (Mathieu, 1995). In addition to these

Figure 8.1 Shede dish

Figure 8.2 Su Dongpo dish

Figure 8.3 Jinchan yinling soup (with Jinchan cicadas in the bowl)

permanent jobs, the apprenticeships offered correspond to Dai Jianjun's training and qualification obligations.

Around twenty-five cooks and forty serving staff work daily at the Longjing Caotang restaurant. The vast majority of employees are local and come from the Zhejiang and Jiangsu provinces. The chef, for example, was born in Hangzhou and has worked for Dai Jianjun since the day the restaurant opened. In this way, Dai Jianjun tries to promote an image of local initiative.

Employees acquire new skills, knowledge, and know-how by working for the company. For example, the chefs learn how to prepare dishes with organically grown agricultural products, discovering a wide variety of plants and animal breeds, cooking without using any artificial colouring or monosodium glutamate. The chefs undertake a second and particularly demanding professional apprenticeship at the Longjing Caotang restaurant. The restaurant is conducive to the development of the chefs' personal tastes. In fact, the recipes listed in the book "Various delights from the Sui Villa" are not very precise. They refer to "a little salt and pepper" or "a little broth." This means that the chefs must vary the seasoning according to the intrinsic characteristics of the product, the season, the variety, the race and their own sensitivity. Innovation is not, however, excluded from the process and, as such, the chefs and Dai Jianjun work together each season to create new dishes.

Likewise, the serving staff are encouraged to develop their personality and build close and responsive relationships with the diners. The training of serving staff, who are responsible for encouraging customers with gastronomic advice and imaginary, enables not only their intellectual and cultural development, but also that of diners who come to feed their bodies just as much as their minds. They must effectively explain and transmit the values of this local and simple cuisine, which is both popular and peasant in origin, but served at high prices. Among this advice and imaginary, the themes of diversity, seasonality, and a return to nature are key. The "beautiful nature" idea is essential here, and as such, the desire to aestheticise the taste, comparable to the technique of Michel Bras in Laguiole, for example (Etcheverria and Bras, 2004; Etcheverria, 2011a, 2011b).

With regard to vocational training, Dai Jianjun plays a role in awarding his chefs and serving staff high-level qualifications. In 2008, he established a partnership with the Institute of Tourism at Beihai University, which aims to promote lifelong learning and guarantees the recruitment of qualified staff.

Dai Jianjun describes the organisation of his business using the image of a tree: "Like the roots, the boss may be present but sometimes absent, so the managers are the trunk to hold everything together, the employees are the leaves, and finally the customers are the clouds." Dai Jianjun is therefore directly concerned with the individual development and personal fulfilment of his employees. He demands a great deal from them, but at the same time he wants to promote confidence and self-esteem in line with paying higher salaries than usually offered in the hotel and catering sector in China. Hence, Dai Jianjun never publishes a job offer and never creates a job description; he builds together with employees, according to their individuality and personality, the framework of the post related to their skills and his needs. Dai Jianjun seeks to develop the spirit of initiative, a taste for quality, and respect for nature (and the seasons).

3. At the scale level of the restaurant's catchment area: stimulate and revitalise local agriculture with qualitative objectives

In "Pour une agriculture marchande et ménagère," Edgar Pisani and the Seillac Group (1994: 67) stress that,

> Not only for ethical reasons, although these are sufficient, but for reasons related to changes in thoughts and attitudes: yesterday's consumers paid little attention to the ways in which the food arriving on their plates was produced; it is and will be less and less so; farmers must be convinced of this: organoleptic and organic quality will be growing in importance year on year.

In China, a first issue is that of food safety for agricultural products (the biological quality that Edgar Pisani refers to). To qualitatively promote the development of local agriculture, Dai Jianjun coordinates and guides several thousand producers in the restaurant's catchment area. The agricultural development project is based on enhancing the idea of proximity, the management of diversity, the respect for seasonality, and the quest for complementarity in supply among the small local producers with whom he works.

In Chinese, *yuan* means origin, and much of Dai Jianjun's emphases revolve around this concept. He prioritises *yuanshengtai* agricultural products (*shengtai* means ecology), which therefore come from organic or biodynamic agriculture. His central objective is the management of local diversity by reintroducing animal breeds (yellow huangzhongji chickens from Xiaoshan, for example) and varieties of fruit and vegetables (soy, for example) that have gradually been abandoned because they are not productive enough. The challenges are on the one hand the reappropriation of a local taste identity known as *yuankouwei* (*kouwei* means taste/natural taste) and on the other hand, the dynamisation of human exchanges based on *yuanzhumin* (*zhumin* means local/village).

Agricultural food products are delivered daily to the restaurant thanks to this diverse and extensive network of producers. Under the control of Mr. Zhou, who is responsible for purchasing, the registers record (Figure 8.4a and 8.4b) the names and details of the market gardeners, breeders, and freshwater fishermen, who must always sign their names when they deliver their farmed produce to the restaurant.

Figures 8.4a and 8.4b Register indicating the variety or breed, information on the producer, geographic location, weight or quantity

Figures 8.4a and 8.4b (Continued.)

In addition, Dai Jianjun and his team regularly invite producers to present their products and production techniques to diners, normally in each of the twenty-four seasons in the Jieqi system. This allows the producers to develop by selling their products to the Longjing Caotang restaurant, which therefore helps in the construction-reconstruction of the local taste identity. The small producers involved in Dai Jianjun's local development project survive because their farmed produce is bought at a fair and realistic price.

The work of Pisani and the Seillac Group (1994) demonstrates the relevance and efficiency of a "market and household agriculture" system, thanks to which people no longer refer to reductions in the number of jobs and exodus, but to concepts of initiative, renewal, and diversification. Dai Jianjun's qualitative strategy helps to boost/revitalise subsistence farming, which is both job-creating (or job-maintaining) and lucrative.

Indeed, Dai Jianjun considers it essential on the one hand to link quality, diversity, and health, and on the other, ensure fair remuneration for the farmers in his network. Pisani and the Seillac Group (1994: 107) insist that:

> They clearly forgot that up until a certain time, really quite recently, any farm was 'naturally' market- and household-orientated, productive and market-garden based. It is the opening of markets, but especially the explosion in the range of techniques and activities that has upset this balance. We need to return to and re-establish this concept, as well as amplify, identify, and compensate the farmer for his work in his non-producing activities.

Each product on the menu comes from organic farming and is local, seasonal, highly flavoured, healthy, clean, and strictly recorded. In the restaurant team, six employees are involved in sourcing and purchasing. They generally ensure long-term cooperation between the various parties. All the producers sign a contract and undertake to comply with the guidelines drawn up by Dai Jianjun, who reserves the right to refuse products if they are unsatisfactory.

As such, for ten years, Dai Jianjun has developed a number of long-term partnerships with around 16,000[1] producers in Zhejiang Province who daily deliver products that may vary.

And yet, these partnerships have required Dai Jianjun and his team to learn new techniques and methods. They have had to introduce a qualitative approach, giving priority to ethically raised animals and plant varieties that taste good. He has also spread the idea that smaller products are both tastier and worth more.

Finally, laying the foundations of a philosophy for urban-rural relations, Dai Jianjun believes that by visiting his restaurant, the urban population must finance the development of a form of agriculture with qualitative objectives and the desire to maintain the diversity of rural areas.

This qualitative type of agriculture is organic. Producers in Zhejiang (and in China generally) do not know much about organic farming. Thanks to Dai Jianjun, who is self-trained, they are discovering and acquiring skills, knowledge, and know-how related to agriculture that respects the land, water, plant and animal diversity, production areas, and the taste of products grown there. Finally, they are learning to respect themselves and all the diners they feed through their products. This agriculture requires a learning curve and the acquisition of skills, as well as new methods and reflections.

Local development is therefore accessible and receptive in terms of income, agricultural knowledge, and know-how, but also rural jobs.

4. At the scale level of the province: encourage people to stay or stimulate a return to the countryside, change and spread new practices linking quality and diversity

The Gonggeng Shuyuan school-farm was set up in 2009 in the hamlet of Huangniling (with nine hundred inhabitants) linked to Suichang Village, 270 km southwest of Hangzhou and considered one of the most overlooked and impoverished villages in Zhejiang Province. Totally isolated, the village has witnessed a huge rural exodus, and the area is covered with abandoned farmland.

The school-farm is at the centre of a group of thirty-five families (about one hundred inhabitants who all have the same surname). One of the six restaurant employees in charge of supply and purchasing discovered this difficult-to-reach village (you have to cross a lake by boat to reach the hamlet of Huangniling) while searching for good chickens. After several visits, Dai Jianjun decided to create his school-farm there based on three factors: the land and air are unpolluted, the hamlet contains a source of particularly pure spring water (it is the source of two rivers, the Qiantang and the Ou), and the penniless local inhabitants needed his help.

The school-farm was built in the same style and according to the same principles of yin-yang theory as the Longjing Caotang restaurant. It consists of:

- a hotel with a few rooms where Dai Jianjun's friends and visitors, such as journalists and researchers, are housed
- several equipped meeting rooms
- a kitchen
- three dining rooms
- an experimental farm

The experimental farm aims to conserve and rediscover the local flora and fauna diversity and to train local inhabitants in techniques related to qualitative agriculture. *Gonggeng Shuyuan* means a "school where you learn to undertake agricultural activities together." It is here that Dai Jianjun and his eleven farm employees produce their crops (traditional varieties of glutinous rice and late-season rice, for example) and their farm animals (rice-fed poultry, for example) in an area consisting of rice paddies (ten mu^2), orchards, vegetable gardens (six mu) and terraced tea-oil gardens. The cultural model is that of permaculture. The farm is 100% organic and is directly involved in supplying the restaurant with rice, tea-oil, chicken, pork, eggs, etc. Agricultural experiments help revive the production of endangered agricultural products that may not be very productive or are seen as too difficult to produce. Such a project has helped save yellow Xiaolin ginger (Figure 8.5), of which there remained only one producer. They have now restarted production by signing contracts with five young producers. These specific agricultural food products are characterised by Pisani and the Seillac Group (1994: 96) in the following way:

> They occupy an ever growing space in the markets and on the tables of the consumers. And they still do so today despite the crisis. They become one of the symbols of societal evolution. They are infinitely diverse, and it would be pointless to try and count them. There are old classics like certain wines or cheeses. There are others which have developed to become sought-after products while before they were simply by-products. There are some that sold at the market direct from the farm and others that are only sold after spending time in the cellar or in the kitchen.

On the one hand, Dai Jianjun tries to keep the farmers in the hamlet from being attracted to the city of Hangzhou, where they hope to find jobs and better lives. The Gonggeng Shuyuan school-farm therefore has a very close relationship with the families living in the Huangniling hamlet. On the other hand, as soon as he moved to the village, Dai Jianjun set up a project to rejuvenate the numerous agricultural plots of land abandoned by farmers who had left for the city. He either leases their land for a certain sum based on the

Figure 8.5 Yellow Xiaolin ginger

sharecropping mode or encourages a return to the land by paying those farmers interested in this project. He gives them a monthly salary of around 1,800 yuan, which is equivalent to the income they could get from working in the city. In so doing, these farmers are able to rediscover their roots, their homes, and their families, while no longer needing to pay rent and bear the extra costs associated with life in the city.

Thanks to the Longjing Caotang restaurant that serves as a showcase and embassy, Dai Jianjun has launched an initiative to boost the rearing of a local breed of chicken. Not only are the chickens appreciated in the restaurant where they are served, but this project has also helped develop a new trade in quality, fresh, organically produced and tasty Huangniling eggs, which are sold at prices well above the usual market rates. As a result, Dai Jianjun has successfully created the "Huangniling Egg" trademark.

Ten women are also employed on the estate and provide housekeeping and administrative services. When there are no customers, they use the time to make handicrafts that are sold at local markets.

Agriculture and culture are closely linked at the school-farm. Nonprofit associations and organisations offer cultural activities at the school, including lessons for local children in Chinese, English, geography, and maths. The school itself offers training in organic farming and calligraphy, and the director of the school is in fact a Chinese calligraphy grand master.

All the costs incurred at Gonggeng Shuyuan are financed by the restaurant takings and private patronage. In fact, Dai Jianjun invites artists to come to the estate for several days who in return agree to finance cultural programs or participate directly in the summer courses for local children.

For Dai Jianjun, life at the school-farm can be summed up with the following phrase, "Get up with the sun, work in the fields and read to acquire physical and mental stimulation, and then rest once the sun goes down." Dai Jianjun therefore encourages individuals to keep or find, within the village, jobs related to a way of life that gives priority to the family structure and the comfort of having contact with an emotional environment. It also helps rejuvenate the age pyramid for the village inhabitants and those in the surrounding area. Dai Jianjun's wish is to keep the countryside full and alive and promote a living environment that contributes to both individual respect (as these farmers do not get the respect they deserve in the city) and personal fulfilment.

Finally, to provide three meals a day for the children being taught and for guests, Dai Jianjun buys agricultural food products from farmers according to the same criteria he applies at the Longjing Caotang restaurant. These meals, based on quality products from organic farms, can on the one hand help combat malnutrition or lack of nutrition, and on the other hand provide a way to educate people in taste and taste diversity. Zhu Yinfeng, who became the school-farm manager in 2009 (after serving as chef of the Longjing Caotang restaurant from 2006 to 2009) sees these two elements as critical factors from a culinary point of view.

The agricultural and cultural apprenticeships offered free of charge to local children, especially during the summer courses, have lead Dai Jianjun to believe that they will encourage this next generation to respect the land, and that they will to stay, work, and live in the village, boosting their level of self-fulfilment. Following Dai Jianjun, these children will play a central role in future local development.

Dai Jianjun's guests at the school-farm stay for free. In exchange, they are invited to buy their products from local farmers, thus boosting the local economy and direct sales. However, the local development generated by the school-farm does not only affect the agriculture and cultural sphere. It has also contributed to improving the living environment. The Huangniling hamlet is now connected to the electricity grid and has running water, public lighting, and selective waste sorting. The kitchens and toilets have been improved to meet current hygiene standards (with tiling in kitchens, for example). The residents of the hamlet have also been able to buy refrigerators and televisions. This improvement in their living standard has also allowed the men to think about getting married.

In addition, with this agriculture that has a qualitative and ecological objective, the inhabitants of the hamlet are able to reclaim their local culinary culture. For example, they collect the organic rice straw that they then burn and use the ashes to make a cake following a local recipe (hui zhi tuan).

5. Conclusion

At different scalar levels, Dai Jianjun's "central" role as a visionary entrepreneur driven by a philosophy of life based on self-fulfilment and solidarism is evident in his ability to foster quality and diversity, as well as his ability to initiate, energise, and enhance activities, knowledge, skills, discourses, and imaginaries. The local development that Dai Jianjun advocates is both agricultural and specialised. Indeed, he asserts and reaffirms the nurturing role of farming. He expresses this more through a process of sedimentation than a reticular logic. This has resulted in establishing 16,000 partnerships and the regeneration of an agricultural area affected by the exodus of its people to the city, and which was in the process of desertification. The agricultural dynamics at work in both the area around the restaurant and the village of Suichang reveal that farming activity rather than just the sector is a useful geographic means of thinking and rethinking agricultural development.

The local development Dai Jianjun fosters is also rural, promoting and simplifying a new way of looking at the organisation and dynamics of rural areas, particularly in a polarised rural area. In Longjing, he suggests we redefine the relationships of dependence and complementarity that exist between the city and the countryside, while at the same time reinventing the logic of proximity and diversity. In Huangniling, this has exposed hidden energy and offers a new way of living by combining traditions with modernity.

Dai Jianjun's entrepreneurial project (his restaurant and school-farm) reveals a range of challenges – socioeconomic (the permanence of peasantry and the economic performance of agricultural activities), cultural (the transfer of techniques and local recipes, and the rediscovery of a local taste identity directly related to seasonality), and environmental (the promotion of agricultural food products from organic and biodynamic agriculture, and the preservation of the landscape).

Notes

1 This very important figure announced by Dai Jianjun during our meeting in June 2016 is explained by the fact that the sale of a very large number of agricultural food products is strictly seasonal and produced in very small quantities. For example, the supply of fresh eggs may involve several dozen hen and duck farmers every day.
2 mu = a unit of area equal to 0.0667 hectares.

References

Brunet, R., Ferra, R., and Théry, H. (1992). *Les Mots de la Géographie, Dictionnaire Critique*, Paris: GIR RECLUS/La Documentation française.

Christaller, W. (1932). *Die zentralen Orte in Süddeutschland: Eine ökonomisch-geogr, Unters. über d. Gesetzmäßigkeit d. Verbreitg u. Entwicklg d. Siedlgn mit städt. Funktionen*, (doctoral dissertation), Iéna: Fischer.

Etcheverria, O. (2011a). Le restaurant, outil de développement local? *Numéro Thématique de la Revue Norois*, Rennes : Presses Universitaires de Rennes, 219/2, pp. 7–71.

Etcheverria, O. (2011b). Les tensions fondatrices du développement local autour du restaurant Bras à Laguiole: centralité, qualité et créativité. *Numéro Thématique de la Revue Norois*, Presses Universitaires de Rennes, 219/2, pp. 57–71.

Etcheverria, O. and Bras, M. (2004). *Existe-t-il un goût de l'Aubrac in Géographie des saveurs, Revue Géographie et Cultures*, L'Harmattan, Paris, pp. 63–76.

Lösch, A. (1940). Die Raumliche Ordnungder Wirtschaft. Jena: Gustav Fischer. English translation (1954): *The economics of location*, New Haven, CT: Yale University Press.

Mathieu, N. (1995). *L'emploi Rural. Une Vitalité Cachée*, L'Harmattan, Paris, Collection Alternatives Rurales.

Pisani, E., and Groupe de Seillac. (1994). *Pour une agriculture marchande et ménagère*, La Tour d'Aigues: Editions de l'Aube.

9 The Cognac vineyard region

Territorial quality as a focus of tourism development in the context of a globally consumed product

Jérôme Piriou

1. Introduction: cognac, local production, and worldwide consumption

Cognac is an alcoholic *eau de vie*[1] produced in the grape-growing area of the same name located in southwest France just north of the Bordeaux wine-producing region. The Cognac region extends from the Atlantic Ocean to the banks of the River Charente, where the town of Cognac is situated. The particularity of this vineyard area is that 97.7% of production in terms of volume is sold for export to 160 countries,[2] with 179 million bottles sold in 2016.[3] For example, China, one of the largest importers in terms of value, has been a major market since 2011 due to the demand from the country's growing middle-class population that also increasingly visits France. The records show that in 2010, 573,039 Chinese visitors came to France on business or leisure trips.[4] Although Paris remains the preferred destination (70.8% of visits in 2011), visits to the French coastal and winegrowing regions are also increasing, including to Cognac, which is in close proximity to the Bordeaux vineyards (Taunay et al., 2013). However, despite the worldwide dissemination of the product, the name of the town, and its vineyards, local tourist activity is statistically lower than the sale of bottles, since the average length of stay in the town of Cognac is only a day and a half.[5] However, the major cognac houses have developed activities based around their production facilities, including blending, ageing, and visitor tours. Our research question therefore examines which territorial qualities are highlighted in the tours organised by the cognac houses for the purposes of tourism development.

To answer this question, we conducted an observation study in August 2013 of the visitor tours of seven cognac houses in the town of Cognac: Bache-Gabrielsen, Baron Otard, Camus, Hennessy, Martell, Meukow, and Rémy Martin. So as to observe the visit in its usual conditions and not disturb the smooth running of each tour, we acted as normal tourists. At the end of the tour, we introduced ourselves to the guide, explained the aims of our study, and requested any further relevant information. During the visits, we conducted our study using a pre-prepared observation grid designed to focus on the elements we sought to analyse in depth and enable standardising our observations (Berthier, 2010). As the initial grid proved incomplete, we added new categories. The final observation grid contained two main sections, the first relating to the description and presentation of the territorial quality via the product and its anchorage, and the second focusing on how the place and the territory were represented.

2. The territorial quality of Cognac

Territorial quality is defined as the combination of a product's intrinsic quality, its ties to a specific place, and that location's history and know-how (Lacroix et al., 2000). From an economic perspective, it is considered a form of organisational rent, as it reflects the ability to create institutional processes that, when associated with the product's environment, are capable of harnessing consumer willingness to pay (Pecqueur, 2001: 38). The approach to quality that focuses on a label or convention to control conformity is not the same as that used in geography, where quality is studied as a process in which the delimitations of productive territories are de-classified and re-classified (Pilleboue, 1999: 6). We will therefore specify what constitutes Cognac's territorial quality, not only in terms of the quality of the product, but also the role of the actors involved and the ties with the local territory.

2.1. The production process

Cognac is essentially made from the *Ugni Blanc* grape variety that has a high level of acidity but low alcohol content. Once the grapes have been harvested and pressed, the resulting juice is fermented. It is then distilled in an alembic copper still (*l'alambic charentais*) that is particular to the Charente territory and performs the double distillation process. Since its emergence in the late-eighteenth and early-nineteenth centuries, the *alambic charentais* apparatus has become inextricably linked with cognac distillation expertise. The two separate heatings, or *chauffes*, are carried out between the boiler located under the alembic still-head and the coolant tank (referred to as *la pipe*) connected by a swan-neck tube. The preheater helps save energy. The distillation process results in three distinct distillates: the heads *(les têtes)*, the heart *(le brouillis)*, and the tails *(les queues)*. The originality of cognac lies in its second distillation of the heart fraction (approximately 30% of the volume produced), which is known as *la bonne chauffe*. The heads and tails are redistilled with the next batch of wine.

The expertise of each cognac house depends on the olfactory skills that characterise its master blender, or *maître de chai*. The master blender buys the *eaux de vie*, monitors their ageing, tastes and blends those from different crus[6] to produce the distinctive characteristics of each brand and product. The heart of the second distillation, which has an alcohol content of 70%, is used for ageing and will become cognac. Ageing takes place in wooden oak barrels that help impart changes in the colour and aromas of the cognac. The oldest *eaux de vie* are kept in a cellar known as *le paradis*. It is the master blender who decides when to end the aging process and transfer the spirit from very old barrels to glass demijohns called *Dames-Jeanne*. The cognac ageing process allows the alcohol to evaporate. This causes the growth of a microscopic fungus called *Baudoinia compniacensis*, which feeds on the evaporated alcohol and blackens the cellar walls. The evaporation is known as the angels' share (*La Part des Anges*) and is said to amount to a loss of more than 20 million bottles a year.

Several types of cognac are on sale to consumers, each categorised by age. The "V.S." (Very Special) is a cognac in which the youngest *eau de vie* in the blend is at least three years old; the youngest *eau de vie* in the "V.S.O.P." (Very Superior Old Pale) is at least five years old; and the youngest in the "X.O." (Extra Old) is at least seven years old. But as we will see, depending on the cognac house, it is the brand names that are the main drivers of sales.

2.2. The role of the various actors in the cognac production process

In the cognac vineyard area, the distribution of tasks is clearly defined by the controlled appellation of origin (*appellation d'origine contrôlée*) specifications. The winegrowers produce the wine, the cognac houses buy the *eaux de vie* and monitor the ageing process so as to fine-tune the "cuts" and meet their clients' expectations. The interprofessional organisation, the Bureau National de l'Interprofession du Cognac, is responsible for promoting the product internationally. This body plays a major role in fixing the price of the grapes sold to the cognac houses. No fewer than five thousand wine-growing farms work under contract – exclusive or non-exclusive – with the major cognac houses. By definition, a cognac house, as in other wine-growing regions, buys the product once it has been distilled and aged and then manages the blending and bottling. For quality purposes, the houses implement a bottom-up integration approach, namely, they control the production and limit the power of action available to distillers. Each cognac house has its own production method and, via the distillers, each imposes its particular distilling and ageing system.

The market power of certain cognac houses enables them to control the entire production chain, from establishing contracts with the winemakers based on specifications for cultivating the vines, to the management of points of sale, to the commercialisation of sales across the world. Some of the major houses also belong to international groups. Even if there are a multitude of cognac houses, the market is highly concentrated: Four major cognac houses account for 80% of cognac sales (Hennessy, Rémy Martin, Martell, and Courvoisier). Indeed, the ability to resist global economic fluctuations or the vagaries of the weather derives from the fact that many of the great cognac houses belong to multinational companies listed on the stock exchange and headquartered in Paris (Hennessy with LVMH, Martell with Pernod-Ricard), New York (Courvoisier with Fortune Brands) or Bermuda (Baron-Othard with Bacardi).

These firms seek to reinforce their dominant positions in the global cognac market by taking advantage of large volumes and their brands.

2.3. Anchorage: from **terroir** *to territory*

The term "anchorage" relates to the concept of being attached to a fixed point. In his thesis, Julien Frayssignes (2005: 88) defines anchorage as a process that defines both the strategic action of "anchoring oneself down" and the state of "being anchored." Anchorage may be of a tangible nature, as in physical geography terms, or intangible in a social geography perspective. In the study of vineyards, anchorage to a specific terroir is the one most frequently examined. Terroir is an "area characterised by specific agronomic conditions" (Plet, 2003a: 919), which can include a type of soil, a micro-climate, or the availability of water. Nevertheless, given the prime importance of the human role, a review of the definition of terroir may be required. Roger Dion, geographer and historian at the Collège de France, suggests, "the role of the terrain in the production of a grand cru hardly goes beyond that of the raw materials used in the production of a work of art" (Dion, 1990: 26; author's translation). We can retain Jean-Robert Pitte's definition of terroir as a "relatively homogeneous portion of rural space, which is more or less large, whose contours are sometimes strictly defined or sometimes blurred and whose boundaries vary across time, at man's volition" (Pitte, 1999: 86; author's translation). Anchorage within a territory indicates the creation of a relation-ship between the product and its production area, both dependent on each other as specified in the regulations for controlled appellations of origin (AOC in French). According to the European regulation,

> designation of origin means the name of a region, a specific place or, in exceptional cases, a country, used to describe an agricultural product or a foodstuff: originating in that region, specific place or country, and the quality or characteristics of which are essentially or exclusively due to a particular geographical environment with its inherent natural and human factors, and the production, processing and preparation of which take place in the defined geographical area.[7]

The Cognac vineyard area is similar to a traditional wine-producing terri-tory in the sense that it relies upon a controlled appellation of origin consisting of six distinct vineyard areas, known as crus: Grande Champagne, Petite Champagne, Borderies, Fins Bois, Bons Bois and Bois Ordinaires.

Terroir therefore plays a determining role in the production of Charente wine. However, in terms of anchorage, the ties between the cognac sector and its territory cannot be limited to terroir alone. For this reason, it is interesting to analyse the territory as a whole, with the terroir as one component of it. The anchorage of a product creates the link between the methods the producers use and the relationship with the territory (Margetic, 1999). As for the anchorage of a firm, this creates a history and builds a community of shared destinies so that the future of the economic or agricultural activity is bound to that of the territory (Zimmermann, 1995). In this case, territorial anchorage can be defined as "the sharing of a piece of history that the company and territory have in common" (Zimmermann et al., 1998: 218; author's translation). The anchorage process therefore results from the taut organisational pull between a community, sector, or industry, and the territory when their rationales and ultimate aims diverge. Indeed, the professional circles dealing with production, sales, and promotion may all be required to adjust their actions, and this may occasionally cause conflicts. However, the organisation of wine territories fosters the valorisation of the winegrower's role as an added value (Couderc, 2005; Mauracher et al., 2016). Know-how is showcased in relation to tasting, olfactory, and visual skills, not just concerning the wine's flavours but also the feel and look of the bottle. The vintages, the blending, and also the glassware are unique components that all link the wine to its territory. Know-how is passed down in wine-producing families with the aim of maintaining professional heritage across the generations (Bessière, 2004). Anchorage in this case refers to the impression of being an integral part of the territory. Such a sense of belonging relates to a differentiation between the institutionalised version of the territory and the practical version experienced on the ground (Plet, 2002). Thus, on the one hand, there is the theoretical Cognac territory – with an environmental ecosystem that includes types of soil, environmental conditions, the hillsides' exposure to sunlight, the varieties of grapes and vines, and the age of the vine, all of which are characteristics of a controlled appellation of origin; and on the other hand, the practical aspects of the Cognac territory, i.e., the geographic and socioeconomic environment within it (Dion, 1993).

3. Tourism development in accordance with the territorial quality of Cognac

Local development, which we define as "a multi-dimensional and multi-actor dynamic within a local society, and which consists in the achievement of a development project centred on and endogenous to that society" (Plet, 2003b: 251; author's translation), depends on the mobilisation of actors within territories (Colletis-Wahl et al., 2001). Within the vineyard areas, local development can be organised by implementing territory-focused tourism. This approach has emerged as a means of energising a sector that faces worldwide competition (Lignon-Darmaillac, 2009; Duarte Alonso et al., 2015). However, the development strategy is often based on a quest for identity. Tourism provides an important means of valorising a territory's resources (Laurens, 1999; Cohen and Ben-Nun, 2009), and as a result, these resources constitute an instrument for local development based on the mobilisation of actors, particularly within a context of spatial proximity (Pecqueur, 1996). To be noted is that the motivation is not purely economic, as the various actors also seek recognition and legitimacy. Winegrowers seek to diversify their activities via tourism, whereas the interprofessional wine organisations focus on improving communication. Tourist offices, for their part, play a role in showcasing the territory and directing visitors towards vineyard estates, wine merchants, or other actors involved in the winemaking sector (Desbos, 2008). Sometimes actors from two different sectors cooperate, such as when a vineyard is promoted based on heritage and tourism factors: the combination of the winemaking sector and that of tourism thus fosters mutual enhancement. Two approaches are therefore presented, one considering tourism as an instrument for showcasing wine, the other seeing wine as a "catalyst" for the tourism identity of the territory (Desbos, 2008). In both cases, local development is based on expertise in the production and commercialisation of wine, and this requires local actors to appropriate the local heritage.

3.1. Turning the activities of the major cognac houses into tourist attractions

Today, the major cognac houses have started to develop discovery tourism as an economic activity by offering guided tours of their wine cellars to allow visitors to discover more about their vineyard products. Thus, for the major houses, tourism is similar to a sales communication strategy in that it seeks to strengthen the brand's reputation (Desbos, 2008). The reasons that lead a vineyard to develop tourism activity may be strategic, so that the winegrowers can diversify or improve their communication and sales. Faced with global competition, offering tourism activities is an effective way of developing the sector (Lignon-Darmaillac, 2009). In European winegrowing regions, receiving tourists is a longstanding tradition (Hall et al., 2000; Croce and Perri, 2010), but there will always be difficulties associated with visitor reception and the level of tourism professionalism demonstrated by the wine-producing actors (Frochot, 2000; Di Francesco, 2016). The major cognac houses, most of which are located in Cognac itself, have developed visitor tours. Their focus goes beyond their industrial production site and takes into account the territory's economic activity (Morice, 2008). This is a type of economic discovery tourism, i.e., a company visit for tourists (Potier et al., 2000). However, behind the outwardly touristic focus, we will show that the major cognac houses establish their brand and their production within the context of a winemaking heritage that owes as much to its territory as it does to the people who live within that territory.

3.2. Inclusion of the territorial dimension in the valorisation of the cognac production process

In their visitor tours, all the cognac houses emphasise the territorial characteristics associated with their production of spirits. These may be the physical characteristics (soil, grape varieties) or their industrial production techniques (double distillation using an alembic charentais still). Each visitor tour includes at least one information section about the territory. The houses first present the different crus and sections of land that contribute to the particularities of their production. The Camus House, for example, has named one of its cognacs Île de Ré. This is because the wine comes from the Bois cru, a terroir situated on the island of the same name and located in the most westerly region of the Cognac appellation. Thereafter, and depending on the visitor pathway each cognac house proposes, a connection is made with the history of the town of Cognac. For instance, as part of the visit, Martell offers a theatrical representation of barrels being loaded from the quays in Cognac onto a traditional *gabare* barge, thus illustrating the way barrels are transported either to the commercial ports or to other wine cellars along the River Charente. At Rémy Martin, the new wine cellars built on the edge of the town are carefully covered with the black traces of the *Baudoinia compniacensis* fungus that feeds on the evaporating alcohol. This detail, which seeks to promote the value of the building, is testament to the desire to place the cognac house's production process firmly within the traditions of its territory. And the Baron Otard House, which has owned the Royal Castle of Cognac since 1796, uses the Renaissance wing of the building to provide a biographical history of King François I, who was born at the castle − a technique that associates the brand with the territory through the intermediary of a historical figure. Furthermore, beyond the narratives that vary according to the technical or historical information provided, the cognac houses also seek to be involved in the town's cultural life by hosting temporary events. The Hennessy museum hosts international exhibitions, and Meukow organises classical music concerts. Finally, in the attempt to establish a relationship with their visitors, the houses share with tour-goers their distinctive expertise, traditions, and family values.

3.3. The cognac houses' brands reflect local territorial quality as part of their tourist development

By proposing services for tourists via their guided tours and various culinary and tasting experiences, the cognac houses hope to win over customers to their brand. Thus, in addition to the entertainment value provided by the guided tours, they also enable visitors to learn about Cognac, its terroir, and its crus, as well as the production process. To foster identification of their house with its symbols, the houses also make the connection between their company's history and that of France or the region. As mentioned earlier, Baron Otard recounts the history of François I and then that of the baron himself via anecdotes from the French Revolution. The visit at Hennessy begins with a boat trip across the River Charente. This enables visitors to discover the architectural heritage on view along the river banks, as well as the history of the town and the cognac house. Identification with the brand is a highly visible feature of these tours. At Meukow, for example, visitors are immersed into plush surroundings with subdued lighting and music when suddenly a panther appears on a screen to tell the story of the cognac house and its products. Here, as the symbol of the brand, the panther expresses power, suppleness, elegance, and sensuality, all reinforced by the black, amber, and gold colour code. At Rémy Martin, the symbol of the centaur is also represented by a colour code used in the reception room, in the tasting room, and on the products to ensure a sense of coherence throughout. In addition, to emphasise the expression and transmission of know-how for tourism purposes, the cognac houses encourage visitors to partake in a sampling experience. For example, Rémy Martin offers a wide range of restaurant and catering services within its premises to extend the experience of discovering the local terroir and its flagship product. The Camus House offers its visitors the opportunity of smelling different *eaux de vie* and cognacs and discerning their main flavours. This house also offers visitors the chance to produce their own cognac – thereby transforming them into individual master blenders who concoct a cognac suited to their own tastes. In essence, the type of experiences the cognac houses propose to their visitors via their guided tours provide a means of attracting visitors, while showcasing the local heritage provides an account of the expertise involved in producing cognac. Thus, by a process of co-construction that transcends the boundaries of a mere visit, the cognac houses aim to sell their products while developing a loyal relationship with their visitors.

4. Conclusion

The guided tours of the cognac houses offer a socioeconomic view of the territory from a technical, historical, and cultural perspective. They highlight the landscapes of the Cognac vineyard area and also place particular emphasis on the equipment and installations that have been a daily feature of local life across the ages to today. The tours also emphasize the ways in which territorial quality relates essentially to the cognac product itself, with its special characteristics developed by blending different *eaux de vie* and ageing. Moreover, the cognac houses use their own brands and symbols to valorise their particular product. The Cognac winegrowing region relies on the international reputation of the product to enhance its tourist development, particularly by organising tours. However, although presented as a resource for cognac production, the territory itself only makes a partial contribution to the valorisation of territorial quality. The cognac houses capitalise more on the expertise of their cellar master, glassmakers, and coopers (barrel makers), ensuring the development of a strong brand image that is conveyed through product marketing rather than territorial marketing.

Notes

1 French for spirits, literally, "water of life."
2 Source: Bureau National de l'Interprofession du Cognac. http://www.cognac.fr/cognac/_en/4_pro/index.aspx?page=chiffres_ac.

3 Ibid.
4 According to the Tourism Directorate's Hotel survey, 573,039 Chinese visitors came to France in 2010.
5 According to an interview conducted with the director of the Cognac Tourist office on 17 April 2013.
6 A vineyard or group of vineyards of recognized superior quality.
7 Art. 2 of the Council regulation (EEC) N°2081/92 of 14 July 1992 on the protection of geographical indications and designations of origin for agricultural products and foodstuffs, *Official Journal of the European Communities*, N°L208, 24.07.1992, https://eur-lex.europa.eu/legal-content/EN/TXT/PDF/?uri=CELEX:31992R2081&from=EN

References

Berthier, N. (2010). *Technique d'enquête*. Collection Cursus. Paris: Armand Colin.

Bessière, C. (2004). Les arrangements en famille: Equité et transmission d'une exploitation familiale viticole. *Sociétés Contemporaines*, 4(56), pp. 69–89.

Cohen, E. and Ben-Nun, L. (2009). The important dimension of wine tourism experience from potential visitors' perception. *Tourism & Hospitality Research*, 9(1), pp. 20–31.

Colletis-Wahl, K. and Pecqueur, B. (2001). Territories, development and specific resources: What analytical framework. *Regional Studies*, 35(5), pp. 449–459.

Couderc, J.-P. (2005). Poids économique de la filière viti-vinicole française et création de valeur. in d'Hauteville F. et al. (eds.). *Bacchus*. Paris: Dunod. pp. 191–207.

Croce, E. and Perri, G. (2010). *Food and wine tourism*. Wallingford: CABI.

Desbos, F. (2008). Le partenariat viticulteurs-institutionnels du tourisme: Clé de voûte d'un oenotourisme performant. *Market Management*, 8(2), pp. 62–73.

Di Francesco, G. (2016). Food and wine tourism and urban local development. *Transnational Marketing Journal*, special issue, 4, pp. 133–142.

Dion, R. (1990). *Le paysage et la vigne. Essais de géographie historique*. Paris: Payot.

Dion, R. (1993). *Histoire de la vigne et du vin en France. Des origines au XIXe siècle*. Paris: Flammarion.

Duarte Alonso, A., Bressan, A., O'Shea, M. and Krajsic, V. (2015). Perceived benefits and challenges to wine tourism involvement: An international perspective. *International Journal of Tourism Research*, 17(1), pp. 66–81.

Frayssignes, J. (2005). *Les AOC dans le développement territorial Une analyse en termes d'ancrage appliquée aux cas français des filières fromagères*. Thèse de doctorat en géographie, Toulouse: Institut National Polytechnique de Toulouse.

Frochot, I. (2000). Wine tourism in France: A paradox? In Hall C.-M. et al. (eds.). *Wine Tourism around the world, development, management and markets*. Oxford: Butterworth-Heinemann, pp. 67-80.

Hall, C.-M. et al. (2000). Wine tourism: An introduction. In Hall C.-M. et al. (eds.). *Wine Tourism around the world, development, management and markets*. Oxford: Butterworth-Heinemann, pp. 1–23.

Lacroix. A., Mollard. A. and Pecqueur, B. (2000). Origine et qualité des produits alimentaires: du signal à l'attribut. *Revue d'Economie Régionale et Urbaine*, 4, pp. 683–706.

Laurens, L. (1999). Le long parcours de l'Aubrac... productions de qualité, développement local et affirmation d'une identité micro-régionale. *Sud-Ouest Européen*, 6, pp. 51–60.

Lignon-Darmaillac, S. (2009). *L'oenotourisme en France: Nouvelle valorisation des vignobles: Analyse et bilan.* Bordeaux: édition Féret.

Margetic, C. (1999). Filières agro-alimentaires "de qualité" et territoires: l'exemple des filières viande dans le Nord-Pas-de-Calais. *Sud-Ouest Européen*, 6, pp. 61–68.

Mauracher, C., Procidano, I. and Sacchi G. (2016). Wine tourism quality perception and customer satisfaction reliability: The Italian Prosecco District. *Journal of Wine Research*, 27, pp. 284–299.

Morice, J.R. (2008). Un trait d'union entre les mondes du travail d'hier et de demain: La visite d'entreprise. In Morice, J.-R. and Zarate, M. A. (eds.). *Visite d'entreprise et tourisme: Contexte espagnol et perspectives européennes.* Angers: Presses de l'Université d'Angers, pp. 20–31.

Pecqueur, B. (1996). *Dynamiques territoriales et mutations économiques.* Paris: L'Harmattan.

Pecqueur, B. (2001). Qualité et développement territorial: L'hypothèse du panier de biens et de services territorialisés. *Economie Rurale*, 261, pp. 37–49.

Pilleboue, J. (1999). Les produits agro-alimentaires de qualité, remarques sur leurs liens au territoire. *Sud-Ouest Européen*, 6, pp. 69–83.

Pitte, J.-R. (1999). A propos du terroir. *Annales de géographie*, 108(605), pp. 86–89.

Plet, F. (2002). Vignobles et villes: Les formes nouvelles d'une vieille liaison. *Cahiers Nantais*, 58, pp. 111–126.

Plet, F. (2003a). Article Terroir. In J. Levy and M. Lussault (eds.). *Dictionnaire de la géographie et de l'espace des sociétés.* Paris: Belin, pp. 919–920.

Plet, F. (2003b). Article Développement local. In J. Levy and M. Lussault (eds.). *Dictionnaire de la géographie et de l'espace des sociétés.* Paris: Belin, pp. 251–252.

Potier, F. et al. (2000). *Tourisme de découverte économique et visites d'entreprises: Bilan, perspectives et préconisations pour un développement harmonieux et durable.* Paris: Conseil National du Tourisme.

Taunay, B., Violier, P., Li, L. and Piriou, J. (2013). L'accès des chinois au tourisme international: tout change et rien ne change. *Géo-regards, Revue Neuchâteloise de Géographie, Presses Universitaires Suisses*, 5, pp. 9–24.

Zimmermann, J.-B. (1995). *L'ancrage territorial des activités industrielles et technologiques – une approche méthodologique.* Rapport final, Convention d'Études N°2394, Paris: Commissariat Général du Plan.

Zimmermann, J.-B. et al. (1997). *Construction territoriale et dynamiques productives.* Rapport final, Convention d'Études N°18/1997, Paris: Commissariat Général du Plan.

10 Diversity of local food production models and local development

A comparative analysis of food production strategies

Anne-Emmanuelle Fiamor

1. Introduction

How, by whom, and under what conditions can the diversity of localised forms of food production be a driver of differentiated forms of local development? These are the questions underpinning this chapter. As part of our field study into the diversity of localised food production and its impact on local development in southeastern France (Drôme department[1]), we observed that this diversity is both practical and symbolic.

Indeed, traditionally accepted in the related scientific literature is that localised production develops in association with a site (Bérard, 2011) by mobilizing the knowledge and historical know-how of the place. From this point of view, the current diversity of production forms would be solely organisational, strategic, and linked to the depth of the territorial attachment of production to the site (Frayssignes, 2005).

However, we also discovered from our fieldwork that there are different ways of referring to a place and that mobilizing traditional knowledge assets and technical know-how is no longer the only way to generate localised food production. A place can be described differently than merely by way of its tradition. We therefore assume that localised production covers a diversity of social meanings that refer to its symbolic representations and therefore the symbolic dimension of its promotion. As a result, in constructing our questions, we assume first and foremost the organisational, strategic, but also symbolic diversity of localised food production.

Second, when considering the widely shared observation in literature that the development of localised production is a driver of local development (Bessière, 2000), a second and complementary hypothesis emerges. This hypothesis is based on the assumption that local production is a driver of both practical and symbolic local development, in turn differentiated according to their own practical and symbolic development. Within the framework of this double proposition, we analyse the different forms of practical and symbolic development of food production and simultaneously report on their respective effects on the local development of sites.

Following the social food space model of Jean-Pierre Poulain, we consider that the development of localised production is part of – and participates in – the development of a set of rules, codes, norms, and rituals, structuring social life and the relationship with the physical environment. This social space, which is transmitted but also transformable over generations, forms a social and cultural model at the origin of community development in the space freed up by the various constraints to which this community is subject (Poulain, 2002, 2017). This interpretation tool allows us to identify the different practical and symbolic ways of fitting into a physical space, thus making it a social food space. From this point of view, the activities but also the symbolic representations of a place (viewed through their food components) are promoted through the development of localised production. In this context, local growth engendered by the expansion of food production is the practical and symbolic development of the local social food space in which each local production is included and valued as it develops. Thus, the practical and symbolic diversity of production presupposes a diversity of local, social, and cultural developments and, correspondingly, a diversity of forms of local development from the point of view of food.

To underpin this scientific proposal, we first present the field under study: the Drôme department, a territory in southeastern France. The methodological presentation explains our assumption that there is both practical and symbolic diversity in the development of localised production but also aims to enable understanding the impact of the development of each type of localised production on local development.

In a second step, we present the tool used to analyse the systems of actors and actions that each producer is part of by reconstructing their strategies enabling the inclusion of production in a localised social food space. We present the results of this analysis in a third and final stage, reporting on the two production strategies most frequently found in the Drôme region. The first is development through the certification of traditional knowledge and know-how; the second, promoting knowledge and know-how that are part of a "cultural here and now" through an independent network of producers. The analysis of the production strategy concerns the inclusion of production in a local social food space and, as such, the local, practical, and symbolic development that the strategy generates. Inclusion in a local social food space and local development are therefore considered one and the same.

2. A field survey of the multidiversity of the promotion of local food production in the Drôme department

2.1. *The multidiversity of the Drôme region and the objective of our sponsor, the Drôme Local Authority*

The analysis presented here is the result of a field survey we undertook in the Drôme department between 2007 and 2010. This project consisted in establishing a typology of the production strategies for local food production in this department on behalf of our sponsor, the Drôme Local Authority.[2] Although sociology tends not to choose the relevant geographic category *a priori*, we circumscribed our research to the department administrative level. However, bearing in mind that the geographic reality does not necessarily remain within the borders of Drôme, we tested whether the department's actions were significant enough to be a relevant study unit, and hence the importance of reporting on the local development of each form of local production. Local food production is intended as associated with a place, as defined by Laurence Bérard (2011, 2012). The objective of the study was to render the diverse, dense, and entangled social reality intelligible, since Drôme was at that time a department with a "multidiversity" of forms of localised food production development.[3]

Indeed, the exploratory phase of the field study showed that the development of production in Drôme was characterised by a diversity and density of different elements including:

- Local food production (around forty listed local food producers[4]).
- Producers and modes of production (businesses, craftsmen, farmers, cooperatives, and independent farmers promoting themselves through a local network).
- Certifications: the Drôme department had nineteen protected geographical indication (PGI)/protected designation of origin (PDO – AOC) certifications in 2007 but was also the top-ranking department in France for organic agriculture in terms of number of farms and proportion of agricultural land used in 2010 (Agreste, 2011).[5]
- Tourist and territorial promotion initiatives: festivals linked to local production, Suze la Rousse University of Wine, two regional natural parks, etc.

These dense and diverse combinations of factors develop at different infra-departmental scales, implying the potential involvement of numerous actors in agricultural and agro-food development, as well as territorial authorities in the development of production. Drôme is a fragmented territory in the administrative sense with two regional natural parks, several administrative areas and districts that in some cases overlap. Drôme is also divided into five tourist and cultural entities that the Departmental Tourism Committee promotes: Drôme des Collines, Drôme Provençale, Vercors, Diois, and Plaine de Valence (Figure 10.1).

This multidiversity and density thus created an "effervescent" development, which was difficult for the Drôme Local Authority to understand and promote. The objective was to obtain an analysis that would allow identifying the actors involved, the missing links in promotion, as well as their assets in the sector, to better develop their food-related potential.

PRESENTATION DU DEPARTEMENT DE LA DROME

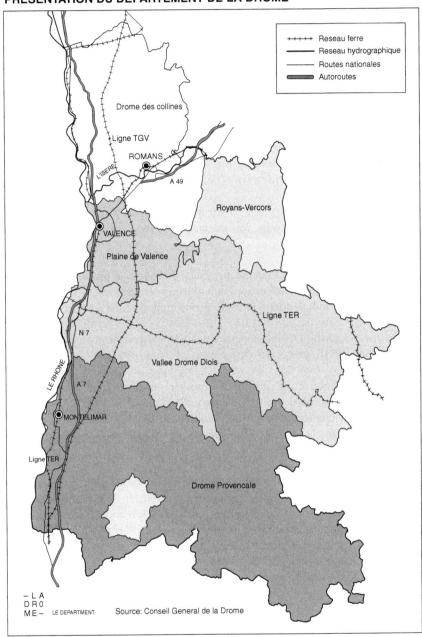

Figure 10.1 Map of the Drôme department and its five tourist entities

2.2. A transversal study of actors and territories: snowball effect development

Our aim was to find transversal variables for this diversity that would reveal the different patterns and elements of cohesion. Within this comprehensive framework, we undertook a qualitative study of the Drôme region, transversal to this multidiversity, which would enable us to establish who works with whom, how, and under what conditions; since when; and in what stage(s) in the production process (culture/breeding, processing, distribution). Based on a categorisation of the different actors,[6] an inventory of production, and a mapping of the different intra-departmental territories, we began our survey with a balanced sample of the different actors involved in the development of production in different sub-departmental territories, thus allowing the survey to develop in a snowball effect (Olivier de Sardan, 2008).

2.3. 139 semi-directive interviews and 14 participant observations

In this context, we conducted 139 interviews, including 90 semi-structured and 49 expert interviews with the various categories of actors, 26 "flash"[7] interviews and 14 participant observations with "eaters," according to the term of Poulain and Corbeau (2002). We also conducted extensive literature searches. The survey took place over two years between 2008 and 2010.

A key finding that emerged from the exploratory analysis of the field data is that the effervescent promotion consisted of a triple diversity: organisational diversity, strategic diversity, but also symbolic diversity. "Symbolic diversity" means that what is understood and valued as local food production can have different definitions. In this case, we observed that local food production was no longer based solely on the traditional aspect to be recognised as such but also on other types of characteristics. Our objective was then to construct a study that would allow us to take this triple diversity into account and understand the territorial development generated by the promotion of the different types of production.

3. The development of the local social food space as a local development dynamic

3.1. Understanding local development through local food production

The impact of food production development on local development has been the subject of much research. Numerous studies show that the development of localised food production can drive local development. Indeed, local development can be considered agricultural, artisan, and the industrial development of goods and services, which, using local resources and carried out by and on behalf of local actors, generate human and physical resources as well as a network of social links specific to a given place or spatial area (Pecqueur,

2000). In this context, this type of development covers very broad areas of investigation.

However, concerning purely the impact of agricultural and food development on local development, we refer to the analysis of the territorial anchoring of agricultural and agro-food enterprises (Frayssignes, 2005), the analysis of localised agro-food systems (Muchnik, 2010), and the analysis of baskets of goods (Hirczak et al., 2008), generally included in the context of human geography, economics, and/or socioeconomics. Nevertheless, none of these studies suffice to analyse the strategic, organisational, and above all symbolic diversity that may have an effect on the development of the Drôme territories.

3.2. The social food space as a way of interpreting local development, both practically and symbolically

On the other hand, the notion of a social food space (Poulain, 2002, 2017), which stems from the sociology of food, offers a useful framework to consider local development in both its practical and symbolic dimensions. The framework extends to whether the development of localised production has an impact on the development of goods and services at the local level, and also on the development of the social and cultural representations associated with the place.

Local food production, like any form of agricultural and food production, can be considered as developing through a set of gestures, rules, norms, standards, codes, and rituals regarding the choice of potential foods selected in the physical environment and designated as edible, as well as the methods of collection, culture, consumption, seasonality, social differentiation, and so forth.

This ensemble, structuring social life, is invariably rooted in a particular space-time. It is the expression of the specific link that a community has with the physical environment through which it develops and is transmitted, adapted, and transformed from generation to generation, as the group evolves and the context develops (Fischler, 1990; Poulain, 2002, 2017). This practical ensemble relates to a set of representations, values, and beliefs that give life to it and make sense both within and outside the space concerned (Poulain, 2002, 2017). This cultural combination, both practical and symbolic, constitutes what Jean-Pierre Poulain called a cultural food model; we perceive it as much by the activities, spaces, and mobilised objects as by the representations we make of them. They are implicit models, internalised in the course of socialisation, forming part of everyone's routines (Giddens, 1984). However, the dynamics of industrialisation and globalisation have contributed to greater reflexivity (Lahlou, 1998) towards our food models (Fischler, 1979, 1990; Poulain, 2002, 2017), especially since the end of World War II.

In this context, historical local food models can be considered as substructures of more general (particularly national) models (Poulain and Corbeau, 2002). Since the end of the old regime and the rise of regionalism up to the modern day, local food models are increasingly mobilised and valued because they respond to the need for cultural identification of human food in an industrialised and de-territorialised context (Fiamor, 2014). In the final part of this social construction process of food location, in the 1990s and 2000s, local food production became a resource in the face of food crises (Bessière, 2000; Fiamor, 2014) and, as we have seen, a resource for local development (Bessière, 2000; Casabianca et al., 2005; Pouzenc et al., 2007; Muchnik, 2010; Fiamor, 2014).

Nevertheless, in relation to this sociohistorical dynamic, we must also consider that, starting from the same ecological and technological constraints, several food models can develop in the same place, since these cultural structures are above all the result of choices, borrowed from the representations that a community is likely to make of itself and its physical environment. From this point of view, local production, however diverse it may be, is always the valued expression of a production system in a localised social food area. With this production, the social food space through which it develops is valued, endures, and is potentially transformed in terms of both the activities and representations conveyed. In so doing, the places corresponding to this space are equally valued. As a result, the goods and services, as well as the representations associated with the food component of a place through the development of local food production, are differentiated according to the food model valued by the production in question – hence, the need to analyse the differentiated inclusion of local production in the social food space to differentiate the local development that it helps foster.

Finally, with regard to the Drôme region, to be noted is that this depart-ment straddles two historic social food areas originating from two former royal provinces: Dauphiné, which historically covers most of the Drôme area, and Provence, which historically covers some of the most southerly Drôme regions. However, due to the climatic boundary (from a meteorological point of view, the south of France begins at the Donzère Gap, near Montélimar) and the current promotion of the whole of the southern Drôme under the heading "Drôme Provençale," a large part of southern Drôme emphasises Provençal recipes and production, while the centre, northern, and part of the eastern Drôme focus on Dauphine recipes and production. However, as explained above, although historic food models undeniably constitute a basis for the development of local production, they are not the only possible models.

3.3. Analysing the systems of actions and actors to understand the integration of local production in the local social food space

How can we analyse and thus differentiate the inclusion of local production in a local social food space? According to Poulain (2002, 2017), the social food space can be broken down into six broad social dimensions that are interwoven and transversal to the systems and actors: the regulation of what is edible, the food system, the culinary space, the space relating to consumption habits, the space relating to food temporality, and the space relating to social differentiation (Poulain, 2002, 2017). Based on this model, we consider that these six dimensions will develop through articulating the production system and the consumption system. We are particularly interested here in the production system (production,[8] processing, distribution) envisaged as intrinsically linked to the consumption system. Indeed, these two systems are built on and legitimise each other, and their shared evolution is achieved by adjustments between these two parts of the same construction. Food production, whatever its type, always responds to a social demand and adapts to it but also participates in influencing it. In this context, through distribution, producers will seek to legitimise their production as local by promoting their inclusion in the local social food space. This legitimisation can take various forms. The "eaters" will, from their point of view, legitimise this production as local (and hence the message that it provides) by buying it, preparing it, eating it, and spreading information about it (Fiamor, 2014).

To analyse the practical and symbolic inclusion of food production in a local social food space, we analyse the activities and all the links that the producer maintains at the different levels of production. This allows us to reconstruct its system of actions[9] and the entire system of actors of which the producer is part (Crozier and Friedberg, 1980; Bernoux, 1985).

This analytical step leads to several data. First, it allows us to account for the variables through which producers place their production in the food system of the social food space (the second dimension of the social food space that interests us here). The numerous possible variables concern not only the local production stage(s) but also the spatiotemporal recording of activities mobilised for this purpose. These variables can be broken down as shown in Table 10.1.

These variables best represent the idea of the production promoted by the producers during distribution and through which they will thus seek to legitimise their production as local. These are the expressions of their system of actions and therefore their production strategy.

Second, as a result, we can also reconstitute the organisation[10] through which the producers concretise their strategy (Is it part of a collective, individual dynamic? Is the authority centralised? etc.) and the motivations behind such strategy. The organisational analysis is important because it influences the way we think about production: a cooperative organisation will not give the same impression of a local social organisation as a small, independent producer.

Third, an analysis of the organisation and distribution activities makes it possible to reflect on the form of legitimisation on which the organisation as a

Table 10.1 Variables for recording activities in a local space

Valued production steps	+	*Spatiotemporal inclusion of promoted activities*
Production (culture, breeding, harvesting)		Here − present
		Here − past
Transformation		Elsewhere − present
Distribution		Elsewhere − past

whole is based. According to Max Weber (1921), there are three main types of legitimisation: the tradition, the charisma, and the legal-bureaucratic system. This is a typology with no possible variants in the classification.

The form of legitimisation is also important for the analysis of the local food mode, since it influences, aside from the organisation, the representations we make of the production and therefore the places associated with it. Legitimising by means of an official mark of quality or relying on family tradition does not give the same impression as with the local food model.

This set of data is complementary to account for the local food model valued by a producer and therefore to account for the form of practical local development as a symbol the producer is involved in developing. This analysis is linked to the analysis of the forms of tourism actions developed by each type of localised production strategy. We here link the articulation of the local social food dimension with the tourist sphere already largely identified (especially in Bessière, 2000), considering that the actions developed in the tourist sphere are part of the production system the producers belong to. These contribute to the value-added food model and are therefore of interest. Thus, by defining inclusion in the local social food space through the analysis of the production strategy, we can differentiate the various strategies and therefore the various food models valued, and thus the different forms of local development that these strategies potentially generate.

4. The tradition-labelled and the "cultural here and now" strategies of small-scale producers within a network: two differentiated local food models

The analysis of local food production strategies led to the identification of seven strategies. Six of these have, unsurprisingly, a spatiotemporal element of their practices in the historic past of the sites – either Dauphinois or Provençal – while only one strategy developed a new spatiotemporal element. Moreover, when considering the number of producers represented in each of the strategy types, as well as the tourism action styles that each generates, we can consider five of the strategies as variants of the first, which we will present here. For this reason, and due to space restrictions, we report here only the two most representative and significant local development strategies.[11] We have named each of these strategies by associating the spatiotemporal recording of their practices with their form of legitimisation. We first present the tradition-labelled strategy followed by the "cultural here and now" strategy of small networked producers.

4.1. Local development of the tradition-labelled strategy

4.1.1. Structuring around traditional know-how that is legally certified

The first type of strategy we outline is that of producers structured around a legally certified form of traditional regional know-how with an official sign of quality and origin (SIQO): PDO-PGI.[12] Five producers in the sample use this type of strategy: *"bleu"* cheese from Vercors Sassenage, the guinea fowl market, Picodon from Drôme, olive oil from Nyons, and garlic from Drôme. Most of these are collective actors: joint farming associations, cooperatives, Economic Interest Groupings, companies, etc., although also individuals and farmers in some areas.

The characteristic feature of producers in this type of system is that they must be part of a union for the protection of their production, which is a *sine qua none* condition to obtain the official quality mark from the National Institute of Designations of Origin (INAO) and the European Union, and thus to obtain legal recognition of their production.

These certified sectors are structured at the production level[13] and, where appropriate, processing level. As part of their legal certification, producers are obliged to source locally. This structuring is particularly visible in the dairy sector linking milk producers with cheese processors. However, over and above the production and processing stages, the local temporal anchoring of knowledge and know-how is put forward to legitimise production and obtain validation with the required quality sign. This certification is based on the creation of specifications that homogenise production. The official sign of quality protects production on the market and allows producers to distribute it in mass distribution channels, nationally and sometimes internationally. That said, in the case of producers in the Drôme department, supermarket distribution mainly concerns south-eastern France.

Internal distribution within the territory depends on the sector. Some sectors are very well represented in the local market, in some supermarkets, in cheese shops, and restaurants (Picodon from Drôme, *"bleu"* cheese from Vercors Sassenage). Others are almost nonexistent in the local space (Pintadeau and garlic from Drôme) due to a distribution objective that is entirely oriented towards the outside world. Finally, the case of olive oil from Nyons is unique. It is indeed well distributed locally (supermarkets, delicatessens, producers' own shops, luxury stores, markets) but at the same time is poorly represented among restaurateurs due to a much higher-than-average cost (nevertheless greatly valued in high-end starred restaurants). In this context, in culinary terms, Picodon is the product most frequently found in restaurants, all ranges combined, which has led to numerous culinary innovations. The next most frequently found product is *"bleu"* cheese from Vercors Sassenage, while the last three products are almost nonexistent in everyday catering.

The power in this type of organisational system is vertical and centralised around the defence union, which itself is subject to INAO regulations. External state and European bodies provide legitimacy. While this legitimacy is firm, well established, and very difficult to change, it allows production to be recognised beyond its local area. The producers' objective in this type of system is to sell a protected and calibrated product and thus be able to list it in the mass distribution channels. Relationships linked to the structuring of the system, particularly at the production and processing levels, are therefore relationships of interest in the professional sphere. The actors in this type of system are in a relationship with the technique with which they reproduce an adapted version of the technical constraints of a bygone era. In fact, they reproduce and promote knowledge and know-how (by adapting it) from a time-space in which this knowledge and know-how were originally developed to meet a need, often for conservation purposes. This is particularly true in the case of cheese making and butchery processes. They do so because these processes have become cultural elements of the local food space. Their localised production strategy is therefore related to respect for traditional knowledge and know-how from the Dauphinois and Provencal cultural spaces. In terms of social structuring, they are part of a centralised system, guaranteeing the homogeneity of the desired production, validated by an impersonal and external system (legal-bureaucratic, according to Weber, 1921). The production is therefore legitimated as local because it reproduces traditional know-how and knowledge validated by a legal, impartial body outside of the social food space. The objective of this structuring is economic, valorising a traditional food model reproduced by setting its practices.

4.1.2. A link to tourism development that may be nonexistent or even institutionalised

We now ask what kind(s) of link(s) is/are established between systems based on the tradition-labelled and tourism enhancement schemes, beyond the aforementioned catering. A first fact noted in our sample is that systems registered as part of a tradition label may be linked to tourism development schemes or may in fact not be linked to them at all. In this context, we will see that olive oil from Nyons, "*bleu*" cheese from Vercors Sassenage, and Picodon from Drôme are the sectors linked to tourism development schemes, whereas the others are not represented at all (garlic and guinea fowl from Drôme). Then, when these relations do exist, are they linked to any of the territorial actors? Indeed, this link takes place through relationships whose objective is the territorial promotion of valued production. By territorialised promotion of production, we mean that producers in this type of system, linked by their membership to a union for the defence and management of their production, can structure themselves with territorial actors to promote their output. The objective of the measures put in place is to promote production, but is associated with the development of a defined territory. We have listed two forms of this type of relationship, which we explain below. To note, however, is that we have added Côtes du Rhône wine to the five sectors from the sample because it is a significant example in terms of links to territorial development, and in addition, this industry is associated with others from the tradition-labelled sector.

4.1.3. Structuring so as to create a place where production can be embedded

The first form of territorialised promotion identified is the association of producers in a production sector and the territorial actors who join forces to create an association for the territorialised promotion of production and a place dedicated to it. These two cases are the Wine University in Suze la Rousse and the Olive World Institute. The Wine University is an association created by a group of twenty trade union representatives from the different appellations of the Côtes du Rhône to boost their sector, which at the time needed fame (1978). For the association headquarters, they rent from the local authority the (very large) Castle of Suze la Rousse in the town of the same name in southern Drôme. In exchange, the local authority has a seat on the association's board of directors. Over the years, it has developed a training centre specialising in sensory and organoleptic analysis of production, first for professionals and then for amateurs, enabling it to be financially self-sufficient.

Several other local products from Drôme are also promoted: Nyons olive oil, apricots from the Baronnies, and several aromatic and medicinal plants (lime blossom, lavender). However, only products with an official SIQO designation are promoted, and moreover, include only those from a specific area referred to as "Another Provence,"[14] also represented on the association's board of directors. This is therefore a structure linking sectors and territorial actors (local authority, town hall, etc.) favouring acquaintanceship and reciprocal interests around some labelled products and an administrative territory (in this case, the "Another Provence" area).

The second case, the Olive World Institute, is similar in terms of structure. This is a nonprofit association created in 1997 in Nyons in the south of Drôme by representatives from the sector (the director of the Nyons cooperative, the director of the black olive union in Nyons) and several elected local representatives who also sit on the board of the Drôme local authority. Their aim is to develop the olive oil production culture that exists throughout the world, including, of course, that of Nyons. The association is linked to the French olive oil production body. Its concerns the discovery of the organoleptic qualities of olive oils and their relationship with the local culture. They organise training for schoolchildren and tourists (during the week only) and an exhibition with olive oil tastings. Thanks to this association, the olive-growing sector has forged links with local and elected departmental officials and is in the process of acquiring a territorial showcase in addition to positioning itself as the olive oil representative throughout the world.

These two cases of territorialised promotion give rise to an underlying network of reciprocal interests. Indeed, the actors in these cases also form an underlying network that has been brought to life thanks to the presence of actors from one of the organisations (agricultural and territorial sector) on the board of directors of the other organisation. As such, members of the Olive World Institute (and therefore the olive oil industry), the University of Suze la Rousse (and therefore the wine industry), the Baronnies Regional Natural

Park, the local authority with its councillors, the tourism offices and "Another Provence" all share seats on the board of directors and form a network of mutual interests around labelled productions and their territorial promotion in an area that covers part of the southern Drôme region.

4.1.4. Structuring so as to create a festive event

The second type of territorialised promotion we identified is the networking of territorial actors and sector managers, working together to set up a local festive event. The actors in a specific sector combine forces with one or more territorial actors (regional natural park or town hall, assisted by the local authority) to put on a festive event. The exhibition is then organised and managed by the agricultural sector. No specific nonprofit association is created, as in the first case, but there is territorialisation through the association of production with a symbolic site. We identified three cases of these events involving two agricultural sectors. First, the "Bleu" Cheese Festival: an ongoing event that takes place each year in a different village in the Vercors Regional Natural Park (always within the park due to its long-standing links with it). The festival brings together around 15,000 people, with stands exhibiting and explaining the life and history of this agricultural sector, the local cheese, and the Vercors Natural Park. This territorialisation enables identifying "*bleu*" cheese with the Vercors Regional Natural Park territory. Next, two Picodon celebrations take place in Saou and Dieulefit, two villages in the centre of Drôme. This cheese production is also associated with the central Drôme region known as Dieulefit.

This type of festive event also allows promoting localised production in other types of strategies related to local production that we have not detailed here, and that of the "cultural here and now" of small producers in a network that we consider next. This type of event therefore positions, in several ways, the products from the tradition-labelled strategy as carriers of other types of local products during these events. Finally, it allows "gastronomising" products (Poulain, 2011), highlighting the innovative and emblematic dishes produced, as is the case for "Vercouline," a raclette made with "bleu" cheese from Vercors Sassenage, a dish invented by and sold at the "bleu" Festival every year. Of the six agricultural sectors constituting this sample, three have set up festive events: "bleu" cheese at the "Bleu" Festival, olives from Nyons with the "Olivades" and "Alicoque" parties, and Picodon with the events at Saou and Dieulefit. To conclude on the links between the tradition-labelled strategy and tourism development, this connection is either almost non-existent (as in the case of guinea fowl and garlic from Drôme) or institutionalised and territorialised. That is to say, it is strongly associated with and interdependent on territorial powers associated with particular sites. As part of this institutionalisation and territorialisation process, we can identify a heritage boost to production and, by extension, to the places to which it refers. This is a matter of enhancing the value of a production area and a traditional culinary space that can be preserved, encouraged, and from which innovation can stem.

5. The local development of the "cultural here and now" strategy of small-scale producers in a network

5.1. Create and form a group independently, and adapt to the physical environment rather than the practices of traditional social food spaces

The type of strategy that we detail here is that of small producers structured around direct sales and short distribution channels in various areas of Drôme. Nineteen producers – mainly neo-rural producers, French, or foreign (Swiss, Dutch, Scottish) – were identified as part of this form of strategy. They own small-scale farms[15] and sell the food products they harvest, produce, and process on their farms[16] via direct sales and to local networks. They use and value practices adopted from both the local area and from elsewhere, from the traditional social food spaces of the Drôme region (Dauphinois and Provence), to other regional food spaces in France (Savoie, for example), to foreign spaces and practices (Swiss, Dutch, Scottish, and Indian). They thus choose their raw materials and their production and processing practices because they have adapted to the local physical environments and not because they emanate from a traditional Drôme social food space. They therefore give themselves total freedom of production in relation to the latter. Following this logic, they sometimes produce historic products (Picodon, Banon, olive oil, walnut oil, etc.) and sometimes culturally innovative products (chutneys, biscuits, spreads, sweets, etc.). By the same logic, they reformed the space of the historic edible,[17] including, for example, the gathering and consumption of wild aromatic herbs, flowers, and roots.

These producers organise themselves both very individually and in terms of group practices. They are rather reluctant to allow any interference in their choices of production (harvesting, cultivation, breeding), processing, and distribution, even from those who represent them (Chamber of Agriculture, for example). They accept advice and even training in their relationship with production, as long as everything fits with their logic. However, in parallel to this individualistic development, these actors are part of a "multi-affiliation" to groups that exchange ideas and to sales networks, both formal and informal, created through either the agricultural associative world[18] or completely autonomously (on-farm collective points of sale set up and managed informally by producers or small networks of mutual aid between neighbours). This multi-affiliation allows diversifying the distribution methods, which in the context of Drôme is essential for the sustainability of this type of system.[19] However, this multi-affiliation also makes it possible to create inter-knowledge networks that promote the exchange and dissemination of practices. This multi-affiliation structure allows a better dissemination of the practices of these groups in the local social food space. The producers' individualism, combined with their multi-affiliation to production and distribution networks, engender a network organisation with no centralisation of power. Producers, within the framework of these groups, have the objective of both selling and forming a group locally as a way of avoiding dependence on their peers and the various institutional actors. Producers therefore remain individuals, while at the same time participating in groups.

In terms of the relationships with local production, these are first of all voluntary and chosen practices adapted to the physical environment over the limited choice of local traditional practices and, as such, express an environmental value. It can be said that these small producers voluntarily respect the physical environment in their choices over traditional social spaces by choosing to include and/or adapt any production-related practice or idea as a resource, provided these are suitable for the physical environment. Their objective, in addition to sales targets, is constituting and belonging to a group while maintaining their individuality. Indeed, these individual producers are equal to those with similar practices but without the formal dominance of some members over others. They disseminate their knowledge with a view to creating best practices; within the framework of this constitution and relationship with the environment, the transparency of their practices and networks forms their legitimacy. This strategy permeates an environmental but also a social value linked to the representation of these producers in their environmental milieu. This strategy will thus have a double impact on the local social food space, not limiting it to traditional spaces and the spatial scale of their networks, covering more or less the entire Drôme and neighbouring departments (Ardèche, Isère, Vaucluse, Hautes-Alpes).

To conclude on this type of strategy, production is here legitimised in a conventional way by a networked system and the legitimisation of production as local. This is combined with the fact that it is produced, processed, and sold locally by small producers or their peers, whatever the origin of the production knowledge and know-how, within an autonomous framework of locally shared practices and knowledge, according to a social and environmental commitment. This leads to products that are rooted in a "cultural here and now," driven by environmental and social motivations.

5.2. An internal and intimate link between tourism and the production system

Producers with this type of strategy are to some extent present in the tourism development mechanisms of the tradition-labelled strategy presented earlier. Small farmers can be found at festive events, such as the "bleu" cheese and Picodon festivals.

Regarding the way in which these small-scale producers are linked to the development of tourism in local networks, several forms exist that we now present. First, out of the nineteen actors interviewed, only one producer did not belong to incoming tourist networks linked to farming activities. She is a Vercors-based farmer who, when we met her, regretted not being able to do so because of the location of her farm.[20]

The tourism development networks in which the eighteen other actors are involved are part of the multi-affiliation described above. Several types of these networks have developed in addition to the farms' sales activities and greatly help promote them.

First, these producers coordinate tourism development through structures dedicated to welcoming visitors to the farm on the one hand and greeting tourists in general on the other. In Drôme, the "Welcome to the Farm" network (at the Chamber of Agriculture) and the CIVAM[21] network are very well developed. Membership of the "Farm Guesthouse" and "French Cottage" networks is also well represented. The CIVAM centres of innovation offer opportunities to meet the producers, develop initiatives, and test new practices. Even more, three CIVAM producers we interviewed also offer pedagogical initiatives. For example, one producer offers school visits related to solar energy production on his farm, and another organises walks with tourists to teach them how to recognise and pick aromatic and medicinal plants.

Through the Farm Guesthouse and French Cottages networks, six of the nineteen producers promote one or more holiday cottages, welcoming their guests for overnight stays, feeding them, and selling them their produce. In addition, again through the Farm Guesthouse network, two producers offer guests dinner-only options. Finally, beyond our sample, there are other examples of tourism activities linked to the farms and developed through these networks in this type of system, such as donkey rides. For the producers, these types of activities represent either an important resource in financial terms or a peripheral revenue stream (20% to 30% of their income), yet correspond to their way of life and the welcome they can offer. As well, various agricultural, agro-food, and territorial development structures are also linked to tourism development. For example, APAP, an association of farmers in the Vercors Regional Natural Park, is an agricultural extension of the park. This organisation has created the "the Vercors Farms" network that runs several one-off or annual activities. For example, each year, they organise several farmers' markets on individual farms, but also a series of meals and demonstrations on the farm where the producer provides the food and the venue.

The Chamber of Commerce and Industry (CCI) also runs two networks. The first is national, called Country Bars, and aims to sustain the last shop-restaurants in a village on the condition that they buy at least part of their produce locally and provide contact details of the local producers. The CCI also runs another network exclusively based in Drôme, the Gourmet Walk in Drôme, a network in which the CCI links producers with restaurants and asks them to create recipes based on local products. Each restaurateur offers at least two local products. A guide to the restaurants and their recipes is produced and widely distributed in Drôme. These products may also be SIQO labelled, but the CCI addresses farmers individually and never through a defence union.

Another link between tourism and food production, the agricultural vocational training and promotion centre[22] at Die in Diois,[23] organises an annual event: the regional taste conference that takes place in the town of Die. This is a cultural and agricultural organisation for tourists and the local population with different types of events that take place all year round. The aim is to meet producers and "eaters" and to engage the former as guides for the latter to allow them to discover the local specialties. Finally, several local representatives from specific areas have created directories of farm producers in their respective regions. These are widely available in the tourist offices and food stores in Drôme.

To conclude on the link between tourism development and this type of production strategy, in around half the cases, income from tourism and income from food production are equal and therefore interdependent. In addition, the tourism development mechanisms, linked to welcoming people to the farms, are embedded within the production system and in the producers' way of life. This offers tourists an opportunity to enter, get a glimpse of, or in some cases, even immerse themselves in the production system and the way of life of small farmers. The inter-knowledge associated with producer networks and to which tourists have access through visits and, if necessary, stays in the cottages, potentially helps this immersion.

Therefore, this type of production strategy enables tourists to benefit from an intimate tourist offer within the production representation of these producers, within their networks, and within a part of the local food life that these producers represent. As producers share their products and lifestyle with their customers, the environmental and social values linked to their production concept are disseminated and potentially shared.

6. Conclusion

Different systems of local food production can generate different local development dynamics, especially tourism, and value different social food spaces. The inclusion in a social food space is, as we have seen, practical and symbolic, social and political. Indeed, inclusion in a particular local social food space means a relationship with the physical environment and the involvement of the community in that environment guaranteed by a particular social structure. It is this model in its entirety that generates local production, providing its specificity and uniqueness, and may or may not be linked to the tourism development strategies corresponding to the social structure. The values, the logic of action, and the representations conveyed through the two local production strategies give rise to tourist actions that resonate with their logic. The originality of our contribution is in allowing us to systematically understand why the forms of development of local food production are carried out in a specific manner, emanating from the producers' motivations, the resulting logic of action, and the values and representations they convey.

In the context of this chapter, a key point of comparison between the forms of social food spaces that lead to developing the two strategies under study concerns the relationship between the past and tradition, a pivotal point of differentiation between these forms of development.

As we have seen, the tradition-labelled strategy is legitimised by the traditional aspect of the knowledge and know-how mobilised, itself legally validated.

Moreover, the "cultural here and now" strategy of the small-scale producer network is legitimised based on a "cultural here and now" that carries social and environmental values, validated by the proximity link between producers themselves and between producers and "eaters." This second cultural model, by virtue of its being based on a new form of legitimacy (and thus a new form of social structuring), should be seen as the emergence of a new model rather than a simple innovation derived from the traditional model. Indeed, a change in the legitimacy of an organisation model is more than just a variation, it is a new vision of the meaning given to actions and relationships, under which norms, rules, codes, and social rituals will be reorganised in accordance. From Max Weber's (1921) point of view, the emergence of a new organisational model (he speaks of an authority model) is a sign of the lack of meaning of a previous model in a given context for a part of the community or society. The hegemony of tradition and the overinvestment to which it has been subjected from a food point of view since the end of the former regime in France (Bérard, 2011) has given way over the last few decades to a greater environmental commitment that is visible in the present (Fiamor, 2014). In this emerging model, the traditional aspect is not rejected – it is not even subject to competition but is integrated, is "part of" but does not constitute anything more than the pivotal validation around which the whole system develops. Moreover, the form of legitimisation that here is in the hands of the "eaters" and producers of this type of system questions the limitations of official, external, and impersonal labelling. Thus, the symbolic aspect we highlight here should not be minimised when considering the development of a food model as a model of local development in its own right. The emerging model of the "cultural here and now" strategy of small networked producers is another symbolic development space deployed both for local food and for the places concerned as a whole.

Notes

1 France is divided into regions, which are then divided into 101 departments.
2 Within the framework of a CIFRE research contract between the French National Agency for Research and Technology, the Drôme Local Authority, and the University of Toulouse 2 Jean Jaurès, between 2007 and 2010.
3 To limit the research to feasible dimensions, we worked on solid foods, excluding all alcoholic beverages but including fruit producers who process or sell fruit to make fruit juices.
4 Picodon from Drôme, blue cheese from Vercors-Sassenage, Pogne from Romans, Swiss biscuits from Romans, olive oil from Nyons, walnuts from Grenoble, plants with aromatic and medicinal properties, Bergeron apricots, Baronnies apricots, peaches, honey, etc.
5 http://agreste.agriculture.gouv.fr/IMG/pdf_D2611A01-2.pdf.
6 The territorial authorities, the actors of agricultural development, the actors of territorial development, as well as the "eaters" were into account in addition to the actor-producers (operators, craftsmen, companies) and distributors.
7 Flash interviews are short interviews (maximum fifteen minutes) used as part of the participant observations.

8 The term "production" is understood here as the first stage of agricultural development: cultivation, animal husbandry, harvesting. With production system, we intend all the stages of food production, processing, and distribution.

9 From Crozier and Friedberg's definition (Crozier and Friedberg, 1980; Bernoux, 1985), we understand an action system as all the actions that contribute to defining the local producer's strategy. We are mainly interested in the production action system, which we define by means of production/processing/distribution actions that, in this case, are interdependent (if I produce like this, it is to sell like that...). Everything contributes to a determined, specific social production in a system of actions. The system of actions is embedded in a system of actors. In this sense, an actor system potentially includes many systems of actions, which may create agreement or conflict, may complement or support each other, etc. (Fiamor, 2014).

10 "Organisation" means the whole system of authority and therefore the power relations in which the producer is involved.

11 For a complete analysis of the seven strategies, see Fiamor (2014).

12 Protected Designation of Origin (formerly French controlled designation of origin) and Protected Geographical Indication.

13 Understood in the narrow sense of culture, breeding, harvesting.

14 This is a French administrative unit.

15 Between two and eleven hectares.

16 Founded between 1979 and 1998, except one that was established in 2005.

17 First dimension of the social food space. Conf. Infra. Part 3.3.

18 Centres for initiatives to promote agriculture and rural areas (CIVAM), Chamber of Agriculture, Regional Natural Park, informal networks, etc.

19 Contrary to other contexts in which this multi-affiliation either does not exist or is weakened and not necessary for sales and takes place entirely on the farm. This is the case of the Ariège department in France under study.

20 This producer of aromatic and medicinal fragrant plants has cultivable land and other property from which they gather their production. She has a drying workshop under her house but is unable to develop her sales activity there because the road leading to the workshop is a shared-access road and her neighbours are unwilling to allow access.

21 Centres of initiatives to promote agriculture and rural areas.

22 This type of centre is a public agricultural training structure that exists throughout France.

23 Diois is a mountainous territory in the east of Drôme, south of the Vercors mountain range.

References

AGRESTE (2011). La statistique agricole. Agriculture et espace rural de la Drôme. Paris: Ministère de l'agriculture et de la pêche.

Bérard, L. (2011). Du terroir au sens des lieux.In Delfosse, C. (ed.), *La mode du terroir et les produits alimentaires*. Paris, Les Indes savantes, pp. 41–58.

Bérard, L. (2012). Productions alimentaires localisées. In Poulain, J.-P. (ed.), *Dictionnaire des cultures alimentaires*. Paris, Presses Universitaires de France, pp. 1093–1096.

Bernoux, P. (1985). *La sociologie des Organisations, Initiation*. Seuil, Coll. Paris, Points Essais.

Bessière, J. (2000). *Valorisation du patrimoine gastronomique et dynamiques de développement territorial: Le haut plateau de l'Aubrac, le Pays de Roquefort et le Périgord Noir*, Thèse de doctorat en Sociologie. Toulouse, Université Toulouse 2.

Casabianca, F., Sylvander, B., Noël, Y., Béranger, C., Coulon, J.-B. and Roncin, F. (2005). Terroir et Typicité: Deux concepts-clés des Appellations d'Origine Contrôlée. Essai de définitions scientifiques et opérationnelles. *Programme transversal de l'INRA "Pour et Sur le Développement Régional" PSDR. Symposium international "Territoires et enjeux du développement régional"*, Lyon http://www.ara.inra.fr/Delegation-regionale-Rhone-Alpes/liste/dossiers/112031.

Crozier, M. and Friedberg, E. (1980). *Actors and systems*. Chicago, University of Chicago Press.

Fiamor, A.E. (2014). *Changement dans la construction sociale de la production alimentaire localisée, analyse à partir du cas drômois*. Thèse de sociologie. Toulouse : Université Toulouse 2.

Fischler, C. (1979). Gastro-nomie et gastro-anomie.In *Communications. 31. EHESS: La nourriture. Pour une anthropologie bioculturelle de l'alimentation*. Paris, Seuil.

Fischler, C. (1990). *L'homnivore, le goût, la cuisine et le corps*. Paris, Odile Jacob.

Frayssignes, J. (2005). *Les AOC dans le développement territorial, une analyse en termes d'ancrage appliquée aux cas français des filières fromagères*. Thèse de doctorat en Géographie. Toulouse, Institut National Polytechnique de Toulouse.

Giddens, A. (1984). *The constitution of society. Outline of the theory of structuration*. Cambridge, Polity.

Hirczak, M., Mollard, A., Pecqueur, B., Rambonilaza, M. and Vollet, D. (2008). Le modèle du panier de biens. Grille d'analyse et observations de terrain. *Économie Rurale*, 308, pp. 55–70

Lahlou, S. (1998). *Penser-manger: Alimentation et représentations sociales*. Paris: Presses universitaires de France.

Muchnik, J. (2010). Localised agri-food systems: Concept development and diversity of situations. *Sviluppo Locale, XIV*, 35 (2/2010), 3–20. https://prodinra.inra.fr/?locale=fr#!ConsultNotice:40937.

Olivier de Sardan, J.-P. (2008). *La rigueur du qualitatif. Les contraintes empiriques de l'interprétation socio-anthropologique*. Louvain-La-Neuve, Ed. Bruylant.

Pecqueur, B. (2000). *Le développement local, mode ou modèle?* Paris, Éditions Syros Alternatives.

Poulain, J.-P. (2002). *Sociologies de l'alimentation, les mangeurs et l'espace social alimentaire*. Paris, Presses Universitaires de France.

Poulain, J.-P. (2011). La gastronomisation des cuisines de terroir: Sociologie d'un retournement de perspective. In Adell, N. and Pourcher, Y. (ed.), *Transmettre, quel(s) patrimoine(s)? Autour du Patrimoine Culturel Immatériel*. Paris, Michel Houdiard, pp. 239–248.

Poulain, J.-P. (2017). *Sociology of food. Eating and the place of food in society*. Bloomsbury Academic.

Poulain, J.-P. and Corbeau, J.-P. (2002). *Penser l'alimentation. Entre imaginaire et rationalité*. Toulouse, Ed. Privat.

Pouzenc, M., Coquart, D., Pilleboue, J., Olivier, V. and Guibert, M. (2007). Diversification des modèles de qualité territorialisée des produits agroalimentaires: Risque ou opportunité pour les terroirs? *Méditerranée*, 109, 31–40. http://journals.openedition.org/mediterranee/111.

Weber, M. (1921). (posthumous). *The theory of social and economic organization*. (Talcott Parsons' translation of volume 1 of *Economy and Society*, 1947). Ann Arbor, University of Michigan, Free Press.

Part III
The link between quality, innovation and creativity

11 Craft beers and beer festivals

Exploring the potential for local economies and gastro-tourism in the UK

Ignazio Cabras and Katie Ellison

1. Introduction

In the UK, the number of breweries has increased significantly since the 1980s, with many small and micro-businesses successfully diversifying their offers and expanding their operations well beyond their local areas. The implications for the industry deriving from this growth have been investigated in a number of studies (Slade, 2004; Cabras and Bamforth, 2016; Cabras and Higgins, 2016), with more recent research focusing on the impact of new beers and brewing on local economies and on the development of business strategies targeting the growing demand for diversified artisan beers (Danson et al., 2015; Moore et al., 2016), including the organisation of beer-related events and festivals.

Although a number of studies have focused on regional food festivals, there appears to be very little research into the role and relevance of these events for the local economy. The increasing number of beer festivals organised in the country, and the general lack of in-depth knowledge on these events, clearly indicate the need for more research addressing their role within local economies so that local brewers and local authorities can capture and harness opportunities in terms of regional tourism development.

The study proposed in this chapter aims to investigate the impact of beer and related events, such as festivals, on local economies and tourism. First, we present and discuss information gathered from micro- and small breweries and by the Society of Independent Brewers (SIBA). Second, we focus on the city of York, in Northern England, analysing primary data collected via means of a survey questionnaire administered during the annual beer festival organised locally in 2016. Particular attention is placed on the potential of micro- and craft breweries to expand their reach and market across different type of outlets – for instance, gastropubs and fine dining – and on the opportunities beer festivals offer in terms of educating consumers and building a beer-destination brand.

2. Literature review

2.1. Food-related events and tourism

In recent years, the number of food-related festivals and gastronomic events has significantly increased worldwide. Local authorities as well as national governments have started to see these events as drivers of international tourism and, particularly in developing countries, a potential source of economic growth (Tiwari, 2011). Several empirical studies on tourism-led growth (Gani, 1998; Cantavella and Balaguer, 2002; Oh, 2005; Jang et al., 2006; Louca, 2006; Proença and Soukiazis, 2008) indicate tourism as an effective contributor to long-run economic growth. The travel and tourism industry accounted for 9.8% of the world's GDP in 2015, with this figure set to increase by about 11% by 2026. Considering direct contributions, such as hotels and passenger transportation, the industry now employs one in eleven workers globally (UNWTO, 2017). Given its potential to create jobs, promote growth, and generate tax revenue, the benefits from tourism can cascade to a wider range of the population (Sinclair, 1998), with positive effects on residents' income (Dritsakis, 2004).

At a local level, event tourism – thus tourism associated with specific cultural or gastronomic events – frequently involves whole communities in their organisation and management, increasing the level of exchanges among residents and unlocking resources and benefits in terms of community cohesion and social capital (Emerson, 1976; Woodley, 1993). However, residents' participation and active engagement in these events mostly depends on what they believe they will gain from encouraging tourism in their area: "Benefits are essentially value domains, and in tourism, economic and noneconomic value domains may influence an attitude toward tourism" (Wang and Pfister, 2008: 86).

There are also some negative externalities associated with event tourism. For instance, in case of food and drink festivals, environmental factors, such as noise pollution, litter, and waste management, become relevant issues (Andereck, 1995). "Binge-drinking tourism" also generates several concerns among administrators and local residents: In Europe, low-cost airlines have made the organisation of bachelor parties more affordable and accessible to a broader range of consumers, with parties slowly becoming stag/hen weekends characterised by drunkenness and extreme behaviours (Thurnell-Read, 2012). With countries in central and eastern Europe becoming more open to international tourism (Broad, 2009), historical cities such as Krakow, Prague, Budapest, and Riga have become increasingly popular destinations for this type of tourism, with locals often referring to the individuals as "drunk invaders" (Rohrer, 2006).

Recent years have seen a surge in the number of new festivals, creating a more competitive business environment (Getz and Frisby, 1988). Competition is positive for consumers, as it ensures choicer and better quality experiences, although frequently poor organisational and management skills, particularly in small communities, are an issue for both organisers and participants (Getz and Frisby, 1988). There is also a general lack of goal-setting strategies amongst organising committees, e.g., whether or not the particular event achieves the specific goals set. In their study on community reasons for staging festivals, Mayfield and Crompton (1995: 42) find that the main reasons for holding such events include "revenues, community spirit, education/culture, recreation, and tourism." Strategic decision-making in tourism events relates to examining the benefits and costs associated with a particular event, and organisations pursue advantages over potential competition through unique selling points (such as location, products, ticketing; Tribe, 1997). Through strategic decisions, organisers are more likely to offer an event that has economic, social, and environmental benefits. Hence, successfully executing the chosen strategy leads to the "development of goals, objectives, and action statements" (Higham and Ritchie, 2001: 41).

Specifically related to the organisation of food and beverage festivals, Higham and Ritchie (2001: 39) examine the influence festivals have on rural communities in New Zealand, finding that these events have become popular in both urban and rural communities for reasons that include social and community improvement in addition to developing tourism attraction. Higham and Ritchie (2001) also find that successful events/festivals help rural regions in southern New Zealand by improving their reputation, attracting visitors, and generating extra revenue for residents.

Place branding – that is, the conscious effort (aspiring tourist destinations make) to create a unique identity to position themselves above competitors in the market (Ketter and Avraham, 2012) – is also important in the organisation of gastronomic festivals. Place branding includes all the inputs and outputs that contribute to form and inform people's perceptions of different places before, during, and after the event. In their analysis of the role of place branding within food festivals, Blichfeldt and Halkier (2014) report the case of Løgstør, a small rural community west of Aalborg in North Jutland (Denmark). In 2005, the municipality of Løgstør began organising two festivals every year: the Mussel Harvesting Festival in April and the Mussel Festival in July. Since their launch, the two events have enhanced the image of this small village with their branding based on the association with mussels, resulting in a progressive increase in the level of tourism. Residents at Løgstør, however, are aware that place branding will not suffice when it comes to tourism success, and they work as a community to ensure visitors obtain quality and value from their experience. In this context, the two festivals become a receptacle for a human and sensorial relationship: Tourists are left with a memory of Løgstør that is the "net result of the interaction of a person's beliefs, ideas, feelings, expectations and impressions about an object" (Chon, 1990: 4). This aspect is particularly relevant: Notwithstanding the rise of communication technologies, predominantly social media, word-of-mouth recommendations and re-visits are still more important with regard to building a reputation and profile in the tourism industry (Allen, 2007).

2.2. The rise of beer festivals in the UK

Place branding presents challenges in terms of the local community's commitment and alignment with the branding objectives and plans. Allen (2007) notes that anyone with whom tourists interact can affect how tourists perceive the brand image. This is particularly pertinent when festivals involve alcoholic beverages.

An example is the Oktoberfest, the famous global event that annually takes place in Munich, Germany, since 1810. By hosting this event, Munich promotes its image on a global scale (Xiao and Smith, 2004): 5.6 million people travelled to attend the seventeen-day-long festival in 2016, with the event generating massive benefits for the city's economy (Herrmann and Herrmann, 2014). For instance, the increase in demand for accommodation arising from the flow of visitors into Munich resulted in a major hotel and accommodation price increase, with room prices in the festival period as much as 850% higher than the average price (Nicolai, 2012).

The success of the Munich festival has resulted in multiple copycat festivals springing up globally. Kitchener-Waterloo in Ontario (Canada) has even created its own Oktoberfest. Particularly in Northern and Western Europe, local administrations and city councils tend to select beer as their beverage of choice in the organisation of food and drink festivals (Smith et al., 1999), and many cities have started to use beer-related events to market themselves in the tourism market (Waitt, 1999, 2003). This has resulted in increasing competition among cities and towns to garner the attention of important stakeholders, including consumers, investors, and policymakers (Richards and Wilson, 2004: 1931).

Beer festivals, in general, are associated with a number of negative externalities predominantly related to alcohol consumption and abuse and antisocial behaviour. Xiao and Smith (2004) find a wide variety of opinions on beer festivals in local communities: Supporters find the event fun, with a great and friendly atmosphere that can be enjoyed by all different cultures, while detractors deem the festival noisy, crime ridden, and full of drunks. Such externalities are among the reasons for imposing taxes to cover costs, such as policing and cleaning up.

In the UK, beer festivals are a tradition, although the number of these events has spiked in recent years. Cabras (2017) indicates this as a consequence of the growing number of craft and micro-breweries, which grew from 142 in the late 1980s to more than 1,500 in 2016 (British Beer and Pub Association, 2016), registering an astonishing ten-fold growth within this period. The rise of these businesses has been described as three consecutive interrelated waves (Bamforth and Cabras, 2016; Cabras, 2018).

The first wave, arriving between the late 1970s and mid-1980s, was mainly due to a general dissatisfaction with the decline in the variety of beers available. This situation led to the creation of CAMRA (Campaign for Real Ale), a movement of beer enthusiasts who lobby for the revival of real ale – cask-conditioned ales brewed with traditional methods. CAMRA's relentless activities and campaigns increased awareness of traditional ales and helped create a potential customer base for new breweries as an alternative to mass producers (Mason and McNally, 1997). The many opportunities related to the increasing demand for real ales attracted a variety of entrepreneurs, many with some prior experience in the brewing industry (Mason and McNally, 1997). The second wave arrived in the early 1990s and was mainly characterised by the entry of new founders with little or no previous connection with breweries or brewing, such as retirees or beer enthusiasts in search of a career change (Knowles and Egan, 2002). Two factors characterised this period: the rapid increase in the number of new businesses brought the development of specialised real-ale producers, which enabled many new breweries to start with more efficient and more cost-effective brewing equipment; and the introduction of the Beer Orders of 1989, which forced the larger brewers to either sell or free up a large number of their pubs (see Pratten, 2004; Preece, 2016). The third and most recent wave arrived early in the 2000s and saw a further and sharper increase in the number of micro- and craft breweries, sustained by cheaper and easier-to-install equipment (Mason and McNally, 1997; Wyld et al., 2010) and the introduction of Progressive Beer Duty (PBD) to support smaller brewers, granting these businesses a lower tax levy than large brewers. The PBD boosted the growth of micro-brewing throughout the country, shaping the size of new businesses, which tended to keep their production volumes low to take advantage of the tax break.

The growth of micro- and craft breweries has undoubtedly increased interest in beer and real ales in the UK. The micro- and craft brewing movement saw a surge in the number of new businesses at almost the same time, often located just a few miles from each other, creating an interesting entrepreneurial environment in the industry. In addition, the support of the intensive campaigns promoted by CAMRA has contributed significantly to developing and consolidating domestic demand for British beers over the years.

In contrast to the tremendous growth of micro- and craft breweries, the number of pubs in the UK has significantly decreased since the 1980s, from about 64,000 to slightly over 50,000 during the period 1990–2015 (British Beer and Pubs Association, 2016). The most recent financial crisis hit large pubcos severely, forcing them to put large parts of their estates on the market, creating more opportunities for small breweries to acquire their own pubs (Preece, 2016; Cabras, 2018).

The broad range of styles of beer and ales has widened consumer choice in the UK. This has increased opportunities for beer-related events and festivals in different parts of the country. By examining several sources in the public domain and mainly provided by CAMRA, it is estimated that between 800 and 1,100 beer festivals were organised across the country in 2014 (Cabras, 2017). The figure comprises events supported by CAMRA as well as events organised independently. Local CAMRA branches alone set up and organised 215 across the country (CAMRA, 2015), with all the work undertaken on a voluntary basis. Frequently, beer festivals are associated with beer contests, mostly organised by SIBA, where brewers have the opportunity to introduce their beers and compete to win titles at regional and subregional levels. The evolution of these events has been exponential with regard to both the number of beers showcased and sold and the level of attendance.

3. Methodology and data analysis

3.1. Data

To develop our study, we focused on two main data sources. The first is information extracted from the British Beer Report, prepared by one of the authors for SIBA (2016). SIBA represented about 840 independent small and micro-breweries in 2016, around 55% of the total number of breweries operating in the UK. SIBA collects information on the state of its membership on a regular basis. The growth of UK micro- and craft breweries continued in the period 2010–2015, although the pace has now stabilised (Cabras and Bamforth, 2016).

The second source is primary information collected at the Knavesmire Beer Festival (KBF). The KBF is an annual event organised in the historic city of York in North Yorkshire, a local authority in Northern England. York is home to nearly 250 pubs that supply a population of 208,000 (according to the UK 2011 Census). Most pubs serve beers brewed in local proximity: 120 breweries are located in North Yorkshire, amongst the highest concentration of breweries per local authority in the UK.

Since 1978, the first year it was organised, the KBF has evolved significantly. Initially, the festival was held on small premises in the city centre with a maximum capacity of three hundred people, forcing organisers to apply a one-in/one-out policy for health and safety reasons. In the mid-1980s, the festival moved to a number of buildings across town; while this increased capacity, the level of attendance tended to remain at an average two thousand visits during the three-day event. Issues related to beer storage and distribution, alongside restrictions imposed by enclosed premises, pushed organisers to search for alternative solutions. In 2008, York City Council (YCC) proposed moving the festival to a field relatively close to the famous York Racecourse, known as Knavesmire. The organisers accepted the proposal and the festival was rebranded accordingly. Attendance passed from about 4,000 in 2008 (three day event) to above 11,000 in 2014 (four-day event), with similar numbers in 2016.

KBF is run entirely by volunteers, mostly members of the local CAMRA branch. The organisational machine runs for twelve months, during which different aspects of the event are carefully planned and managed (e.g., gathering appropriate authorisations to use public spaces, selection of volunteers to be allocated to different roles/duties, identification of providers/suppliers of diverse goods and services). The organising committee purchases the beers directly from breweries at market prices. Beers and ciders are then sold on the premises in different price ranges and three different measures: full pint, half pint, and one-third pint. Sales revenue is used to refund initial purchases and investments, with profits recorded at between 5% and 10% in most recent KBF editions (2014 to 2016).

3.2. The economic impact of micro- and craft breweries on local economies

The data presented in this section are based on information gathered from 301 member breweries surveyed by SIBA, about 35.6% of total membership. According to the responses, beer production amounted to a cumulative total of 1.64 million hectolitres (mhl). This equates to roughly 287 million pints produced by the respondents and translates into approximately 532m pints brewed by SIBA members. Figure 11.1 shows the level of production by packaging and compares 2015 figures with production estimated in 2013 and 2014, and those forecast for 2016. Cask beer still represents the bulk of production, with a relatively steady increase in the amount of bottled/canned beer, although less than 5% of the surveyed breweries reported bottled beers accounting for the majority of their brewed output.

The vast majority of beer produced fell into two alcohol-by-volume (ABV) ranges: between 3.5% and 4.2%, and between 4.6% and 6.0%, with an average strength of 4.3%. Just five breweries reported brewing low-alcohol beers, which in any case accounted for very low proportions of their total production in 2015 (mostly below 5%, with only one brewery reporting up to 10%).

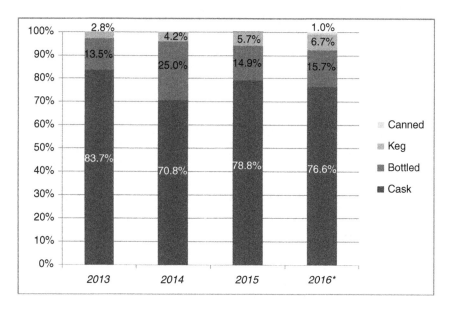

Figure 11.1 Proportion of beer production according to packaging (2013–2016)

Conversely, ninety-six breweries reported brewing beers with an ABV higher than 6.0%, which accounted for over 20% of total production in five cases.

The beer styles brewed regularly by the surveyed breweries are reported in Table 11.1. The regular production of Golden Bitter/Ale beers is indicated by over 90% of respondents, followed by traditional bitter ales, stout/porters, and strong bitter IPAs also brewed by the majority of brewers. Only a handful of breweries indicated gluten-free and low-alcohol beer in regular production, although roughly one out of three regularly brewed organic and speciality beers. About 85% of respondents indicated having more than four different brands regularly brewed at their premises, with a quarter indicating at least seven different brands in regular production. Engagement with seasonal or "one-off" beers is also significant, with almost all respondents reporting brewing seasonal products in 2015. Nearly one out of four brewed more than ten seasonal beers in the period considered and only twenty-one breweries (less than 7%) did not brew any.

The surveyed breweries provided valuable information on the employment their activities generated. The total workforce captured by the survey comprised 1,669 staff employed in the breweries under study. The vast majority were full-time equivalent (1,187 – equal to nearly 71% of the total), with men representing approximately three out four employees. About 43% of part-time employees worked between ten and twenty hours per week, with another 26% working more than twenty hours.

Figure 11.2 classifies employees by age bands and residency. Almost half the employees surveyed were aged between 35 and 54 years on average, with

Table 11.1 Types of brands and seasonal beers*

Beer styles	Percentage	Beer styles	Percentage
Pale golden bitter/ golden ale	94.7%	Strong ale/barley wine	20.6%
Traditional brown/ copper/amber bitter	83.4%	Lager-style beer	20.6%
Stout/porter	74.4%	Local ingredients beer	19.6%
Strong bitter/IPA	67.4%	Themed series of beers	16.3%
Bottle-conditioned beer	38.9%	Wheat beer	14.3%
Speciality-ingredient beer	30.9%	Foreign-style ale	11.3%
Traditional mild	30.6%	Super-premium bottled beer	11.3%
Special hop beer (e.g. single variety, green)	29.2%	Unfined cask beer	9.6%
Strong mild/old ale	23.6%	Gluten-free beer	1.7%
Craft keg beer	22.9%	Lower-alcohol beer (<2.8%abv)	1.3%

* Percentages calculated on total responses per category
Source: SIBA (2016)

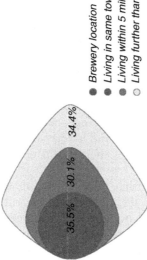

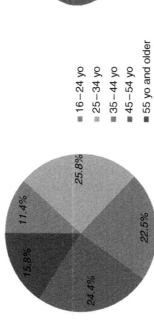

Brewery location
● Living in same town/village
● Living within 5 miles
○ Living further than 5 miles

■ 16–24 yo
▨ 25–34 yo
▨ 35–44 yo
■ 45–54 yo
■ 55 yo and older

35.5%

30.1%

34.4%

25.8%

11.4%

15.8%

24.4%

22.5%

Figure 11.2 Workforce categorised by age bands and residence
Source: SIBA (2016)

more than one out of three employees aged below 34. Interestingly, the number of employees grouped in the oldest age band (55 years and above) outnumbered those grouped in the youngest category (16–24 years old). The majority of workers live in the same town or village of the brewery, with about two out of three employees living within five miles of their brewery. These findings indicate the level of importance of breweries in terms of impact on local employment. In addition, the vast majority of breweries surveyed indicated the intention to increase their staff in the next twelve months, with three out of four breweries planning to recruit two or more new employees.

Free trade pubs, owned pubs, and wholesalers are the main channels for beer sales across the surveyed breweries, with an average 56% of brewery production supplied to free trade pubs and about 9% to owned pubs. The majority of responses indicated a largest proportion of production (80% and above) sold within close spatial proximity: about one out of three breweries sold more than one-fifth of their beers beyond a forty-mile radius, with just twenty breweries selling more than half their production farther away from their location.

With regard to pub ownership/management, about one out of five breweries in the survey indicated they own, lease, or rent pubs. In particular, the total number of pubs owned by breweries captured by the survey was 294, while those leased/tenanted were 161. The majority of respondents (forty-two) owned at least one pub, while four respondents directly own more than ten pubs each for a cumulative total of 147 controlled pubs. The numbers related to leased/tenanted pubs were smaller, with twenty respondents controlling at least one pub under this type of management, and another sixteen with more than two.

3.3. The economic impact of beer festivals: the case of York

The data gathered for this study were collected at the KBF held on September 2016, the greatest event of the series ever held (at the time of this study), with more than 480 beers and over 100 ciders showcased. We collected the data by means of a survey questionnaire comprising very specific questions in a multiple-choice format and through interviews conducted with festival organisers and local breweries partaking in the event. The survey questions aimed at evaluating respondents' expenditure, expected attendance (number of days at the festival), any overnight arrangements in York, and travel to the festival venue. The data collection was conducted for the full four days of the festival, generating input from 268 respondents. It is estimated that about 11,000 people attended the KBF considered for this study. The responses account for approximately 2.7% of the total; although this is a small fraction, it provides an interesting picture of the impact of the festival.

The largest attendance across the four days was on Friday and Saturday. The vast majority of respondents (240; 89%) indicated attending only one day of the festival, 21 respondents (8%) indicated at least two days, and 7 respondents

(3%) indicated more than two days. A key feature of any festival is the degree to which it can attract a wide range of participants beyond its locality. Arguably, the more widespread the participation, the more renowned the festival, and the more successful in building a destination brand (Lee and Arcodia, 2011). The questionnaire asked participants to indicate the first four digits of their postcode, enabling us to map their location of departure/ residence. As Figure 11.3 illustrates, respondents travelled distances between less than 20 miles to 280 miles to attend the KBF. Those travelling within a 20-mile radius represent local and subregional participants, such as from North Yorkshire, Humberside, West Yorkshire, and South Yorkshire. However, nearly half the respondents (45%) had travelled more than 20 miles to get to the festival. Of these, over 70% had travelled 40 miles or more, showing that nonregional attendance has a wide reach. Travel distances exceeding 40 miles imply attendance from other UK regions and conurbations, such as Manchester, Nottingham, and beyond, confirming York as an important destination for beer lovers.

Participants were asked to disclose their planned expenditure whilst attending the KBF. This was defined as expenditure related to any consumption on the festival premises, including food and drinks, but excluding entry fees. We carried out an analysis of mean planned expenditure per distance category, as Table 11.2 illustrates. The figures range from little more than £32 to nearly £38, although the analysis indicated no clear pattern between travellers' expenditure and distance travelled. However, significant data concerned the

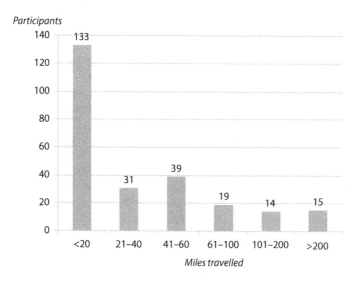

Figure 11.3 Miles travelled by respondents to attend the KBF

Table 11.2 Average expenditure per distance travelled by respondents

Distance category (miles)	Frequency	Planned expenditure (£/Means)
<20	133	33.05
20–40	31	37.91
41–60	39	33.59
61–100	19	33.55
101–200	14	35.95
>200	15	32.32

analysing of responses from participants planning to stay in York overnight. The survey results indicate that fifty-six respondents intended to spend at least one night: thirty-nine respondents (13%) stayed in a hotel/B&B/rented accommodation during the KBF, with a further seventeen respondents (6%) camping in the nearby caravan park.

To determine the expenditure associated with these overnight stays and the impact for the local economy, we asked the respondents to provide the price-per-person for their accommodation during their stay at the KBF.[1] In total, accommodation generated £5,963 in expenditure across the four days. About 79% of the overnight stays were concentrated on the last two days of the KBF (Friday and Saturday), although nearly half of those surveyed indicated spending three or more nights in the city. This figure signifies that those visiting the KBF and staying overnight spent about £106 each. When correlated with the distance travelled data, the analysis indicates that the vast majority of those that chose to stay in York had travelled over eighty miles.

Aside from the economic impact generated by visitors to the KBF, the organisation of the festival has an impact on the local supply chain. To investigate this aspect, we conducted a number of in-depth interviews with festival organisers and brewers taking part in the event. In total, twelve interviewees were approached.

The interviews with festival organisers provided valuable insights about the KBF, its organisation, and its impact on the local economy and businesses. As a CAMRA festival that is completely self-funded and entirely run with the support of volunteers, the KBF's main goal is to promote real ales, thus traditional British beers that are cask-conditioned and without additional gas pressure. As Karl Smith, one of the main organisers told us,

> The purpose [of the KBF] is to campaign for real ale. That's what we do. That's why a lot of people give up all their time and energy for up to two weeks because it's our biggest campaign opportunity of the year.
>
> [Interview with the Authors, April 2016]

The search for local KBF suppliers/providers constituted another point of discussion. According to Melissa Reed, KBF chief-organiser, an important objective is to maximise the number of commercial stalls run by local businesses. Any business wanting to take part in the KBF has to pay a pitch fee; the fact that the fees have steadily increased by up to 10% per annum since 2010 does not seem to have had an impact on the number of requests. In 2016, about 80% of KBF suppliers were local (e.g., based in North Yorkshire), although their presence depended heavily on the type of good/service sold:

> The t-shirts and engravers are not [local]. They do a lot of CAMRA festivals. The food stalls, we are trying to get more local but [the challenge is] finding the right balance and finding the contacts. We are working on it.... We have a local pie producer and we are hoping that our fish person is going to be from Leeds, and we had a local cheese person last year.... Most businesses want to come back so they must do well enough.
>
> [Interview with the Authors, April 2016]

Local networking among businesses seems to play a crucial role together with previous experience working at a CAMRA festival in determining the provenance of providers/suppliers at the KBF. Melissa Reed explained,

> Some of them do just go round and do the CAMRA festivals. Of course, this means that people know them. They have contacts, they know that CAMRA festivals work for them, but it is harder to get someone that has not done this kind of festival before.
>
> [Interview with the Authors, April 2016]

In such context, the KBF works as an important driver for breweries, particularly local breweries that are given more visibility and sampling opportunities for their brews. Beers and ciders showcased at the KBF are selected by local experts, and the beer list has progressively expanded mainly due to the increase in micro- and craft breweries in the UK, although the festival also proposes a foreign beer bar and a wine bar. Karl Smith commented,

> What you get is all the beer drinking population of York are interested, and a good proportion, students, as you can imagine are very keen. We do cater for tastes and we did do foreign kegs which some festivals look down on. We sell wine and we also have a well-stocked cider and perry[2] bar. A lot of people come for that. Whatever you drink, we cater for. If you come with friends it's a good social occasion. You don't have to drink beer if you don't want to and you can actually drink soft drinks. So it is pitched at drinking, and it's mainly a social thing but of course, because it's such a big beer festival it gives quite a good choice of beers.
>
> [Interview with the Authors, April 2016]

This has a positive impact not only in terms of sales during the event, but also with regard to visitors' willingness to visit breweries, tap rooms, and pubs in York. A good example of the KBF-local business interplay is the Brew York Brewery. Founded in March 2016, this York-based brewery was given the opportunity by KBF organisers to run a "brewery tap" on festival premises. In this way, the Brew York founders and owners, Lee Grabham and Wayne Smith, could sell their beer directly from an exclusive stall with their name and merchandising on display (instead of having it sold amongst other lined-up cask beers), under the condition of donating ten casks (normally sold at a retail price of £75+VAT). Wayne Smith stated,

> If we had just left it to volunteers to run, we might have just gone through an extra couple of casks which meant obviously that we would have lost money on the entrance fee. They have to manage how many beers they have and the number of beers they sell so we were getting a lot of traffic to our bar but they still had 350 other beers they needed to sell at the time.
>
> [Interview with the Authors, April 2016]

The platform that KBF provided enabled Brew York to reach a wider audience, and the event itself was used as advertising for the brewery's own facilities in town. As Lee Grabham stated,

> The KBF definitely promoted our brand.... We put an advert in the programme which entitled people to 10% off their beer if when staying in York City Centre they came in here [the tap room] and had a drink. We didn't track that closely how many came down and took up that offer but we definitely know that a few did.
>
> [Interview with the Authors, April 2016]

During these years, the KBF obtained logistics support from YCC. Until 2015, the festival pavilion used to be assembled at the Knavesmire field, owned by the council, at no charge. However, the most recent edition was held at the York Racecourse, a large property owned by and run as a private commercial business. The York CAMRA Branch pays for the site, although they must still apply for licensing to the YCC. Karl Smith explained,

> We have to submit a licence application and they have to approve that. Then they come and check – they do a health and safety check before we open, usually the morning before... So now the council is not our landlord anymore but still have to approve our licence.
>
> [Interview with the Authors, April 2016]

The active involvement of the YCC with the KBF raises some doubts about the potential risks associated with antisocial behaviour due to alcohol consumption (Arseneault et al., 2000), often at the expense of local authorities. However, when asked about issues related to antisocial behaviours at the KBF, Amanda Reed stated that the police had never been called to the site since the KBF had been running, and that any potential problems that might occur are dealt with by volunteer stewards operating on the premises. The KBF does not seem to affect residents within the local proximity either. As Karl Smith confirmed,

> Locals are used to similar events with the racecourse being nearby, and there is a procedure we follow in order to make the locals aware. The council requires that we print some leaflets to let them know it is happening and explain what is going on.... We have to monitor the noise levels like any responsible organisation to make sure we don't exceed them.
>
> [Interview with the Authors, April 2016]

4. Exploring the potential of gastronomy and local development

The findings presented in the previous section provide a wide overview of the British craft beer movement and multiple avenues for reflection with regard to economic development. The significant increase in the number of micro- and craft breweries in the UK has widened opportunities for consumers in terms of access to more diverse beers, not only through large distribution and super-markets, but also through beer festivals and related events. It would seem that the steady growth of the micro- and craft brewing movement has created a new market segment for craft beers, mainly intended and perceived in the UK as cask-conditioned ales with low carbonation using traditional techniques (Cabras, 2018). Much of the appeal of micro-brewed/craft beer is that it rejects national, or even regional, culture in favour of something more local (Danson et al., 2015).

Micro- and craft breweries in the UK appear to have consolidated their presence and level of recognition within their respective areas also in social and economic terms, as the strong relationship between local beers and beer festivals demonstrates. Local breweries and brewers are almost always actively involved in organising these events, and they obtain significant returns in terms of visibility and appreciation. Moreover, breweries rely heavily on the local workforce, and the majority of investments these businesses make are within spatial proximity of their premises. This emphasis on geographic origin has now become a sort of trend characterising the existence of many new firms, with inevitable clashes and overlap in the same areas.

New micro- and craft breweries are likely to remain small, mostly to profit from the support in the form of tax breaks (see Cabras, 2017). Many breweries tend to differentiate their production in line with the reduced market they serve, trying to preserve the original niche in which they started. In such context, the increasing number of beer festivals in the country seems to be functional to the development of an "appreciation strategy" that leads con-sumers to identify themselves with their local breweries. This attitude, by reflection, can be also associated with the resurgence, among consumers, in recognising the significance of local food and recipes in the British pre-imperial tradition. The two concepts, local beer and typical food, can be combined and strategically used to promote tourism at the regional and subregional level, involving and expanding the local supply chain.

The case of the KBF in York seems to corroborate this assumption. The festival organisers tend to select their suppliers and businesses within a spatially constrained supply chain, which brings advantages with regard to local custom. Similarly, breweries showcasing their beers at the KBF generally supply pubs within a range of a few miles (longer distances would result in higher transport costs; see Danson et al., 2015). This strengthens the relationship between craft beers and local provenance, profiling brewers and expanding the level of recognition among consumers. The example of Brew York and their pre-ference for a branded stall rather than having their beers sold amongst those available at the festival's bars supports this statement.

The findings from the SIBA annual survey indicate that about two-thirds of the beer brewed by members goes to pubs, still the main distribution channel. Many breweries own pubs and use these premises as outlets for their beers. In addition, breweries still tend to supply the bulk of their production via casks and kegs, although alternative forms of packaging, such as bottles and cans, are used increasingly. This is likely to expand the provision of beers from bars and pubs, the traditional outlets, to the off-trade market, expanding access to craft beers from mostly pub-goers or ale connoisseurs to different types of con-sumers. The expansion in terms of the offer and customer base could raise the profile of beers also in relation to fine dining – for instance, in hotels, restaurants, and gastropubs, a new form of pub in the UK that combines high-quality cuisine with a pub atmosphere. In such context, new opportu-nities may arise in increasing knowledge among consumers regarding pairing specific types of food and recipes with ales.

This appears to be the strategy that the KBF organisers have thus far pursued: The success in terms of participation and tourism has engendered opportunities to reach consumers and widen their knowledge on how specific beers can accompany specific types of food. The last editions have seen an increasing number of cooking sessions and tutorials organised on the KBF premises, with attendance levels growing year by year. In parallel, the YCC Tourism Office launched the "York Food and Drink Festival," organised in the city since 1997. Originally a small underground event, the festival now runs for ten days (York Press, 2016). The event has seen a growing participa-tion of local retailers and licensers over the years, particularly pubs that offer tailored menus in which beer is a significant component.

The case of York shows interesting potential for gastro-tourism related to beer. Overnight stayers indicated their expenditure could increase significantly by expanding the offer to beer-related dining. However, the "quality" of beers is an issue to consider. The interpretation and perception of beer varies significantly with regard to different contexts and issues related to markets and societies (Bamforth and Cabras, 2016). While quality is an extremely subjective concept, the increasing variety of beers available to British consumers poses some questions about their standards and characteristics. Educating consumers on key aspects and features of beers – for instance, different brewing styles, ingredients, and their provenance – would definitely broaden their knowledge and level of appreciation.

According to Bamforth and Cabras (2016), as much as consumers, it is also extremely important to invest in educating the brewers. Today, a significant number of brewers, mostly operating in the craft and micro-brewing sector, have little or no formal training and enter the market without the necessary knowledge to increase their chances of survival, in addition to increasing the quality of the product they brew. It is certainly possible for extremely talented and natural individuals to develop world-class operations with no formal credentials; however, obtaining a consistent product requires a thorough understanding of the complexities of malting and brewing allied to genuine practical experience gained "on the job." Hence, systemic efforts in training providers, business agencies, and government bodies are needed to upscale opportunities for the UK craft-brewing industry. The fact that most of those employed in the industry are relatively young provides multiple avenues to implement policies that effectively address this aspect.

Educating both brewers and consumers is likely to create the conditions to further expand the offer of beers, from pubs and festivals to restaurants and fine dining outlets. In the UK, the rise in gastropubs is not necessarily associated with a more conscious and expert combination of food and beer, as these places rely heavily on wines as the main beverage with meals. This is not only driven by price (a bottle of wine in UK licensed premises sells at an average £18–22, versus £3–5 for a pint of beer) but also due to the scarcity of knowledge on how to pair beers with recipes. Hence, increasing the level of understanding among consumers would enhance their power of choice in relation to which beer to select for a meal. Likewise, enhancing brewers' expertise regarding the characteristics and features of their beers would increase their power when placing their portfolio across restaurants and licensees. In this way, the British craft beer industry would increase its profile and market share, involving more businesses in its distribution channels.

5. Conclusions

The study presented in this chapter explores and examines the UK micro- and craft brewing movement in relation to opportunities and challenges with regard to local development and gastro-tourism. The steady growth of the movement has created a new market segment for craft beers, mainly intended and perceived in the UK as cask-conditioned ales with low carbonation using traditional techniques (Cabras, 2018). Nonetheless, despite the impressive choice now available to consumers, craft beer sales remain marginal in the British market, with just an 8% market share in 2016.

From the analysis presented, it appears that new opportunities for craft beers can be created by expanding the offer from pubs and bars to restaurants and fine-dining outlets. However, doing so requires increasing and refining knowledge of beer across brewers and consumers. Our analysis indicates that pale ales, traditional brown ales, and stout porters are the most-brewed types of ale, but many breweries tend to differentiate their production as a function of the reduced market they serve, trying to preserve the original niche in which they started. However, with the expansion of bottle packaging, an increasing number of micro- and craft breweries are starting to compete with large brewers on a greater scale, increasing their output and enlarging their range of products by significantly investing in innovation and marketing (Cabras and Bamforth, 2016). This poses some questions in relation to the types of beers offered and whether consumers continue to perceive micro- and craft breweries differently from mass producers.

This chapter adds to the literature on breweries and the brewing industry in general, which tends to focus more on large-scale production processes and marketing strategies implemented by large breweries, at times neglecting the marketing and gastronomic aspects that contribute to shaping their development, business trajectories, and ways to attract new customers. As a result, there is a general paucity of information with regard to micro- and small breweries. Given the resurgence of real ales and craft beers and the growth of these businesses in the past decades, more studies on micro- and craft breweries would help predict future behaviours in the UK beer market and beyond and enable a better understanding of their potential in terms of local development and gastro-tourism.

Notes

1 Prices were provided in five ranges, from under £20 to more than £100 per night. Price bands were formulated on estimates based on average prices on Booking.com during the KBF event.
2 Perry is similar to cider but made from pears instead of apples.

References

Allen, G. (2007). Place branding: New tools for economic development. *Design Management Review*, 18(2), pp. 60–68.

Andereck, K. (1995). Environmental consequences of tourism: A review of recent research. *Intermountain Research Station, USDA Forest Service*, INT-323, pp. 77–81.

Arseneault, L., Moffitt, T., Caspi, A., Taylor, P. and Silva, P. (2000). Mental disorders and violence in a total birth cohort: Results from the Dunedin Study. *Archives of General Psychiatry*, 57(10), pp. 979–986. http://dx.doi.org/10.1001/archpsyc.57.10.979.

Bamforth, C. W. and Cabras I. (2016). Interesting times: Changes in brewing. In I. Cabras, D. Higgins, and D. Preece (eds) *Beer, brewing and pubs: A global perspective*. London: Palgrave Macmillan.

Blichfeldt, B. and Halkier, H. (2014). Mussels, tourism and community development: A case study of place branding through food festivals in rural north Jutland, Denmark. *European Planning Studies*, 22(8), pp. 1587–1603.

British Beer and Pub Association. (2016). *Statistical handbook*. London: BBPA.

Broad, M. (2009). Strong euro stems stag party flood. *BBC Business*. http://news.bbc.co.uk/1/hi/business/7875415.stm.

Cabras, I. (2017). The capitals of ales: How beer is revitalizing cities and local economies in Britain. In N. G. Chapman, J. S. Lellock and C. D. Lippard (eds) *Untapped: Exploring the cultural dimensions of craft beer*. Morgantown: West Virginia University Press. ISBN-13: 978-1943665686.

Cabras, I. (2018). Beer on! The evolution of micro- and craft brewing in the UK. In C. Garavaglia and J. Swinnen (eds) *Economic perspectives on craft beer: A revolution in the global beer industry*. London: Palgrave Macmillan.

Cabras, I. and Bamforth, C.W. (2016). From reviving tradition to fostering innovation and changing marketing: The evolution of microbrewing in the UK and US, 1980–2012. *Business History*, 58(5), pp. 625–646.

Cabras, I. and Higgins, D. (2016). Beer, brewing, and business history. *Business History*, 58(5), pp. 609–624.

Campaign for Real Ale (2015). Brewery boom hat trick as British brewing grows by 10 percent for third consecutive year. http://www.theguardian.com/lifeandstyle/2012/jul/29/flavoured-beers-popularity-food-pairing.

Cantavella-Jordá, M. and Balaguer, J. (2002). Tourism as a long-run economic growth factor: The Spanish case. *Applied Economics*, 34(7), pp. 877–884.

Chon, K. (1990). The role of destination image in tourism: A review and discussion. *The Tourist Review*, 45(2), pp. 2–9.

Danson, M., Galloway, L., Cabras, I., and Beatty, C. (2015). Microbrewing and entrepreneurship: The origins, development, and integration of real ale breweries in the UK. *International Journal of Entrepreneurship and Innovation*, 16(2), pp. 135–144.

Dritsakis, N. (2004). Tourism as a long-run economic growth factor: An empirical investigation for Greece using causality analysis. *Tourism Economics*, 10(3), pp. 305–316.

Emerson, R. (1976). Social exchange theory. *Annual Review of Sociology*, 2(1), pp. 335–362.

Gani, A. (1998). Macroeconomic determinants of growth in the south pacific island economies. *Applied Economics Letters*, 5(12), pp. 747–749.

Getz, D. and Frisby, W. (1988). Evaluating management effectiveness in community-run festivals. *Journal of Travel Research*, 27(1), pp. 22–27.

Herrmann, O. and Herrmann, R. (2014). Hotel room rates under the influence of a large event: The Oktoberfest in Munich 2012. *International Journal of Hospitality Management*, 39, pp. 21–28. http://dx.doi.org/10.1016/j.ijhm.2014.01.006.

Higham, J. and Ritchie, B. (2001). The evolution of festivals and other events in rural southern New Zealand. *Event Management*, 7(1), pp. 39–49.

Jang, S., Chen, M., and Kim, H. (2006). Tourism expansion and economic development: The case of Taiwan. *Tourism Management*, 27(5), pp. 925–933.

Ketter, E. and Avraham, E. (2012). *Media strategies for marketing places in crisis: Improving the image of cities, countries, and tourist destinations*. Burlington: Taylor and Francis.

Knowles, T., and Egan, M. (2002). The changing structure of the brewing and pub retailing. *International Journal of Contemporary Hospitality Management*, 14(2), pp. 65–71.

Lee, I. and Arcodia, C. (2011). The role of regional food festivals for destination branding. *International Journal of Tourism Research*, 13(4), pp. 355–367.

Louca, C. (2006). Income and expenditure in the tourism industry: Time series evidence from Cyprus. *Tourism Economics*, 12(4), pp. 603–617.

Mason, C. M. and McNally, K. N. (1997). Market change, distribution, and new firm formation and growth: The case of real-ale breweries in the United Kingdom. *Environment and Planning A*, 29(2), pp. 405–417.

Mayfield, T. and Crompton, J. (1995). Development of an instrument for identifying community reasons for staging a festival. *Journal of Travel Research*, 33(3), pp. 37–44.

Moore M., Reid, N. and McLaughlin, R. (2016). The Locational determinants of microbreweries and brewpubs in the United States. In I. Cabras, D. Higgins, and D. Preece (eds) *Beer, brewing and pubs: A global perspective*. London: Palgrave Macmillan.

Nicolai, B. (2012). München: Zum Oktoberfest steigen hotelpreise um 850 prozent. https://www.welt.de/wirtschaft/article109323216/Zum-Oktoberfest-steigen-Hotel preise-um-850-Prozent.html.

Oh, C. (2005). The contribution of tourism development to economic growth in the Korean economy. *Tourism Management*, 26(1), pp. 39–44.

Pratten, J. (2004). Examining the possible causes of business failure in British public houses. *International Journal of Contemporary Hospitality Management*, 16(4), pp. 246–252.

Preece, D. (2016). Turbulence in UK public house retailing: Ramifications and responses. In I. Cabras, D. Higgins, and D. Preece (eds) *Beer, brewing and pubs: A global perspective*. London: Palgrave Macmillan.

Proença, S. and Soukiazis, E. (2008). Tourism as an alternative source of regional growth in Portugal: A panel data analysis at NUTS II and III levels. *Portuguese Economic Journal*, 7(1), pp. 43–61.

Richards, G. and Wilson, J. (2004). The impact of cultural events on city image: Rotterdam, cultural capital of Europe 2001. *Urban Studies*, 41(10), pp. 1931–1951.

Rohrer, F. (2006). Stagflation. BBC News, 21 June. http://news.bbc.co.uk/1/hi/ magazine/5101628.stm.

Sinclair, M. (1998). Tourism and economic development: A survey. *Journal of Development Studies*, 34(5), pp. 1–51.

Slade, M. (2004). Market power and joint dominance in UK brewing. *Journal of Industrial Economics*, 52(1), pp. 133–163.

Smith, D., Solgaard, H. and Beckmann, S. (1999). Changes and trends in alcohol consumption patterns in Europe. *Journal of Consumer Studies & Home Economics*, 23(4), pp. 247–260.

Society of Independent Brewers. (2016). *British beer: A report on the 2016 members survey of the society of independent brewers*. Burton-on-Trent: SIBA.

Thurnell-Read, T. (2012). Tourism place and space. *Annals of Tourism Research*, 39(2), pp. 801–819.

Tiwari, A. (2011). Tourism, exports and FDI as a means of growth: Evidence from four Asian countries. *The Romanian Economic Journal*, 14(140), pp. 131–151.

Tribe, J. (1997). *Corporate strategy for tourism*. London: International Thompson Publishing Services.

UNWTO (2017). Why tourism? http://www2.unwto.org/content/why-tourism.

Waitt, G. (1999). Playing games with Sydney: Marketing Sydney for the 2000 Olympics. *Urban Studies*, 36(7), pp. 1055–1077.

Waitt, G. (2003). Social impacts of the Sydney Olympics. *Annals of Tourism Research*, 30 (1), pp. 194–215.

Wang, Y. and Pfister, R. (2008). Residents' attitudes toward tourism and perceived personal benefits in a rural community. *Journal of Travel Research*, 47(1), pp. 84–93.

Woodley, A. (1993). Tourism and sustainable development: The community perspective. In Tourism and Sustainable Development: Monitoring, Planning, Managing (J. G. Nelson, R. Butler and G. Wall Eds), pp. 135-147. Waterloo: University of Waterloo, Heritage Resources Centre

Wyld, J., Pugh, J. and Tyrrall, D. (2010). Evaluating the impact of progressive beer duty on small breweries: A case study of tax breaks to promote SMES. *Environment and Planning C: Government and Policy*, 28(1), pp. 225–240.

Xiao, H. and Smith, S. (2004). Residents' perceptions of Kitchener-Waterloo Oktoberfest: An inductive analysis. *Event Management*, 8(3), pp. 151–160.

York Press (2016). York Beer Festival 2016: What you should know – and what you should drink... York Press. http://www.yorkpress.co.uk/news/14733716.York_Beer_Festival_2016__What_you_should_know___and_what_you_should_drink___/.

12 The luxury turn in wine tourism

Still good for local development?

Nicola Bellini and Evelyne Resnick

1. Introduction

The objective of this chapter is to explore the relationship between some recent trends in wine tourism (i.e., the "luxury turn") and local economic development (LED). While the luxury turn certainly draws on creativity and innovation and achieves superior levels of service quality, the actual impact on LED demands a closer and more critical look.

This chapter is not based on original research, but the result of a dialogue that began at the La Rochelle workshop on "Gastronomy and Local Development" in November 2015 between two otherwise "distant" participants – namely, the authors of this chapter: Bellini, with considerable expertise in the research and practice of regional and local development policies and place marketing, and Resnick, with equally considerable expertise in consulting and research in wine marketing and tourism management.

As a starting point, we emphasise that this chapter is based on rejecting any simplified and univocal definition of LED and therefore assumes that there is no simple relationship between gastronomy and LED. This induces researchers to qualitatively investigate the variety of possible links (Barrère, 2013), rather than committing themselves to building and formalizing models with a supposedly generalised value.

A crucial issue, which requires dealing with, is the relationship between LED and globalisation. As convincingly argued in Certomà's (2011) narration of the "scandal" concerning Brunello di Montalcino (one of the most celebrated luxury wines of Italy), a wine's local identity may be as much the result of a particular terroir as the outcome of a web of technical, economic, legal, and political relations of a global kind.

However, the ample literature on this subject suggests that the outcome of a global opening of local systems is not predetermined. To avoid the opposite risks of entropy and disintegration, exposure to globalisation requires balancing the economic and sociocultural dimensions of internationalisation. In practice, this occurs when the local system accumulates all those intangible assets, which are mostly of a cognitive and relational nature, allowing the local to take on a proactive and not just a defensive role in the global context. Actors accumulate such assets through experiential learning, but also through collective institutions and practices (Bellini and Bramanti, 2008).

In the following sections, we first recall the main issues concerning the relationship between wine tourism and local development, including some emerging critical factors. We then look at the luxury dimension and at luxury wine tourism as an expression of contemporary "experiential luxury." In our discussion, we especially emphasise the tensions between the quality contribution deriving from the luxury turn and the potential disconnection from the local heritage.

2. Wine tourism and local development

For the purposes of this chapter, we define "wine tourism" as comprising actors and activities concerned with visiting vineyards, wineries, wine-related events, and occasions when experiencing the attributes of a wine region is the main motivation for the visit or at least a significant and memorable component of the travel experience (definition adapted from Charters and Thach, 2016). Wine tourism is "simultaneously a form of consumer behavior, a strategy by which destinations develop and market wine-related attractions and imagery, and a marketing opportunity for wineries to educate, and to sell their products, directly to consumers" (Getz and Brown, 2006). In a wider perspective, wine tourism combines, in an original way, a specific kind of agritourism with cultural tourism (Lignon-Darmaillac, 2015a) and thus helps to perceive and understand the "real value" of wine, much beyond its mere market value (Perrot, 2014).

Limiting ourselves to an economic dimension, wine tourism impacts on LED in three ways:

- As an (additional) attractor for tourist destinations, contributing to their competitiveness in the tourism market and especially some of its segments.
- Adding to the income of local winemakers in rural areas by internalizing the positive externalities of wine production, such as preserving the landscape or protecting the intangible cultural heritage (Menghini, 2015).
- As a marketing tool for local wine products, especially for lesser-known wine regions, in connection with the increasing relevance of word of mouth, social networks, and other e-reputation media.

On scratching the surface, the relationship between wine tourism and LED is much more complex. First, a variety of actors interact in packaging wine tourism. They are private (individual companies: winemakers, shops, restaurants, hotels and resorts, tour operators), but also of a collective (associations, consortia) and public nature (local authorities, destination management organisations). They belong to the rural context (typically, winemakers) but also to the urban (shops, restaurants, hotels, and cultural institutions, such as wine museums). Individual entrepreneurs or institutions rarely implement successful wine tourism strategies in isolation. On the contrary, success depends on the effective networking of clusters of several local companies that are sometimes complementary but other times competing with each other (Musso and Francioni, 2015). A kind of associational economy is required, implying cooperation between private, collective, and public actors, and rural/urban integration. The quality of the local social capital may have a decisive role in all this (Cooke and Morgan, 1998; Granovetter, 2005).

In other words, local networking (and social capital) is both a precondition and an outcome of wine tourism success. This is especially strengthened with two conditions in place: first, the integration of producers in regional development platforms exploiting the related variety potential that also involves gastronomy and food-related tourism (Lazzeretti et al., 2010); second, the "local accumulation of knowledge, practices, gastronomic and taste-related discourse and images that promote learning and skills' acquisition by the protagonists of the co-construction of the tourism experience," i.e., what has been termed (echoing the Marshallian industrial atmosphere) a "gastronomic atmosphere" (Clergeau and Etcheverria, 2013).

Wine tourism develops in close relationship with "the cultural geography of the landscape" (Mitchell et al., 2012). This brings into play the "terroir," a concept that combines technical features (the biophysical properties of a place) and cultural practices (pertaining to both production and social organisation) that are the objects of a "patrimonialisation" process. A credible reference to the terroir makes the relationship between product and places (at least to some degree) objective and at the same time unique and nonreproducible (Spielmann and Charters, 2013; Charters and Michaux, 2014; Lenglet and Giannelloni, 2016). Wine tourism can therefore be seen as the privileged, coproduced, experiential access to such local uniqueness.

This kind of link between wine and territory does not apply to all geographical situations. The terroir concept is dynamic and context-specific (Spielmann and Charters, 2013). On the one hand, consumers' perception of the authenticity of New World wines appears to be related to specific references to the technical terroir, while Old World wines rely on the subjective and hedonic dimensions of an "internalised authenticity" (Moulard et al., 2015). In some cases, however, New World wines also draw on collective identities: this is the case of immigration vineyards (Italian vineyards in South America, Huguenot vineyards in South Africa) that are emotionally reconnected to the winemaking tradition of the countries of origin (Perrot, 2014). On the other hand, emerging wine cultures and markets, such as China, India, and Russia (sometimes labelled New World or the Third World of wine; Banks and Overton, 2010), seem far less able to establish such links and therefore lag behind in the creation of wine tourism experiences.

Due to its apparent uniqueness and nontransferability, the link between wine and territory, when present, is easily translated into overlapping images and brands of the former and the latter. Place branding, especially in rural areas and regions, often uses terroir-based products and especially wine as a reference, mirroring the use of the place-of-origin reference of products. Wine brands are an integral part of a large number of tourist destination brands.

This is especially obvious when the names coincide and the fame of the product brand may contribute to that of a possibly less visible location: Cognac, Bordeaux, Champagne, Cahors, Chianti, Montalcino, Barolo, Valpolicella (just to mention some French and Italian examples) are territories whose fame is linked to the wines they produce. However, wines also contribute to defining the distinctive profile of territories with much more recent traditions. In some cases, this adds a sense of exclusivity and innovation (as in the case of the Bolgheri region in Tuscany, brought to worldwide attention as the home of the famous Sassicaia), or greater authenticity, a less commercialised approach, quality of life, and "affordable luxury" (as in the case of Tri-Valley in California, i.e., the valleys of Amador, Livermore, and San Ramon, an area often shadowed by its more famous neighbours, Napa and Sonoma) (Resnick, 2008).

In most cases, wine (in the same way and often more than other terroir-based products) helps materialize the storytelling of places and their otherwise intangible cultural assets. This is most effectively achieved through the interactive, fluid, and uncontrolled creation and re-creation of "sincerity" and inclusive meanings linked to the emotional value of brands, rather than through technocratic, top-down processes managed by marketing professionals (Beverland, 2005; Resnick, 2008; Rabbiosi, 2016).

3. Critical factors in wine tourism

The contemporary dynamics of wine tourism present a number of critical features that may impact on the relationship with local development. First, the growth of wine tourism increases the analytical and practical relevance of market segmentation to target the increasing share of nonexpert visitors (as profiled by the literature), and especially the in between categories, i.e., regular drinkers with no special knowledge and yet interested in a meaningful learning experience (Charters and Ali-Knight, 2002; Marzo-Navarro and Pedraja-Iglesias, 2010). Thus, profiling a successful wine tourism experience requires effectively managing emerging cultural attitudes in consumer behaviour, such as the foodies phenomenon (Getz et al., 2014).

An additional consequence is the possibility of also adopting tourism practices for analogous products, therefore competing with wines (and spirits, such as cognac or whisky). Non-terroir-based beverages, such as beer, provide a challenging alternative. Local breweries contribute to entertaining tourists in many locations (as discussed in the Cabras and Ellison chapter [11] in this book). The Guinness Storehouse in Dublin has been a benchmark experiential attraction, and beer is also used synergistically with place branding, as in the recent case of the place-inspired promotional campaign of the Sardinian beer brand Ichnusa (a brand owned by Heineken).

Dealing with this scenario calls for differentiation. This occurs through thematisation, i.e., building distinctive narratives, which in turn are realised through the consistent integration of core and other services, as well as through wine-related and other attractors within the "increasingly complex, multi-directional geography" outlined by contemporary wine routes (Lignon-Darmaillac, 2015b).

Thematisation may take several directions. It may emphasise: history and ethnography; geography and landscape; wine education; wine trade; arts (architecture; performing arts); hospitality (wineries as hotels); gastronomy; ecotourism (harvest tourism); event organisation (business meetings, team building events, weddings etc.); animal parks; sports (horse riding, biking, etc.), and open-air activities (Lignon-Darmaillac, 2015a; Byrd et al., 2016; Rico, 2016; Bellini et al., 2017). Thematisation also implies a consistent approach to the microdimension of the "winescape" (Quintal et al., 2015) and may be supported by technological innovations, such as mobile apps, augmented reality, etc. New formats are being implemented, including theme parks (such as the "Hameau du Vin" established in 1993 in Burgundy's Beaujolais region) and a new generation of wine museums, which are characterised by a multifaceted presentation of wine culture, an experiential approach, and the massive use of multimedia technologies. Examples of the latter are WiMu in Barolo, opened in 2010, and especially the "Cité du Vin" in Bordeaux, inaugurated in 2016. The latter case involves landmark architecture, a visible addition to the skyline of a French city, and a global approach, as the museum consistently refers not just to the local heritage but to wine civilisations (plural!).

Wine tourism markets are also made more complex by internationalisation. This is a twofold process. On the one hand, the number of wine tourism destinations in the New World countries has rapidly increased. This implies not only a higher level of competition but also competitive challenges linked to a different approach to designing wine tourism packages, namely, those less constrained by heritage and therefore more customer oriented than product oriented. On the other hand, the share of international, long-distance tourists (vs. regional/domestic tourists) is increasing (Getz and Brown, 2006), implying a growing number of visitors from countries with no indigenous tradition in wine production and consumption accessing wine tourism. This dramatises intercultural issues in dealing with them.

These trends imply a number of serious managerial challenges. Wine tourism originally developed as a result of intuitions more than planned strategy. Notwithstanding the fast professionalisation that is visible especially in some major wine regions (Rigaux, 2015), the lack of specific managerial competences is still a significant problem, especially for small winery companies. It affects the design of distinctive tourist experiences, the efficiency of management, the effectiveness of communication, the appropriateness of market positioning and targeting, and the ability to manage intercultural relations (Rico, 2016; Nicolosi et al., 2016).

4. Luxury wines...

A relevant trend in wine tourism is the emergence of wine tourism packages and destinations that may be characterised as "luxury." Luxury in this sense is a relatively new term but not a new concept in the wine industry (Wolf et al., 2016). A "luxury wine" is commonly a synonym for an expensive wine.

According to standard segmentations, wines can be considered luxury when priced over $50 US per bottle and super-luxury when priced over $100 US (on the US retail market).[1] Recently, a more articulated Luxury Wine Price Continuum was proposed, taking into account the full range of consumer perceptions. This continuum is based on the following segmentation: Affordable Luxury ($50–$99 US), Luxury Wine ($100–$499 US), Icon Wine ($500–$999 US), and Dream Wine ($1,000+ US) (Thach et al., 2017). In Europe, high prices are especially linked to scarcity, i.e., to the limited number of bottles producible from a specific terroir, as well as strict regulations, expensive land, and the use of sophisticated technology. However, both the literature and professionals agree that price must be combined with other dimensions of luxury, such as aesthetics, sustainability, high quality, symbols, and a sense of privilege that goes much beyond the financial dimension.

Therefore, reputation plays an important role. The region of origin is a decisive attribute for luxury wine. Especially in Europe, the association with a region with a long and distinguished tradition in this production supports the customer's perception of the luxury character. This is strengthened by the certified rarity and exclusivity of the wine, as in the case of the Bordeaux Premier Grands Crus (according to the 1855 classification); and by narratives linking wines to some outstanding entrepreneur (e.g., Mario Incisa della Rocchetta for Sassicaia) or the centuries-old continuity of family ownership (e.g., for some châteaux of the Bordeaux region), even if presently framed in larger corporations (Resnick, 2008). Accordingly, branding and marketing strategies will aim to pursue the emotional connection to consumers by focusing on the wine-region link and – as a professional recently put it – by "being as local as possible."[2]

Wolf et al. (2016: 121) stress that "the existing understanding of consumer perceptions of luxury in general may not be sufficient in developing an adequate conceptualisation of luxury wine." According to these authors, the lack of consensus on what exactly constitutes luxury wine also derives from the fact that producers and consumers have differing perceptions of luxury. The producer's perspective predefines the luxury character by assuring and communicating a high level of technical quality, unique authenticity, and translating all this into a high price. The consumer's perception has a subjective dimension and is affected by the variety of characteristics (knowledge, income, lifestyle, etc.) that determine the motivation and perception of the wine consumption.

Thus, only some segments of wine consumers (the "connoisseurs" and the "aspirational drinkers," according to the classic definition of Spawton, 1990) will include luxury wine consumers. At the same time, luxury wine consumption may be shaped by wider social and psychological needs, such as communicating an acquired status or a quality-oriented lifestyle to others. Luxury wine consumption can be part of lifestyles that range from "frugal hedonism"

(McMillan, 2017) to big spending, tempered by taste and knowledge. This, in turn, will influence perception. In sum, luxury wine consumption is thus mostly explained by the self-congruency theory: "Consumers are more likely to purchase brands which they believe match their self-image" (Wolf et al., 2016).

In building self-congruency, a number of factors and trends may nonetheless contribute to reducing (or at least confusing) the relevance of the relationship of luxury with a specific territory and a specific heritage of production excellence in the consumers' eyes. In the case of Champagne, the luxury qualification is the result of a sequence of resilient myths that made it an "integral social marker of status and membership" for the bourgeois society on a national and international scale (Rokka, 2017). As a consequence, storytelling keeps the reference to a specific terroir alive, but the distinctive features relate to translocal practices and meanings. More recently, the term "artification" expresses the process by which luxury goods no longer derive their legitimacy from their objective rarity but from their status as works of art. In the case of luxury wines, this shifts the balance in communication towards the entrepreneurs' innovative personality and artistic role, as in the cases of Robert Mondavi and Bernard Magrez, while de-emphasizing the technical terroir dimension (Passebois-Ducros et al., 2015). The same effect emerges when wines are associated with other luxury products, as they are integrated into a wider strategy (as in the case of LVMH, with several wine and spirit brands managed by Moët Hennessy) or named after and packaged by fashion designers (e.g., Stefano Ricci's wines at the Enoteca Pinchiorri in Florence, Roberto Cavalli's wine selection, etc.).

Self-congruency is influenced by the meanings attached to the concept of luxury. Thus, it is important to note the emergence of transnational identities in food consumption through the identification of luxury with high-quality exotic or "culturally contaminated" food – i.e., Western in the East and Eastern in the West – as well as the diffusion of affluent social groups practicing a kind of "inconspicuous consumption" nurtured by anticonsumerist countercultures (Winterhalter, 2011). Parallel to this, the democratisation of luxury exposes wider social groups to at least some luxury products (as in the case of Champagne, available in supermarkets) and allows "luxury nibblers" to partake in luxury consumption occasionally, within the limits and opportunities of their income.

Finally, globalisation suggests that luxury wines may adapt to international customers and their drinking habits. In some cases, this occurs by re-originating the product (Pike, 2015), i.e., associating it with the consumption market rather than the production region through communication and packaging (as in the case of the 2016 Moët & Chandon campaign to introduce a new rosé vintage to the North American market, with a limited edition honouring ten iconic US cities). Other new translocal luxury products have been proposed as well, such as the Franco-American "OpusOne" or the more recent Chinese Chandon sparkling wine.

5. ... and luxury wine tourism

The relationship between luxury wines and luxury wine tourism is not an obvious one. Essentially, luxury wine tourism is the result of integrating experiences concerning high-quality (but not necessarily very expensive) wine into a framework of luxury hospitality, where consumers respond to a combination of functional, hedonic, and symbolic/expressive values (Yang and Mattila, 2016; Swarbrooke, 2017). This means that the implication of luxury wines is a possibility but not a necessity. Still, luxury wine tourism is mostly influenced by the same dynamics that we briefly discussed in the previous section.

Luxury wine tourism positions itself fully within the global trend of experiential luxury, i.e., the shift from the luxury of exclusive "having" to the luxury of exclusive "being," with its related managerial implications: a well-argued emphasis on uniqueness and heritage, in-store staged experiences, meaningful links to art and culture, exoticism and/or authenticity (Abtan et al., 2014).

"Luxury wine tourism" refers to only one trend in a wider spectrum of proposed wine-related tourist experiences where more traditional types still prosper. Provisionally, let us accept high(er) prices as its basic defining element (Sjostrom et al., 2016). However, its characterisation needs to be more articulated.

First, a significant feature in the product design is that it takes place in exceptional buildings. These may be the ancient chateaux of the Bordeaux region or new, unique architectural landmarks. The best example is the Marques de Riscal Winery in the Rioja region (Spain) designed by Frank Gehry. This is an obvious extension of the more general trend of assigning the construction of new wineries to world-renowned architects. These "wine temples" add aesthetic value to both their functional role in wine production and to the surrounding landscape – and often in an unconventional and controversial way (Lazzeretti et al., 2010).

With regard to customers, luxury wine tourism addresses mostly long-distance and international visitors. Luxury services are provided to resident guests as well as to participants in special events, such as weddings or corporate events. This element is emphasised in, for example, Bernard Magrez' Château Fombrauge estate in the Bordeaux region. Although integrated in relatively expensive wine experiences, classes, vineyard visits etc., they tend to reproduce features common to most top hotels worldwide, including the possibility of personalised services for VIPs (helicopter flights, Rolls Royce rides, private events, etc.).

Wine-related services go beyond mere tasting and learning. A major trend concerns wellness. A well-known example is the French five-star countryside resort Les Sources de Caudalie and its spa, which offer distinctive wine therapy (whose products are successfully commercialised under the Caudalie brand). Therapy consists of beauty treatments, massages, and baths using the properties of the residue of winemaking (pips and pulp).

Last, one should consider the emergence of a luxury consumption that makes sustainability and responsibility an appealing feature and often a selection criterion. Ethical luxury tourism is a niche market developed by specialised tour operators (e.g., Luxethica in Paris), with a focus also on "responsible hedonists". Eco-wine tourists purposely visit wineries that produce organic and biodynamic wine (Holohan and Remaud, 2014). Luxury resorts are established in wine regions like Tuscany through the sustainable reconversion of old, abandoned villages (Cucculelli and Goffi, 2016).

The exclusivity of this kind of luxury tourism is mitigated by at least two phenomena. On the one hand, within the same area, different approaches may coexist. In the case of Champagne, the ambivalent character of the product (accessible by standard mass markets; exclusive for wealthy elite consumers) is reflected in the different positioning of producers. Some position themselves in the luxury segment; others target wider audiences with group visits to cellars and vineyards, festivals, and popular festivities (Gatelier et al., 2012, 2014). On the other hand, a democratisation of wine luxury experiences is taking place, mostly by providing some affordable features for luxury nibblers in the form of special packages (weekends and short stays in off-peak seasons), simple access to some wellness services, one-day visits, introductory tastings, and so forth.

6. What kind of wine tourism for what strategy of local economic development?

Does the luxury turn lead to a weakening of the local link, and does this mean a less significant contribution to local development?

Differences in market approaches may reflect the heterogeneous nature of the wine tourism actors, e.g., in the case of the Champagne region, the big traders (*maisons de négoce*) tend to address exclusive market targets with an approach based on the individual heritage and luxury symbolism, while the growers place greater emphasis on the collective, territorially specific heritage (Gatelier et al., 2012, 2014). Luxury wine tourism seems to be an option for companies that are clearly positioned in the global market. The advantages of referring to the local, natural, and heritage specificities must then find compromises with cosmopolitan standards of luxury and with the need to authenticate experiences within the customer's cultural frameworks that may be at an extreme psychic distance from local ones, also with regard to wine consumption, as in the case of Chinese tourists (Bellini et al., 2014). In fact, the state-of-the-art of luxury wine tourism suggests a tension between those aspects that seem to confirm that distinctiveness is rooted in the unique features of the local environment and those that, on the contrary, mark a departure from it.

Overall, luxury wine tourism cannot renounce designing and giving value to an appealing tourist terroir or winescape, both in macro and micro terms (Sparks, 2007; Quintal et al., 2015). Reference to the technical terroir will be especially relevant when other features (history, tradition, reputation, etc.) are not available, typically for New World wineries (Moulard et al., 2015). However, as for wines (Sjostrom et al., 2016; Wolf et al., 2016: 121), the luxury perception of wine tourism is heavily influenced by the region's reputation. This may be related to the exclusivity and quality of wine production (e.g., in the Bordeaux region) but also to a mix of intellectual and emotional components that lead to identifying (at least some) of the tourists as belonging to socioeconomic elites (e.g., in the case of Tuscany: Bellini et al., 2010).

In other cases – e.g., California – tourists may be sensitive to a more holistic perception of the local lifestyle, combining relaxation, wellness, fine dining, and luxury within a distinctive European elegance evoked by the urban landscape inspired by the Spanish Revival style (Rae, 2013; Jones et al., 2015). The case of Tri-Valley in California is especially interesting in this respect. Its fame is shadowed by its more famous neighbours, Napa and Sonoma. Napa Valley is the oldest and most famous California wine region, home to Mondavi Vineyard and Wines, pioneer of the wine industry and advocate of the European-style way of life combining wines with food and elegance. Sonoma Valley houses more than four hundred wineries, within a winescape characterised by the Pacific coastline and the redwood forests. Both places enjoy an upscale image in terms of restaurants, hotels, and wine tourism. Tri-Valley does not benefit from the same notoriety. Its name comes from its geographic location at the corner of three valleys (Amador, Livermore, and San Ramon). Its four cities (Pleasanton, Livermore, Dublin, and Danville) constitute a high-quality suburban area linked to San Francisco and San José. As emphasised in a ten-year-old communication campaign, Tri-Valley's strength originates from its combination of small-town hospitality and big-town amenities (events, restaurants, cafes, galleries, theatres, and shops); its relevance as a business hub that is less pressured, more laid-back, friendlier, and with more beautiful scenery than its Silicon Valley neighbour; and its milieu that is less commercialised than Napa Valley. Within this framework, wine and wineries appeal to the tourist who is culturally sensitive, in search of elegance and sincere authenticity, luxury-oriented but in more affordable terms. In all this, wine is not as central as in Napa or Sonoma. The valley offers a beer trail and an ice cream trail alongside the traditional wine trail, and those unusual trails attract a younger crowd, including families with young children. Wine is not critical per se but as a component of an overall and wider image consisting of relaxation, quality of life, and sustainability (Resnick, 2008).

Within this more articulated scenario, luxury wine tourism may thus propose a series of eclectic compromises responding to the global-minded expectations of cosmopolitan elites, with culinary preferences that comply with transnational identities (Winterhalter, 2011). Rather than referring to strictly local or regional specificities, wine tourism may be presented and perceived in more generic terms, e.g., as an initiation to some stereotypical (French, Italian, etc.) lifestyle (Lignon-Darmaillac, 2015a).

One should also take into account the cultural and personal limits in tourist adaptation, such as the unwillingness to relinquish certain standards of comfort or fully comply with local eating habits and tastes, for religious motivations, different health standards, etc. Moreover, the investment scenario in the wine and wine tourism industry testifies to the relevance of international and large companies (and even status-driven investors following a conspicuous production model), shaping wine production and wine tourism activities around internationally recognizable standards (Qiu et al., 2013; Hojman, 2015; Overton and Banks, 2015).

As in the tourism industry as a whole, the Chinese are providing opportunities and challenges in wine tourism also. In China, the increasing consumption of wine is an element of self-identification for the middle class in its (partial) convergence towards cosmopolitan consumption patterns. Curiosity about wine and the desire to learn (e.g., the art of matching wines with food) is fostering the rapid growth of visits to wineries both domestically and internationally. The Chinese already hold a significant share of the wine tourism market in both Australia and California (Qiu et al., 2013; Lee et al., 2016).

The growth of Chinese wine tourists in Europe is thus easy to forecast, thanks to the increasing number of European destinations promoted specifically to Chinese markets, and also as a result of Chinese investments in the European (and particularly French) wine industry. These investments, although limited in size, have great visibility, as they are often motivated by prestige and fascination with wine heritage. Such is the case of the four-hundred-year-old Château Monlot (in Saint-Emilion), bought as an *achat de plaisir* (pleasure purchase) by the Chinese international film star Zhao Wei in December 2011. In other cases, the investments are clearly framed in a luxury strategy, as with Richard Shen Dong Jun, owner of the Château Laulan Ducos in the Medoc, selling his wine (and wedding packages) in his jewellery shops.

Looking at the tourist product, some of the most successful luxury features are not linked to a specific terroir but can be transferred to, and reproduced in, other wine regions. For example, wine therapy and grape-based wellness treatments are rapidly spreading in resorts and spas in Europe, the US, Australia, South Africa, etc., with substantially similar patterns.

In conclusion, there is no doubt that the luxury turn coincides with an increase in the quality of the experience in wine tourism, and this is achieved through creative linkages and additions, taking this kind of experience far beyond the original wine tasting. Yet, in this case, the relationship between LED and quality remains open to different assessments influenced by different visions of LED and its relationship with the globalisation process.

Optimists will easily stress the contribution to the quantity and quality of the local economy's growth. More specifically, on the positive side, luxury wine tourism may act as an effective attractor of higher value and the apparently growing segment of the tourism market. It will certainly contribute to the marketing and market positioning of local wines (and food), even when they are not luxury products as such, and increase the international exposure of local wine and wine tourism clusters. This, in turn, will promote an image of excellence and world-class quality, with positive consequences on the overall attractiveness of the area – not just with regard to tourism but also to inward investments.

Perhaps more important, it will add to the knowledge and skills available in the area to exploit the tourist potential and allow management of the new flows of culturally distant tourists. It will also increase the ability to intercept new consumption practices and the demand for sustainable and responsible tourism that characterises at least some luxury consumers.

Conversely, critics will focus on the lack of sustainability of the tourist configurations that luxury investments impose on rural areas due to their negative effects on the environment and on the social sphere, mainly through the loss of cultural identity. Parallel to this, the luxury approach may cause the destruction of the potential for community-type tourism and the creation of tourism monocultures that will be highly vulnerable and depend on external decision-makers (Belletti et al., 2013). Overall, the outcome may be passive compliance with globalised consumption patterns, which are substantially disconnected from the local heritage.

Further research is certainly needed to clarify and provide more substantial evidence for both arguments, to measure the impact of luxury wine tourism on the local-global relation underlying LED, and to assess whether a luxury turn in wine tourism adds to the territories' assets for balanced internationalisation or – on the contrary – promotes disruptive colonisation by external actors. At this preliminary stage, we can only note that some evidence supports both lines of argument. In a normative perspective, the rationale of managerial choices must be explored: To what extent can and will exogenous investors localise their business models when addressing the luxury market? This is also a matter for policy discourse: What mix can be found between actions targeting outsiders (e.g., as potential inward investors) and actions strengthening the insiders' capacity to interact with an increasingly global and plural wine culture?

Notes

1 See: http://winefolly.com/update/reality-of-wine-prices-what-you-get-for-what-you-spend/
2 Michael Havens as quoted in https://www.winesandvines.com/news/article/50453/How-to-Determine-a-Wine-Brands-Value

References

Abtan, O., Achille, A., Bellaiche, J.M., Kim, Y., Lui, V., Mall, A., Mei-Pochtler, A. and Willersdorf, S. (2014). *Shock of the new chic: Dealing with the new complexity in the business of luxury*. Boston, MA, The Boston Consulting Group.

Banks, G. and Overton, J. (2010). Old world, new world, third world? Reconceptualising the worlds of wine. *Journal of Wine Research*, 21(1), pp. 57–75.

Barrère, C. (2013). Patrimoines gastronomiques et développement local. *Mondes du Tourisme*, 7, pp. 15–36.

Belletti, G., Brunori, G., Marescotti, A., Berti, G. and Rovai, M. (2013). Is rural tourism sustainable? A reflection based on the concept of "rural tourism configurations." In Figueiredi, E., Raschi, A. (eds.) *Fertile links? Connections between tourism activities, socio-economic contexts and local development*, Firenze, Firenze University Press, pp. 93–106.

Bellini, N., Baratta, V., Loffredo, A. and Rovai, S. (2014). Chinese tourists in Tuscany: Redefining the relationship between heritage and authenticity. Proceedings of the Heritage, Tourism and Hospitality International Conference HTHIC 2014. Istanbul: Boğaziçi University, pp. 104–115.

Bellini, N. and Bramanti, A. (2008). *Sustainable glocalisation: A framework to analyze the international relations of local and regional governments*. Working paper no. 14, Milano: CERTET – Bocconi University.

Bellini, N., Loffredo, A. and Pasquinelli, C. (2010). Managing otherness. The political economy of place images in the case of Tuscany, In Ashworth, G. and Kavaratzis, M. (eds.). *Towards effective place brand management: Branding European cities and regions*, Cheltenham: Edward Elgar Publishing.

Bellini, N., Pasquinelli, C. and Piat, R. (2017). Innovative entrepreneurship and value co-creation in the management of rural tourism: An exploratory study of harvest tourism in France. In Proceedings of the Sinergie – Sima 2017 Conference on "Value co-creation: Management challenges for business and society," Napoli: June 2017.

Beverland, M.B. (2005). Crafting brand authenticity: The case of luxury wines. *Journal of Management Studies*, 42(5), pp. 1003–1029.

Byrd, E.T., Canziani, B., Hsieh, Y.C.J., Debbage, K. and Sonmez, S. (2016). Wine tourism: Motivating visitors through core and supplementary services. *Tourism Management*, 52, pp. 19–29.

Certomà, C. (2011). Standing-up vineyards: The political relevance of Tuscan wine production. *Environment and Planning D: Society and Space*, 29(6), pp. 1010–1029.

Charters, S. and Ali-Knight, J. (2002). Who is the wine tourist? *Tourism Management*, 23 (3), pp. 311–319.

Charters, S. and Michaux, V. (2014). Strategies for wine territories and clusters: Why focus on territorial governance and territorial branding? *Journal of Wine Research*, 25(1), pp. 1–4.

Charters, S. and Thach, L. (2016). Introduction and overview of wine tourism. In Charters, S. and Thach, L. (eds.) *Best practices in global wine tourism*, Putnam Valley, NY, Miranda Press.

Clergeau, C. and Etcheverria, O. (2013). La mise en tourisme et le développement local par la création d'une atmosphère gastronomique. Analyse à partir du cas de Vonnas. *Mondes du Tourisme*, 7, pp. 52–67.

Cooke, P. and Morgan, K. (1998). *The associational economy: Firms, regions, and innovation*. Oxford, Oxford University Press.

Cucculelli, M. and Goffi, G. (2016). Does sustainability enhance tourism destination competitiveness? Evidence from Italian destinations of excellence. *Journal of Cleaner Production*, 111, pp. 370–382.

Gatelier E., Barrère C. and Delaplace M. (2014). Le développement de l'œnotourisme en Champagne: L'hétérogénéité des acteurs et de leurs stratégies. *Mondes du Tourisme*, Hors série, pp. 69–81.

Gatelier E., Delaplace M. and Barrère C. (2012). L'œnotourisme en Champagne: entre valorisation d'un produit de luxe et développement territorial de la Champagne. Journée Internationale de Recherche: Stratégies des territoires vitivinicoles. Clusters, gouvernance et marque territoriale, organisée par le pôle de recherche Wine-Place-Value (Reims Management School). Reims, 1er juin 2012.

Getz, D. and Brown, G. (2006). Critical success factors for wine tourism regions: A demand analysis. *Tourism Management*, 27(1), pp. 146–158.

Getz, D., Robinson, R., Andersson, T. and Vujicic, S. (2014). *Foodies and food tourism*. Oxford, Goodfellow Publishers.

Granovetter, M. (2005). The impact of social structure on economic outcomes. *The Journal of Economic Perspectives*, 19(1), pp. 33–50.

Hojman, D.E. (2015). Radical innovation in luxury Carménère wine from Chile. *Journal of Wine Research*, 26(1), pp. 40–63.

Holohan, W. and Remaud, H. (2014). The impact of eco-friendly attributes on Bordeaux wine tourism and direct to consumer sales. In Procedings of the 8th International Conference of the Academy of Wine Business Research, pp. 1–13.

Jones, M.F., Singh, N. and Hsiung, Y. (2015). Determining the critical success factors of the wine tourism region of Napa from a supply perspective. *International Journal of Tourism Research*, 17(3), pp. 261–271.

Lazzeretti, L., Capone, F. and Cinti, T. (2010). The regional development platform and "related variety": Some evidence from art and food in Tuscany. *European Planning Studies*, 18(1), pp. 27–45.

Lee, K., Madanoglu, M. and Ko, J. Y. (2016). Exploring key service quality dimensions at a winery from an emerging market's perspective. *British Food Journal*, 118(12), pp. 2981–2996.

Lenglet, F. and Giannelloni, J. L. (2016). Does a terroir product tell the same story to tourists, day-trippers and local consumers? The moderating role of variety-seeking tendency and perceived authenticity. *International Journal of Tourism Research*, 18(5), pp. 494–505.

Lignon-Darmaillac, S. (2015a). Les grandes orientations de l'œnotourisme: Modèles européens, modèles californiens. *Territoires du Vin*, 8. https://pepiniere.u-bourgogne. fr/territoiresduvin/index.php?id=1336.

Lignon-Darmaillac, S. (2015b). Trouver sa route ou se perdre dans le vignoble? Les routes du vin, une géographie multidirectionnelle, la nouvelle alliance du tourisme et du vin. In Bourdeau L. & Marcotte, P. (eds.). *Les routes touristiques*, Québec, Presses de l'Université Laval, pp. 139–150.

Marzo-Navarro, M. and Pedraja-Iglesias, M. (2010). Are there different profiles of wine tourists? An initial approach. *International Journal of Wine Business Research*, 22(4), pp. 349–361.

McMillan, R. (2017). *State of the wine industry 2017*. St Helena, CA, Silicon Valley Bank Wine Division.

Menghini, S. (2015). The new market challenges and the strategies of the wine companies. *Wine Economics and Policy*, 4, pp. 75–77.

Mitchell, R., Charters, S. and Albrecht, J.N. (2012). Cultural systems and the wine tourism product. *Annals of Tourism Research*, 39(1), pp. 311–335.

Moulard, J., Babin, B. J. and Griffin, M. (2015). How aspects of a wine's place affect consumers' authenticity perceptions and purchase intentions: The role of country of origin and technical terroir. *International Journal of Wine Business Research*, 27(1), pp. 61–78.

Musso, F. and Francioni, B. (2015). Agri-food clusters, wine tourism and foreign markets. The role of local networks for SME's internationalization. *Procedia-Economics and Finance*, 27, pp. 334–343.

Nicolosi, A., Cortese, L., Nesci, F.S. and Privitera, D. (2016). Combining wine production and tourism. The Aeolian Islands. *Procedia-Social and Behavioral Sciences*, 223, pp. 662–667.

Overton, J. and Banks, G. (2015). Conspicuous production: Wine, capital and status. *Capital & Class*, 39(3), pp. 473–491.

Passebois-Ducros, J., Trinquecoste, J.F. and Pichon, F. (2015). Stratégies d'artification dans le domaine du luxe. Le cas des vins de prestige. *Décisions Marketing*, 80, pp. 109–124.

Perrot, M. (2014). L'imaginaire de la vigne et du vin: un patrimoine culturel à préserver. *Cultur-. Revista de Cultura e Turismo*, 8(3), pp. 62–75.

Pike, A. (2015). *Origination: The geographies of brands and branding*. Chichester: John Wiley & Sons.

Qiu, H.Z., Yuan, J., Ye, B.H. and Hung, K. (2013). Wine tourism phenomena in China: An emerging market. *International Journal of Contemporary Hospitality Management*, 25(7), pp. 1115–1134.

Quintal, V.A., Thomas, B. and Phau, I. (2015). Incorporating the winescape into the theory of planned behaviour: Examining "new world" wineries. *Tourism Management*, 46, pp. 596–609.

Rabbiosi, C. (2016). Place branding performances in tourist local food shop. *Annals of Tourism Research*, 60, pp. 154–168.

Rae, C. (2013). *Pearl Chase. First Lady of Santa Barbara*. Seattle, Olympus Press.

Resnick, E. (2008). *Wine brands. Success strategies for new markets, new consumers and new trends*. Basingstoke, Palgrave Macmillan.

Rico, J.-C. (2016). Oenotourisme et expérience touristique: Un état des lieux et des perspectives. Paper presented at the 2016 AFMAT annual conference, Chambery, May.

Rigaux, C. (2015). L'œnotourisme en Bourgogne: De la valorisation du patrimoine à l'élaboration de compétences. *Territoires du Vin*, 8, https://pepiniere.u-bourgogne.fr/territoiresduvin/index.php?id=1353.

Rokka, J. (2017). Champagne: Marketplace icon. *Consumption Markets & Culture*, 20(3), pp. 275–283.

Sjostrom, T., Corsi, A.M. and Lockshin, L. (2016). What characterises luxury products? A study across three product categories. *International Journal of Wine Business Research*, 28(1), pp. 76–95.

Sparks, B. (2007). Planning a wine tourism vacation? Factors that help to predict tourist behavioural intentions. *Tourism Management*, 28(5), pp. 1180–1192.

Spawton, T. (1990). Marketing planning for wine. *International Journal of Wine Marketing*, 2(2), pp. 2–49.

Spielmann, N. and Charters, S. (2013). The dimensions of authenticity in terroir products. *International Journal of Wine Business Research*, 25(4), pp. 310–324.

Swarbrooke, J. (2017). *The meaning of luxury in hospitality, events and tourism*. Oxford: Goodfellow Publishers.

Thach, L., Olsen, J., Cogan-Marie, L. and Charters, S. (2017). What price is luxury wine? Research Studies Unclear. https://www.winebusiness.com/news/?go=getArticle&dataid=180699.

Winterhalter, C. (2011). Gastronomic fashions, luxury concepts, consumption practices and the construction of identity. In De Witt-Paul A. & Crouch M. (eds). *Fashion Forward*, Oxford, Inter-Disciplinary Press, pp. 287–296.

Wolf, H.L., Morrish, S.C., Morrish, S.C., Fountain, J. and Fountain, J. (2016). A conceptualization of the perceptions and motivators that drive luxury wine consumption. *International Journal of Wine Business Research*, 28(2), pp. 120–133.

Yang, W. and Mattila, A.S. (2016). Why do we buy luxury experiences? Measuring value perceptions of luxury hospitality services. *International Journal of Contemporary Hospitality Management*, 28(9), pp. 1848–1867.

13 Urban experiential value creation platforms

The case of Eataly in the city of Florence

Cecilia Pasquinelli

1. Introduction

This chapter analyses and discusses the relationship between gastronomy brands and city brands, with particular attention to their mutuality. While place-of-origin studies (Bilkey and Nes, 1982; Johansson et al., 1985; Insch and McBride, 2004) focus on the dynamics enabling the firms' creation, appropriation, and exploitation of geographical associations, scholars of city and region brand management (Ashworth and Kavaratzis, 2010; Go et al., 2015) have largely overlooked this topic. As such, place brand positioning within urban brand networks (including product, person, institution, and corporate brands) remains understudied (Pasquinelli, 2017), particularly the creation, or conversely the destruction, of value from the multiple connections and mutual relationships between diverse brands that coexist within the urban brand network.

We here consider the case of Eataly, a food retail and restaurant chain with the declared mission of disseminating the Italian eating style, attention to quality food, regional traditions and diversity, and global distribution of regional agro-food products. Specifically, we focus on the Eataly store in the city centre of Florence, Italy. Inaugurated in 2013, Eataly Florence consists of 2,000 square metres bringing together and featuring food, art, and culture. Eataly replaced the library housed in the prestigious location near the Piazza Duomo, Brunelleschi's Dome, and Giotto's Bell Tower, which are part of the historic centre's most visited tourist precinct and listed as a UNESCO World Heritage Site since 1982. Through an analysis of a sample of Eataly Florence reviews on TripAdvisor, this study discusses the relationship between Florence as a cultural tourist destination and Eataly to identify mutual value creation mechanisms for both the food chain brand and the city brand. The hypothesis we investigate is whether their coupling facilitates the self-production of value of Eataly customers and urban travellers.

The rationale for this analysis is based on a key premise. The "experiential turn" of the contemporary economy has had an impact on the meaning of value and on the value creation process (Prahalad and Ramaswamy, 2004), with significant consequences for brand management (Arnoud and Thompson, 2005; Brakus et al., 2009). Gastronomy literature analyses tourism destinations as experiential platforms that enable customers to undergo a situated first-hand culinary experience. Also acknowledged is that, in turn, gastronomic products contribute to the construction of the tourism experience by helping customers/travellers make sense of the location (Hjalager and Richards, 2002; Kivela and Crotts, 2006).

This experiential turn suggests that the value creation agenda needs to be broader. Dialogue across diverse fields of knowledge, such as branding, geography, and urban studies, can provide further insights on the role of cities in value creation. Nigel Thrift (2004) highlights that cities and public urban spaces increasingly take part in fostering emotional pressure points and forms of symbolic product innovation. Cities – and particularly some districts, squares, and buildings within them – function as experiential platforms for value creation, increasingly designed to satisfy market needs, but not without effects on urban regeneration and development.

The analysis of the Eataly-Florence relationship highlights various aspects of value creation. By offering local products under the umbrella of a global brand industrialising the agro-food experience, how and to what extent does the Eataly brand draw value from its presence in Florence? How and to what extent does Eataly support Florentine tourists in creating valuable relationships with the city throughout the development of individual experiential projects? Do the Eataly and Florence brands co-create value? Does the Eataly-Florence coupling trigger forms of city brand building? What (if any) specific aspect of Eataly's connection with the city produces effects on local development? These questions are particularly relevant for a research agenda on the relation between gastronomy and local development, scrutinising not only the potential synergies but also the tensions at stake in the search for innovative interplays between globalising and (re)localising the food experience, between industrial and artisanal gastronomy, between the narration of history and contemporaneity. In line with the exploratory aim of this chapter, the next sections will question the conventional interpretations of the relationship between cities and gastronomy by emphasising that beyond forms of value creation, value destruction may emerge in the urban brand network.

2. Value creation in the urban brandscape

This section models the mechanisms of value creation by stressing the importance of considering the urban dimension, especially in light of the aforementioned experiential turn. This begins from the customer service logic (see Grönroos, 2008) stating that customers play a leading role in creating value for themselves through service consumption. Defining "value" and "value creation" is not easy. Grönroos proposes using a "simple working definition" (2008: 303), according to which value is the consumers' capacity to feel, right after participating in a self- or full-service process, "better off than before." Based on this perspective, value is not embedded in a product or service (value-in-exchange) but spills from the act of using or the act of experiencing it (value-in-use).

Consumers can only create value autonomously if they possess the appropriate resources and skills. Indeed, a key aspect of value (co-)creation is the customer's endowment of resources and skills, which are the means for value generation in the hands of the value creator, that is, the customer. Such resources include information and knowledge, a conglomerate of goods and services, as well as a psychological and emotional background. These are particularly salient to experiential consumption, which is thereby unique and highly subjective. In light of the value facilitation model (Grönroos, 2008), the customer is not the only agent, despite being the protagonist of a postmodern act of self-identity production and autonomous value creation. The supplier plays the important role of value facilitator by providing customers with a cue or foundation for individual value creation, offering support through key resources, and facilitating the acquisition of skills.

Complementing Grönroos' model, this chapter argues that acknowledging the role of the urban context (Figure 13.1), which is a physical space particularly dense in symbols, enhances the framework.

Resource integration and exchange, as well as fostering opportunities between the facilitator and the value creator, are crucial value-creation mechanisms. These processes do not occur in a vacuum, but rather in a context, which is neither neutral nor inert. This may, of course, be a virtual space (consider digital platforms, for example), but can also be a physical (i.e., urban) context. Value-in-context literature (Ger et al., 1999; Chandler and Vargo, 2011) recognises the role of a relational context in which resources are integrated and exchanged, thus enabling value creation. The hypothesis is that such a relational context is not a mere "container" of value creation but is instead an active participant in the value creation mechanisms.

In this chapter, as stated, the city – or, better, some part of it – is the relational context under scrutiny. In particular, we refer to the part of the city

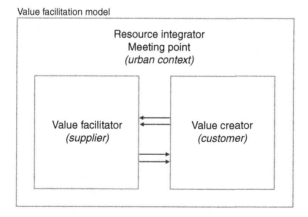

Figure 13.1 The urban dimension of the value facilitation model

that the "urban brandscape" reflects (Bellini and Pasquinelli, 2016), namely, the urban population of commercial (i.e., product and corporate) and non-commercial (i.e., cultural institution and person) brands. This does not necessarily coincide with the city's administrative borders, since large portions tend to be excluded. Such networks of brands constitute the city's symbolic capital, that is, the set of images, symbols, and meanings that authenticate products and services. This provides customers with historic coordinates, cultural background, visual identities, as well as opportunities for "sincere" and not purely commercial encounters with brands (Pasquinelli, 2014). The definition of an urban brandscape as a network of brands aims to emphasise the mutual pollination that may occur in such a web of brand connections.

The urban brandscape is evidence of the constant symbolic production in the urban space, taking shape in streets, buildings, private and increasingly public spaces. Here brands are – consciously or not – consumed and experienced. The brandscape is, in this sense, an urban experiential platform that facilitates or, even better, enables a certain type of urban experience for residents and travellers. It contributes to the creation of the urban atmosphere (Löfgren, 2014) shaped not only by the city's physical architecture and constructed environments but also by brands that, despite their fairly intangible nature, may establish a visible presence in the city, until "polluting" it through their pervasiveness.

The notion of brandscape in gastronomy literature intertwines brands as a source of value creation, albeit without a clear focus. The relationship between city destination brands and gastronomy is often studied in only one direction, whereby gastronomy is an integral part of the tourism experience until it becomes the main motivation for repeated visits (Kivel and Crotts, 2006). Gastronomic heritage may build the city brand (e.g., the "City of Gastronomy"), with positive effects on both local gastronomy and the destination image (Khoo and Badarulzaman, 2014). By acknowledging the reciprocity and mutual pollination across different brands, food encounters in the city can be sold to tourists through strategically linking cultural heritage towns and cuisine by way of narrating traditions through a selection of elements and historical facts. However, this carries the risk of delivering a static rhetoric that simplifies the richness of both the urban heritage and the cuisine heritage (Staiff and Bushell, 2013).

3. Eataly in the Florentine brandscape

Eataly's first store opened in Turin in 2007 on the premises of an old factory that had previously been owned by a vermouth producer. Today, the company has fourteen stores in the country and ten worldwide, employing approximately four thousand people (GoNews, 2014), although not without controversy regarding work conditions. Eataly is a food space that combines the sale of wholefoods, restaurants, and food courts in a megastore where visitors are provided with information, including maps showing the geographic origins of the food, workshops, and courses. The company provides quality food and attempts to combine the local dimension of production with global distribution.

The concept behind the name "Eataly" is to convey not only the Italian food tradition but also the Italian eating style. The brand markets its products as "high foods" through the "faces, production methods, and stories of people and companies who make the best Italian high quality food and wine."[1] "Lifestyle," which can be summarised in Eataly's narration as quality, genuineness, and authentic origins, is the link between the various products. An important component of Eataly's brand is learning, based on the narration of lifestyle as a culture to be learned.

Eataly is deemed a "new" model of Italian gastronomic promotion, globally exporting the country's specific local and regional food traditions through significant logistical, organisational, and marketing innovations (Barrère, 2013). Eataly successfully markets local products to geographically or culturally distant markets by increasing the products' perceived symbolic, historic, and intellectual content. The Slow Food movement philosophy, the growing global mass interest in food (largely supported by the mass media), the strong image of Italy as a country of origin for reputable food products and distinctive eating style – these have combined to create a global niche market that Oscar Farinetti, Eataly's founder, has captured. His business model has innovated food distribution and codified a means of creating economic value in the Italian food system.

Opening Eataly stores usually entails significant investments, as in the case of Eataly Rome, for which an investment of 80 million euros was made in purchasing and refurbishing a building at the Ostiense Rail Station (De Nolac, 2012). Originally built to be integrated with the Fiumicino International Airport, this part of the station was inaugurated in 1990 in connection with the FIFA World Cup, but it was abandoned afterwards. Eataly's corporate philosophy includes integrating the stores within the host city contexts, with a contribution to urban regeneration. The reuse of iconic brownfield sites, sometimes within the framework of broader regeneration plans, or single abandoned buildings with historic value for the city characterise various Eataly stores. For example, Eataly Torino Lingotto is in the historic industrial district that formerly hosted FIAT; Eataly Milano Smeraldo replaced a closed theatre; Eataly Genoa occupies a historic building in the Ancient Port; and Eataly Bari is hosted within the *Fiera del Levante*, a trade show that was established in 1929 and is in serious need of relaunching.

In November 2017, Eataly opened an 80,000m^2 theme park dedicated to high-quality food in Bologna called the *Fabbrica Italiana Contadina* (FICO) Eataly World, located in the city's Centre for Food and Agricultural Products (CAAB). CAAB is a public organisation that manages one of the country's largest food and vegetable logistic hubs and market. However, like similar organisations, it is facing decline due to extensive changes in food distribution. Including forty farm factories, twenty-five restaurants, cultivation and production sites, food markets, shops, didactic laboratories and itineraries, and a congress centre, FICO Eataly World is considered an opportunity to relaunch CAAB and its associated firms. The theme park, which the media has nicknamed "Food Disneyworld," aims to attract approximately six million tourists a year, with significant attention to the promotion of children's attendance and school visits. However, the project has raised issues related to visitor logistics and transport links with Bologna city centre, which need to be addressed in the medium term to fully exploit the park's tourist potential. The theme park is intended to become an attraction for a city that has significant food production and consumption traditions. However, doubts have been raised regarding the area's transformation: the creation of a global brand tourist attraction that will displace smaller food producers and distribution networks; the brand's lack of attention to "real" biodiversity; and precarious employment conditions (linked to the criticisms of Eataly's employment policies in other stores in Italy). The international media has also dedicated critical attention to this opening in Bologna, speculating on whether FICO Eataly betrays Italian gastronomy, being more "a US-style megamart, a Wholefoods on steroids" for mass consumer culture, in evident contrast to the "Italian way" which – according to Seymour (2017) – denotes farmers' markets in old towns and "small producers in remote hilltop towns."

In Florence, Eataly occupies an empty brownfield location that is not in a peripheral district of the city, but in the most central and crowded area, frequented by approximately five million tourists a year. Inaugurated in 2013 and defined as a "shop-library-laboratory," Eataly replaced the *Marzocco* library in the city centre. Founded in 1840, the library then became the *Libreria Martelli*, a reputable cultural spot in the city that hosted writers and intellectuals over time. The Martelli Library closed in 2011.

Localisation in Florence's city centre is not without controversy. Residents and the city council recently took part in a lively debate on the appropriate food style for the historic centre of Florence, which received significant coverage in the national media. This resulted in local mobilisation against the opening of a McDonald's in *Piazza Duomo*, the main square of the old town, not far from the Eataly store. The debate echoed national concerns on the proliferation of fast food and "tacky" shops, generally tagged by the media as "McDonald's and kebab," in the historic centres of Italian cities. In 2016, this concern drove the central government to approve a decree allowing mayors to forbid establishing commercial activities in historic towns that are not compatible and coherent with the protection and promotion of the local cultural heritage.

The historic centre of Florence is listed as a UNESCO World Heritage Site. In 2015, UNESCO requested clarifications of the management plan for the historic centre and warned the city about excessive tourism pressure, the insufficient management of tourist flows, and the absence of a tourism strategy (ICOMOS, 2015). For some, Florence is at risk of becoming "the next Venice" due to the progressive expulsion of residents and its transformation into a luxury historic theme park (Montanari, 2015).

The historic centre is symbolic of the Italian Renaissance, unique for its concentration of art and cultural landmarks: Michelangelo's David, a symbol of the city and icon of Italian artistic genius, and Brunelleschi's Dome are two such examples. In addition to cultural tourism, fashion shopping has become an increasingly important driver of tourism in Florence. To revive its past as a 1950s fashion capital, the city promotes the local presence of global luxury brands and designers, such as Gucci, Ermanno Scervino, and Ferragamo, as well as other reputable fashion houses and fashion events. In turn, fashion brands have built visible links with the cultural heritage of the city (Bellini and Pasquinelli, 2016).

In this context, and especially at its opening in 2013, Eataly proposed a Florentine footprint in the store echoing the Renaissance age (Corriere Fiorentino, 2013). A museum itinerary devoted to the Renaissance was designed by an Italian writer; it offered audio guides to Eataly's visitors, narrating stories about Florence as the cradle of Italian culture. According to Montanari (2013), this was about packaging a commodified summary of local culture and identity, which should have been tasted in the streets of Florence instead of within a store belonging to an international food chain:

> Wouldn't it be better to establish a dialogue with Florence instead of making a summary of it? We are not in Sydney or Beijing: why should Florentines or tourists waste their time listening to a series of banalities instead of seeing with their own eyes the Renaissance that is all around?
>
> (Montanari, 2013, author's translation).

Eataly attempts to connect with Florence's popular culture by offering local street food at the store's premises. Eataly's *lampredotto* indoor kiosk sells a typical sandwich made from a cow's fourth and final stomach, which is an icon of the city's culinary tradition. This is usually eaten in the streets of Florence and in the city's markets. A relationship with Florence and the local popular culture was also built through Eataly's presence in another key position in the city, i.e., the San Lorenzo Central Market. Located in the old town, it was founded in the nineteenth century and refurbished in 2014 to restore the old central market atmosphere.

3.1. Methodology

The case analysis began with desk research reviewing various web sources, including Eataly's official website and various local and national newspapers, describing the company's profile, the geographic context of Eataly Florence, and the characteristics of its presence in the city. A sample of reviews of Eataly Florence on TripAdvisor was then analysed to empirically test the revisited value facilitation model. By means of qualitative content analysis (Gunter, 2000; Berg, 2001; Krippendorff, 2004), the sampled reviews were categorised as "Quality" (text fragments assessing the quality of the product, service, and overall experience), "Authenticity" (text with a clear reference to geographic origins), and "Culture/Art/Architecture" (a sort of control variable highlighting the specific Florentine location). Each of these three categories is a specification of the other, with "quality" encompassing "authenticity," which is then specified as "culture, art, and architecture." The text in each category was then grouped according to two criteria: first, according to the positive or negative value expressed, and second, its association either with the specific location (Florence) or with the company (Eataly). This enabled distinguishing the role of Eataly and Florence in facilitating visitors' value creation.

Of the 1,159 reviews in the public TripAdvisor archive (retrieved 1 March 2017), we sampled and analysed 113. We analysed 50 reviews (28 in Italian and 22 in English) starting from the most recent ones available, calculating the percentages of each evaluation category for the entire set of reviews used to compose the sample (Table 13.1).

An additional 63 reviews were retrieved using keywords (up to 10 reviews for each keyword were sampled), that is, *Florence/Firenze, Art/Architecture, City, Duomo, Quality, Culture, Touris*, San Lorenzo,* and *Lampredotto.* In this case, we applied the evaluation percentages calculated for the entire set of retrieved reviews. The result of this pilot study, based on the qualitative content analysis of a small sample of reviews, is a mosaic of fragments that sheds light on some aspects of the Florence and Eataly brands and their intertwining. This partial insight aims to determine not the absolute strength of value creation but its various mechanisms.

3.2 Findings

An initial overview of the retrieved sample indicated that overall, Italian-speaking reviewers were relatively less satisfied than English-speaking reviewers, with 57.8% of the former evaluating Eataly Florence as "excellent" or "very good" compared with 77.1% of the latter. Of the Italian reviews, 18.5% evaluated Eataly Florence as "poor" or "terrible," compared with 10.4% of non-Italian reviews.

Table 13.1 Sample composition based on the TripAdvisor evaluation percentages calculated for all Eataly Florence reviews

	Excellent	Very good	Average	Poor	Terrible
Language					
All	31.3%	35.9%	18.7%	9.4%	4.7%
Italian	22.4%	35.4%	23.8%	12.7%	5.7%
English	42.2%	34.9%	12.4%	5.6%	4.8%

Under the "Quality" category in relation to Eataly (with no specific mention of the place), the positive elements prevailed. Reviewers expressed a great deal of satisfaction for the retail products (the "high-quality ingredients") and for the wide variety. The service and overall Eataly experience were positively valued. It is a "unique Italian experience" for an English-speaking reviewer, while for an Italian-speaking reviewer, the direct contact with chefs over a fast and informal high-quality lunch was a valuable experience. The fact that staff members speak different languages due to being part of an international food chain was also mentioned, as well as their willingness and kindness in answering questions and providing information. In addition, for some reviewers, the opportunity to enter the store and walk around without feeling pressured to buy and consume products made the Eataly atmosphere different from many "tourist traps."

Regardless of its localisation, the value of the Eataly experience is also evident in a review that positively assessed the brand concept as "fresh air" in the Italian context, in which "shopping is still stuck up and stuck back in medieval times." Similarly, one reviewer stated that it is "much more modern than you expect in Florence but still very Italian," and another claimed that "it's bright, airy, modern but still very Italian!" Some reviews stated that Eataly is positively valued *despite* its localisation in Florence: in the title of the review, one reviewer said that it was "a lovely contrast to medieval Florence" and then "I LOVE the architecture and art in Florence … so I didn't expect to like this place." In other cases, previous knowledge of the Eataly brand was the reason for visiting the one in Florence. Various reviews reported on the Eataly New York City experience while commenting on Eataly Florence either as a sort of guarantee to encourage people to visit Eataly when in Florence or as a type of benchmark.

On the negative value side concerning the Eataly brand itself, fragments from the sample reported the lack of "substance" and the standardisation of all Eataly stores. For some, the comparison with the store in New York resulted in disappointment in the Florence store, which did not meet their expectations; it was even positioned amongst the reviewers' worst culinary experiences.

Concerning the fragments referring to Florence as Eataly's localisation (focusing on Florence as the main driver of positive value), reviewers emphasised the "beautiful" and "elegant" building that the store occupies. The fact of being located "one block from the *Duomo*" made the size of the store and the variety of products "astounding." The prestigious location justified the higher prices for one reviewer, making the visit worthwhile and special. Although the food was not of high quality for another reviewer, Eataly was an appropriate lunch break after having visited the city's museums. Eataly Florence is considered a good place to buy good local products and food, such as *lampredotto*, "in an easier way." The fact that the location is "easy to find and convenient [to get to/from] many of the important sites in the city" was frequently mentioned in the sampled reviews. In addition, for one reviewer, Eataly was "a little more user friendly than the *Mercato Centrale* and more attractive than regular super-markets," and "if you are tired of looking for restaurants or need a break from the touristy sites you should check out this place." The ease with which outsiders, who have no knowledge of the place or local traditions, are able to access good food in a tourist destination emerged as a clear point of value.

One reviewer defined the store as "the Apple Store of Florence food and drink," emphasising the short distance from the *Duomo* and the fact that it is clean, hip, cool, and has Wi-Fi. According to this reviewer, it is a bit expensive, but this is justified by its "location and décor." Despite acknowl-edging the significant tourist presence in the store, one reviewer stated, "Touristy but who cares!" because it is a good place and "an easy spot to stop off even if you aren't too familiar with Florence." For others, the good quality, cleanliness, professional service, and central location made it a special place that is better than other tourist traps. The tourism topic was highly present in the sampled reviews. One reviewer even commented that spending hours visiting Eataly has become "a tourist attraction in itself" and is to be repeated when in Florence.

In contrast, the main critical points of the Florence localisation concern the "expensive tourist trap" that contributes to the worse positioning of the store compared to others, including the one in New York, where charm and quality are perceived as higher. For instance, "We love Eataly NY, so it just seemed to make sense that Eataly Florence would put NY to shame. Not so! This place is small, touristy – well, we are in Florence – with mediocre food and service." Even when the touristic character of the store was embraced, there were complaints about the limited opening times of Eataly's restaurants and the lack of knowledgeable staff to help customers who, in the case of tourists, are even more in need of support. With no customer care service, a reviewer would prefer to buy from any other small shops in the city. A comparison with the myriad smaller shops and local restaurants in Florence's city centre was a frequent topic: "I felt silly after going here…. Should have gone to any number of other places serving equal or better food."

Under the "Authenticity" category, emphasising geographic origin as gen-erating value, which may be considered a specific aspect of quality, we distinguish the positive/negative value deriving from the Eataly brand and that deriving from Florence. Eataly per se is considered the expression of Italian style in contemporary and modern fashion. It is the place where the right ingredients ("100% Italian products," "the excellence of our Italy," "Italian taste," and "Italy in its finest") can easily be purchased to cook dishes in the Italian culinary tradition using products from all the Italian regions. In contrast, some reviews did not acknowledge Eataly's authenticity, claiming the chain sells products that can be found in regular supermarkets or just "products for tourists." The lack of interest in Italian wheat production is mentioned, raising issues of responsibility towards Italian producers: "[only one] loaf made of Italian flour as [if] it was a museum's piece of art....." For one Italian-speaking reviewer, the Eataly concept was "innovative" on paper, but the reality resembles an Italian-style McDonald's or, for an English-speaking reviewer, "an Italian version of a Costco or Walmart," characterised by mass food production appealing to tourists.

The authenticity deriving from the localisation in Florence concerns the expectations created by the idea of visiting the Eataly prototype: an experience of the "original Eataly" and "the real thing" just for being located in an Italian city. The presence of local patrons in the store contributes to the authenticity of Eataly Florence, even though, for one reviewer, it was unclear why Florentines make purchases at Eataly despite having better and cheaper alternatives in their own neighbourhoods. However, the perception of local patrons amongst customers helped simulate a residential experience for visitors to Florence, creating a sense of distance from other tourists, as is evident from the following comment: "An amazing find ... [it] was heavily patronised by local Florentines. A great evening in our lovely apartment, and on our balcony, drinking wine and watching the tourists enjoying the sunshine in the amazing Piazza Duomo." The authenticity of the location, its décor, its style, and the artwork on the walls were highly valued, as was the presence in the central market of San Lorenzo, which has great "energy" and "ambiance."

Conversely, other reviews suggested a lack of authenticity of the Eataly store in Florence. These focused on the paucity of the city's traditional dishes, the lack of Tuscan customs – such as serving wine in a carafe instead of providing bottled wine only – and high prices. None of these aspects coincided with the idea of presenting local excellence to tourists. For some, there was an evident appeal to the "unprepared tourist" who does not realise that higher quality can be found in the nearby supermarkets (*Sapori e Dintorni*, opened by the *Conad* supermarket chain and dedicated to traditional regional food, was mentioned). In addition, one reviewer maintained that the space that hosts Eataly has no distinct personality and is "in between a *trattoria* and a corporate canteen." The comparison with the many local wine bars, restaurants, and bistros in the city reduces Eataly's authenticity in Florence to a location that has less charm than the surrounding "original food temples," and hence the suggestion to go to real local food stores and restaurants instead, since these provide a better experience.

4. Discussion and concluding remarks

The findings show that Eataly plays the role of value facilitator (Grönroos, 2008) by providing customers with key elements for individual value creation, primarily information and access. As emerged from the sampled reviews, Eataly represents a gateway to quality food not only for providing easy access due to its location in central Florence but also for the learning experience that is made possible through the provision of information in foreign languages. To prove the importance of knowledge acquisition and learning, a reviewer reported the problems encountered when English-speaking staff were not on duty at the store; in this case, the reviewer argued, it would be better to buy from small local shops. Indeed, learning about the eating style that the brand seeks to represent is a key component of the Eataly experience. Providing access to information and learning opportunities related to the food on sale is crucial to the facilitation mechanism. As one reviewer stated, Eataly represents facilitated access to the world of Italian food that is suitable or "user friendly" for outsiders who often struggle to find the right local places where they can consume good food. This could arguably be relevant for Italians visiting the store due to the regional variety of food on Eataly's shelves. However, this aspect of facilitation is especially relevant to international visitors who benefit from the efforts to explain the eating style in a relatively fast, affordable, and understandable way.

Providing information and speaking English in the Eataly Florence experience seem to suggest a value creation opportunity that also benefits the tourist destination. In fact, according to the sampled reviews, Eataly is part of the tourist precinct (one reviewer even suggested that Eataly itself is a tourist attraction), because it creates a quality comfort zone for visitors, giving them access to a food experience that would otherwise not be possible for many tourists who may have neither the money nor the time to allocate to it. Eataly seems to participate in intercultural adaptation to a tourist destination, playing the role of a "metaworld" (Hottola, 2004), namely, a place for escape and rest from other public spaces where the difference and richness of cultural stimuli may create forms of stress and fatigue for visitors. Consequently, Eataly seems to support the construction of a relationship between the destination and tourists who make use of the Eataly experience to fulfil their own tourist project.

Thus, Eataly plays a role in local development in relation to the support it provides tourists in the value creation process at the destination. In addition, Eataly seems to trigger a distinctive experience by infusing the traditional view of the local food culture with a taste of modernity and contemporaneity, as variously mentioned in the sampled reviews. This might contribute to providing visitors with an interpretive cue to the urban experience, breaking stereotypes through the "unexpected" signs of modernity in the Florentine context. In other words, simply because Eataly has this dissonant modern character, i.e., different from what is generally perceived as "typically Florentine," it succeeds in adding value to the city's brand image.

However, for other customers who have more extensive or simply different background knowledge, and who consequently face a different path of "cultural confusion" (Hottola, 2004), the facilitation mechanism may be perceived as *over-facilitation* – a summary of culture and identity without any "substance," as one reviewer stated – and highly standardised. From this perspective, the presence of Eataly seems to hamper the development of the tourist destination due to the lack of specificity regarding its connection with the place (Barrère, 2013). However, the notions of "connection" and "specificity" need to be better articulated and discussed in their different nuances, especially when intersecting historic town planning and management issues. As stated, in Italy, recent laws enable local governments to forbid the establishment of commercial activities that are not compatible with the protection and promotion of the local cultural heritage. In the case of Florence, the opening of Eataly in 2013 was not without criticism, while the opening of a McDonald's was actually prohibited. Where is the boundary between specificity, compatibility, and coherence benefiting the regeneration and development of historic centres on one hand, and standardisation and lack of coherence on the other? Is Eataly sufficiently original, specific, and authentic to be a part of the historic town of Florence?

The facilitation model suggests that there is a trade-off between standardisation and "existential authenticity" (Wang, 1999). Standardisation consists of designing experiential practices through the codification and de-codification of meanings and symbols for the industrialised agro-food experience, such as that which Eataly offers. Standardisation leads to forms of "staged authenticity" (McCannel, 1973), which reduces customer uncertainty and anxiety towards the perceived risk of not being able to infiltrate the "back region" without grasping the taste of the place. Instead, existential authenticity refers to "a state of being" (Wang, 1999) activated by the individuals' activities, allowing the tourist to find their "authentic self," which responds to an ideal of authenticity that is imbued with nostalgia and romanticism in postmodern society. Existential authenticity derives from the individual efforts of de-codification (as an individual activity), which is often a time-consuming and demanding process of learning jealously maintained as exclusive as possible. Moreover, there is certainly a romantic and nostalgic ideal of the authentic food experience inspiring the construction of the authentic self. This vision in many cases is based on the idealisation of small, local family restaurants and shops, on escaping to the countryside where "real" food is produced and can be purchased directly from farmers, who are seen as rigorously remaining distant from global markets: Farming and craft production in this idealisation are the romantic opponents of global distribution.

Complementing the value facilitation model, Florence – and especially the old town – functions as a resource integrator by providing an emotional and psychological background that is particularly salient to experiential consumption. The prestigious location and the building that hosts the store play a key role, as they contribute to magnifying the experience (the "astounding" variety of products, the size of the store, and the special visit) and even help justify the high prices that some reviewers reported. At the same time, localisation in the heart of the tourist city challenges value creation and may even contribute to value destruction for some customers. Despite the fact that the location is likely to boost the volume of sales, given the crowds of tourists visiting the Florence city centre, value destruction may emerge in relation to the definition of value that Grönroos (2008) proposes, that is, as the consumer's capacity to "feel better off than before," linking back to the existential authenticity mentioned above (regardless of the actual volume of purchases).

In terms of value destruction, it seems that Eataly's presence in the historic centre of Florence "touristifies" the store, which is described by some as an "expensive tourist trap," food for "unprepared tourists," and mass food production for mass tourism. Such "touristiness" makes a great deal of sense because, according to one reviewer, "Well, we are in Florence." Value destruction is evident when Eataly Florence is compared to the New York City store, since the former, being "the real thing" and the original prototype in Italy (actually, the NYC store has a longer history than the one in Florence), should be much better than the latter. However, there is significant disappointment on realising that the New York store provides a better atmosphere and sets a standard that is unmet in Florence, in one reviewer's words.

Florence also challenges Eataly customers' value creation as an arena for significant competition with the "original food temples," meaning the many local wine bars, restaurants, and bistros surrounding Eataly; it affects the perception of its "objective authenticity" based on the existence of the original (Wang, 1999). From the perspective of existential authenticity, one reviewer even felt "silly" when visiting Eataly, as they "should have gone to any number of other places serving equal or better food" instead of choosing the "easier" option, facilitated by a multinational corporation that runs an international food chain. Let us say that in this case, the urban context provides an emotional and psychological background that challenges the customers' Eataly brand experience.

Finally, beyond appreciation for the localisation and location, the reviews do not link the culture, art, and history of Florence with the Eataly experience. A commodified summary of the city risks proposing a series of empty "banalities" (as commented on in a newspaper [see above]) and determining overfacilitation. Consequently, a sharp boundary is created between the in-store and the urban "lived experience." A key question emerging from this analysis is: What other dialogue and relationships can be established between the city brand and the product/corporate brand?

Note

1 https://www.eataly.net/eu_en/who-we-are/about-eataly/

References

Arnoud, E. and Thompson, C. (2005). Consumer Culture Theory (CCT): Twenty years of research. *Journal of Consumer Research*, 31(4), pp. 868–882.

Ashworth, G. and Kavaratzis, M. (2010). *Towards effective place brand management: Branding European cities and regions.* Elgar, Cheltenham.

Barrère, C. (2013). Patrimoines gastronomiques et développement local: Les limites du modèle français de gastronomie élitiste. *Mondes du Tourisme*, 7/2013, pp. 15–36.

Bellini, N. and Pasquinelli, C. (2016). Urban brandscape as value ecosystem: The cultural destinationstrategy of fashion brands. *Place Branding and Public Diplomacy*, 12(1), pp. 5–16.

Berg, B. (2001). *An introduction to content analysis. In Qualitative research methods for the social sciences.* Allyn and Bacon, London.

Bilkey, W.J. and Nes, E. (1982). Country-of-Origin effects on product evaluations. *Journal of International Business Studies*, 13(1), pp. 89–112.

Brakus, J., Schmitt, B. and Zarantonello, L. (2009). Brand experience: What is it? How is it measured? Does it affect loyalty? *Journal of Marketing*, 73, pp. 52–68.

Chandler, J.D. and Vargo, S.L. (2011). Contextualization and value-in-context: How context frames exchange. *Marketing Theory*, 11(1), pp. 35–49.

Corriere Fiorentino (2013). Apre Eataly in via Martelli Con dedica al Rinascimento, Corriere Fiorentino, 16 December 2013. http://corrierefiorentino.corriere.it/fire nze/notizie/cronaca/2013/16-dicembre-2013/apre-eataly-via-martelli-dedica-rinasci mento-2223806773013.shtml.

De Nolac, P. (2012). Eataly guarda già oltre Roma. http://cinquantamila.corriere.it/ storyTellerArticolo.php?storyId=0000002205876.

Ger, G., Askegaard, S. and Christensen, A. (1999). Experiential nature of product-place images: Image as a narrative. *Advances in Consumer Research*, 26, pp. 165–169.

Go, F.M., Lemmetyinen, A. and Hakala, U. (2015). *Harnessing place branding through cultural entrepreneurship*. Palgrave, Basingstoke.

GoNews (2014). Vicenda Eataly, raggiunto l'accordo sulla stabilizzazione del personale. http://www.gonews.it/2014/09/03/vicenda-eataly-raggiunto-laccordo-sulla-stabiliz zazione-del-personale/.

Grönroos, C. (2008). Service logic revisited: Who creates value? And who co-creates? *European Business Review*, 20(4), pp. 298–314.

Gunter, B. (2000). *Media research methods*. Sage, London.

Hjalager, A.-M. and Richards, G. (eds). (2002). *Tourism and Gastronomy*. Routledge, London.

Hottola, P. (2004). Culture confusion. Intercultural adaptation in tourism. *Annals of Tourism Research*, 31(2), pp. 447–466.

ICOMOS (2015). Analisi tecnica di ICOMOS del rapporto sullo stato di conservazione della proprietà del Patrimonio Mondiale "Centro Storico di Firenze" – Allegato I. http://www.eddyburg.it/2015/11/altro-che-degrado-nardella-risponda.html.

Insch, G.S. and McBride, J.B. (2004). The impact of country-of-origin cues on consumers perceptions of product quality: A binational test of the decomposed country-of-origin construct. *Journal of Business Research*, 57(3), pp. 256–265.

Johansson, J.K., Douglas, S.P. and Nonaka, I. (1985). Assessing the impact of country of origin on product evaluations: A new methodological perspective. *Journal of Marketing Research*, 22, pp. 388–396.

Khoo, S.L. and Badarulzaman, N. (2014). Factors determining George Town as a City of Gastronomy. *Tourism Planning & Development*, 11(4), pp. 371–386.

Kivela, J. and Crotts, J.C. (2006). Tourism and Gastronomy: Gastronomy's influence on how tourists experience a destination. *Journal of Hospitality and Tourism Research*, 30, p. 354.

Krippendorff, K. (2004). *Content analysis: An introduction to its methodology*. Sage, London.

Löfgren, O. (2014). Urban atmospheres as brandscapes and lived experiences. *Journal of Place Branding and Public Diplomacy*, 10(4), pp. 255–266.

McCannel, D. (1973). Staged authenticity: Arrangements of social space in tourist settings. *The American Journal of Sociology*, 79(3), pp. 589–603.

Montanari, T. (2013). Eataly, il Bignami del Rinascimento: L'ultima idea per vendere paccheri. http://www.ilfattoquotidiano.it/2013/12/27/eataly-il-bignami-del-rinasci mento-lultima-idea-per-vendere-paccheri/825951/.

Montanari, T. (2015). L'allarme Unesco "Cemento e degrado il centro di Firenze sorvegliato speciale." http://www.eddyburg.it/2015/11/lallarme-unesco-cemento-e-degrado-il.html.

Pasquinelli, C. (2014). Innovation branding for FDI promotion. Building the distinctive brand. In Berg, PO and E. Björner (eds) *Branding Chinese mega-cities: Strategies, practices and challenges*, Edward Elgar, Cheltenham.

Pasquinelli, C. (2017). *Place branding. Percezione, illusione e concretezza.* Aracne, Roma.

Prahalad, C.K. and Ramaswamy, V. (2004). Co-creation experiences: The next practice in value creation. *Journal of Interactive Marketing*, 18(3), pp. 5–14.

Seymour, S. (2017). Eataly world opens but leaves a bad taste in Bologna. http://www.theguardian.com/travel/2017/nov/17/eataly-world-bologna-megamarket-betrayal-italian-gastronomy.

Staiff, R. and Bushell, R. (2013). The rhetoric of Lao/French fusion: Beyond the representation of the Western tourist experience of cuisine in the world heritage city of Luang Prabang, Laos. *Journal of Heritage Tourism*, 8(2–3), pp. 133–144.

Thrift, N. (2004). Intensities of feeling: Towards a spatial politics of affect. *Geografiska Annaler, Series B: Human Geography*, 86, pp. 57–78.

Wang, N. (1999). Rethinking authenticity in tourism experience. *Annals of Tourism Research*, 26(2), pp. 349–370.

14 Are social eating events a tool to experience the authentic food and wine culture of a place?

Magda Antonioli Corigliano and Sara Bricchi

1. Introduction

Over the centuries, food has evolved from its primary function as nourishment to a type of continuous innovation in the search for pleasure, an essential part of a community's culture and a social identifier: The choice of what we eat and how we do it is influenced by cultural fashions and trends (French et al., 1994; Fischler, 1988).

With the rise of globalisation and the consequent homogenisation of cuisine, and with standardised dishes easily available around the world, two different trends have emerged.

On the one hand, supermarkets now offer all the ingredients needed to cook a good meal (also from different cuisines) and eating in restaurants has become an important leisure activity and a great opportunity for socialisation. Studies show that people are less interested in what they consume than in the overall experience associated with consumption (Hughes, 2004).

On the other hand, even if the relation between food and culture has always been close, interest in regional cuisine and local food has recently emerged as a way to reaffirm local traditions and values (Richards, 2002; Mirosa and Lawson, 2012). While residents turn to local productions as they perceive them as healthier (Pearson et al., 2011) or more socially responsible behaviour grounded in environmental and ethical sustainability (Jones et al., 2004), and restaurants serve dishes cooked with locally grown ingredients to add value to the customers' eating experiences (Pieniak et al., 2009), tourists look more and more for typical taste sensations and food experiences (Gymóthy and Mykletun, 2009; Björk and Kauppinen-Räisänen, 2016).

Indeed, the consumption of different foods is also a way to experience different cultures, transforming it into a type of "tourist attraction" (Cohen and Avieli, 2004; Smith and Costello, 2009; Hillel et al., 2013). Food and the related experiences are an essential part of holiday activities (Kivela and Crotts, 2006; López-Guzmán and Sánchez-Canizares, 2012) and constitute a significant portion of travel expenses (Hjalager and Antonioli Corigliano, 2000; McKercher et al., 2008).

For some traveller segments, particularly the so-called "foodies," food experiences can even affect the destination choice (Basil and Basil, 2009; Robinson and Getz, 2014) and/or post-trip behaviour, with local products taken home as souvenirs (Björk and Kauppinen-Räisänen, 2012; Swanson and Timothy, 2012). Local gastronomy and the consumption of foods and goods deeply rooted in a territory, beyond a way to experience the culture, have also become synonymous with authenticity and genuineness (Sims, 2009; Kauppinen-Räisänen et al., 2013).

Wine and food tourism has high potential in promoting the development of a rural destination's attractiveness and imagery, where visitors can enjoy a living experience in the production environment (Antonioli Corigliano, 1996, 1999, 2016; Hjalager and Richards, 2002), forming the link between the terroir[1] and its typical productions. Beyond the material component linked to ingredients (typical and traditional local products), it can also act as a gateway to understanding the destination's intangible heritage and culture (Björk and Kauppinen-Räisänen, 2016). Recipes, expressions of local traditions and values, become an important element of the characterisation and promotion of the territory, especially in a country such as Italy, which is marked by the absence of a unique institutionalised national cuisine that favours the origin of many regional or local recipes, based on specific ingredients that can only be found in those regions. Italy was for centuries composed of independent territories very rich in local traditions and wine and food productions; for instance, more than five hundred varieties of cheese, three hundred varieties of ham and salami, and more than two thousand wines have been categorised (Antonioli Corigliano, 2016).

Wine and food are an important segment of Italian tourism. According to Città del Vino (2016), visitors to wine producers and cellars in 2015 were estimated at 13.709.600, for a turnover of about 242.5 million euro. Considering the correlated activities and expenditure (travel, accommodation, meals, etc.), the same study determined the impact of wine and food tourism in Italy at 1.2 billion euro for the same year. To also consider are all the travellers who visit for other reasons, with a more casual attitude towards food, but who like to experience local cuisine as a way to directly relate to the local culture (Hall et al., 2003).

Given the importance of the food and wine offer in Italy, and the positive perceptions usually associated with Italian gastronomy, this chapter aims to explore whether visitors to Italy perceive new technologies, and particularly social eating events, as a tool to experience authentic food and the genuine gastronomic culture of a place. A qualitative review of the events offered in Rome on different national and international websites is our starting point to identify connections among these elements. The fast and widespread introduction of information and communications technologies (ICT) has led to the diffusion of new business models in tourism, more than in other sectors (often affecting existing operations), changing the relationships among the economic actors (Antonioli Corigliano and Baggio, 2010; Antonioli Corigliano and

Mottironi, 2016). With reference to demand, internet has favoured the active involvement of travellers, turning "personalisation" and "interaction" into two mantras for the entire industry. Currently, little is known about the link between home restaurants and food and wine tourism, and the objective of this work is to understand whether and how the innovation brought by this new form of socialisation has changed the relationship between gastronomy and local development.

2. The development of social eating and the importance of interaction in the dining experience

The last few years have seen the development of a new form of economy, the so-called collaborative or sharing economy: Thanks to the possibilities offered by new technologies, people organised in community-based networks can obtain and share access to goods and services with strangers around the world on a mass scale (Botsman and Rogers, 2010; Hamari et al., 2013). With new IT solutions offering safer online payment methods and the general search for social interactions, new food-related digital platforms have been created to facilitate peer-to-peer marketplaces in real time (Privitera, 2016).

The social eating phenomenon, also known as home restaurants, defined as the practice of inviting strangers to home with the purpose of cooking a meal for them against a payment, has also emerged in Italy. ICT and new forms of media have engendered social eating and the desire to share the experience, turning amateur cooks into hosts for those interested in tasting new dishes and spending an evening in an informal environment with other individuals with similar interests (Celata and Sanna, 2014).

According to a recent analysis (CST – FIEPET Confesercenti, 2015), in 2014, home restaurants in Italy generated revenues of 7.2 million euro, involving more than 7,000 cooks who organised 37,000 events with the participation of around 300,000 paying guests, with an average price per person of 23.70 euro. The majority of these events took place in Lombardy (16.9%), Lazio (13.3%), and Piedmont (11.8%).

Since time immemorial, eating together has been synonymous with conviviality (Surinder et al., 2015): the concept of "feeling at home" linked to that of a reunion, of time spent in the company of friends while sharing something with others, usually a meal, which makes individuals feel comfortable (Hughes, 2004). As stated, food in this sense transcends its nourishment nature: The pleasure a person derives is not only linked to taste satisfaction but also to the act of sharing, to living a collective and pleasurable experience (Fischler, 1998; Pietrykowski, 2004). Even if the experiential component is poor, this does not affect the nutritional value of food and/or the sense of fullness at the end of the meal, but it will have a strong negative effect on the overall satisfaction of the dining companions, as the pleasure from food predominantly derives from the commensality aspect of eating (Simmel and Hughes, 1949; Symons, 1994; Simmel, 1997; Sobal, 2000; Kerner et al., 2015).

At the same time, as an experiential good (Nelson, 1970), a specific food does not necessarily satisfy the needs of an entire category; on the contrary, the more delicious, the more people are tempted to taste different dishes from the same cook. This is also at the base of the curiosity for trying traditional cuisine and, while visiting new places, looking for homemade and authentic food.

3. The role of the community in social eating events

In a sort of paradox, the internet and social media enable a first contact among people who share the same interests (but are geographically distant) and would like to develop physical relations in the real world. Indeed, eating together has gained the attention of researchers for its ability to connect different social groups and reinforce cultural identities (Murcott and Gamarnikow, 1983; Mennel et al., 1993; Mestdag, 2004; Blake et al., 2008). In this way, an established social habit has been transformed into a new trend, leading to the growth and development of the social eating phenomenon thanks to ICTs and a new need for sociality and human contact born as a reaction to globalisation and the pervasiveness of new technologies themselves.

When taking part in a social eating event, the most relevant factor is the experience lived. People primarily look for affinities with the other individuals attending the event; they want to be part of a sort of community. Food consumption patterns and cuisines are a means of status and group identification (Pietrykowski, 2004). As in the case of literary cafes in the nineteenth century, where the upper classes used to meet to discuss, share ideas, and network with those with a similar mentality, home restaurant events today enable people to be part of a chosen community. Discussing common interests, the community turns itself into an amplifier of suggestions, advice, and practices that spread amongst its members, influencing their habits and consumption behaviours. Individual taste is validated through the elaboration of shared values (Dolfsma, 2002), which in turn shape the individuals' attitudes and beliefs (Etzioni, 1996; Bagozzi and Dholakia, 2002).

From a sociological point of view, an exchange in social capital leads to an exchange in economic capital, which goes far beyond the price expressly agreed and paid to partake in the meal (which in the community logic is simply a type of reimbursement to the host for organizing the event). These social eating platforms have in fact started to add sections that give visibility to third parties with shared community values – local products, organic or natural ingredients, seasonal foods, etc. – enabling them to present their offer.

On the other end, the diffusion of social eating platforms and the consequent wider offer and personalisation of the service enhance the potential links with the tourism industry. Food has the power to connect travellers to a place in a way that is probably closer, more immediate, and more engaging than anything else they could encounter during their trip (Peltier, 2015). According to the World Food Travel Association, just 5% of the expenditure in food tourism can be attributed to restaurant purchases (Oates, 2016). Travellers look for experiences and want to learn more and more about how their meals are prepared and where they come from. Thanks to the sharing economy, foodies have a new tool to experience food and wine once at the destination, directly meeting locals willing to share their culinary knowledge and expertise. According to Le Cesarine (one of the most important Italian associations in the field of social eating events), it is only at the family table that local products and culinary traditions can be combined to obtain dishes that are not only tasty, but also tell the story of those who passionately prepare them (Manuelli, 2015).

Nevertheless, foodies wanting to taste the local gastronomy and experience genuineness and authenticity are only one of the two main tourist market categories of users of this phenomenon. The other category are visitors already experiencing the possibilities of the sharing economy in other sectors, such as, for example, accommodation and transport. For these tourists, the human factor is as important as the role the community plays, reinforcing their membership of a social group also thanks to a reputational mechanism.

4. Objectives and methodology

This qualitative study has the purpose of reviewing the current offer in the Italian social dining events market to assess whether tourists currently perceive social eating platforms as a tool to experience authentic food and local gastronomic culture. In particular, we investigate whether a link can be found between the menus presented online by hosts and some type of promotion of regional cuisine, of local ingredients and, ultimately, of the territory itself.

We formulate three hypotheses:

- H1: Cooks offer dishes from the local cuisine.
- H2: In promoting the social eating event, hosts give attention to the aspects that can create a connection between the dish and its territory (respect for traditional recipes, homemade products, use of local ingredients, etc.).
- H3: Social eating is a new form of promotion for territories and destinations.

We selected six social eating platforms (three Italian and three non-Italian) operating in Italy but with different characteristics:

- Gnammo: An Italian community mainly targeting residents and offering the possibility of organising/attending scheduled events and offering/ choosing a menu to be cooked on request.
- Le Cesarine: An association whose mission is to promote local Italian dishes and traditions; members can attend scheduled events or choose from culinary itineraries on request.
- Cene Romane: A community of affluent citizens in Rome offering tourists a dinner – a fixed menu but open dates – to appreciate the destination from a different perspective.

- VizEat: An international community founded in France with the objective of connecting people who want to host travellers and visitors who would like to discover a new culture (the website offers fixed menus with open dates).
- EatWith: An international community marketplace founded in Israel with the aim of connecting hosts (amateurs and professionals) with visitors who would like to discover local and authentic food.
- NewGusto: An international platform to post pictures of the dishes cooked, promote them, share comments, and create events – which other members can attend – based on the published menus.

We selected Rome as the best destination to test the hypotheses for several reasons. First, with its 4.3 million inhabitants (Istat, 2016), it is the biggest Italian city located in one of the regions where the phenomenon is more advanced (CST- FIEPET Confesercenti, 2015) and where the probability of social eating events is higher.

Moreover, with nearly 25 million nights spent in its accommodation structures in 2016 (Istat, 2016), Rome is the most popular Italian tourist destination, part of the "Grand Tour," and gastronomy is a very relevant attractor of the Italian offer: Visitors want to experience authentic Italian cuisine while touring the country. Indeed, the restaurant industry is very relevant for the city. With its 19,465 restaurants, the majority of which are situated in Rome, Lazio is the second Italian region for number of eating places, with 11.3% of total businesses operating in Italy (FIPE, 2016). As in the hospitality sector with hotels and short-rentals serving guests with different needs, the data suggest that there is room for growth in the dining industry, and the relationship between restaurants and social eating is marked much more by complementarity than competition.

Finally, Lazio is one of the Italian regions with the highest number of products with a protected designation of origin, both for wine and food (European Commission, 2017; Federdoc, 2017), and as Rome has a distinctive and popular local cuisine, regional dishes can easily and unambiguously be identified.

We classified and reviewed the events listed on the aforementioned websites for the month of October 2015 with the objective of assessing the size of the phenomenon (in terms of number of events, number of cooks involved, and price scheme) and to test the hypotheses, considering the type of cuisine offered to guests (Roman or other), and whether attention is given to aspects related to the territory (authenticity, use of local ingredients, etc.). We repeated the same analyses in May 2017 to see whether and how the phenomenon evolved over the eighteen months.

5. Results

Based on the data collected (see Table 14.1), the number of events promoted is still limited; only three websites out of the six offered more than fifty events for the entire month of October. Conversely, the number of cooks involved is rather high, pointing out that the number of events offered per capita is low

Table 14.1 Number of events promoted, chefs involved, and price scheme (October 2015)

Website			N° of events	N° of chefs	Price Avg.	Min.	Max.
Italian websites	Gnammo	Events	25	19	25.44€	12.00€	60.00€
		Upon request	50+	30	25.04€	5.00€	100.00€
	Le Cesarine		31	22	NA	NA	NA
	Cene Romane		50+	19	43.52€	25.00€	78.00€
International websites	VizEat		50+	35	27.94€	3.00€	80.00€
	EatWith		32	6	45.38€	28.00€	65.00€
	NewGusto		17	9	NA	NA	NA

(no more than two per month), with the exception of EatWith, where, in Rome, a small number of cooks hold the same events at least once a week.

The prices vary both among the different websites and also within each channel according to the menus offered, ranging from 3 euro for an afternoon tea to 100 euro for a multiple course dinner. Two sites, Le Cesarine and New Gusto, do not declare prices.[2] The other four websites are divided into those offering cheaper events (Gnammo and VizEat) and those targeting a more affluent audience (Cene Romane and EatWith), with average prices ranging respectively from around 25 euro in the first two cases to 45 euro in the second (see Table 14.1).

Concerning the type of dishes offered, only Le Cesarine has a majority of menus based on Roman cuisine (65%); for all the other platforms, meals consisting exclusively of Roman dishes are less than one-third (see Figure 14.1). Between 10% and 20% of the cooks (excluding those on Le Cesarine and NewGusto) offer traditional cuisine menus but from other Italian regions (especially southern Italy), while the percentage of those offering menus generally inspired by Italian tradition but mixing dishes from different local cuisines varies greatly among the websites analysed. However, except for Gnammo, the majority offer menus referring to Roman, regional, and, more generally, Italian cuisine (Le Cesarine and EathWith cover the entire supply), suggesting a sort of connection with the country as a whole and its culinary tradition.

On the EatWith website, the cooks make more explicit reference to the use of local ingredients (25%) and to the fact that dishes are completely homemade in all the preparation processes, from raw materials to the finished product (for example, pasta, bread, and pizza) (38%). The percentage of completely home-made dishes is higher compared to those cooked with local products (local ingredients are never mentioned in the Le Cesarine, Cene Romane, and NewGusto menus), but both values are quite low – well under 20% (Table 14.2).

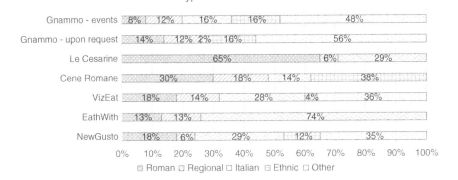

Figure 14.1 Type of cuisine offered (October 2015)

Table 14.2 Percentage of menus explicitly mentioning homemade preparations and local ingredients (October 2015)

Website			Homemade	Local ingredients
Italian websites	Gnammo	Events	16%	12%
		Upon request	14%	16%
	Le Cesarine		13%	0%
	Cene Romane		4%	0%
International websites	VizEat		14%	2%
	EatWith		38%	25%
	NewGusto		12%	0%

Emerging from same analysis in May 2017 (see Table 14.3) is that NewGusto is no longer active. On the other platforms the number of events and hosts has remained stable over the last year and a half (cooks host on average between 1.7 and 2.6 events per month per platform), while the offer has changed. Indeed, with the exception of Le Cesarine, all the other websites also offer cooking classes, with higher percentages for VizEat (22%) and EatWith (14%). The two international platforms also sell other activities: shopping for wine and food products at open-air markets, food tours, sightseeing tours of the destination with stops at local restaurants, or ending with a meal at the host's house, wine and food tastings, etc. The variety of activities implies a greater variance in the price of the experiences offered. However, in terms of meals, a general tendency is a significant increase in the average price: Excluding Le Cesarine, whose prices were not published in 2015, but for which the membership fee including the first meal was 50 euro, and EatWith, whose events are on average 9% more expensive, the average price of

Table 14.3 Number of events promoted, chefs involved, type of event, and meal price scheme (May 2017)

Website		N° of events	N° of hosts	Event type			Price (meal per person)*		
				Meal	Cooking class	Other	Avg.	Min.	Max.
Italian websites	Gnammo Events	20	19	96%	4%	-	44.56€	19.00€	120.00€
	Upon Request	77							
	Le Cesarine	32	19	100%	-	-	51.25€	41.00€	81.00€
	Cene Romane	53	22	94%	4%	2%	61.34€	21.00€	160.00€
International websites	VizEat	134	35	62%	22%	16%	41.28€	15.00€	78.00€
	EatWith	29	6	76%	14%	10%	49.31€	20.00€	69.00€

* Price per cooking class and other activities not considered
Source: Antonioli and Piona, 2017

Figure 14.2 Type of cuisine offered (May 2017)

Table 14.4 Percentage of menus explicitly mentioning homemade preparations and local ingredients (May 2017)

Website		Homemade	Local ingredients
Italian websites	Gnammo	34%	10%
	Le Cesarine	34%	0%
	Cene Romane	8%	6%
International websites	VizEat	36%	1%
	EatWith	38%	3%

Source: Antonioli and Piona, 2017

Cene Romane, VizEat, and Gnammo increased respectively by 41%, 48%, and 76%, suggesting a shift in the target audience.

Furthermore, a change in the type of cuisine offered suggests an evolution of the phenomenon, which, compared to 2015, now seems to address visitors more than residents. Indeed, other than the activities proposed and the price, the percentage of cooks offering Roman cuisine has greatly increased on all platforms, ranging from a minimum 25% for VizEat to 100% for Le Cesarine. Moreover, we observe that the menus inspired by the Italian culinary tradition (given by the sum of the Roman, regional, and Italian cuisine percentages) now represent the entire offer for three websites out of five, and over 80% in the other two cases analysed (see Figure 14.2).

Probably also due to the extension of the offer to cooking classes, attention to homemade preparation has increased: the percentage of cooks explicitly mentioning homemade products (pasta, bread, or pizza in particular) on Gnammo, Le Cesarine, and VizEat has more than doubled, representing more than one-third of the total. No clear trend can be detected instead in the case of local ingredients, despite the introduction of food tours and shopping at open-air markets: While in some cases the number of cooks promoting them has increased, in some others, it has decreased. On all the websites, however, it now represents a very low percentage (see Table 14.4).

6. Discussion

Even if the analysis is of qualitative nature and focuses only on a specific destination (and comprehensive conclusions are therefore left to more in-depth studies that combine a qualitative-quantitative review of the offer with specific surveys of demand), some interesting points of discussion emerge.

First, at the time of data collection, despite a second review of the offer eighteen months later, social eating can still be considered a relatively new phenomenon in Rome and, more generally, in Italy, as the number of events promoted on the different platforms is still low. Furthermore, not all the events published reach the minimum number of bookings needed, resulting in even lower figures.

The offer is very heterogeneous, both in terms of dishes cooked and prices, ranging from afternoon tea for 3 euro to dinners for almost 100 euro per person. Moreover, the variance has grown over time, with the introduction of new types of activities offered: from cooking classes to food tours and tastings. However, in general, compared to traditional restaurants, the prices proposed on average are not as cheap as one would think (especially for events targeting primarily tourists), signalling a current positioning mainly oriented to affluent consumers and, again, indicating that the phenomenon in Italy has not yet become a mass trend as in other countries.

If in 2015 the websites analysed were characterised by different offers reflecting the varying nature and aims of the platforms, the current data suggest an evolution of the phenomenon, moving from the concept of commonality at the base of the sharing economy to a more exclusive experience. As a consequence, while in the first phase different types of communities were easily recognizable, with different target audiences (tourists vs. residents), diverse spending power, dissimilar expectations, and, above all, seeking a different kind of experience and relation with the host and other guests,[3] today's guests seem to look for a memorable experience, with willingness to pay linked to the uniqueness of the emotions lived, the intimacy, the authenticity, and genuineness of the proposal. The importance of the social component withstands in the role of the host, more and more seen as an expert guiding the guests, be they foreigners or residents, to the discovery of local gastronomy/cuisine secrets, unknown to the former, forgotten by the latter.

H1: Cooks offer dishes from the local cuisine.

Excluding Le Cesarine, the percentage of cooks offering menus exclusively based on dishes from the local cuisine are not high. This phenomenon could be partly explained by the fact that the majority of cooks are amateurs (as also confirmed by the low number of events realised per capita per month) and tend to offer the dishes they have mastered. Moreover, a minimum number of participants is required to host an event, and the hosts tend to try to meet their guests' tastes and expectations.

However, from 2015 to 2017, the number of users proposing menus linked to Italian culinary traditions (be they Roman, from other regions, or a mix of the two) has grown significantly on all the platforms, now representing the entire offer for three out of five websites, and more than 80% in the other two cases analysed, thus suggesting on the one hand a link at least with Italy as a whole, and on the other, cooks' growing interest in targeting tourists, increasingly attracted by the possibility of living local experiences as a way to better discover the destination. (Not to be forgotten is that culinary experiences, cooking classes, and more generally, food tourism, are today amongst, if not the most important, elements that tour operators and other tourist intermediaries use to sell Italian destinations, especially on foreigner markets.)

Even in the case of Gnammo, an Italian community initially targeting mainly residents and offering dishes from other cuisines or themed events (such as women-only nights with beauty treatments, dishes seen in the movies, karaoke, etc.), the number of menus based on Italian cuisine has grown significantly, from nearly 50% to 84%, suggesting an evolution of the phenomenon. Even if the social function/community component is still a relevant dimension of partaking in the event (of interest on this matter is that Gnammo partnered for some of its dinners with Meetic, an online dating service), the type of dishes offered points to the fact that Italians are starting to re-evaluate dishes from their tradition – also thanks to a new desire for authenticity, genuineness, and more simplicity, seen as opposed to globalisation and the frenzy of contemporary urban life.

H2: In promoting the social eating event, hosts give attention to the aspects that can create a connection between the dish and its territory (respect for traditional recipes, homemade products, use of local ingredients, etc.).

Hosts dedicate modest attention to the promotion of food as entirely "homemade" (with reference to all the steps of the production process, as in the case of pasta and pizza dough prepared with natural yeast/sourdough starter), also as a way to prove the authenticity and neutrality of what is served. In particular, in the transition from 2015 to 2017, the percentage of cooks explicitly mentioning homemade products in their events description doubled on most platforms analysed. This is probably also due to the expansion of the services offered and particularly the introduction of cooking classes.

The use of local products, instead, is still not equally advertised, nor can a clear trend be detected over the two years considered.

H3: Social eating is a new form of promotion for territories and destinations.

If in the first phase we detected no clear link between the social eating events reviewed and the promotion of the territory – probably also due to the novelty of home restaurants in Italy – the analyses of the events conducted eighteen months later suggest an evolution of the phenomenon with the promotion of Italian culinary traditions.

In 2015, only Le Cesarine (an association whose objective is the conservation, transmission, and promotion of the culture and traditions of regional recipes) and partially Cene Romane offered a significant number of events based on local dishes. By 2017 this percentage had grown for all the websites considered, as had a more general tendency to promote Italian dishes.

In addition to the menus, this trend can be seen both in the diversification of the offer and in the evolution of the business. The general and significant increase in average prices suggests that consumers, be they locals or visitors, seek not only a delicious meal and conviviality, but also a unique and memorable experience. As mentioned, tourists eager to interact with the resident community increasingly appreciate the opportunity to "live like a local," and social eating seems to fulfil this function more than ever. This explains the expansion in the activities offered, going beyond a simple meal, to convey to participants something more about the culture and traditions of the destination: cooking classes, shopping at street markets, but also food and mixed tours that combine oeno-gastronomy and street food with sightseeing under the guidance of the host-"expert."

This tendency is also visible in the transformation of the social eating website business model: Some platforms more linked to the original concept of social eating have closed down (as in the case of NewGusto), new ones have been created with the objective of offering experiences connected to the promotion of local wine and food products (such as the Italian Faberest), while others (VizEat and Le Cesarine) have started signing partnerships with travel agents and local tour operators to promote their offer together with sightseeing tours and other leisure activities on the broader tourist market.

Currently, however, and differently from other European countries[4] that explicitly take advantage of social eating as a tool to promote gastronomy and hence the destination, in the cases analysed, no references to home restaurants can be found on Rome or Italy tourism websites. Thus, all is left to the initiatives of individual hosts, who can take advantage of the popularity of the Italian cuisine to promote themselves and their events.

7. Conclusions

The role of food has changed over the centuries, adding a sociocultural component to its primary function of nourishment. In particular, with the rise of globalisation, the interest in local productions and regional cuisine has emerged as a way to reaffirm local traditions and values. In tourism, this phenomenon results in the consumption of local dishes and in engaging in food-related experiences as a means of making contact with locals, directly knowing the culture of the destination and, ultimately, living the territory.

While new technologies enable contacting geographically distant people with similar interests, the home restaurant phenomenon has its roots in a distant past, originating from the pleasure of spending time in the company of friends, sharing a meal, and conviviality. In fact, a key element of social eating is the community: Hosts and guests are usually proud to be part of a group whose social and economic influence goes far beyond the actual event. Yet social dining events, as all other sharing economy phenomena, are also a way for tourists to directly experience a destination, its customs, manners, and values, living like and with the locals.

This study aimed to understand whether the innovation introduced by new technologies through the home restaurant phenomenon has changed and favoured the relationship between gastronomy and local development, assessing whether there is a connection between the actual social eating events offered in Rome and its territory. What emerges is that different platforms provide different types of offers, with some addressing residents and others targeting tourists. Apart from one of the cases analysed, the link with Roman cuisine tends to be weak, while the majority of menus promoted are to some extent inspired by Italian and local gastronomy. However, over the course of a year and a half, the phenomenon has evolved towards a more touristic direction: The percentage of cooks offering Italian dishes has increased to more than 80% on all platforms; the average price has significantly increased in association with the demand for unique and memorable experiences; the importance of homemade preparation (linked to the widening range of offerings, such as cooking classes, wine tastings, and food tours) has grown, and the first partnerships with tourism operators for the commercialisation of products have been signed.

Given the qualitative nature of the analysis, a complete mapping of the phenomenon is beyond the scope of this work. However, in Italy, social eating is a relatively young trend: The number of events is still limited, and there is room for development in a more territory-oriented way. Destination marketing organizations and institutions could and should try to take advantage of the possibilities that home restaurant platforms offer to engage the resident community and promote regional and local cuisine as an important part of the local heritage.

Notes

1 Originally from the wine industry, the term "terroir" (intended as a set of local resources and distinctive environmental and traditional signs that characterise the place of production) is now also commonly adopted with reference to gastronomy. (Recently, the equivalent term "merroir" has been coined to designate water quality and the properties that influence the features and characteristics of fish and seafood.)
2 As concerns Le Cesarine, the price for the first meal is included in the membership fee, which is 50 euro, but no mention is made of the cost of subsequent meals.
3 In some cases (Gnammo, VizEat and New Gusto), the role of the community is more relevant, with individuals trying to find others with similar interests with whom to establish a hopefully long-lasting relationship. In others (Le Cesarine, Cene Romane and EatWith), the social component is always fundamental, but in the sense of meeting a "local" who can guide the visitor in the discovery of the place, through a shared moment of conviviality, even if the dishes cooked do not always pertain to the local tradition. In this second case, the interaction between the host and guest was more likely to occur only once.

4 A good example in this sense is Visit Finland: the Finnish tourist board within the Food & Tourism strategy 2015/2020, Hungry for Finland (http://hungryforfinland.fi). This aims to develop products and partnerships to grow food tourism in the country; it provides on its visitors' website, through the MyStay platform, different experiences connected to local gastronomy, including social eating events, which are either directly bookable on the DMO or can be reserved by contacting the host through the website.

References

Antonioli Corigliano, M. (1996). *Enoturismo. Caratteristiche della domanda, strategie di offerta e aspetti territoriali e ambientali.* Milano, Franco Angeli.

Antonioli Corigliano, M. (1999). *Strade del vino ed enoturismo. Distretti turistici e vie di comunicazione.* Milano, Franco Angeli.

Antonioli Corigliano, M. (2016). Wine routes and territorial events as enhancers of tourism experiences. In Peris-Ortiz, M., Del Rio Rama, M. de la Cruz, Rueda-Armengot C. (eds), *Wine and Tourism, A strategic segment for sustainable economic development,* Switzerland, Springer International Publishing.

Antonioli Corigliano, M. and Baggio, R. (2010). *Internet e turismo 2.0: Tecnologie per operare con successo.* Milano, Egea.

Antonioli Corigliano, M. and Mottironi, C. (2016). *Turismo.* Milano, Egea.

Antonioli Corigliano, M. and Piona, G. (2017). *Il social eating quale strumento di promozione dell'enogastronomia locale: Il caso della cucina romana.* Milano, Bocconi University, working paper.

Bagozzi, R.P. and Dholakia, U.M. (2002). Intentional social action in virtual communities. *Journal of Interactive Marketing,* 16(2), pp. 2–21.

Basil, M. and Basil, D.Z. (2009). Reflections of ultra-fine dining experiences. In Lindgreen, A., Vanhamme, J. and Beverland, M.B. (eds), *Memorable customer experiences: A research anthology,* pp. 135–147, Surrey, Gower Publishing Company.

Björk, P. and Kauppinen-Räisänen, H. (2012). A netnographic examination of travelers' online discussions of risks. *Tourism Management Perspectives,* 2/3, pp. 65–71.

Björk, P. and Kauppinen-Räisänen, H. (2016). Local food: A source for destination attraction. *International Journal of Contemporary Hospitality Management,* 28(1), pp. 177–194.

Blake, C.E., Bisogni, C.A., Sobal, J., Jastran, M. and Devine, C.M. (2008). How adults construct evening meals. Scripts for food choice. *Appetite,* 51(3), pp. 654–662.

Botsman, R. and Rogers, R. (2010). *What's mine is yours: The rise of collaborative consumption.* New York, Harper Collins Business.

Celata, F. and Sanna, V.S. (2014). Community activism and sustainability: A multi-dimensional assessment. Working Paper, 137. http://eprints.bice.rm.cnr.it/10270/1/Celata-Sanna_CBIs_Assessment_WP.pdf.

Città del Vino (2016). XII Rapporto sul turismo del vino in Italia, Caratteristiche attuali e dinamiche evolutive del turismo del turismo del vino in Italia. http://www.cittadelvino.it/studio_ricerca.php?id=NTI.

Cohen, E. and Avieli, N. (2004). Food in tourism: Attraction and impediment. *Annals of Tourism Research,* 31(4), pp. 755–778.

CST – FIEPET Confesercenti. (2015). *Pubblici esercizi a confronto, quale futuro formativo.* Data were presented during FIEPET National Convention (in Cesena on October 5, 2015), but no publications have been released.

Dolfsma, W. (2002). Mediated preferences – How institutions affect consumption. *Journal of Economic Issues,* 36(2), pp. 449–457.

Etzioni, A. (1996). The responsive community: A communitarian perspective. *American Sociological Review*, 61(1), pp. 1–11.

European Commission (2017). DOOR. EU database of agricultural products and food. http://ec.europa.eu/agriculture/quality/door/list.html?locale=en.

Federdoc (2017). Mappe e vini italiani a denominazioni di origine – Lazio. http://www.federdoc.com/vini-a-d-o/lazio/.

FIPE (2016). Ristorazione 2016. Rapporto Annuale. http://www.fipe.it/centro-studi/news-centro-studi/item/4099-ristorazione-rapporto-annuale-2015.html.

Fischler, C. (1988). Food, self and identity. *Social Science Information*, 27(2), pp. 275–292.

French, J.A., Blair, A.J. and Booth, D.A. (1994). Social situation and emotional state in eating and drinking. *British Food Journal*, 96(1), pp. 23–28.

Gyimóthy, S. and Mykletun, R. (2009). Scary food: Commodifying culinary heritage as meal adventures in tourism. *Journal of Vacation Marketing*, 15(3), pp. 259–273.

Hall, M., Sharples, L., Mitchell, R., Macionis, N. and Cambourne, B. (eds) (2003). *Food tourism around the world: Development, management and the markets*. Oxford, Butterworth-Heinemann.

Hamari, J., Sjöklint, M. and Ukkonen, A. (2013). The sharing economy: Why people participate in collaborative consumption. *SSRN Electronic Journal*, http://papers.ssrn.com/sol3/Papers.cfm?abstract_id=2271971.

Hillel, D., Belhassen, Y. and Shani, A. (2013). What makes a gastronomic destination attractive? Evidence from the Israeli Negev. *Tourism Management*, 36, pp. 200–209.

Hjalager, A. and Richards, G. (eds) (2002). *Tourism and gastronomy*. London, Routledge.

Hjalager, A.M. and Antonioli Corigliano, M. (2000). Food for tourists – Determinants of an image. *International Journal of Tourism Research*, 2(4), pp. 281–293.

Hughes, K. (2004). Food for thought. *Long Term Care Management*, 53(7), p. 43.

Istat (2016). Popolazione residente. http://dati.istat.it/.

Jones, P., Comfort, D. and Hillier, D. (2004). A case study of local food and its routes to market in the UK. *British Food Journal*, 106(4), pp. 328–335.

Kauppinen-Räisänen, H., Gummerus, J. and Lehtola, K. (2013). Remembered eating experiences described by the self, place, food, context and time. *British Food Journal*, 115(5), pp. 666–685.

Kerner, S., Chou, C. and Warmind, M. (2015). *Commensality: From everyday food to feast*. 1st ed. USA, Bloomsbury Academic.

Kivela, J. and Crotts, J.C. (2006). Tourism and gastronomy: Gastronomy's influence on how tourists experience a destination. *Journal of Hospitality & Tourism Research*, 30(3), pp. 354–377.

López-Guzmán, T. and Sánchez-Cañizares, S. (2012). Culinary tourism in Cordoba (Spain). *British Food Journal*, 114(2), pp. 168–179.

Manuelli, M.T. (2015). Le Cesarine, custodi del gusto italiano, nel mirino del private equity. *Il Sole 24 Ore*. http://food24.ilsole24ore.com/2015/07/le-cesarine-custodi-del-gusto-italiano-nel-mirino-del-private-equity/.

McKercher, B., Okumus, F. and Okumus, B. (2008). Food tourism as a viable market segment: It is all how you cook the numbers! *Journal of Travel and Tourism Management*, 31(3), pp. 928–936.

Mennell, S., Murcott, A. and Van Otterloo, A. (1993). *The sociology of food*. 1st ed. London, Sage.

Mestdag, I. (2004). Disappearance of the traditional meal: Temporal, social and spatial destructuration. *Appetite*, 45(1), pp. 62–74.

Mirosa, M. and Lawson, R. (2012). Revealing the lifestyle of local food consumers. *British Food Journal*, 114(6), pp. 816–825.

Murcott, A. and Gamarnikow, E. (1983). *It's a pleasure to cook for him: Food, mealtimes and gender in some South Wales households*. London, Heinemann.

Nelson, P. (1970). Information and consumer behavior. *Journal of Political Economy*, 82(4), pp. 729–754.

Oates, G. (2016). These 3 trends are redefining the next generation of food tourism. *Skift*. https://skift.com/2016/06/20/these-3-trends-are-redefining-the-next-generation-of-food-tourism/.

Pearson, D., Henryks, J., Trott, A., Jones, P., Parker, G., Dumaresq, D. and Dyball, R. (2011). Local food: Understanding consumer motivations in innovative retail formats. *British Food Journal*, 113(7), pp. 886–899.

Peltier, D. (2015). The future of food tourism goes beyond the restaurant experience. *Skift*. https://skift.com/2015/10/23/the-future-of-food-tourism-goes-beyond-the-restaurant-experience/.

Pieniak, Z., Verbeke, W., Vanhonacker, F., Guerrero, L. and Hersleth, M. (2009). Associations between traditional food consumption and motives for food choice in six European countries. *Appetite*, 53(1), pp. 101–108.

Pietrykowski, B. (2004). You are what you eat: The social economy of the Slow Food movement. *Review of Social Economy*, 62(3), pp. 307–321.

Privitera, D. (2016). Describing the collaborative economy: Forms of food sharing initiatives. *Proceedings of the 2016 International Conference on Economic Science for Rural Development*, 43, pp. 92–98.

Richards, G. (2002). Gastronomy: An essential ingredient in tourism production and consumption? In Hjalager, A.M. and Richards, G. (eds), *Tourism and gastronomy*, pp. 3–20, London, Routledge.

Robinson, R.N.S. and Getz, D. (2014). Profiling potential food tourists: An Australian study. *British Food Journal*, 116(4), pp. 690–706.

Simmel, G. (1997). Sociology of the meal. In Frisby, D. and Featherstone, M. (eds), *Simmel on culture*, pp. 130–135, London, Sage.

Simmel, G. and Hughes, E.C. (1949). The sociology of sociability. *American Journal of Sociology*, 55(3), pp. 254–261.

Sims, R. (2009). Food, place and authenticity: Local food and the sustainable tourism experience. *Journal of Sustainable Tourism*, 17(3), pp. 321–336.

Smith, S. and Costello, C. (2009). Segmenting visitors to a culinary event: Motivations, travel behavior and expenditure. *Journal of Hospitality Marketing and Management*, 18(1), pp. 44–67.

Sobal, J. (2000). Sociability and meals: Facilitation, commensality and interaction. In Meiselman, H.L. (ed), *Dimensions of the meal*, Gaithersburg: Aspen Publishers.

Surinder, P., Wills, W. and Dickinson, A. (2015). Is it a pleasure to eat together? Theoretical reflections on conviviality and the Mediterranean Diet. *Sociology Compass*, 9(11), pp. 977–986.

Swanson, K.K. and Timothy, D.J. (2012). Souvenirs: Icons of meaning, commercialization and commodization. *Tourism Management*, 33(3), pp. 489–499.

Symons, M. (1994). Simmel's gastronomic sociology: An overlooked essay. *Food and Foodways*, 5(4), pp. 333–351.

15 Gastronomy, local development, and the quality issue

A provisional conclusion

We often teach our students about the virtuous path that leads from a thorough literature review to a crystal-clear definition of the research questions. In research practice, of course, pathways are much less linear, and often circular. Thus, the reader should not be surprised by the fact that this book also ends with, rather than robust findings, a refined, often revised, and certainly more complex set of research questions.

As mentioned in the introduction, the *fil rouge* of our work through the two workshops and this book is the focus on quality. This choice was supported by the overwhelming evidence of quality as the cornerstone of economically, socially, culturally, and environmentally sustainable, tourism-led local economic development. Undoubtedly, gastronomy can play a role in this dynamic only to the extent that it provides quality – as service management teaches – that meets or exceeds tourists' expectations. And yet, the kind of quality that emerges from the contributions in this book cannot be confined to a mere marketing issue that must be managed predominantly at the company level, nor can it be simply extracted from the physical and cultural, material and immaterial assets of a territory as a type of economic rent.

Let us then try to summarise the lessons learned from our discussions and especially from the chapters here published in line with the three main issues structuring the contents of our book: the identity issue, the diversity issue, and the innovation and creativity issue.

Gastronomy and identity

The chapters in Section 1 of this book clearly confirm that we must consider gastronomy as a cultural resource and an identity marker. Against the background of rapidly evolving trends in consumption and tourism (experience economy), the ability of a dish or a recipe to represent a place, a people, and a culture becomes a fundamental factor. Gastronomy is a territory's cultural resource (as gourmet tourism is fully part of cultural tourism).

Clergeau and Echeverria (Chapter 2) propose the concept of identity quality to describe this very link between quality and identity, and to understand how this identity quality acts as an affordance for the tourist ecumene. In this respect, gastronomy helps to reveal the structuring elements of one territory and its culture: It tells a story of the people, their way of life, their tastes, the constraints they had to face, the land they cultivated, the landscape they see every day, the animals they have domesticated, and those they have hunted or fished. The identity quality of a restaurant reflects not only the chef's personal profile but also the identity of the producers of the food products, as well as of the eaters, and is co-defined with the diners who, in consuming, interactively exchange cultures, discourses, and imaginaries. As Salvador (in Chapter 7) discusses in detail, interest in authenticity is a key driver of contemporary tourists. Although this concept must be managed with great care (due to its instability, rhetoric ambiguity, and plurality of meanings), there is no doubt that tourists nurture a specific and high expectation of some kind of authenticity in gastronomic experiences, often more than for any other component of the travel experience.

Gastronomy determines a process of (using the French term) *patrimonialisation*, becoming a cultural heritage. Ashworth and Graham (2005) remind us that heritage construction is a very selective process where some (and not any) "material artefacts, mythologies, memories and traditions become resources for the present." Gastronomy involves a selection of the past (the food of the tradition), an adaptation to societal needs (e.g., wellness), and sociocultural conditions (such as those imposed by globalisation, including curiosity for the other, and the intercultural contamination of food habits and tastes).

Identity quality results from an interaction between the outsiders' and the insiders' view; it is a learning process where the economic and symbolic value for outsiders does not always match the value for insiders. This dialectic relationship is well known and has been operationalised by the territorial marketing literature and practice. Férérol (Chapter 3) reminds us that a gastronomic identity increasingly contributes as a "marker" to territorial branding in a strong and distinctive way, even in countries little known for their gastronomic heritage. Looking at the rural region of Auvergne in France, she shows that this is enabled (although not always consistently implemented) not just due to the iconic character of some local products, but also thanks to the collective networking action that gives visibility to local resources and talents. The link with the territory is further emphasised by ecogastronomic approaches that, as Venzal (Chapter 4) discusses, pay attention to health and the environment.

The risk of an excessive dependence on tourism and on outsiders' images is also present in Lopes Cardoso's discussion of the Alentejo region (Chapter 5). As she argues, such dependence can only be reduced through wider and more consistent strategies, both future-oriented and deeply rooted in the history; otherwise, gastronomy may also be a vehicle for processes that weaken local identities. Lanquar (Chapter 6) clearly warns of this outcome when signalling the evolution of "authenticity"-minded festivals in Andalusia towards fusion food.

Gastronomy and diversity

At the crossroad of tourism and gastronomy, quality reflects the curiosity for diversity that characterises postmodern tourists. The keynote speech of chef Athinagoras Kostakos at the opening session of the La Rochelle workshop perfectly illustrated the approach to gastronomy through diversity via both its practices and ideologies. He highlighted the surprising and little-known (even to the permanent inhabitants) diversity of Cycladic agricultural food products, thanks to his in-depth knowledge of the islands and the technical skills developed while he trained in Paris. Thus, the extraordinary diversity of products, tastes, and culinary preparations is directly reflected in the diversity of dishes that reveal an aesthetic and sensory link between the landscape and the dish offered to eaters. This in turn contributes to local development: Local food supports local families and builds community, preserving the working landscape, and engaging in a time-honoured connection between eater and grower.

Similarly, biodiversity plays a key role in the case of the Longjing Caotang restaurant presented by Etcheverria (Chapter 8), and as in the Greek case, the chef-entrepreneur's visionary and ideological approach renders this a source of the area's socioeconomic and cultural vitality at different scalar levels.

Diversity may result from different interpretations of the local heritage. By looking at how territorial qualities are highlighted in the tours organised by the cognac houses for the purposes of tourism development, Piriou (Chapter 9) emphasises how territorial qualities are differently shaped by individual brands and their focus on the companies' skills, traditions, and heritage. Fiamor (Chapter 10) convincingly suggests that two different food production strategies may induce two types of local development: one structured around a legally certified form of traditional regional know-how that gives legitimacy to the producers and their tradition; and one based on networks of local producers and on the specificity of the physical setting, proposing culturally innovative products driven by environmental and social motivations.

Gastronomy, innovation and creativity

The globalised world is a stimulus to creativity and a source of innovation for gastronomy. Imagining and realizing new representations of food, new sensations, new ways of cooking that reinterpret tradition, are often related to the chefs' international curriculum and to the possibility of obtaining spices and other food products from all over the world.

Gastronomy is perfectly integrated in its own time, sharing social moods and intellectual trends, evolving and innovating according to new inspirations and technological opportunities. A creative, innovating gastronomy is an integral part of the symbolic dimension (the "soft infrastructure"; Bellini and Pasquinelli, 2016) of a creative milieu, such as contemporary cities, and is in tune with the present discourse on creativity as a cornerstone of the new urban-centred development model. This has been recognised by UNESCO, whose Creative Cities Network covers seven creative fields, one of which is gastronomy, and characterises twenty-six cities worldwide.

Our book suggests different innovation paths. New market segments may derive from the revival of products and techniques, possibly with a significant impact on local economies, as in the case of craft breweries that Cabras and Ellison (Chapter 11) discuss. The luxury turn in wine tourism is presented by Bellini and Resnick (Chapter 12) as an emerging differentiation, combining wine-related experiences with high-quality locations and services to increasingly international customers. This may be beneficial to local economies, although the authors warn about compromises responding to the "global"-minded and stereotypical expectations of cosmopolitan elites that may cause a weakening of local ties and specificities.

Eataly, a successful case of "industrialised gastronomy," is presented by Pasquinelli (Chapter 13). Innovation results in a value facilitating role, which makes the learning experience with regard to a local gastronomic tradition easier and reduces uncertainty in approaching it. This is especially relevant for international, culturally distant visitors, although at the risk of over-facilitation and presenting a simplified, staged, and "touristified" representation of the local culinary identity as part of a commodified summary of the city.

Finally, gastronomic innovation and creativity are confronted with the emergence of social networks and sharing economy platforms. Antonioli Corigliano and Bricchi (Chapter 14) question, in the Italian case, whether and how the innovation brought by these social eating platforms has changed the relationship between gastronomy and local development. Social dining events are also a way for tourists to directly experience a destination, its customs, manners, and values – living like and with the locals. This is a rapidly evolving phenomenon, where the tourist-oriented component is increasing, combining social eating with a wider range of memorable, and potentially more territory-oriented, experiences.

To sum up

As the contributions in this book disentangle the various facets of quality, it has become evident to us that a shared vision emerges with regard to the relationship of gastronomy with local development and the role of quality.

Quality, local development, and gastronomy have a common and fundamental characteristic: all are *social constructs*, the result of locally anchored processes that mobilise many different actors and obey (evolving) social conventions. By its very nature, gastronomy encompasses an economic activity that cannot be confined to isolated, exceptional spots of culinary ingenuity mixed with entrepreneurial visions; it does not exist by itself and for itself, but in the eyes, the mouth, and the senses, the discourses and the imaginaries of eaters who experience it, and in their dialogue with the network (and social/cultural capital) of local chefs(-artists), artisans, farmers, and producers. It is this experience that contributes to qualify gastronomy. It is here that gastronomy comes into resonance with local development.

This approach clearly redefines the research space on gastronomy and local development in terms that cannot be constrained within some disciplinary picket fence. As this book shows, disciplines enrich each other to understand the complexity of relationships and phenomena. The dialogue between geography, economics, management science, and sociology frees us from any separation between economy, society, institutions, culture, the local, and the global.

In our opinion, this approach opens up two large research areas that at the same time impose a reappraisal of managerial and political practice.

The first concerns the relationship with the market. The relationship between the chef and his ecosystem with the gourmet consumer often reveals an exclusive characterisation that is an essential component of the history and the geography of gastronomy, suggesting an "elitist" association with luxury. This goes far beyond the pricing of menus in the most prestigious restaurants and the possibility of cobranding, as the creative inclusion of a Bottura "Osteria" in the new Gucci Garden in Florence has recently reminded us.

And yet, gastronomy as a system of discourses and imaginaries has never been just for some elites. Today it also appears to be a lifestyle dimension that is increasingly attractive to wider segments of the market and contemporary societies. In reaction to the abuse in the food industry and the dead end of "McDonaldization", gastronomic craft and professionalism reassure consumers seeking quality, significant, and original (and therefore memorable) experiences. New trends have emerged: Chefs create from local products, guarantee production chains, and also invent recipes that aim to feed better, for example, by eliminating meat or diminishing the use of sugar. In other words, successful gastronomic experiences meet – in a holistic way – all the expected dimensions of quality for contemporary consumers (hedonism, symbolism, hygiene, productive processes, self-congruency, identity…). A down-market movement of elite lifestyles is also taking place through occasional consumption by "temporary gourmets", the expansion of media addressing the curiosity and learning needs of "foodies", the digitalisation of consumption practices, and the emulation of high-level gastronomy in some of its features, even with provocative contaminations (such as the McDonald burgers "signed" by Gualtiero Marchesi in 2011). How should this process be interpreted? Positively, as the pervasiveness of the quality values that characterise gastronomy? Or negatively, as a challenge to quality deriving from its necessary standardisation and industrialisation?

The second area for research and practice concerns the policy framework that could sustain the role of gastronomy. Also in this field, quality often seems to call for standards and labels. Undoubtedly, this is a necessary tool with a proven record, but from this book we derive the strong conviction that quality refers first and foremost to partnership building, organisation, co-ordination, and co-operation. In a sense, it is time to move from a "legal" to a "political" perspective. Only this associative power of gastronomy lends substance and strength to its role within local economies and societies. Thus, we need to know more about the "logic of collective action" that is behind gastronomic quality, to what extent this reflects existing social capital or the result of targeted policies, designing networks of actors around gastronomic quality objectives.

References

Ashworth, G.J. and Graham, B. (2005). Senses of place, senses of time and heritage. In Ashworth, G.J. and Graham, B. (eds), *Senses of place: Senses of time*. Aldershot: Ashgate, pp. 3–12.

Bellini, N. and Pasquinelli, C. (2016). Branding the innovation place: Managing the soft infrastructure of innovation. In Hilpert, U. (ed), *Handbook on politics and technology*. London: Routledge, pp. 79–90.

Index

Printed in the United States
by Baker & Taylor Publisher Services